Military Life
in Dakota

MILITARY LIFE IN DAKOTA

The Journal of Philippe Régis de

TROBRIAND

TRANSLATED AND EDITED

FROM THE FRENCH ORIGINAL BY

LUCILE M. KANE

University of Nebraska Press
Lincoln and London

First Bison Book printing: 1982

Most recent printing indicated by first digit below:
1   2   3   4   5   6   7   8   9   10

Library of Congress Cataloging in Publication Data
Trobriand, Régis de, 1816–1897.
  Military life in Dakota.

  Translation of: Vie militaire dans le Dakota.
  Reprint. Originally published: St. Paul : Alvord Memorial
Commission, 1951. (Publications / The Clarence Walworth Al-
vord Memorial Commission of the Mississippi Valley Historical
Society ; 2)
  Bibliography: p.
  1. South Dakota—Description and travel. 2. Great Plains—
Description and travel. 3. Indians of North America—South
Dakota. 4. United States. Army— Military life. 5. Trobriand,
Régis de, 1816–1897. I. Kane, Lucile M. II. Title. III.
Series: Publications (Mississippi Valley Historical Association.
Clarence Walworth Alvord Memorial Commission) ; 2.
F655.T8413 1982   978   81–14740
ISBN 0–8032–1661–0   **AACR2**
ISBN 0–8032–6557–3 (pbk.)

REPRINTED BY ARRANGEMENT WITH THE MINNESOTA HISTORICAL
SOCIETY

Contents

Illustrations

Errata and Additions

P. ix, 1. 23. For *Wilamette,* read *Willamette.*

P. xv, 1. 24. For *die with,* read *decline during.*

P. 22, n. 10, 1. 29. Add the following: Although the name "American Fur Company" remained in common use, successor firms in the Missouri River trade were Pratte, Chouteau and Company from 1834 and P. Chouteau, Jr., and Company from 1838. Berthold was associated with Chouteau in the trade.

P. 22, n. 11. Add the following: The firm, also called the Northwestern Fur Company, evolved from a partnership formed by C. Francis Bates, James A. Smith, and Hubbell & Hawley. The papers of James B. Hubbell and Smith, which the Minnesota Historical Society acquired in 1955 and 1980, respectively, include significant data on the Upper Missouri River fur trade during the 1860s.

P. 28, n. 16, 1l. 1–9 and *passim.* Substitute the following tribal identification: The Santee, the Eastern Division of the Dakota or Sioux, includes Mdewakanton, Wahpekute, Sisseton, and Wahpeton. The Middle, or Wiciyela Division, includes Yankton and Yanktonai. The Teton, or Western, Division includes Oglala, Brule, Sans Arc, Blackfoot, Miniconjou or Minneconjou, Two Kettles, and Hunkpapa. Memorandum by Alan Woolworth, May 26, 1981, in Minnesota Historical Society.

P. 58, n. 37, 1. 8, and p. 378, 1. 14. For *Elliot,* read *Elliott.*

P. 83, n. 48. Add the following: Cagnat, below, was an employee of P. Chouteau, Jr., and Company before joining the Northwest company. See Deposition, Sept. 21, 1865, in James Smith Papers.

P. 122, n. 70. Add the following: "Spotted Tails" may be a reference to Brules led by Chief Spotted Tail.

P. 154, 1. 6. Note 85 is on p. 157.

P. 192, n. 97, 1. 2. Add the following: Gardepie is characterized in an undated memoir by "Frontiersman" in the James B. Hubbell Papers. His first name is not given in the memoir.

P. 224, n. 105, 1. 1, and p. 373, 1. 23. For *Edward*, read *James Edward*.

P. 270, 1. 3. For *Manoouakan*, read *Medicine Bear*.

P. 272, n. 126, 1. 6. For *Breuner*, read *Brenner*, Add the following: The James Smith Papers contain a great deal of information on Robert G. Terry's fur trading business at Fort Totten.

Foreword

WHEREVER IT WAS, the West was the "New World." From the settlements at Jamestown and Massachusetts Bay westward until there was no longer any wilderness, every frontier was part of that New World. What did it look like? What kind of folk were the original inhabitants? What experiences did the traveler and the settler have? What sights did he see? These and a thousand other questions were asked by those at home, whether they lived in Europe or in the older settled regions of America.

No small part of the world's literature has been written in response to these questions, for always there was Odysseus returning from far-off places. The tale he told was just a bit more wonderful because of a receptive audience and because the teller believed he had lived through an exciting and remarkable experience. In the lives of that great company of westward-journeying folk, who traversed the continent until the trails ran out, there was nothing that quite equalled the experience of seeing for the first time a part of this New World. They would tell of it, they would set it down. Those who had never kept a journal before kept one; those who wrote little and seldom sent long, descriptive letters home, and the literature of the New World is richer because of their labors.

Although the most important reason for leaving their old homes for the West might have been the desire for a home on the James, the Connecticut, the Ohio, or the Wilamette, still, who can say how powerful was the urge just to go forth "for to see and for to admire"? Often through their inexperienced eyes, the reader catches glimpses of the New World that only they could give us.

Useful and important as such accounts may be to those who would know the West, they are perhaps less valuable than the journals of the experienced traveler who had been in many places and had seen many things. His powers of observation had been sharpened, his interests had a wider scope, and his insight and understanding were more penetrating. If such an observer were blessed with literary

Philippe Régis de TROBRIAND

skill and power of expression, whatever he might write about the West in which he found himself is of great and lasting value.

When the traveler had the ability not only to put into words what he saw, but also to illuminate his journal with pictures so that the stay-at-homes might see with their eyes as well as with their minds, such a narration is doubly valuable. From Le Moyne's beautiful drawings of the sixteenth-century settlement of the French in Florida to the pictures of W. H. Jackson, the pioneer photographer of the last West, the urge to make people see the New World has produced a whole rich gallery of western history.

In the journal here presented the reader will find a keen, intelligent, and experienced observer who wrote with real distinction and great insight. More than that, he supplemented his journal with sketches of the regions round about, drawings that have in them some of the sweep and clarity of the new land.

Set down on the plains of Dakota at a remote army post, Régis de Trobriand, aristocrat of France, cosmopolite, traveler, and soldier, gave to future readers a picture of that last "New World" which stirred and fascinated and at times repelled him. The literature of the Far West would have been poorer had he not in those long winter evenings in his snow-bound quarters on the banks of the Missouri written of what he saw and thought of this land so far removed from the world he had known.

Translated by a brilliant young scholar who has caught the spirit of the author, this journal of military life in Dakota belongs with the best of those accounts which brought to men everywhere some of the wonder of the land to the West.

ERNEST S. OSGOOD
University of Minnesota

General Editor's Foreword

THE SECOND VOLUME of the Clarence W. Alvord Memorial Commission's publications has been long in appearing. Not that material has been lacking, but that funds, sufficient in 1942 in the revolving fund for publishing a book, have become woefully inadequate since that time because of the rising cost of book production. It is only by special arrangement that the funds have now been stretched to cover the publication of this volume.

Totally different from the first book in this series, the translation of Régis de Trobriand's manuscript diary will have much more interest for the general reader. The writer of the diary, an unusually keen observer of men and scenes, was an author of repute in his own tongue and country. In addition, he was an artist of no mean ability, as the illustrations in this book from his pencil and brush indicate. The tempo of the narrative is quick, and the philosophical character of much of the writing is on a plane calculated to elicit the reader's admiration. Miss Kane has translated the document with genuine understanding of the author's original statement, with its fine shades of meaning and its rather specialized vocabulary. She secured permission to use the manuscript diary, thus producing the first full translation of the journal as it was written.

The present owner of the diary is a grandson of Régis de Trobriand, Waldron Kintzing Post of New York City, who has been almost as enthusiastic as Miss Kane in plans for publishing the diary. To him and to the other members of his family we owe a good deal.

An earlier translation of parts of the journal was published in 1941 as *Army Life in Dakota,* translated by George F. Will and under the general editorship of Milo Quaife. These excerpts are based on the form of the journal that appeared in French in France in 1926 as *Vie Militaire dans le Dakota.*

There are many differences between *Vie Militaire dans le Dakota* as printed in 1926 and the original manuscript. When the printed form was compared with the manuscript, it was found that twenty-eight pages of the original had been omitted, that paragraphs originally in English had been translated into French with no warning to the reader, that the transcriber had substituted words on many occasions, and that there were errors in copying. Moreover, the sketches and paintings of De Trobriand have never been utilized beyond the reproduction of a few items. So the Commission has felt justified in issuing a full and complete translation of the manuscript by a competent French student, illustrated by the author's own handiwork, and with other data not supplied by the two earlier editions. Miss Kane's translation has been checked not only by the general editor of the series, but more expertly by Mr. Mortimer Naftalin of the Department of Romance Languages, University of Minnesota.

Something of the book's format and style should be mentioned here, so that the reader will understand Miss Kane's method of editing. Since De Trobriand wrote well in English, his style in that language has been copied by Miss Kane in her translation, for his letters in the National Archives in Washington, D. C. have been available for study. At the place in the diary where the author makes mention of a person for the first time, Miss Kane has given the Christian name of that individual and has pointed out the irregularities in the author's spelling, if it was defective in any way. She has not identified minor officers beyond this point, for their service records may all be conveniently found in Francis B. Heitman, *Historical Register and Dictionary of the United States Army* (Washington, D. C., 1903) in alphabetical sequence.

When any variation in spelling from that of the original manuscript has been employed, a footnote explains the correction. After the author's error in a spelling has once been noted, the correction has not been repeated. All additions to the manuscript have been enclosed in square brackets. Italicized words in brackets at the beginning of certain paragraphs are merely substitutes for the author's marginal topic headings, which have proved too awkward and too expensive to include in this volume as they appeared in the manuscript. Only major divisions in the narrative now begin with these headings; and De Trobriand's own words are reproduced in translation within the brackets.

GRACE LEE NUTE
Chairman, Alvord Memorial Commission

Acknowledgments

To THE PEOPLE who helped produce *Military Life in Dakota*, I extend sincere thanks. Mortimer Naftalin of the University of Minnesota helped collate the French manuscript with the printed French edition of *Vie Militaire dans le Dakota,* in order that we might have a complete record of the differences between the two. He then checked most of the translation. Anne McDonnell of the Montana Historical Library, John B. Martin and Elizabeth Drewry of the National Archives, and Robert G. Athearn of the University of Colorado have been generous in uncovering De Trobriand manuscripts. Professors Herbert Heaton and Rodney C. Loehr of the University of Minnesota read the manuscript before it was submitted to the Alvord Memorial Commission. Louise P. Olsen of the University of Minnesota typed the final copy of the manuscript. June D. Holmquist, Esther Jerabek, Mary W. Berthel, Polly Canfield, Bertha L. Heilbron and Kathryn Johnson of the Minnesota Historical Society assisted in putting the manuscript through the press. Leona Kane and Dorothy Kane collated the manuscript each time it was retyped. Mr. and Mrs. Emery Kane provided money for research trips. Dean Theodore C. Blegen, Graduate School, University of Minnesota, provided help at various points through the years of preparation.

Waldron Kintzing Post, grandson of General de Trobriand, has shown me many kindnesses. He allowed me to borrow the French manuscript of "Vie Militaire," granted access to the family papers, had copies made of the pencil sketches and oil paintings, and talked with me about the De Trobriand family.

Professor Grace Lee Nute read the manuscript, criticized the translation and editing, and undertook the labor of seeing it through the press. I appreciate deeply the help she has given me by keeping before me always her high standards of scholarship. I thank, too, the other members of the Alvord Memorial Commission, and Mrs. Clarence S. Paine of the Mississippi Valley Historical Association.

Any attempt to express the measure of my debt to Professor

Philippe Régis de Trobriand

Ernest S. Osgood of the University of Minnesota must fall short of the mark. He gave me, as one of his graduate students, the job of translating and editing the De Trobriand manuscripts, directed the work until it was ready for the Alvord Memorial Commission, and spent months of his time in helping solve the many problems that arose. *Military Life in Dakota* is, therefore, one of the many products of his seminars in the history of the American West. With a generation of his students, I thank him for his inspired teaching and his unselfish attention to the training of historians.

LUCILE M. KANE

St. Paul, Minnesota
August 30, 1950

Editor's Introduction

Philippe Régis de Trobriand, Colonel in the Army of the United States, veteran of the volunteer forces in the Civil War, stood at the wharf in Omaha in 1867, waiting to take passage on the steamboat *Deer Lodge* for his new post at Fort Stevenson, Dakota Territory. To reach this desolate outpost on the edge of the American Desert, he had come far from Paris in his native France, far from the metropolitan centers of the eastern states. World traveler, novelist, journalist, artist, and soldier, Colonel de Trobriand was no stranger to adventure; yet this assignment to the command of a tiny post in the heart of Sioux country was for him a completely new experience.

At his feet the Missouri swept in its impetuous course from the headwaters of the Jefferson Fork to St. Louis, 2,547 miles below, where its yellow waters poured into the Mississippi. A river of history, the Missouri was the cord that bound together a far-flung empire. Downstream came the packs of furs gathered from river post and inland rendezvous; downstream came gold from the placers of Alder Gulch. Upstream went blankets and beads for the traders; shingles, flour, and guns for the military garrisons strung out along its banks; picks and beans for the miners digging for fortune in Montana, Idaho, and Wyoming; annuity goods for Indians who had pledged peace and friendship at Laramie sixteen years before.

Since 1832, when the steamer *Yellowstone* made her voyage to Fort Union, traffic on the Missouri had been growing, and now, in 1867, it had reached its peak. It would die with the century as the iron rails of the Union Pacific, the Northern Pacific, and the Great Northern reached out across the plains, but in this year it was the great highway of travel and commerce.

As he moved up the Missouri, Colonel de Trobriand saw from the decks of the *Deer Lodge* a rapidly changing West. Fort Pierre, named for Pierre Chouteau of St. Louis, was one of the first important posts established by the American Fur Company as it penetrated deep into the fur country beyond the Mississippi. John Jacob Astor had enjoyed years of plenty from 1808, when his company was incorporated, until his retirement in 1834. A virtually untapped resource, a wide European market, a country already explored by Lewis and Clark, and a leader with unusual business acumen—these were factors that enabled the American Fur Company to drive almost every competitor from the field.

After Astor's retirement, the Northern Department kept the company name, and the Western Department was called Pratte, Chouteau and Company. The men of St. Louis still dominated the fur trade, beaver pelts and buffalo hides still streamed into that great entrepôt, but by 1867 the trade had lost its exclusive character. Where once the powerful company had disputed for sole right of trade, Durfee and Peck, the Northwestern Fur Company, independent merchants, and numerous transportation companies fought over the leavings.

On the passenger list itself, Colonel de Trobriand could note the growing importance of the mining frontier in the Far West. Men hungry for gold took passage on every river steamer bound for Fort Benton, where they scattered to the diggings in Montana and Idaho. On this raw frontier where law could not reach and where Indian power was still menacing, the miner led a perilous existence. He might not find gold; he might lose his scalp. This was his gamble. But the lines of communication with the States, from St. Louis to Fort Benton, from St. Paul to Virginia City, must be maintained in spite of the raids of the hostile Sioux. For this the miner looked to the military, to the string of posts lining the river and rising on the overland routes across the plains.

As the Sioux watched this growing tide of civilization rolling across his hunting grounds, he knew that here was his last stand. Canny chiefs like Red Cloud of the Oglala and Sitting Bull of the Hunkpapa observed the events of 1867 with apprehension. At Fort Laramie in 1851 they had accepted as their range the country north of the Platte River and had agreed to allow the government to build roads and establish posts in their country. But now, as the rails of the Union Pacific cut into their buffalo empire, as the Bozeman Trail was opened from the line of traffic on the Oregon Trail to the upper Yellowstone, as the stream of miners grew by the year, as the military force of the victorious Union garrisoned strategic points, the Indians of the plains steeled themselves to combat any further white encroachment.

Red Cloud made war on the whites in the Powder River country where Colonel H. B. Carrington had been sent to protect the Bozeman Trail with a string of posts, and on December 21, 1866, a detachment commanded by W. J. Fetterman was led to ambush and annihilation. Red Cloud won only to lose, for although the government yielded to his demand to give up the posts and abandon the road, he ceased to be a power among the Sioux when he signed government papers and ate government beef.

Sitting Bull remained irreconcilable. Scourge of the plains, he led his warrior band to haunt the trails frequented by travelers. At Fort Union in 1867 he expressed his ideas about the government's effort to bring the tribe to ways of peace and agriculture: "I have killed, robbed, and injured too many white men to believe in a good peace. They are medicine, and I would eventually die a lingering death. I had rather die on the field of battle . . . I don't want to have anything to do with people who make one carry water on the shoulders and haul manure. Look at me; see if I am poor, or my people either. The whites may get me at last . . . but I will have good times until then. You are fools to make yourselves slaves to a piece of fat bacon, some hard tack, and a little sugar and coffee."[1] And he made good his boast until 1876, when at the Little Big Horn he led the Sioux against General George A. Custer in their last major engagement with the United States Army. Then, after escaping to Canada, fugitive from his own land, he came in to make his submission and accept his rations.

This story of Indian hostilities, followed by retaliation, concessions, and final concentration on limited reserves was repeated throughout the plains until, by the last decades of the century, the "Indian problem" had become one of their support and education as wards of the government. Right or wrong, the Indian had to give way before the pressure of the young nation as it moved into the West to claim the gold in the earth, the grass on the plains.

The lines along which these pressures were felt cut straight across Sioux country. In the years before De Trobriand went to Fort Stevenson, the routes of overland travel had been marked out by the expeditions of William H. Nobles and James L. Fisk, who had been detailed by the army to guide emigrants to the gold camps. Fisk had met Indian hostility when his third expedition was turned back by the Sioux in 1864. But he tried again, and in 1866 he led a party northward from St. Paul to the Red River, west across the Missouri, and on to Fort Benton and the mines. The same years saw the fortifi-

1 Charles Larpenteur, *Forty Years a Fur Trader on the Upper Missouri,* 2:429–430.

cation of the Bozeman Trail, the building of the Union Pacific, and the chartering of the Northern Pacific, which was to reach Bismarck in 1873.

With the development of these transportation links with the Eastern market, the way was opened for the utilization of the grazing grounds of the plains, and already long lines of Texas cattle were heading north to the land of the buffalo. By the close of the 1870's, the range-cattle industry was at its peak, and cow towns like Abilene and Cheyenne rivaled gold camp and railroad town in the popular imagination.

The efforts of the government to prepare the Indians for the transition from a nomadic life to one of settled existence were made through the Indian Bureau, a part of the Department of the Interior since 1849. In this task, which called for the skill and wisdom of a well-organized central agency, the government was pitifully inadequate. While corrupt Indian agents filched annuities in collusion with the traders, the departments of War and the Interior fought for control of the Indian Bureau. Peace commissioners gave breechloading rifles to Indians who expressed peaceful intentions and then shot at the troops of the United States instead of at buffalo.

The government tried in a number of ways to find a more humane and just method of accomplishing the necessary transition. In 1869, after long agitation on the part of the army for a complete transfer of the Indian Bureau to the Department of War, a compromise was made and officers of the army were appointed as Indian agents. Congress refused, however, to permit this appointment of military officers and the policy had to be abandoned.

When in 1870 the responsibility for the appointment of agents was given to the denominations of the Christian church, optimists saw a ray of hope. The Quakers had already earned praise for the administration of the agencies placed under their direction in 1869, and missionaries like Father de Smet had shown through the years a most sincere and intelligent interest in both the temporal and spiritual welfare of the Indians. But neither the army nor the churches could make the sweeping reforms that were needed. So the tragedy, called by Helen Hunt Jackson "a century of dishonor," was played out to the end.

Colonel de Trobriand, appointed commander of the Middle District in the Department of Dakota, stepped into a military organization that was not prepared to meet the demands of the times. General William T. Sherman headed the Division of the Missouri, divided into the departments of the Missouri, Dakota, the Platte, and the Arkansas. General Alfred H. Terry, able soldier and officer in the Civil War, commanded the Department of Dakota, subdivided into the districts of Minnesota, Montana, Southeast Dakota, and the Middle District.

In the Department of Dakota, virtually unsettled west of the Missouri, ranged the tribes of the great Sioux nation, twenty thousand strong. Garrisoned with infantry, dependent on steamboat and slow-moving wagon train for communication and supply, the posts scattered throughout the department could do little more than maintain themselves and build the forts. Some like Fort Buford were particularly offensive to the Sioux and were under an almost constant state of siege. Although war parties never attacked the fort, their raids on woodcutting parties and hunters made it almost impossible for men to leave the post unless accompanied by a well-armed detachment.

The enlisted men at these Western posts led a life that little resembled that of a soldier. Making adobe brick, hauling rocks from the hills for foundations, pursuing bands of raiding Indians, the soldier on the plains alternately built and fought. His diet of salt pork gave him scurvy. His lodgings were miserable. His pay was too small to support a family. Little wonder that the ranks of the army were constantly depleted as men deserted for neighboring gold fields and for home.

Although the officers had more material comforts than the men in the ranks, their position was far from happy. They were a varied lot, coming from many states of the Union, from Ireland, England, Spain, France. Some were graduates of the Military Academy; some were officers in the volunteer service; some rose from the ranks, commissioned on the field as their superior officers were killed in battle. But most of them had been welded together by a great common experience, the Civil War.

In the period following the Civil War, the government took action to dismantle the military machine it had assembled to save the Union. Officers who had won rapid promotion for valorous service before Richmond or at Chancellorsville were assigned to duty in the West where there were few opportunities to display their military talents. Stationed at an isolated post for months, waiting for the mail to bring news of the outside world, shooting at a few hostiles who sneaked in to steal mules, dishing out rations to hungry bands of Indians who came to beg, making out routine reports to the division commander—this was not an assignment that would win promotion in an army already over-staffed in all ranks from generals to second lieutenants. Many like Fetterman and Custer grew restive, and, hoping to win recognition by a quick, decisive action, led their troops to death or glory against Indians wherever they could find them.

Top military men believed that, given a few regiments of cavalry and freed from the meddling of humanitarians, they could solve the Indian problem in a few months. The great difficulty lay in the fact that neither the American people nor their government had any clear conception of what the problem was or what they proposed to do about it.

General Sherman in two of his reports to the Secretary of War spoke out against this state of confusion that was paralyzing military action: "These Indians are universally, by the people of our frontier and of our isolated Territories, regarded as hostile, and we, the military, charged with a general protection of the infant settlements and long routes of travel, have to dispose our troops and act as though they were hostile; while by the laws of Congress, and the acts of our executive authorities, these Indians are construed as under the guardianship and protection of the general government, through civilian agents." And in another report: "Our people continue to settle on the exposed points of the frontier, to travel without the precaution which a well known danger would suggest, and to run after every wild report of the discovery of gold or other precious metal, thus coming into daily and necessary conflict with discontented and hostile Indians. The co-ordinate departments of our government likewise continue to extend the surveys of public lands westward, and grant patents to occupants; to locate and build railroads; to establish mail routes . . . as though that region of country were in profound peace. . . . Over all these matters the military authorities have no control, and yet their public nature implies public protection, and we are daily and hourly called on for guards and escorts, and we are left in the breach to catch all the kicks and cuffs of a war of races."[2]

It was into an army facing these problems that Colonel de Trobriand came when in 1866 he was mustered out of volunteer service and then accepted a commission in the 31st infantry. The vicissitudes of military life were nothing new to the De Trobriands. Miles Denys,

[2] *House Executive Document* no. 1, 39 Congress, 2 session, p. 20; *House Executive Document* no. 1, 40 Congress, 3 session, p. 1.

an ancestor of Irish descent, won the fiefs of Kereden and Trobriand in 1385 fighting for Jean de Montfort in Brittany. Through the centuries that followed, the De Trobriands fought both for kings and against them in the wars of France.

When Denis de Trobriand, grandfather of Régis, was implicated in a conspiracy against the Governor of Brittany, he fled to Spain to escape the *lettres de cachet* that were sent out from Paris. In Spain, where he remained until the death of Louis XV brought him back to France, Denis took service in the Spanish navy and married a noble lady of the country, the aunt of Simon Bolívar.

Joseph de Trobriand, father of Régis, was a student at the Collège Louis le Grand when the great revolution broke out in France. He began his long military career when he escaped from the mob and joined the army of princes outside the borders of France. In this army and that of Austria, he fought in almost every European country. Napoleon offered amnesty and commissions to the émigrés, and Joseph returned to France, where he became a trusted officer in the army of the empire. Like many another soldier of his generation, he marched with the French armies through their victories and then straggled back with them from Moscow in the ice and snow of a Russian winter. The title of Baron was added to that of Comte already possessed by the family, and life seemed fair to the warriors of the De Trobriand line.

Eleven times wounded, Joseph de Trobriand ended his active fighting career when Napoleon abdicated in 1814. The Bourbons put him on half pay for six years, since he had not resigned during the hundred days of Napoleon's return, and then restored him to a command. He was a brigadier general when the Bourbons were driven from France in 1830. Not wishing to serve under Louis Philippe, he resigned from the army and forbade his son, already enrolled in the school for pages, to employ the family sword in the service of that king.

Régis, descendant of this line of soldiers that had fought in every major battle of the Republic and the Empire, reluctantly gave up plans for a military career and turned to the study of law, a profession foreign to the De Trobriands. Although he was admitted to the bar when he received a degree from Poitiers in 1837, he never practiced law. When his father died in 1840 and the family estate was divided, he went to Paris to take a position in the Ministry of the Interior.

During this time De Trobriand attracted attention by writing a novel based on the expedition made by the Duchesse de Berry in

1832 to Vendée to fight for the throne for her son, the Comte de Chambord. The appearance of his book, *Les Gentilshommes de l'Ouest,* caused considerable excitement, since the characters in the novel were poorly masked and the sympathies of the De Trobriands for Charles X were well known.

In 1841 De Trobriand made his first trip to the New World that was to become his home. He went with the Comte de MaCarty to New York where he lived the life of a tourist. During the year that De Trobriand spent visiting the principal cities of the United States and Canada, he began his career as an observer of life on the new continent by contributing to *Le Courrier des Etats Unis* articles on the aftermath of the events of 1837 in Canada entitled "Le Rebelle, Nouvelle Canadienne. [*Sic*]" A Canadian editor who reprinted the articles in brochure form was imprisoned for six months.

The introduction of Régis de Trobriand, commentator, was certainly inauspicious, but in the years that followed the talented Frenchman was to perform a real service by illuminating for Americans, as did De Tocqueville before him, features of the national landscape. America of the nineteenth century did not leave him unmoved, and before he died at the close of the century, the aristocrat and royalist became a sincere convert to the republican form of government for the United States. Washington Irving welcomed the new writer on America to this country when he wrote in 1841: "You have a new World before you in which you may win laurels and gain an enviable and lasting reputation."[3]

The next years were pleasant ones; "silk and gold" he himself called them. New York society cordially received the charming and handsome Baron de Trobriand who could paint a picture, compose a verse, write an essay, and turn a phrase. After his marriage in Paris to Mary Mason Jones of New York, he and his wife went to Venice where they joined the court circle of the exiled Bourbons. For three years De Trobriand studied painting, music, and history, while enjoying the pleasant companionship of old friends in exile. In 1847 he left Venice to return to America by way of Paris. Writing to the Comte de Chambord from Paris, he commented on his own land: *"Il est évident que nous marchons aux catastrophes."*[4] The revolution broke out the next year, and he returned from a visit to Paris completely disgusted.

In 1847 De Trobriand became a regular contributor to *Le*

[3] Marie Caroline Post, *Life and Memoirs of General de Trobriand,* p. 59.
[4] *Ibid.,* p. 148–151.

Courrier des Etats Unis. His articles on the opera received wide attention through the translations of Nathaniel P. Willis of the *Home Journal.* His literary charm and artistic skill were welcomed by the journalists of New York, and a well-wisher hoped "that he will think it worth his while to graft himself on our periodical literature, and give it an effervescence it needs."[5]

So warm was the reception given to the new writer that he believed the time was ripe to aid the fusion of French and American culture by founding in the United States a French literary magazine. *La Revue du Nouveau Monde* had a short but brilliant life. Although the list of contributors includes names like Lamartine, De Vigny, and Gautier, the four volumes are pervaded by the spirit of the editor. In poem, story, essay, and critique, he demonstrated the breadth of his interest and his skill. When at the end of a year the journal ceased publication, Régis de Trobriand had contributed considerably to American letters. Although an essay on flirtation written to amuse the reader of the day may well repose in the dusty rows of a periodical file, the notes on his travels in America and Cuba deserve to be rescued from oblivion. In these, as in *Quatre Ans de Campagne à l'Armée du Potomac* and as in *Military Life in Dakota,* he is an articulate observer of things American.

After three years in France (1851–1854) De Trobriand returned to America again, this time to accept a position as subeditor of *Le Courrier des Etats Unis.* His column, *Les Feuilletons du Lundi,* a weekly chronicle of social, literary, and artistic events, appeared regularly in *Le Courrier* from 1854 until the outbreak of the Civil War.

And thus, living on two continents, "a Frenchman in France, an American in America," the Baron passed his life until 1861. Then, on April 18, Régis de Trobriand heard the beating of drums, saw the national colors floating in the wind as the Sixth Massachusetts Regiment passed down the streets of New York in response to the President's call for troops. "And I thought," he says in his memoirs of the Civil War, "despite myself of those familiar sights of my childhood, when the French battalions defiled before the starry epaulets of my father; and I wondered vaguely if the destiny that had deprived me of the heritage of his sword had not in reserve for me in America some compensation, in the ranks of these volunteers marching to fight for a cause which had immortalized Lafayette."

His decision made, Baron de Trobriand became a citizen of the

5 Post, *Life and Memoirs of General de Trobriand,* p. 172.

United States, joined the Lafayette Guard, and fought by choice for the cause of the Union. Through battles at Fredericksburg, Chancellorsville, and Gettysburg he led his regiment, happy to pay a debt of gratitude to his adopted country. When he was breveted major general for his services during the war, he became the only Frenchman other than Lafayette to hold that rank in the army of the United States.

After mustering out of volunteer service, he went to France to write *Quatre Ans de Campagne à l'Armée du Potomac* from the notes he had made during the war. Written to explain to the French the civil conflict as he saw it, the two volumes held much for American readers. The observations of the new citizen on high-ranking officers and on military strategy were both applauded and denounced as the reviews of the French edition were issued.

While General de Trobriand was compiling his memoirs of the Civil War, he received notice that he had been appointed to the regular army as colonel and that he was to report for duty with the 31st infantry. A leave of absence was requested and granted, and after the completion of his volumes, De Trobriand joined his regiment at Fort Stevenson. Adam Badeau, who was then writing a biography of General Grant, wrote to his friend: "You are indeed plunged from one extreme to the other of life. From Paris to the American Wilds, from the opera to the Indians. But then you are a man of the world."[6]

And the "man of the world" made good use of his talents in the American West. The vistas of the prairies, the sweep of the plains fired his great imagination, and with paint and pencil he recorded the look of the Dakota land: the lazy Missouri curving from bluff to bluff past an old Indian village; a painted chief posed stiffly in ceremonial robes; an army post rising on the empty plains like a phantom bastion; a supply train moving slowly across the plains toward a distant fort. Like those of Catlin, Bodmer, Miller, Mayer, and other artists of the frontier, his sketches and paintings are documents that should not be ignored by historians who are trying to picture the West as it was before the Indian hunter accepted his reservation and the white man's plow turned the sod of the hunting ground.

Coming to the West as a writer and artist as well as a soldier, De Trobriand felt the grandeur of the country, its immensity, its loneliness, and his journal is as much the record of the impact of the country on a sensitive man as it is a narrative of military life. In the

6 Adam Badeau, Washington, D. C., to Gen¹ de Trobriand, Fort Rice, D. T., May 27, 1867. De Trobriand Family Papers.

daily entries he writes expressively of the country—of hot winds burning the Dakota plains, of winter snows blanketing the land, of summer storms that brought no rain, and always of the great plains rolling away to nowhere.

De Trobriand brought to the West a mind free from the prejudices that colored the thinking of officers who had seen long service in Indian country. From the philosophers and writers of France he had gathered impressions that were to be tested by actual contact with the American Indian—from Jean Jacques Rousseau, who a hundred years before had made popular the concept that man was most noble in his natural state, from Chateaubriand who gave the idea eloquence in his idyllic novels.

In New York he had heard both the philanthropic Easterner who listened with sympathy as Red Cloud told of his people, and the practical frontiersman who believed that good Indians were dead Indians. But determined to see for himself, he waited on his own experience, then told what he saw in uncompromising language.

This assignment to Dakota Territory was the beginning of more than ten years' service with the regular army. When he was transferred after two and one half years at Fort Stevenson to Fort Shaw, Montana Territory, he organized the campaign against the Piegans executed by Baker; later, in Utah, he parleyed with the Mormons in the perilous days of near-revolution. After service at Fort Steele, Wyoming Territory, he was sent to Louisiana where his arrest of one of the two legislatures meeting in 1875 gained him a certain notoriety. After his retirement in 1879, he spent his summers in Paris and Bayport, Long Island, and his winters in New Orleans, where he died in 1897.

In the scope of this edited journal, there is no place to tell the full story of this remarkable citizen, who, like many another son of a foreign land, contributed so richly to the diversity of culture that is America's boast. But much of the man, Régis de Trobriand, can be discerned in the pages of the journal written by lamplight in his lonely quarters at Fort Stevenson. Here then is *Military Life in Dakota,* the journal of a man who learned the West and told its story well.

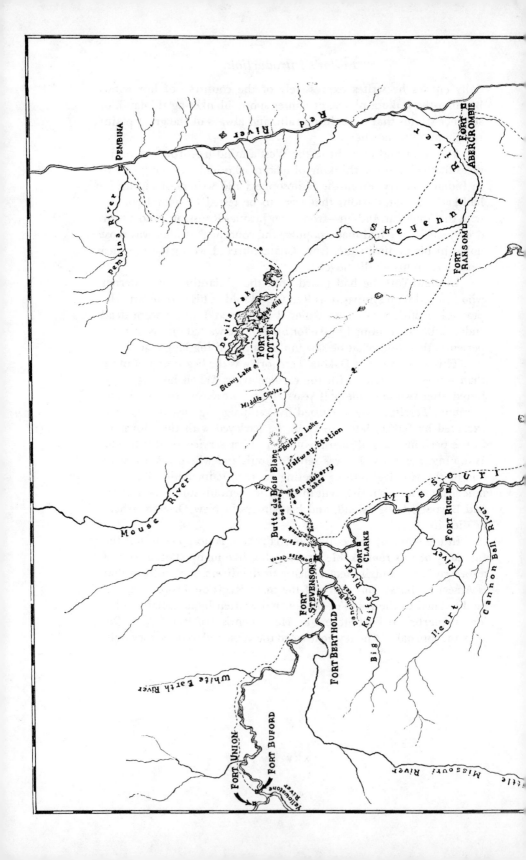

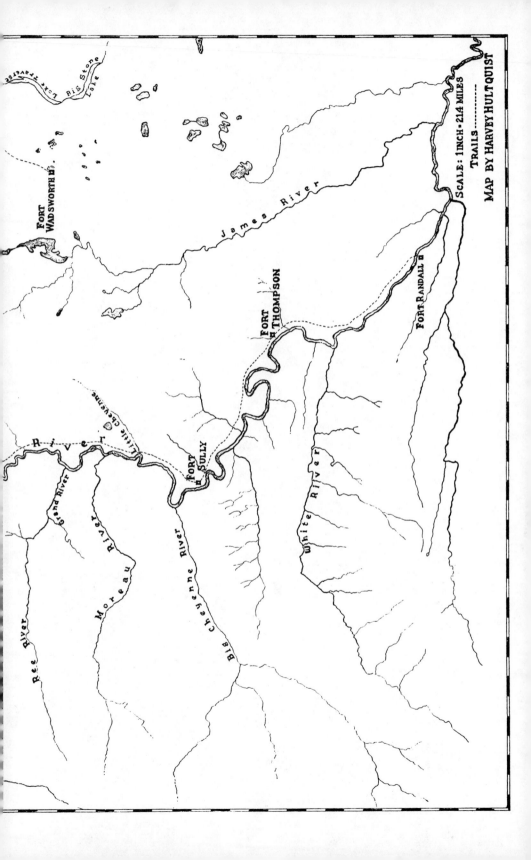

FORT WADSWORTH

Big Stone Lake

Lake Traverse

James River

FORT THOMPSON

FORT SULLY

Little Cheyenne

River

Grand River

Ree River

Moreau River

Big Cheyenne River

White River

FORT RANDALL

SCALE: I INCH = 214 MILES

TRAILS ----------

MAP BY HARVEY HULTQUIST

Military Life in Dakota

The Journal of Philippe Régis de

TROBRIAND

Notes

I left Paris Tuesday, June 11, 1867, a festive Paris at the height of the Universal Exposition, welcoming travelers from every country in the world and celebrating the visits of foreign sovereigns. In the official world there were rounds of great banquets, receptions, balls, festivities of every kind. For the common herd, theaters and places of amusement were in full swing, horse races were held two or three times a week everywhere, and important newspapers vied with one another to honor today the Emperor of Russia, tomorrow the King of Prussia, next the Sultan, then the Emperor of Austria. Crowned foreigners were literally running in the streets: Emperor Alexander disguised his majesty in an *incognito* in a box at the Varieties, hearing *La Grande Duchesse de Gerolstein;* the King of Prussia drank his mug of beer in true bourgeois style at the cafe; the heir to the British crown—we shall not mention him. And every afternoon at the Bois de Boulogne so many Royal and Imperial Highnesses, Dukes, and Princes appeared at the edge of the lake that they could scarcely be distinguished from one another. From nine o'clock in the morning to six o'clock in the evening, the people crowded the curved walks of the Champs de Mars, along which extended the marvelous galleries of the Exposition.

The great whirlpool had seized me an hour after I arrived. It carried me along a few weeks and released me only an hour before I left. I left Paris to go straight to the Upper Missouri. From the brilliant peaks of civilized life, I was to plunge straight into the dark pit of savage existence. Never was there a greater contrast, but contrasts are the spice of life; they banish monotony and boredom, and give life a variety that cannot be found in a settled existence. In order to know life, one must experience all kinds of it, examine it from different points of view. The most excellent book on education is that of personal experience. In its different chapters, gradations only dull sensations, I fear, and impair our judgment of them. The more contrasts one meets, the stronger are his impressions and the keener are his appreciations of them. In such cases, the intellect takes a Russian bath, and in going from Paris to Dakota, my Russian bath was like going from the sweating room to a cold shower.

[*The crossing*] I devoted the last ten days of my stay in France to my family, and on June 22, 1867, I embarked at Brest on the *Ville de Paris,* en route to New York. On the two most important lines, the French *Compagnie Transatlantique* and the English Cunard Line, the crossing is a matter of nine or ten days; other lines take from twelve to fifteen days. The time has long passed since it took sailboats thirty to sixty days to make the same trip, the time varying with the circumstances, especially with the wind.

Wonderful weather favored our departure. The sky was blue, the sun shone, the sea was calm, the air was still. It was pleasant to consider this an omen of a quick and happy crossing for us. At the captain's table, everyone but me believed this. They urged me to explain the reasons for my skepticism about the auguries, and I did not have to be coaxed, since the enforced absence of many of the passengers made our group at meals small for the first few days. "Without making any statement of belief or disbelief in the omens," I said, "I am always curious about comparisons that can be interpreted this way, and because of this, I have, since anchor was weighed, looked over my fellow passengers quite carefully, for if any favorable or unfavorable influences can be exerted on sailing conditions, it seems to me more natural and logical to attribute them to active life and to thinking beings who, perhaps unconsciously, put mysterious forces in motion than to inert causes such as the weather."

"Aha! the evil eye," said the doctor.

"Exactly. Well gentlemen, although the analysis I have made is in general satisfactory, I am apprehensive about one of the passengers."

"Which one? Which one?" they immediately asked, for it is interesting to note that no matter how skeptical any person may claim to be about the occult, his interest is caught as soon as the subject is mentioned.

"Take a look out of the corner of your eye at the next to the last man at the purser's table," I said to my companions.

"He is a strange person," remarked the postal agent.

"I have noticed how queer he is," said the captain.

"I believe he is a little crazy," added the doctor.

"I do not know if he is or not," I continued, "but one thing seems certain to me: if we must have a bad omen, it will come from him."

My companions laughed at the joke.

"That man," I went on, without taking part in the hilarity of the others, "has an *idée fixe.* He has an unkempt appearance, his

PHILIPPE RÉGIS DE TROBRIAND

face is haggard, his walk nervous. Since we left port, he has continually paced the deck, oblivious to everything around him. He went down to the salon and came back up again, chewing on the stub of a dead cigar, and never for a moment losing his air of preoccupation. Two or three times he has looked at me without seeing me. But deep in his eyes I have seen the shadow of mysterious things; I have seen in his face the mark of a predestined fate which has reached the time of fulfillment. That man will die a violent death, or I am badly mistaken. Will the evil influence which dominates him spread to others? I should not want to say so, but perhaps we shall know before the end of the trip."

Since dinner was over, everyone went up on deck, and there was no more speculation about the realm of the unknown.

The next morning, just as I was sitting down at the breakfast table, my neighbor said to me: "Do you know what has happened?"

"No, I don't. What?"

"You remember the man with the evil influence whom you pointed out yesterday at dinner?"

"Yes, what about him?"

"Well, he cut his throat with a razor and is dying right now."

The doctor soon came in and furnished us with fuller details. It seemed that the suicide belonged to a respectable merchant family in New York. He was wealthy and had made his fortune in business. Whether he had worked too hard and had upset his mental balance or success in speculation had caused his derangement, the fact remains that he had become insane and that he had undergone treatment in one of the most famous private hospitals in Paris. After a time the illness seemed to respond to treatment, and the cure was considered complete enough for the convalescent to return to his family. In order to make provision for the dangerous consequences of a relapse, which is always possible in such a case, our man was confided to the care and surveillance of a fellow countryman, Doctor ———, who was about to return to America. The American doctor took charge of the patient in Paris, took him to Brest, and sailed with him, not revealing to anyone the condition of his traveling companion. These circumstances were known only after the tragedy. "When the first bell rang," related the ship's surgeon, "the steward assigned to the suicide's cabin thought he heard groans, but supposing him to be seasick, he ignored them and went on. However, since the breakfast bell had rung, Doctor ——— went to his traveling companion's door and found it locked from the inside. He called and got no answer.

He pounded on the door hard and there was no response. He was worried and went to the captain, and, explaining the circumstances, asked that the door be forced, which was done. They found the unfortunate crazed man stretched out on the floor in a pool of blood. He had cut his throat from ear to ear with so steady a hand that although he is still breathing and we are giving him every possible care, it is physically impossible for him to live more than an hour or two. He has not been restored to consciousness. The lamp is still smoking, but it is almost extinguished, and nothing can make it burn again."

The news of the tragedy spread among the passengers immediately, and the usual comments were heard on deck after breakfast. The man died about eleven o'clock. When his doctor reappeared on deck he was, of course, subjected to every sort of question that curiosity could prompt. The doctor was a tall, large man with an unruffled composure that can withstand shocks. Nevertheless, he seemed very surprised about what had happened. His amazement seemed strange when it was revealed that he knew perfectly well the mental condition of the patient entrusted to his care and surveillance, and yet he had allowed him to get: 1. A pair of razors—we know how he used them; 2. A fully loaded revolver that was found in his baggage; 3. A vial of morphine containing enough poison to kill about twelve people. This was a strange kind of surveillance, and the surprise was post-mortem indeed. The trait is essentially American.

The man was dead, and since he died the day after departure, the only thing to do was to sew him in a sack with two weights and consign his mortal remains to the deep. But at this juncture the care and surveillance of the doctor, aroused rather late, were now devoted to the dead rather than the living. He vigorously opposed burial at sea, and in the name of the bereaved family he claimed the body so it could be buried in its native country. It was just a matter of keeping it on ice, like the fresh supplies brought from Brest. But a serious objection was raised. After an investigation of the ice supply, it was found that the quantity over and above the estimated needs of the passengers was far too small to carry out the proposed plan. In a case like this, the question was, of course, settled in favor of the living rather than the dead.

The doctor did not consider himself defeated, and he now suggested that the body be preserved in a barrel of rum. The family was wealthy; they would be willing to pay the expense, and he himself would guarantee it.

Finally the head of a barrel of rum was knocked in, and the man who had cut his throat was plunged into it in a position which would be very embarrassing to a living person, but which, as far as is known, makes no difference to the dead. After this was done, the barrel was closed with care, and the *Ville de Paris* continued to plow the waves as if nothing had happened.

"Upon my word," said the postal agent, addressing me, "I think you are a prophet, and in the future, I shan't doubt your theories of the evil eye. But now the episode is closed, the evil influence is gone, and there is nothing that should prevent us from having a short and pleasant crossing."

"Don't be too sure of that," I answered. "You might be disappointed yet."

"How? Is there more bad luck in store for us?"

"Perhaps. For my part I do not like this human body being sealed in rum. It is true that the soul has gone to take up a new life, but who knows what mysterious forces can still be stirred up around that corporal shell vacated so recently? My opinion is that it would have been better for us to send it to rest on the bottom of the ocean."

"That's what the sailors are saying," said the ship's doctor. "They believe that the presence of the dead will give us a rough crossing."

"And maybe the sailors are not as wrong as you think they are, Doctor. I am not predicting anything, but before the voyage is over, we shall know all that is going to happen to us, whether it is explained as a chance coincidence or as an inexplicable consequence."

The next day the sun set with all the signs that warn the sailor's eye of the approach of bad weather. The head wind grew in violence during the night, the sea became worse and worse, and the *Ville de Paris,* slowed down in her course considerably, soon began to toss around in the furious water.

The officers explained to me that we were entering a region of the Atlantic called the "devil's hole" because of the frequency of bad weather in a radius of a few hundred miles. But after a bad night, the day turned out to be still worse. The raging wind roared in the rigging, howled around the smokestack, and the maddened sea crashed against us like ranks of moving mountains. The steamer (a remarkable ship) rolled terribly, pitched horribly at times, creaking in all her timbers and groaning like a giant in agony. Sometimes she shot up toward the sky, resting on the shifting back of some enormous wave; then she plunged down into the abyss, the sea retreating under her, and she was swallowed up more completely than ever in the ava-

7

lanche of tempest-driven water that rushed in. The billows broke against the side of the ship, rebounded in torrents on the bow, ran like a deluge over the deck, dashed from bow to stern and back again, poured from port to starboard, and finally ran off through the scuppers provided for that purpose. The propeller struggled bravely but with much effort in a rapidly changing situation: at times it was slowed down and almost swallowed up by the violence of the sea; at times it speeded up when it came out into the air and met no resistance. A whole day passed like this. Scarcely a dozen of the two hundred passengers came to the table. The dead man was playing his pranks.

When evening came, things grew still worse, for the storm, changing its direction, turned into a hurricane and came from all points of the compass. The second night was terrifying. Reversed by the sudden veering of the wind, the great waves crashed together, and the entire power of the steamship was needed to keep her from foundering in such a turbulent sea. We did not advance a mile. All the officers and sailors were on deck; the passengers stayed in their cabins, very uneasy both mentally and physically. At intervals the masses of water beating around the deck broke through to the interior, rushed in cataracts into the corridors separating the cabins, and even went into some cabins. Then were heard the sharp, distressed cries of some passenger who believed that his time had come, the loud swearing of someone doused by the deluge, and the characteristic moaning which accompanies seasickness. No one could sleep a wink, for even if one were exempt from any worry or seasickness, it was necessary to brace oneself with hands and knees at the edge of the bunk in order not to be thrown to the floor by the most terrible rolling I have ever gone through. Finally, in the morning, the storm seemed to have spent its fury and the man in the rum his evil influence. The wind steadied and died down somewhat, but it took the ocean forty-eight hours to regain its calm.

The next morning my companion, who had been kept in his cabin by the storm, reappeared on deck and said to me, "I hope that this time we are done with mysterious influences."

"I hope so, too," I answered. "In any case, the worst has passed. It is possible that some of these influences, like sparks that fly up from warm coals after a fire, are still stirring around the rum barrel and might cause us some minor misfortunes. But that isn't important."

As a matter of fact, for two more days we had to go through banks of thick fog which slowed us down and which made the captain fume almost as much as the storm, although, it was not important in the opinion of the passengers.

On the morning of the third day, a blast of wind took my hat out to sea. "Is that another omen?" asked one of the passengers.

"Undoubtedly," I answered, "it is the last breath of evil influences; now we have only good fortune before us."

From that time on, the sky and sea were all smiles for us, and the obliging wind blew just enough to speed us up and help us make up for the time we had lost.

I disembarked at New York on the morning of July 3. We spent the night at anchor before quarantine. We made the crossing in ten days and a few hours in spite of hurricanes, fogs, and the man in rum.

The first thing I did was to announce my arrival to the adjutant general of the army and to spend with my relatives the few days I had before the orders of the War Department sent me off. These orders arrived on the twelfth, and on the sixteenth, after I completed my preparations and passed before the examining committee prescribed for all officers transferred from voluntary to regular service, I started on my way to join my command on the Upper Missouri. Fort Rice in Dakota was designated as my general headquarters. I was to get there by the shortest possible route.

Journal

MILITARY LIFE IN DAKOTA

Left New York the morning of the sixteenth, arrived at Chicago (Illinois) the evening of the seventeenth, after traveling for thirty-six consecutive hours by railroad. Stayed at the Sherman House. Spent the morning looking over this town, which is remarkable for the rapidity and extent of its development. You must remember that only thirty years ago there was no Chicago. Then it was a village built around a military post of two companies quartered in log houses surrounded by palisades.[1] It was a squalid settlement bogged down in prairie mud, built in a natural cove at one end of Lake Michigan. Only two years before, the government had bought it from the Indians, who had sold great areas of land in this region and who were then sent farther up the Missouri.[2] Bears and wolves were still plentiful in the surrounding country, and there was almost no commerce.

Now the impossible had happened. The population which in 1836 was less than 2,000 passed the 200,000 mark in 1866. It increased a hundredfold in thirty years. The amount of grain shipped out in 1838 was 78 bushels of wheat; in 1866 the figure rose to 55,000,000 bushels, not counting more than 3,000,000 hogs slaughtered, salted, barreled, sold and shipped, almost half a million head of cattle brought in and shipped out in different forms, and over 600,000,000 feet of lumber. Thirty years ago, the only way to get to Chicago was by horse or crude cart of some kind. The first locomotive got there in 1849, and today an average of two hundred trains come and go every twenty-four hours. The city is the hub of a network of track radiating for 5,000 miles around. Everything else has progressed at the same

1 Fort Dearborn was established in 1803.

2 By the treaty made at St. Louis on August 24, 1816, the Ottawa, Chippewa, and Pottawatomi ceded to the United States a strip of territory north and east of the Kankakee River as far as Lake Michigan, including the present site of Chicago. De Trobriand is apparently referring to the treaties signed at Fort Armstrong with the Winnebago, September 15, 1832, and with the Sauk and Fox, September 21, 1832. In these treaties the Winnebago ceded lands south and east of the Fox-Wisconsin River line, and the Sauk and Fox all claims to areas east of the Mississippi River. Charles C. Royce, *Indian Land Cessions in the United States,* Eighteenth Annual Report of the Bureau of American Ethnology, 2:682; Charles J. Kappler, *Indian Laws and Treaties,* 2:132–133.

pace. It is reported that Mr. Richard Cobden said to one of his friends leaving for America: "There are two things you must see in America if you see nothing else: Niagara and Chicago." I have seen Niagara and Chicago as well as other things, and I have not seen everything yet.

[*Chicago to Omaha*] Left for Omaha at three o'clock in the afternoon. The sleeping cars on the train from Chicago to Omaha are not as luxurious as those which are so pompously called "silver palaces" on the New York–Chicago route. There are no separate compartments, there is less glass, and the decorations are duller. But they are comfortable enough, indeed a good deal more so than one might expect, since this road serves as no connecting link to a center of population, a city, or a market town, but instead runs straight across four hundred and ninety miles of almost deserted Iowa prairie to end at a miserable village on the bank of the Missouri, for the railroad stops at Council Bluffs, four or five miles from Omaha on the other bank of the river.

My trip across Illinois and Iowa gave me a glimpse of the spectacle of the Great Plains of the West, as seen from a flying locomotive. These great level spaces without mountain or hill, where a thin stream of water scarcely marks a bed in its lazy course, are called the prairie. Only scattered clumps of trees obstruct the view of the horizon where the earth and sky meet. The prairie still seems rather boggy to me. Earth has been taken to build an embankment for a solid roadbed, and this leaves ditches on both sides with endless sheets of water. Many aquatic plants grow on the surface of this water, and the waterfowl have become so accustomed to the trains that they look at them with more curiosity than fear. This man-made border of stagnant water often merges with the great, green natural swamps stretching away in the distance on the plains. It is hard to define their limits, for they seem to be a part of the dry land which surrounds them. Since there is little difference in land level, the only thing that distinguishes these two areas from each other is the difference in the color of the vegetation.

The population of the prairie is still so sparse that one can go for miles without seeing a log house surrounded by a cultivated field or shaded, perhaps, by a clump of young trees. No roads anywhere, hardly a path for the pedestrian or beast of burden. The only wagon roads that I have noticed are the long, muddy, narrow ones which are found near the railway stations, where rude houses scattered around a waiting room and a storehouse for merchandise form the pretext for calling it a village. These endless plains are not without character. There is grandeur in their immensity, but they are monotonous too. Since horizon after horizon is just alike, looking at the country grows tiresome. The trip from Chicago to Council Bluffs has few attractions for the traveler. More and more one feels that civilization is being left behind as one goes into this great open domain which man has not yet converted from its natural state, but on which he has already laid his hand.

The travelers match their country. They are for the most part rough Westerners, men who are not at all refined, who are still crude physically and morally, but who are gifted with tremendous energy, and who utilize fully the gifts that God gave them. Inside the car as well as in the surrounding country, it is evident that the centers of civilization are far away, although here, as everywhere else, one meets the ingenious Yankee, the precocious fruit of Eastern culture.

In the group of fortune seekers, there are some who have already found it. They are more easily identified by their air, their jewelry, and their language than by their manners. Almost without exception, these men are adventurers who have earned their money by the sweat of their brow and at great personal risk. They have come up from the dirt and have never had time to dust themselves off. Because they live among savages, or half savages, and are completely absorbed with business affairs, they do not worry very much about elevating themselves above the material comforts and crude pastimes they can buy with their money. They may be clever, intelligent, energetic, and even honest, but they are not gentlemen, although they often assume the title. In fact, they do not even know the real meaning of this word which has been so distorted since it left England and arrived on the banks of the Missouri.

[*Council Bluffs*] It was around four o'clock in the evening, July 19, when the train stopped at the end of the line in sight of the Missouri. No station. After we passed the village of Council Bluffs, we were out in the middle of the prairie. We could see houses scattered up the side of a height where a few years ago the Indians had come in to hold council. That is how it got its name. Everyone jumped out of the car, and ran pell-mell for a line-up of coaches and wagons on the other side of a second track, which was blocking the way with empty cars. They got settled as well as they could, pushing, piling on top of one another, some on the steps for lack of any other place, until it seemed to me that they were all taken care of at last. The heat was terrific and the dust asphyxiating, but it could have been

13

worse: if it had rained, we should have been between water from the sky and mud from the ground.

The railroad checks baggage only up to Council Bluffs, so it must be checked again for Omaha. Time is lost, but it is done quickly and the baggage is then stacked up pyramid fashion, rather than inverted-cone fashion, in a large baggage wagon with flare-boards, drawn by six horses. Considering the height of the load, its width toward the top, and the laws of gravity, I do not understand why the load didn't fall off nine times out of ten. However, everything arrived safely, although the road was not macadamized. Good Lord! There isn't any road, with or without macadam, between the terminus of the railroad and the steamboat which crosses the river. Many trails are made by wheels across the prairie. When they are passable, they are used. When they are broken up with ruts, they are deserted and others are made. They go over grass, stones, stumps, brushwood and thickets, following the inspiration of the driver, or at best, the keenness of his vision. One is jolted, bounced, and upset, but the vehicle always overcomes all obstacles. The baggage follows. When the jolting becomes too dangerous, the driver leaves the trails and goes across fields. Since the steamboat must wait for the baggage, another mile makes no difference. Anyway it is better than having the baggage upset and using the time to reload it, to say nothing of possible damage to the bags and of the labor involved.

Since we were unfortunate enough to arrive when the water was already very low, the ferryboat had to make a long detour to cross the river, and it was moored four or five miles away, waiting for us. What heat, dust, and sweat! After the baggage finally arrived, we were transported to the other bank amidst a conglomeration of horses, mules, bipeds, and vehicles of every kind that were crowded on the deck. The loading and unloading of the carriages by a drawbridge, part of which was buried in the bank, deserves a description in itself, but we shall not take up time with such port details. A one- or two-mile road, marked only by tracks, led us joltingly to Omaha. The carriage dropped us off at the door of a large, square brick building. It was the Herndon, the hotel of the town (the only one in existence at that time, since the Cozzens Hotel was not yet finished). The baggage arrived next. I must admit I was worried about it. In spite of everything it had gone through, it had escaped injury, for I considered it of no great consequence that the corner was broken off my most elegant Parisian bag. Since I had feared the worst, I considered myself fortunate to get off with so little injury.

Omaha City was—I do not speak in the imperfect because things were in an imperfect state then, but because in such a devil of a country as this, things change so rapidly that they cannot be recognized from one year to the next. Some cities have grown more rapidly than the generation born with them; villages have become cities before children have become men. The Omaha of 1867 was undergoing so rapid a development that the sketch I make now probably will not apply to the Omaha of 1870.

In the month of July, 1867, Omaha was no longer a village and not yet a city, properly speaking, although she gave herself the proud name of Omaha City. The title really has no significance, for a dozen huts sometimes give themselves such a name *motu proprio* in anticipation of the future. Take Sioux City for example. However, I was assured that the population of Omaha was almost ten thousand. It did not seem so big to me; I should say that five or six thousand was closer to the truth, but I am probably mistaken. Two or three blocks of stores, shops, offices, and a theater, half brick and half planks, formed the hub of the town which hummed with activity. The main street, Farnham Street, connected this business section with the bank of the river. On this street there were two or three half blocks of brick houses, a number of shops built of planks, as many bars and eating houses of low quality, ending in the Herndon Hotel on the edge of the plateau above the high-water mark of the Missouri. There the street becomes a mere trail and plunges through an opening in the escarpment down the slope, across the tracks by the depot of the Pacific Railroad to the bank of the river.

Some day there will certainly be quays built in this place; perhaps there are now. But at that time the steamboats, unmoored and at the mercy of the current, loaded and unloaded their cargoes on the sandy bank. Evidently all this must be under water in the spring when the thaws raise the level of the river to the foot of the cliff. The railroad then moves out temporarily and the trains stop some distance away on higher ground. Then when the water recedes, the railroad company takes the rails from the siding and again uses the marshy ground.

Note: It was in the drainage ditches of these lowlands that I saw the first crayfish in America. Urchins were fishing many of them from the dirty, muddy water. They are smaller than the French crayfish, and I suppose they are inferior in taste. I do not know any more about them. We shall get back to the subject of Omaha proper.

Since Farnham Street is the only one that goes to the river bank,

Philippe Régis de TROBRIAND

it is, and will be for some time, the main street and artery of business. All the other open streets, seen traced on a large map, stretch at a right angle and for equal distances, parallel or perpendicular to the river. This is the uniform plan of cities in the United States, large or small.

According to this plan, starting from the center as I have indicated, there are spread out in every direction buildings of all sorts, cottages, small houses, huts, and shanties interspersed with fenced and unfenced land, mostly unfenced. All of this is on a vast extent of land which slopes gently from the banks of the Missouri up to the summit of a chain of hills surrounding the city on the west and south and terminating at the river. This chain of hills forms a pleasant amphitheater from the top of which two large buildings, magnificent because of their isolation and location, dominate the countryside. One is the Capitol, which has been without a legislature since the capital of Nebraska was transferred to [Lincoln].[3] The other is the convent of St. Mary devoted, I believe, to the education of young girls.

Catholicism is remarkable, among other things, for the way it follows up movements of population with educational institutions. By getting possession of the youth, it insures its future.

The site of Omaha was well chosen. Until the railroad bridge is constructed, the city is the terminus. It serves as a depot for goods which are going west onto the plains. That is why there is such feverish business activity, such restless energy; that is why population is growing so fast and construction is going on apace. That is why speculation is rampant in lands and buildings, etc. The future will answer this question: when the Pacific Railroad crosses the Missouri as it has already crossed the Mississippi, when Omaha becomes just a way station or perhaps a supply depot instead of the head of the line, when the branch line from St. Louis on one side and the direct line from Chicago on the other meet to distribute goods across the plains up to the Rocky Mountains, and direct communications with all the territories to San Francisco are established, will all this activity which is now going on in Omaha stop, and will the business so flourishing today be reduced to a special trade in agricultural products?

It is quite probable that the city, deprived of the profits which now accrue to her in provisioning the Pacific line, will not keep the

[3] Lincoln was chosen as the site of the new capital at the fourth session of the state legislature, May, 1867.

16

partial provisioning of the posts of the Upper Missouri either. Sioux City will furnish what St. Louis does not, for it is located two hundred and thirty miles up the river, and next year a new railroad line coming directly from Chicago by way of Dubuque will end there.[4] Two lines of rails are already being built. But even if the development of Omaha slows down or even halts completely, the progress already made will not be lost. Cities may stop going forward in the United States, but they never go backward.

[*Men of the plains*] It can easily be concluded from what I have just said that there is nothing unique about Omaha and that, taken as a whole or in part, it is just like any other American city in this period of growth. That is true. However, there are a few characteristic details that warn the stranger that he has reached the fringes of civilization and that he is now in the far, far West. In the streets one constantly meets hardy, sun-tanned men with long hair and beards who carry unconcealed in their belts the hunting knife and revolver, inseparable companions of the plainsman. If these men leave the city, whether by coach, wagon, or horse, they almost always take with them a carbine, just as people in other parts of the country would take an umbrella or walking stick. In any season, they wear a woolen shirt and a great coat, which is sometimes replaced by a deer- or antelope-skin jacket. The Indians usually seen on the Omaha streets are not remarkable. They are dirty beggars, half dressed in filthy rags, and they show their long black hair and brick-colored faces at kitchen doors more than at any other place.

In spite of their rough looks and rude manners, the Westerners are usually good natured and obliging. They do not hesitate to talk to strangers, they ask many questions, and gladly answer all that are asked them. They are so friendly that they will go further than that and will tell you about themselves, where they live, what they do, and what brings them to town, etc. Their adventures in the desert among the Indians are often really interesting, and it seemed to me that they were conscious of the attention they gained because of them.

It is very evident that I was taking advantage of every opportunity to learn as much as I could about this new country in which I was going to live. So I had a good many talks with Western pioneers while I got some fresh air at the hotel door in the evening. The ideas,

4 In 1867 the Illinois Central Railroad leased the Iowa Falls and Sioux City Railroad, which was still building. It was not completed to Sioux City until 1871. Henry V. Poore, *Manual of the Railroads of the United States, 1871–1872*, p. 497.

manners, and customs of the Indians were a subject to which I returned constantly, especially since my informants were not at all in agreement on the matter. Most of them believed that the only way to settle the Indian question was to exterminate *all this vermin.* This is the opinion held by the majority of frontiersmen, particularly those in the cities and settlements of some importance. Others who were more moderate or more just held that the white man was far from being blameless and that he was really responsible for the outbreaks during the war and now. These people were not numerous, and I believe that even if they did maintain that the poor Indians had been treated like dogs, deceived, cheated, pillaged, and massacred, they would have been just as quick as anyone else to shoot on sight any suspicious looking redskin who appeared on their road. The destiny of the white race in America is to destroy the red race, and in the rising tide of civilization which is moving toward the setting sun, there is no one who would hesitate to deal the final blow. Only the government temporizes and buys peace, so it does not have to do the job that individuals are going to do in spite of everything. For example, in Montana, in the heart of the Indian country, the Indian must go when gold brings in the miners. If he tries to defend his land, he is wiped out. The miner, excited by his work and dreams of fortune, is in a terrible mood. He needs complete security and protection from retaliatory raids. He leaves no stone unturned to get this security, and when he attacks the redskin, everyone, warriors, women, children, becomes food for the wolves or fertilizer for the soil. In many frontier settlements, they do not see any other answer to the question, and when the settlers ride away on an expedition, they don't bring back any prisoners.

Since I shall have every possible chance to study the Indians myself and to speak from my own experience, there is little use in discussing them further at this time.

I stayed in Omaha for sixteen days, sixteen days of heat, dust, boredom, and regrets, for since there was no communication with the place to which I was going, might I not have been able to spend about twelve more days with my relatives in New York and Newport and still arrive at my post at the same time? Fortunately, it is not my nature to torture myself with "ifs." What is done is done.

The first thing I did when I got to Omaha was to find out when the next steamboat would leave going up the river. No one could tell me, since there was no definite day of departure, the departure depending entirely on the freight that the steamboats could pick up.

Because of this uncertain state of affairs, I looked in the two most important St. Louis newspapers to find out which boat was leaving first and when she was starting. In this way, I learned that the *Deer Lodge*, Captain Clark, was to leave St. Louis on the nineteenth. A few days later I read that her departure was postponed to the twenty-fifth. She finally got under way on the morning of June 29.

General [Edward S.] Meyer, chief quartermaster of the Department of the Platte, whose headquarters are in Omaha, gave me excellent reports on the *Deer Lodge*. "She is," he told me, "one of the best steamboats on the Upper Missouri, and one of those that always makes the quickest trip. You are fortunate to have such good luck." But what was there to do in Omaha while waiting for the *Deer Lodge?* General [Christopher C.] Augur, commander of the Department, whom I had known during the war, was away. He was selecting, at the foot of the Rockies, the site for a new city, which was still in the planning stage but which will be populous in a few years. It was named Cheyenne before it was born.[5]

But even when General Augur returned after a few days, time still hung heavy. I became acquainted with a few officers and citizens of the town. Among the latter was a young man named Kimball, who had served in the Army of the Potomac. After the war, he became a wholesale grocer, and almost every day I loafed an hour or two in his store, watching the customers who came in a steady stream and admiring the Yankee energy with which my new acquaintance managed the business in the absence of his partner, who was then traveling in the East. The intelligence, skill, and enthusiasm of this young man were really remarkable. He spared himself nothing. He received the customers, discussed their needs, took their orders, got the merchandise around, made entries in the books (his clerk had typhoid), and took care of the correspondence. I would go in and take a chair. If he wasn't busy at the moment, we talked. If he was busy, I would pick up a paper or smoke a cigar, and business would go on as if I weren't there. Otherwise, of course, I would not have stayed. There I met a curious class of men who were strange to me. Because of their lack of education and the nature of their work, they were common people, but they had gone through great ordeals and had had strange adventures. A few officers came in, too, especially in the evening after dinner when the day's business was finished. Then we could get a breath of fresh air on the steps or talk war or politics

5 General Augur was on this trip locating Fort D. A. Russell near the town of Cheyenne. 40 Congress, 2 session, *Executive Document* no. 1, p. 60-61.

around a bottle of whiskey in the room behind the store where Mr. Kimball lived.

One Sunday, Mr. K———— took me to see the country around Omaha in a light wagon drawn by two good horses. I had no idea that we were right at the gate of the desert. In fact, when we reached the top of the hills around the city, the plains in all their immense solitude stretched out before us. The unfinished road which passed the gate of the convent led us to two isolated farms, but beyond these we saw no trace of cultivation or habitation. In order to return to Omaha by a different route (we were only four or five miles from there) we had to cross fields, for there was no road of any kind past the second farm. We came upon some miserable Irish shanties by a muddy stream, where some geese and ducks were playing and the inevitable hogs were wallowing. Irishmen and hogs always go together. In front of one of these shanties, we crossed the Pacific Railroad, and we stopped to gaze after the train disappearing far away into the prairie desert. I returned to the city firmly convinced that Omaha was an ultimate outpost of civilization.

Sunday, August 4. Finally I am on board the *Deer Lodge.*[6] She arrived at Omaha about six o'clock this evening and moored to the bank for the night. As I had been expecting her momentarily for days, I was all ready to embark immediately. My preparation didn't take long. Just enough time to close a bag or two, pay my hotel bill, and have my baggage loaded on a wagon ordered for that purpose, and I was at the wharf. I much preferred getting on board that night and going to sleep, without any worry about leaving time, to staying at the hotel, getting up before dawn, and going through all that last minute confusion.

Moreover, I accumulated much more baggage at Omaha. Enlightened by information gathered from officers accustomed to military life in the frontier posts, I had bought some necessary furnishings. I can get the rest later if I need them. Minimum essentials, no matter how few they are, cannot be put into an overnight bag. I am taking a bedstead, a mattress, covers, sheets, table linen, hand linen, chinaware, glassware, and a couple of rocking chairs. These things and four bags make quite an amount of luggage, and my servant just succeeded in getting them on the spring wagon.

[6] The log of the *Deer Lodge* telling of the incidents of this trip up the Missouri River was published in *National Waterways*, February, 1930. De Trobriand's description of the journey is more complete than the log, but this record does supply some information not included in the journal.

Captain Clark seems to be a fine fellow. His clerk, Mr. Corbin, who supervises the business transactions of the trips, is a very polished young man. Both of them were extremely gracious, and gave me the best cabin they had. My baggage was loaded quickly. Two of the bags were carried to the cabin I occupy alone: my servant will sleep on a mattress in the salon near my door, and it looks as if I am going to have as comfortable a trip as can be expected.

Brevet Lieutenant Colonel [Alexander] Chambers, a major in the 22nd, boarded an hour after I did. He had been waiting longer than I at the Herndon Hotel for the steamer which was to take him to his post. He was accompanied by his young wife and an orphaned maid they were bringing up, who went with Mrs. Chambers everywhere and waited on her. The major is assigned to the command of Fort Randall, the first post above Sioux City; consequently, he will not be with us for more than a few days.[7] He is taking with him a light carriage, a horse, and two magnificent greyhounds.

Mrs. Elliot and her two children are also on board. She is going to join her husband, a captain in the 22nd, who is stationed at Fort Sully, where General [D. S.] Stanley, commander of the District of Southeast Dakota, has his general headquarters.[8]

Last of all, the most pleasant acquaintance I have made on the steamer is that of Mr. Marshal, my adjutant, who is returning from leave, bringing with him his bride of a few weeks.[9]

Mr. Marshal made a very favorable impression on me. He holds the rank of first lieutenant and took his military training as a cadet at West Point, and although he is too young and too recently out of the military academy to have been in the war, the duties that he has performed make it evident that he is a good officer. He gave me all

[7] Established by General William S. Harney in 1856 when Fort Pierre was abandoned, Fort Randall was planned as one of the posts designed to protect advancing settlement. It was the first in the line of forts that was to extend up the Missouri River to Fort Benton. George W. Kingsbury, *History of Dakota Territory*, p. 66; *South Dakota Historical Collections*, 8:84; *Report on Barracks and Hospitals with Descriptions of Military Posts*, Circular no. 4, War Department, Surgeon General's Office, p. 386–87.

[8] De Trobriand uses two spellings for Thomas I. Elliott's name. It appears in the journal most often as "Elliot."

New Fort Sully was built in 1866 twenty miles below the mouth of the Cheyenne River after old Fort Sully was abandoned because of its unhealthful site. It was built for four companies and was located about halfway between Fort Rice and Fort Randall. The mail wagons, important to the communications of the upper river posts, ran from Fort Sully to Sioux City. *Report on Barracks and Hospitals*, p. 388–390.

[9] De Trobriand usually spells the name of James M. Marshall with one "l." It appears as "Marshall" in all official military registers.

possible information about my regiment and posted me on details that are valuable to know beforehand. Through him I learned that there are three posts in my command: Five companies at Buford located at the juncture of the Missouri and Yellowstone; three companies at Fort Totten on Devils Lake to the northeast of the big bend that the Missouri makes below Fort Berthold; two companies at Fort Stevenson, fifteen miles below Fort Berthold.[10] Fort Stevenson is my destination, since it is my general headquarters. Fort Berthold is also under my command, but the garrison has been withdrawn, and now the only occupants are some agents of the American Fur Company of the Northeast and some white traders.[11] An Indian village is built around it, where the remnants of three once powerful and warlike tribes cultivate their corn in peace.

After procuring some general information, I was presented to the ladies. General Augur, the officers of his general staff, and others I had met in Omaha came on board to bid me goodbye. There is action everywhere.

[10] Fort Buford was built as a five-company post by Colonel W. G. Rankin in the summer of 1867 on the site selected earlier in the year by General Alfred H. Terry. Situated in the heart of the buffalo country, this post was particularly offensive to the Sioux, who harassed the garrison with attacks on herds, communications, workmen, and soldiers. From the first days when the post was being built, the soldiers at Fort Buford kept their rifles beside them to fight off bands of Sioux who tried to make the post untenable. *Report on Barracks and Hospitals*, p. 400–405; 41 Congress, 2 session, *Executive Document* no. 1, 2:58. In the manuscript journal, Fort Buford is spelled "Bufford" throughout the first three hundred pages. In the rest of the manuscript, the spelling is correct, but De Trobriand is not always consistent. In *Vie Militaire dans le Dakota* (Paris, 1926) the word is spelled consistently as "Bufford." The editor of this translation has spelled the post name as "Buford" throughout the book.

On his expedition of 1867, General Terry selected the site for Fort Totten, one of the posts in the chain to be built for the protection of the overland route from southern Minnesota to western Montana. The rolling plains, timbered hills, and lake made this post one of the most attractive military stations on the plains. Occupied in July, 1867, "the fort arose as if by magic," but the hastily constructed buildings were replaced by more permanent ones in 1869–1870. *St. Paul Pioneer*, July 14, 1867, April 30, 1868; *North Dakota Historical Collections*, 3:178–179, 187–325.

Fort Berthold was established in 1845 by the American Fur Company and named in honor of one of the founders, Bartholomew Berthold. In 1859 an opposition company erected Fort Atkinson close to the village of the three tribes (the Mandan, Rees, and Gros Ventres) and after the American Fur Company bought it in 1862 it was renamed Fort Berthold. It was occupied by the military from 1864 when General Sully left a contingent of soldiers there as a protection against the Sioux until the building of Fort Stevenson in 1867 made further occupation unnecessary. *Report on Barracks and Hospitals*, p. 395.

[11] When De Trobriand mentions the Fur Company of the Northeast, he means the Northwest Fur Company.

The freight that was waiting for the *Deer Lodge* is being loaded by the light of pine-knot torches. Everything will be on board soon, and probably when I wake up in the morning we shall be far from Omaha.

Monday, August 5. Here we are, on our way on the great Missouri. At lunch, I found that there were more passengers on board than I mentioned yesterday: the wife and children of a carpenter employed at Fort Rice,[12] common people with whom I shall have no relations, and a big strapping fellow who doesn't look too promising, but who introduced himself to me as the Indian agent at Fort Berthold. Here is another source of information. The country is monotonous. The river banks are flat, bordered here and there by bare hills. The river is capricious in its course and changes its channel frequently. For some years it has been forming magnificent alluvial plateaus; the vegetation is verdant and abundant; trees grow rapidly here and reach a great height. Then one day the Missouri sets out to destroy its own work and eats away foot by foot the same plateaus it has built up. Along the banks, in the great woods, woodcutters hew down the trees which belong to everyone, cut them into the desired lengths, and cord them in long piles on the bank. Steamboats which are short of wood moor by the piles. The price is discussed, the sale is concluded, the crew goes ashore and loads the purchased wood on the run. Then they leave without further delay. Woodcutting is profitable and pays well for the season's work. A cord of wood brings from three to six dollars per cord, and sometimes even seven dollars, depending on the supply and whether the place where it is found is near or remote.[13] An able and ambitious man can cut up to two cords a day. Even if he does not cut more than forty cords a month, at five dollars a cord, he gets an income of *two hundred dollars* a month, and he has no expenses other than food. Since the river is navigable six months a year, he can earn from one

12 Fort Rice was established in the summer of 1864 by General Sully on his punitive expedition against the Sioux. Located on the right bank of the Missouri about seven miles above the mouth of the Cannon Ball River, this post was important in the period of this journal to the mail communications of Fort Stevenson with the East. Although an agent of the Post Office was appointed at the post as early as 1866, the carrying of the mail was in the hands of the military. *Report on Barracks and Hospitals*, p. 390–394.

13 Eight dollars a cord was the minimum price charged for wood by the cutters located above Fort Randall. "Wood hawks" was the name given to these frontiersmen by the steamboat captains. Joseph M. Hanson, *The Conquest of the Missouri*, p. 116.

thousand to twelve hundred dollars a year if he works from April to October. Isn't that worth risking Indian attacks and living in absolute solitude from thaw to freeze?

Tuesday, August 6. Arrived in Sioux City at sunset. This is the last village of any importance that we are going to pass. Here we must definitely say goodbye to the last traces of civilization we are leaving far behind us. The country we passed through today is a little more varied. Here and there among the trees we noticed some sawmills surrounded by miserable huts, where whites and Indians live together in misery and filth, at least to judge by appearances. There is nothing remarkable about the village. A badly kept inn, some shops along a wide street, and frame houses scattered about. There are also two churches, I believe, and there must be a print shop somewhere. Barrooms, of course. But all this will grow tenfold, perhaps a hundredfold, in a few years. The railroad from Dubuque is coming toward Sioux City. When it gets here, it will bring business activity and a movement of population which will quickly change the village to a city. This explains the land speculation that is already boosting the price out of proportion to the present condition of the place. A bend in the river by Sioux City forms a natural cove which can be greatly improved and used for the service of steamboats. With the protection of a pier, it would provide a place for boats to winter, and that would be an important advantage for the commerce of the Upper Missouri, for the provisioning of military posts, and for trade.

[*Missouri River steamboats*] The steamboat *Deer Lodge* is built on the same plan as all the boats which ply the Missouri and Mississippi. Its general construction is very simple. The hull is quite flat, almost without a keel, made to displace as little water as possible. When completely loaded, it does not draw more than four feet of water. Its average is from three to three and one-half feet. Under the first deck, the hull forms the hold where the merchandise is stacked. One-half to two-thirds the length of the boat, the forward deck is open. The stern is closed in a room to protect the engines and to serve as a repair shop. The furnaces and boilers are on the deck, forward of the engines. They pile the firewood port, starboard, and forward, leaving a passage for the crew on each side of it. In front of the furnaces, there is an open stairway which leads up to the upper deck. This deck, supported the length of the boat by cast-iron columns, encloses a dining room or salon in the center, from which all the cabins open on port and starboard.

Because of this arrangement, the anterior part of the salon is directly above the boilers, which heat the floor both summer and winter. Outside the cabins on both sides there is a gallery, onto which each cabin opens by a glass door. In summer, when the two opposite doors are open, there is a pleasant breeze throughout the boat. On the *Deer Lodge,* the two rows of cabins and the salon end in open decks, one forward and one aft. Finally, there is a stairway to the roof of the salon, but although there is a better view from this height, it is not used very often. The reason for this is that if the sun shines, one roasts, and if it rains, one gets soaked, and if there is neither rain nor sun, burning cinders shoot from the two smokestacks, fall on the deck, and burn openwork in any clothing they touch. The only real difference in construction that divides steamboats on the Missouri into two classes is this: some have wheels on the side and others have just one at the stern. The *Deer Lodge* is of the latter type. The great paddle-board wheel which propels her is as wide as the stern.

A propeller cannot be used because of the shallowness of the water, the swiftness of the current, and especially because of the many hazards in the river bed—dead trees, sand bars, etc. To complete the description, I should mention the pilot's house, which contains the wheel and is located forward on the upper deck between the two high smokestacks, a little astern.

The person on the bank who watches a steamboat of this type pass gets quite a different impression from that given by a steamer of the East, the country of deep waters. The Missouri River steamer looks like a long, flat cabin built on piles which the water left high and dry when it receded and which was then carried with its supports on a huge barge. There is certainly nothing elegant about it, but it must be very well suited to the navigation of these swift Western waters since it is the principal form of transportation used in these regions. The engines are low pressure and powerful. They breathe noisily like giants puffing under the weight of a mountain. They sometimes wrench themselves loose. Some day the boat will probably founder, ripped open by a snag, but she usually gets people to their destination.

Thursday, August 8. The landscape varies little. There are always thick woods or vast prairies on the alluvial plateaus along the river, beyond which there is on each side a chain of green hills covered by grass, more or less thick, but where not a tree grows. Today navigation has been slow and labored. The river bed was full of trees uprooted by the current gnawing at the bank, and there were many obstructions in the channel. These obstructions, as you know, are dead trees with their branches ripped off, which are dragged by the current and fixed in the river bed by their weight and the tangling of roots. The top of the trunk and the large broken branches, if there are any left, float beneath the surface of the water at a more or less acute angle, or even at the surface, if the water is shallow enough. There are two kinds of obstructions: those which float with the current and are called snags, and those which are counter to the current and are called sawyers. Both are very dangerous when their heads are completely under water, for if a steamboat strikes them squarely, the collision makes a hole in the hull, and the boat founders in a few minutes. A number of steamboats have met this fate. But sawyers are the more dangerous, for since the boat goes down the river faster than she comes up, the shock is much more violent. It is not nearly as dangerous to strike an obstruction pointed in the same direction as the boat is going. They sink down deep, bending under the shock, and the hull scrapes over them with more noise than harm.

In addition to these obstructions, we had to contend with banks of quicksand. Sounding line in hand, we had to steer our course among them, scrape bottom in the shallow water, back up, try another channel, and even force through sand with the keel to keep going. We went through these trials twenty times today. When the boat runs on a sand bar while going full speed, there is sometimes such a shock that it seems as if the whole thing is going to fall apart. The boat literally bends, throws herself right and left, or sticks fast on the bar. Then they reverse the engines, back off full force, and try another channel. These collisions are inevitable, for the water of the Missouri is yellow, dirty, and muddy, and nothing can be seen a few inches below the surface. If the river bed were rocky instead of sandy and muddy, navigation would be so dangerous that very few people would risk it.

A Negro from the crew fell into the water. He was brought up by the current for a second and then was swallowed up forever. The engines, which stopped for a few minutes, started up again. It was useless to try to save him. I suppose that the poor devil had his head crushed or his back broken by the moving paddle wheel astern. The incident seemed to make only a slight impression. No one mentioned it an hour after it happened.[14]

[14] The log of the *Deer Lodge* has this entry for August 8: "A negro rousta-

We arrived at Yanktown [Yankton] in wonderful weather, the heat tempered by the breeze. This town is a little settlement of a few cabins, but it has been designated as the capital of the Dakota Territory. Some merchandise and a few cases of ammunition were unloaded here, and the boat left immediately.

Above Yanktown the landscape becomes a little less monotonous. Occasionally there are beautiful amphitheaters of hills, but trees do not grow on them. We are beginning to see a few Indian huts. In the afternoon we stopped to buy some wood at one of their little encampments of four or five lodges. Almost all the men wear woolen shirts and trousers of American manufacture. The women wear short skirts, leggings, and brown or red blankets in which they wrap their heads, shoulders, and waists—no shoes or boots. All of them have moccasins on their feet. One squaw wore in her ears copper rings four or five inches in diameter and seemed to be very proud of that unusual ornament.

We moored for the night at another camp thirty or forty miles below Fort Randall. We completed the rest of our next day's wood supply there. The Indians (male) who sold it to us came on board to get their money. There were half a dozen of them, evidently very poor. One of them was dressed in just a red blanket. Another had in addition to this a pair of ragged trousers and a pipe with a metal bowl. A child of about six or seven who was with them was *in puris naturalibus*. None of them had their hair cut. All of them wore it hanging on their shoulders in masses black as jet, straight as horsehair, and very bushy. The night is calm and beautiful, but the mosquitoes are very annoying.

Friday, August 9. A series of rocky cliffs worn almost sheer by the current and separated by gullies as regular as the big waves of the ocean. Some bushes and stunted trees grow in these gullies. The cliffs are from one hundred to three hundred feet high and form the first terrace in a group of hills which become almost twice as high farther back.

Passed the agency of the Yanktonah Indians.[15] It is composed of fifty or sixty lodges and about twenty cabins, around which there

bout named Dick Johnson fell overboard and was drowned about eight miles below Yanktown." *National Waterways*, February, 1930.

15 This was not the Yanktonai agency, but the Yankton. The Yanktonai agency was farther upstream at Crow Creek. Frederick W. Hodge, *Handbook of the American Indian*, 2:989; Kappler, *Indian Laws and Treaties*, 2:776–780.

De Trobriand spells "Yanktonai" as "Yanktonah" throughout the manuscript.

are some fowl. Horses and cattle graze on the prairie outside the fields of corn. These Indians are forced by their poverty to begin the cultivation of the soil, like the Santees we passed yesterday. These various bands belong to the Sioux nation, but they have become peaceful and have given up war and a nomadic life since the buffalo has disappeared from these regions.[16]

Met the steamboat *Little Rock,* loaded with miners coming from Montana to spend the winter in the States.[17]

[*Fort Randall*] We arrived at Fort Randall around noon. Through the tall trees growing on the bank we saw the buildings, only part of which are surrounded by a palisade. It is more a post than it is a fort, for the fortifications do not amount to anything. We left there Major Chambers, his wife, the orphan, the chambermaid, the horse, and the two greyhounds in the midst of about twenty Indians who were helping with the unloading. Then after handshakes and the customary goodbyes, the steamer took her course again and continued the trip.

After leaving Fort Randall, the two chains of high hills follow the river, which twists and turns in its sinuous course when the alluvial plateaus or great sand banks encroach on one side or the other. These hills are very undulating. Beyond their crests, the land retains this character and forms what is known as rolling prairies. Cottonwood grows almost exclusively near the river banks. This tree closely resembles our Italian poplar, and I strongly suspect it belongs to the same family. The cottonwood grows very high. It is a beautiful tree. The wood, however, is quite spongy, which makes it useless for construction purposes. When the weather is dry, it shrinks, leaving cracks along the edges; when the weather is damp, it swells pro-

16 The Santee, like the Yankton, are one of the eastern tribes of the Sioux nation moved from Minnesota to this reservation immediately after the Sioux Outbreak of 1862. William Watts Folwell, *A History of Minnesota,* 2:259–262. The chief tribes of the Siouan family are the Yankton, Yanktonai, Two Kettle, Sans Arc, Miniconjou, Brulé, Santee, Oglala, Hunkpapa, Sisseton, Teton, Assiniboin, Wahpeton, Mdewakanton, Wahpekute. The eastern Sioux were involved in the outbreak on the Minnesota frontier in 1862, and against the troops that pursued them into Dakota from 1863 to 1865. J. W. Powell, *Fourth Annual Report of the Bureau of American Ethnology,* p. 97–98; Hodge, *Handbook,* 2:577–579.

The buffalo had not completely disappeared in 1867, but by this year they had become rare enough on the northern plains to cause comment when they appeared. Harold E. Briggs, *Frontiers of the Northwest,* p. 156–157.

17 Large numbers of miners began to rush to Montana in 1862 after James and Granville Stuart built their sluices on Gold Creek. By 1867 mining was in full swing in Virginia City, Alder Gulch, Helena, and Bannack City in Montana, as well as in Wyoming and Idaho. Briggs, *Frontiers of the Northwest,* p. 16–22.

portionately. The name comes from its flower, which looks like a ball of ripe cotton.

Willows grow abundantly on the banks of the Missouri, but they never attain the height of trees. In some places ash trees grow in with the cottonwood, and they are a welcome addition. Some stunted pines embed their roots on the steep slopes of the cliffs. Some cedars grow in the gullies going down to the river, but other than that, there is not a tree, unless it is along a stream. "This is the general rule," as military school theory goes.

At sunset, passed the steamboat *Nymph No. 2,* completely loaded with Montana miners.

Saturday, August 10. The two chains of high hills which border the river and form the river valley are becoming still higher. Here and there they are marked with large, dark patches where even grass does not grow and where there is no vegetation of any kind. These sterile areas are saturated with alkali and form what is called "the badlands." Nothing can be grown here, but if industry were to come to these lands, the caustic bases which make them alkali would probably be exploited. They would be real mines of potassium and sodium.

[*The White River*] Around the middle of the day, we passed the mouth of the White River. Properly speaking, this is nothing more than a big creek, and it is the first since Omaha which flows into the Missouri. The tributaries on the entire course of the river between the Platte and the Yellowstone are few and unimportant. This explains why the Missouri keeps about the same volume of water in that long course of *sixteen hundred miles.*

From the mouth of the White River, the mountains get lower and recede from the river banks. The river makes a wide bend to the west (going up), and on the left bank the heights level off to gentle slopes which form a magnificent slanting plateau where the yellow grass looks like grain ripe for the harvest. Perhaps some day this horizon will be dotted with houses and cultivated fields, and this uninhabited desert will feed a vast population. The left bank is like this for thirty or forty miles more.

We lost a lot of time this afternoon. At a wide place in the river where it is divided into two arms by a long island covered with willows and by a large sand bank, we took the channel with no navigable outlet. We had to go back more than a mile, but then we ran into a sand bar twenty to thirty yards wide. To get across this obstacle, we had to make a passage or channel by steampower with the help of two props with which the bow of the boat was lifted. These props were two strong spars suspended from a powerful crane above each cathead.

The crew rests the ends of the spars on the river bed, which is only two or three feet deep here. Then a system of ropes and pulleys is attached to an enormous ring on the front of the boat; one end fastened to the end of the spar and the other to a steam-driven winch. Lifted by the bow, the boat slowly forces her way on the surface of the sand, which is kept in motion by the current. After an hour or more of repeated effort, we got back into the channel again, and went on our way. Needless to say that before beginning this operation, the ship's boat sounded out the best course, or, to be more exact, the least bad.[18]

Because we are now in desert country where neither Indians nor whites cut any wood for the steamboats, it is up to us to get our own fuel. So this evening, no sooner were we moored to the bank than the Negroes of the crew jumped ashore and gathered all the dead trees they could find around the point where the steamboat stopped. This dead wood makes wonderful fuel, but it burns so fast that about twice the usual amount is required to keep the furnaces going.

The steamboat burns around twenty cords of wood a day. It costs *one hundred dollars* a day if it is bought already cut. If the crew gathers its own wood, the loss of time prolongs the trip, and in reality the economy is not appreciable. Consequently, captains use their own crews to gather wood only when they are forced to do so.

Sunday, August 11. We did not go very far today. Part of the afternoon was spent in finding a channel in the low water that

[18] There are many descriptions of the process of "walking the boat over the bar" or "grasshoppering." The crew lowered two huge spars, set them in the sand, lower ends pointing downstream so a pull on the lines would lift the boat and crowd it ahead. They then hauled the lines taut, threw them over the capstans, and "walked" the boat. "Warping" was the method used if the rapids were too steep. The boat headed for shore when she reached the foot of a rapid. The men got off, the first carrying a pick, spade, and stakes, the second a stick of timber, the rest a strong line uncoiled from the boat. Beyond the head of the rapids they planted a "dead man"; that is, they dug a trench three or four feet deep, put in the timber, long dimension at right angles to the river. When the timber was buried with the line fastened to it at the middle, the crew on the boat threw their end of the line around the capstan, and it was then slowly wound in under the power of steam. Hiram M. Chittenden, *History of Early Steamboat Navigation on the Missouri River*, p. 121–122; Hanson, *The Conquest of the Missouri*, p. 87.

seemed to stretch across the river and then in forcing our way through with the help of winches. At eight o'clock in the evening, we moored at some woodcutters' huts, where five French-Canadians were living. The place is called St. John. It is located about one hundred miles this side of Fort Sully on an alluvial plateau where many tall trees grow.

While they were loading the wood that was purchased, I had time to talk to the inhabitants of the place. As I have just said, these five men who have settled here to sell wood to the steamboats are French-Canadians. This is the only work they do. With them are their Indian wives who bear them half-breed children. All summer they live in lodges or skin tents, and in the winter they move into log cabins built for this purpose. They do not cultivate the land because they say that grasshoppers would devour the crops; they do not raise vegetables because they say the animals would eat them; they do not raise sheep because they say the wolves would kill them. The only animals they have are horses, oxen, and two or three cows to furnish milk. One can see what kind of men these lowest specimens of the Canadian race are by the excuses they make for their laziness and carelessness.

These men are not nomads. This is the only difference between them and the general run of Indians, whose customs and manners they have otherwise adopted, including polygamy. Their wives are nothing but servants who do the heavy work. The men don't speak Indian; the squaws don't speak English or French. They communicate by signs. It is assumed that the squaws have no personality or individuality. The relation between the sexes is more bestial than human. There are no homes; they merely pair up. The moral and intellectual level of these bipeds (savages by choice) is more that of a brute than of civilized man. They know nothing; they haven't the slightest idea of what is going on in the world. Their ideas don't go beyond the river, and they concentrate entirely on their present needs, worrying no more about the future than they do about the past.

With the income from their wood, they buy necessities, a few clothes, flour, whiskey, and tobacco. After receiving the seventy-five dollars for the fifteen cords of wood, they used some of it to buy the supplies they needed, which were quite expensive, I suppose.

For six months of the year, they bury themselves in their cabins under the snow and come out only when they go hunting. If buffalo come in the winter, it is a blessing for both their larder and their pocketbook. They can get from five to six dollars apiece for the skins if they do not use them themselves. But in addition to the buffalo, they have all kinds of small game: deer, antelope, hare, and rabbits. Wild fowl are plentiful: geese, ducks, prairie chickens, rails, woodcocks, bitterns, and curlews, to say nothing of herons and cranes, which are not edible. As for fish, the river supplies only chunky catfish and a small barbel they call "whitefish."

The reason they gave us for living this kind of life was that in populated centers, especially in cities, poor people have to work too hard for their living. Here their work is easier, and they need to work only enough to satisfy their needs.

When they don't need anything, they quit working until they do. If they work a few months in the summer, they can rest peacefully all winter. What a rest! I wonder how these men spend their time in their cabins, with nothing to read, incapable of thinking: they eat, drink, smoke, and sleep—just that for month after month.

These men spoke to me about "lacking nothing." In the opinion of many people, they lack everything, but they don't suspect it in the least. All the luxuries, comforts, and pleasures of civilized life do not exist for them. They don't even know there are such things. The best of life that they ever see is the simple comforts of the steamboat, and of these they are not envious. On this subject, how many reflections could be made on the real needs of man, on the mastery of habit over him, and on the artificial world that for him is "civilized society"! In this society, how many trivialities have become necessities, and how many natural inclinations have been sacrificed to convention! I think of the Parisian life I left two months ago today and look around me at natural life in its most simple, unrestrained form. Here there are no laws, no taxes, no rules—nothing but space and freedom. And this brings me to remark that civilization and freedom must go together. What are the results when they are separated? Collective degradation or individual abasement.

Monday, August 12. Two stops at the Cedar Islands to buy and load wood. Some soldiers discharged from the army are living here. Their business seems to prosper. They look much better than any woodcutters we have seen so far. Fully dressed and neat in appearance, they wear revolvers in their belts, and carry carbines in case of Indian attacks. They own teams of oxen and mules to haul their wood. We could not see their settlement, which is back in the woods. According to calculations I have made before, it is possible that in two or three seasons they can save enough money to go back to civilized life with one foot in the stirrup. I suppose that is the reason they came out here when they left military service.

Passed by the location of old Fort Sully, which, it must be admitted, is in poor condition. The countryside is bare, gloomy, and treeless, with patches of alkali lands and very little prairie. Of the buildings, only three miserable looking cabins remain, where some trade is still going on with the Indians. The rest have gone through the furnaces of the steamboats.

The chain of hills along the river between the old and new Fort Sully—about forty miles—have a dismal and lonesome look. Grass hardly grows here. The sterile land is blackish and saturated with alkali. Because there are no rocks or solid base of any kind, the crumbling earth, washed by the rain, forms domes, with furrows in their sides. They are great piles of earth rather than hills. They could be called the ash pile for the cinders of creation. Met two steamboats in the afternoon. The moon was clear and wonderful.

Tuesday, August 13. Arrived at the pier of new Fort Sully about ten o'clock in the morning. It is unnecessary to add that the "pier" is nothing but half a dozen piles driven into the prairie where steamboats come to tie up. The post is a mile or two from here, built on a high point where there is not a shrub in sight. It is a group of buildings quartering a garrison of four companies of the 22nd, General Stanley and his general staff, for Fort Sully is general headquarters of the military district. Nothing in the world justifies its being called a fort, for it is completely open, with not even a palisade or a ditch to protect it. General Stanley believes that in dealing with such a contemptible enemy as the Indian, it is better for troop morale to depend on vigilance and breechloaders for protection than to hide behind palisades. I think that the general is quite right.

A thick wood grows at the foot of the hill on which the post is built and extends through a marsh to the very banks of the river, which explains why, at least for the present, the post is built so far from the pier. After leaving Mrs. Elliot and her children with her husband, who came to get them in an ambulance, and after the freight for the post was unloaded, we pulled away from the pier, just as the steamer *Mountaineer* was tying up. She was reported run aground somewhere around Fort Berthold. This must have been a mistake, or else she succeeded in getting afloat again.

We are now entering the region frequented by hostile Indians. Sometimes they hide in the brush and fire on the steamboats when they come near the bank. Some people have been wounded or killed in this way. To protect the passengers, the captain of the *Deer Lodge* has just had . two rows of shingle bundles stacked on top of each other on the upper gallery, which makes a four-foot bulwark against bullets. The sides of the pilothouse are protected by a thick sheet of iron. In addition to these precautions, Missouri steamers are fully armed. We carry two howitzers forward, and in the salon there is a gun rack loaded with rifles and carbines, not to mention the revolver that every male passenger carries as a matter of course for his own protection.

The countryside does not become any more attractive above Fort Sully. Still prominent on the landscape are those huge piles of cinders furrowed by rivulets of rain.

Wednesday, August 14. The river is still very wide; that is why it is shallow. Today we should have lost a good deal of time looking for a channel if the time had not been used to moor the steamer where there were many dead trees for the crew to gather to renew our wood supply while the ship's boat sounded out a course.

I have not yet mentioned the composition of the crew. Here it is: There are on board 30 deck hands, hardly men, all Negroes; 2 pilots, 2 mechanics, 2 boatswains, 6 firemen, 1 clerk, 1 barkeeper, 3 or 4 cooks, 1 barber who also takes care of the baggage, 6 chambermaids, and 1 laundress. Everyone in the last classification is white but the barber, the chambermaids, and the cooks. The operating cost exclusive of firewood is one hundred and fifty dollars a day. This figure is brought to two hundred and fifty dollars when the expense of wood is added to it. In order to cover expenses and realize a profit, the freight charges must be high. From St. Louis to Fort Benton, the rate is about ten cents a pound, and has been as high as fifteen. This makes prices terribly high in the Upper Missouri posts.

While we were stopping around noon, we saw a band of Indians on the heights outlined against the sky. Since they had their baggage, their families, and their tents with them, it is evident that they were not on the warpath. They were going toward Fort Sully.

Before sunset we passed still another band of Indians. They were living at the edge of the river in an open ravine where we could make out about twelve lodges, which means that there were from fifty to sixty persons. Just as soon as they sighted the steamboat, they climbed the cliff and ran to a point where she could pull up to them. And the captain did stop a minute to make them a present of a small barrel of biscuit and some carrots of tobacco. The women of that band were not distinctive, but the men were singularly dressed. The chief wore a pair of striped trousers trimmed with yellow, no shirt, a red blanket, and an old gray felt hat. One of his young braves wore a bolero of the Spanish type, covered with copper ornaments and nail heads such as the upholsterers use on chairs and armchairs. Other than this shoulder garment, the brave wore nothing but a little loincloth, which flapped around in the breeze. He once had some leggings, but he had cut them in strips and hung them from his belt. The only possible purpose in doing this was to keep the flies off his bare legs. Indians very rarely wear a whole pair of trousers. They cut off the largest portion that hinders free movement and keep only the part that can be made into leggings, which they wear fastened to their belt by a string or thong.

While the steamboat stopped for a few minutes, a tall fellow in the prime of life remained apart, standing proudly at the edge of the cliff. He carried on his right arm the bridle of his horse, on his left a rolled blanket, and on his person a kind of loincloth flapping in the wind. The other members of the band were just alike. The most the children wore was a thong around their waists, undoubtedly to indicate that they meant to wear a loincloth some day.

Passed the mouth of the Moreau River and spent the night a few miles up. Moonlight is useful because the crew can gather wood when the boat is moored for the night. All in all, we have not gone very far today.

Thursday, August 15. Feast of the Emperor and all the Marys of the Catholic world.[19] There is a great celebration in Paris today. The banks of the Missouri are utterly indifferent to it. At eight o'clock met the steamer *Viola Belle*. Around ten o'clock passed the mouth of the Grand River, which is just another small stream.

Although big game is plentiful in these regions, we have seen very little of it. A young stag is all we have sighted up to now; no antelope and no buffalo. When a herd of buffalo is crossing the river, they will not let a steamboat break their solid ranks. If this happens, the steamboat must either stop or slow down before this living obstacle. When these animals, whose instincts guide them so poorly, get into quicksand while crossing, many die in it. They can be seen struggling desperately as they go down, exhausting themselves in useless struggles while they disappear little by little until only the

19 August 15 is the birthday of Napoleon I and the feast of the Assumption.

head is left on the surface, where it sometimes remains for a day or two.[20]

Moored the boat at six o'clock in the evening to gather wood. The whole evening was spent thus.

Friday, August 16. A terrible night. We moored at the edge of a wood, and a breeze was blowing from the land. The sun had scarcely set when millions of mosquitoes invaded the boat, and nothing could protect us from them. They were everywhere—on the deck, in the salon, in the cabins. No matter what was done, they slipped in under the mosquito netting. Impossible to sleep a wink. We spent most of the night walking back and forth with our heads and necks covered by a handkerchief or napkin under our hats, hands gloved, armed with green boughs with which we defended our faces. These mosquitoes are a real scourge. All the woods by the river are infested with them, and if the night is spent at the edge of a wood with the wind blowing from the land to the boat, one may as well say goodbye to sleep until the next day. On the other hand, if the night is spent by a sandy bank, or if the wind blows from the boat to the bank, one is comparatively free from these nocturnal invaders.

I do not know if mosquitoes chase Indians and quadrupeds from the woods, but we have seen only birds—eagles, vultures, herons, ducks, geese, and the like. Since these birds of the desert are seldom shot at, a bullet fired by a careless passenger does not frighten them. The boat often comes very close to them. For example, today some eagles perched on dead trees to watch the steamboat pass sixty to eighty paces away. The flocks of young geese and ducks, since they have no wings to fly away, waddle to the edge of the water in that awkward gait which characterizes them. The goslings, led by the mother goose, scramble up on the sand bank where they think they are safe from anything. The ducklings prefer to stick their beaks under water or plunge under stubble or grass until we pass. I have seen the boat pass noisily twenty-five or thirty paces from them without driving them from the water.

The heat of the last few days has been terrible, a hot sun and not a breeze. Worse than that, just enough breeze blows in the direction of our travel to neutralize the current of air caused by the movement of the steamer. A series of misfortunes—we are out of fresh

[20] Migrating herds of buffalo could stop steamboats for several hours while they crossed the Missouri River. When buffalo became entangled in the wheel, they were a real danger to steamboat navigation. Hanson, *The Conquest of the Missouri*, p. 97–98.

Fort Stevenson, Dakota Territory, 1867–69

meat, and the ice is gone. Without ice, it is impossible or rather futile to slaughter a beef brought along to renew our provisions. The meat would not keep twelve hours. So we must wait until we get to Fort Rice. From now on the meals will consist of fried ham, potatoes, and corn cakes. The wine for sale on board is so bad that it is better to drink the yellow, dirty, unpurified, and tepid water of the Missouri. Fortunately, it has been proved that however terrible it may be, it is good for the stomach.

Remember that the furnaces are right beneath the salon and cabins. As a result, the floors are heated, which makes the interior temperature of the boat everywhere that of a bake oven only half cooled off. One would have to be the "incombustible Spaniard" to be comfortable.

Near the mouth of the Cannon Ball River we saw our first antelope galloping along the bank. He is as graceful an animal as the gazelle or roebuck; his antlers are like those of a chamois. I need not mention that he is light and fast, the swiftest animal of all the hosts on the plains.

The Cannon Ball River gets its name from the many large spherical stones found there. They look like big cannon balls. We saw about thirty of them at the edge of the water and still others half embedded in the sandy escarped banks of the river. I do not know what caused this peculiar formation, and no one could tell me. For my part, I have never seen anything like it anywhere, and I do not remember seeing a mention of it in any book.

Felix qui potuit rerum cognoscere causas [Happy is the man who finds out the reasons for things], which an English writer has translated as: "Happy is the man who knows when to take an umbrella."

[*Fort Rice*] We arrived at Fort Rice around dusk.[21] This was my destination, according to the original plan, but now that I have seen it, I thank Heaven I am going elsewhere. On a high point on the right bank of the river there looms a square, palisaded enclosure with two blockhouses jutting out on the corners. This is Fort Rice. There are some traders' cabins outside the palisade; inside, four companies of the 22nd commanded by Lt. Colonel [Elwell Stephen] Otis

21 The log of the steamer *Deer Lodge* provides more details on the stop at Fort Rice than does De Trobriand's journal entry. "Aug 16th—Arrived at Fort Rice at dark and lay there all night: discharged 30,000 feet of lumber, a few passengers and their plunder, and received 8 horses, 4 mules and 10 tarpaulins, government freight for Fort Stevenson, also some furniture and private freight; put off mail for below." *National Waterways,* February, 1930.

have their restricted quarters because they lack space for separate buildings. The officers' quarters are cabins of squared logs and earth. They are low structures, whitewashed with lime inside, and rather poor in appearance. Here as in every other place I have gone, I have met an old acquaintance from the Army of the Potomac. At Randall it was Captain and Bt. Major [Joseph] Bush of the old 5th corps; at Rice it is Lieutenant [Thomas H.] Fisher, old captain of the volunteers on the general staff of General [Gershom] Mott, whose capture by the rebels at Deep Bottom I told about in my *Quatre Ans de Campagnes à l'Armée du Potomac*. There are many Indians around the fort. They are chiefly Yanktonahs and Unkpapahs, both of the Sioux nation.[22] The government has presents distributed to them once a year, and the garrison gives them provisions from time to time. These tribes are divided. Some of them stay near the fort and take no part in the hostilities against the white men, with whom, consequently, they are on very good terms. Others stay out on the plains, lead a nomadic life, have nothing to do with the military post, and commit depredations whenever they get a chance. These are the ones who sometimes fire on steamboats. Their wanderings often take them into the country between Fort Rice and Fort Stevenson, particularly on the right bank of the river.

We leave behind at Fort Rice the steamboat *Last Chance*, which left St. Louis almost a month before the *Deer Lodge*. She is heavy and draws too much water. The crew is a motley lot, for they are not well paid. That is why her progress is so slow and why the company who owns her will lose.

Saturday, August 17. Cottonwood is poor fuel because of its sponginess; dead wood burns too quickly. Standing ash is what steamboats look for. When they come to a high, thick clump of it, the boat moors to the river bank, and the crew armed with axes jumps to

22 The Yanktonai are one of the primary divisions of the Dakota or Sioux. They fought against the United States in 1812, but they did not take part in the Minnesota Massacre of 1862. Both upper and lower bands signed a treaty of peace and friendship in 1865. After the treaty, they were gathered on reservations at Standing Rock and Devils Lake, North Dakota; Crow Creek, South Dakota; and Fort Peck, Montana. Hodge, *Handbook*, 2:990–991.

The Hunkpapa, or Unkpapa, are a division of the Teton Sioux. These people resisted the incursion of the whites into Indian country by refusing to accept annuities and by killing any whites they could reach. They took part in the Fort Kearny massacre, in the Custer battle, and in the sporadic warfare on the northern plains in the 1860's. Hodge, *Handbook*, 1:579–580. De Trobriand calls them the "Unkpapah."

land, cuts down the trees, drags them on board with a machine brought along for that purpose, and lops off the branches. Today we stopped twice to do this, but we made up for lost time by traveling by moonlight until eleven o'clock.

Above Fort Rice, the landscape changes and becomes more pleasant. The alkali lands have disappeared, and everywhere there is a carpet of yellowing grass. In general the banks of the river slope gently and evenly toward rather low hills, which are scarcely more than undulations in the land. Many birds of all kinds; no men or quadrupeds. Many mosquitoes. Met the steamboat *Luella*.

Sunday, August 18.   Even in the desert, there are swallows everywhere. On the banks of the Upper Missouri they nest in the escarpment of the cliffs which here and there rise sheer from the edge of the water. I see no difference in the habits and plumage of these and the more civilized breed which nest in the roses of Carrousel's *Arc de Triomphe* in Paris.

In the morning a thick fog forced us to moor to the bank until the sun dispelled it. Then we had superb weather. The Missouri is always the same. I found it in Omaha just as I find it here—yellow, wide, treacherous. The small streams emptying into it are few and affect the volume of water very little.

The Indians do not bury their dead. They expose them on a platform supported by eight- or ten-foot poles, probably to keep them from the teeth of the wolves. The body is stretched out on its back, wrapped with skins and blankets, and bound from head to foot. There it remains to dry up in the heat of the sun or to decay in the inclemencies of the weather. From a distance we have seen a number of these open-air tombs, usually perched on the top of some hill. Today we passed one of them at the edge of the river. The wind, rain, and vultures had torn away the wrapping, which now looks like jagged tufts of straw matting. The dried up head and feet of the corpse were sticking out from the frayed wrapping, and it seemed to be still looking toward the sky as the sun covered it with its warm rays.

We are still making good time. The *Deer Lodge* has been traveling twenty days. They assure me that this is the fastest trip ever made between St. Louis and the point where we have just stopped for the night. This record is proclaimed in great letters on a wide plank nailed to a big tree in full view.[23] This is the inscription:

23 The entry in the log of the *Deer Lodge* is not in agreement with De Trobriand about the date the sign was posted. The entry for August 19 reads: "Started

Philippe Régis de TROBRIAND

The *Deer Lodge*—20 days out
August 18, 1867.

The *Deer Lodge* will be the admiration and envy of all steamboats which pass this point after us.

The country is becoming more and more one of great plains and distant horizons. We finally saw a band of antelope. Most of them ran when we approached; some stopped to watch the steamboat pass, looking at us with an air of marked astonishment and curiosity. A beaver surprised by the approach of the boat hesitated to throw himself into the water, so he stood there while we examined him at our leisure. Finally he decided to take the plunge.

Superb weather, good traveling. Moored the boat at nine o'clock in the evening. We shall be at Fort Stevenson rather early tomorrow morning. The distance from St. Louis to Fort Stevenson is 2,035 miles, and from St. Louis to Omaha 807 miles. So I have just finished a trip of more than *twelve hundred* miles up the Missouri in twenty days. We averaged exactly sixty miles or twenty-four leagues a day against a very strong current. When one takes into consideration the mooring at night, the number of times we stopped for wood, and the delays necessary to find or to force a channel, he can certainly conclude that such great speed could be made only by a powerful boat.

FORT STEVENSON[24]

August 19, 1867. So here I am off the boat and at my post at last. To get here I have crossed half of France by railroad, seventeen hours; the Atlantic Ocean by steamboat, ten days and a half; 1,400 miles across seven states of the Union, sixty hours; and finally I have gone 1,235 miles up the Upper Missouri in twenty days and a few hours. I have earned a rest. But first, we shall have a look at my future residence.

At the 101st degree longitude west of Greenwich and between the 47th and the 48th degrees latitude north, the Missouri, after

---

out at daylight and landed for wood just before breakfast and lay there two or three hours; put out sign here (twenty days run) being about two hours over on account of not finding a good place for the night before." *National Waterways*, February, 1930.

24 Fort Stevenson was named for General Thomas G. Stevenson, who was killed at the battle of Spottsylvania in 1864. It was occupied by the military from 1867 until 1883, when it was used as an Indian school. Department of Dakota, *General Orders*, 1867, General Field Orders no. 1, July 4, 1867. In *Report on Barracks and Hospitals*, p. 398, there is a diagram and a description of the post buildings.

flowing east for a long time, makes a sharp turn, and takes a new southerly direction. A few hundred yards upstream from this turn and on an elevated plateau forty or fifty feet above the water, the white tents of a small camp of two companies warm themselves in the sun. This serves as a temporary post until the construction of Fort Stevenson. The steamboats stop at a place on the bank less steep than other spots, on the upper part of the sharp bend which the current undermines as it gnaws away the edge of the prairie in a semicircle; here, under temporary shelters, are piled sacks of corn and oats, different provisions, and a quantity of articles needed for the establishment of a new post: cannon, gun carriages, shingles, ambulance wagons, spruce planks, construction wood, bricks, etc. The freight is unloaded at this wharf first and then transported to the storage tents behind the camp. The officers' tents, most of them made of planks, face the river on a kind of natural terrace. The tents of the companies are ranged perpendicularly to the first [the officers' tents] on the slant of the land which slopes downward behind and forms a natural runway for water when it rains, which seems very seldom to me. Below the companies, the quarters of the civilian workmen are built against a double corral which has cattle on one side and horses and work mules on the other. Parallel with the corral and east of it is the steam sawmill where logs are made into lumber, beams, and rafters. The mill is going full blast.

The stores of the quartermaster and the commissary jut out on the right flank of the camp, parallel with the hospital tents.

The only evidence of fortification is a temporary palisade erected behind the officers' tents, less as an effective protection against Indian hostiles than as a means of inspiring the officers' wives with a sense of constant security. Two rifled three-inch pieces and their caissons are placed here ready to fire, waiting for the time they will be needed. Since the establishment of the camp, they have had to be used only once, and two conical shells were enough to disperse a band of two or three hundred Indians who had announced their presence in the neighborhood by stealing four mules and killing a wagoner whom they surprised alone. One of them had his leg shot off by the first cannon shot, another was seriously wounded, and one of their horses was ripped open from a distance of 1800 yards where they thought they were out of firing range. They had enough and ran away on the gallop. Since then, nothing more has been heard about it. The palisade was built as a result of this skirmish.

At this very moment on the prairie behind the camp a convoy of

110 wagons or carts pulled by oxen is drawing up to transport to Fort Totten, which is being built on the edge of Devils Lake, the grains and provisions that the steamboats unload here for that destination. Not far from here, sixty head of beef for the feeding of the garrison graze under the guard of armed soldiers. Again as many will soon arrive for our winter provision.

The countryside is vast, and one has an unobstructed view of it. It is composed of an immense, long plateau, bordered on the north by a chain of irregular hills and on the south by the river which runs from east to west. In its windings, the river leaves uncovered on one side or the other huge sand points or alluvial lands covered with osiers, brush, or wood of full-grown trees. These trees are the only ones visible on the horizon, with the exception of one. This solitary tree, the exception, grows, I don't know why, in the hollow of a ravine which opens on to the plateau, and consequently it can be seen from there. But on the chain of hills to the north and on the high and sharp cliffs which border the right bank of the river to the south, nothing can be seen but some brush growing in the hollows of the land. The rest is a carpet of smooth grass. The plateau stretches out uniformly to the east and west for great distances until it finally merges with the sky. On the Berthold side, the hills draw back to the river, where mounds of alkali lands devoid of vegetation predominate; this is the view eight or ten miles from camp. On the opposite side, the variations in the terrain are very slight, and the eye can take in a still greater distance without meeting any obstacle. Finally, a mile to the east, the plain is cut transversely by the windings of a little river called Douglas Creek. A bridge has been built there since we arrived; but as the water flows between high banks where nothing but willows and brush grow, its course is hard to see, and it is literally necessary to be on the edge of it to find it. There is nothing especially picturesque about all this. The character of the countryside is completely desert-like; space and solitude.

Now, where are the buildings? Hardly begun. The garrison did not arrive here until this June when Fort Berthold was abandoned. First it had to find the best place to build the fort, measure the ground, examine the slopes, look for the most desirable conditions; next, or at the same time, a complete plan had to be made of the buildings to be erected, their location, and their dimensions. When this was done the first task was to lay the masonry foundations and to install the steam engine. But stones are needed for foundations and loose rocks must be brought from the bluffs one and a half or two miles away.

Transporting them is slow work, and when they do get here, they still must be broken into pieces of the desired size. While the masons, civilian workmen for the most part, are busy with this work, detachments of soldiers do fatigue duty, crossing the river in a long boat to the other side where they cut down the large trees which furnish the construction wood. On that side there is a permanent post of ten men, a sergeant, and two corporals, who sleep in log cabins, and guard a yoke of oxen and a team of six mules. After a tree is cut down and the branches hacked off, one end of the trunk is raised and fastened by chains to a skeleton wagon without a box, and in this way is dragged to the river. When they have put ten or twelve of these logs in the river, they bind them together tightly to form a raft which the long boat takes in tow and drags to the opposite bank near the landing. There the logs are drawn onto the prairie up an incline built of timber, and from there they are transported to the sawmill by the same means used to get them to the river. I find that from four to five hundred big trees have already been cut down, and a good part of them have been transported to the left bank. The skeleton of the new fort's principal storehouse already stands in place, and the frames of the doors and windows are set up. The wood is very bad; it is cottonwood, but we have no choice. It is the only thing at hand.

All the walls will be adobe. These are big Mexican bricks, or rather, the idea was borrowed from the houses of New Mexico. They are made by a kind of masonry, half clay, half sand, held together by chopped up hay. These bricks, fashioned quickly by hand in board frames or forms, are then dried and baked in the sun to make them harder. The same mixture of earth is also used to cement them together, and the combination makes good buildings, solid and durable summer and winter. The brickyard is between the wharf and the camp, and extends far back. The bricks, which are being made rapidly, are spread out or piled up, according to the stage they are in. There are already from twenty to thirty thousand of them ready to be used. In two or three days, the men will begin the walls of the storehouse.

In short, the installation of this fort is only begun, and no matter what is said, it seems to me that it will be difficult to make it habitable by winter. There are only 220 men in the garrison, and when civilian employees are added the number is brought to 260. The relieving guard and the guard coming off duty, the orderlies, the men assigned to different bureaus of the post and district, the adjutant, commissariat, and quartermaster must always be reserved—those who are left for fatigue detail must divide up the cutting of trees, escorting of trains, making of adobe, and guarding of cattle. These many tasks occupy everyone all the time. The result is that while the fort is being built, military instruction will be useless. There is not an hour free for drill, except guard duty.

The quartermaster has had two wall tents set up for me, and these will be my temporary lodging for some days. My servant is behind in an edge tent. This is the same setup I had during the war. So I am going to sleep in a tent again. All right then, I shall take up the life of a soldier in the field. In two years I have had time to forget about it, but it will not be hard to get used to it again.

Tuesday, August 20. General Terry, commander of the Department of Dakota, arrived this morning on the steamboat *Guidon,* completing an extensive tour of the districts under his command. Last month, setting out from St. Paul, his general headquarters, he crossed the plains with an escort of one hundred and fifty cavalry. On his way, he visited in turn forts Abercrombie and Ransom,[25] and the new post on Devils Lake (which will be called Fort Totten), and Stevenson. Here, after sending his escort back to St. Paul, he boarded one of the steamers going up the river, and visited Camp Cook[e] and forts Buford, Shaw, and Benton.[26] Above Buford, the Sun River

[25] Fort Abercrombie was established in 1857 by Lieutenant Colonel J. J. Abercrombie on the west bank of the Red River of the North twelve miles north of the confluence of the Bois des Sioux and Otter Tail rivers. It was the terminus of military mail routes from Fort Stevenson via Fort Totten, and from Fort Wadsworth via Fort Ransom. The mail from these posts was forwarded from Fort Abercrombie to St. Cloud and then to St. Paul. It was used as a depot of supply and as an objective point during the campaign against the Sioux in 1863. Fort Abercrombie was the resting place for the three thousand or more teams that went from Pembina and Fort Garry to St. Cloud for supplies. *North Dakota Historical Collections,* 1:412–420; *St. Paul Daily Pioneer,* August 19, 1869.

General Terry in June, 1867, selected the site for Fort Ransom on the Sheyenne River, about seventy-five miles from its junction with the Red River of the North. The post was supplied from St. Cloud, via Abercrombie, and from St. Louis. *Report on Barracks and Hospitals,* p. 380–382.

[26] Camp Cooke was built in the fall of 1866 in Montana Territory near the mouth of the Judith River. It was abandoned as a military post in 1870. Department of Dakota, *General Orders,* 1870, General Order no. 23, March 31, 1870; *Report on Barracks and Hospitals,* p. 410.

Fort Shaw was established in 1867 twenty miles above the mouth of the Sun River to protect the route from Helena to Fort Benton and to prevent the incursions of the Indians into the settlements to the south. The post was first called Camp Reynolds; then it was named Fort Shaw for Colonel Robert Shaw who was killed before Fort Wagner in 1863. The buildings of the post were not completed until 1869. *Report on Barracks and Hospitals,* p. 409–416; Records of the Medical

District, commanded by Colonel [Isaac Van Duzer] Reeve of the 13th infantry, begins. Now General Terry is retracing his course back down the river, stopping at each post. He will then go to St. Louis, where he will join the commission charged with negotiating peace with hostile Indians. This commission of which he is a member is presided over by Lieutenant General Sherman. It will meet with the chiefs of the Cheyenne, Arrapahoe, Comanche, etc., somewhere on the Platte River near the route of the Pacific Railroad, which the Indians are naive enough to claim they can stop us from building.[27]

[*Four military districts*] General Terry, like myself, comes from volunteer service. The capture of Fort Fisher in North Carolina made his reputation and military fortune. He is an excellent officer and a man of great charm. He takes the job of governing his department seriously and devotes himself with energy and intelligence to the welfare of his command. He is responsible for the excellent measure of dividing the Department of Dakota into four districts, each occupied by a regiment and commanded by a colonel of this regiment. The four districts are these: 1. Minnesota, general headquarters at Fort Abercrombie, Col. [Edmund B.] Alexander of the 10th infantry commanding; 2. Sun River, general headquarters at Fort Shaw, Col. Reeve of the 13th infantry commanding; 3. Middle District, general headquarters at Fort Stevenson, Col. de Trobriand of the 31st infantry commanding; 4. Southeast, general headquarters at Fort Sully, Col. Stanley of the 22nd infantry commanding.[28]

History of Post no. 66, Old Records Division of the Adjutant General's Office, National Archives.

Fort Benton is located on the Missouri River at the head of navigation. It was originally built by the American Fur Company in 1846. It was sold to the Northwest Fur Company in 1864. In 1869 it was occupied by troops to receive and forward freight to forts Shaw and Ellis. *Report on Barracks and Hospitals*, p. 405–406.

27 This commission was appointed under act of Congress approved July 20, 1867. The members, N. G. Taylor, J. B. Henderson, William T. Sherman, William S. Harney, John B. Sanborn, Alfred H. Terry, S. F. Tappan, and Christopher C. Augur, had as their objective "to remove, if possible, the causes of war; to secure as far as practicable, our frontier settlements and the safe building of our railroads looking to the Pacific; and to suggest or inaugurate some plan for the civilization of the Indians." The commissioners were to meet in St. Louis on August 6 to begin their work. *Report of the Commissioner of Indian Affairs*, 1868, p. 26–30; O. H. Browning, Department of the Interior, Washington, D. C., to General John B. Sanborn, Washington, D. C., July 29, 1867. Sanborn Papers. Minnesota Historical Society. See below, p. 203. See footnote 61 for information on the Cheyenne and footnote 77 for data on the Arapaho.

28 General Alfred H. Terry was commander of the Department of Dakota from 1866 to 1869. There were twelve posts in the four military districts under

General Terry visited the camp and the work in progress, inquired about what we needed, took notes, gave orders, and left at the end of an hour on his boat loaded with a group of miners coming back from Montana. These people look more like bandits than honest travelers. They make an uproar, swear on any provocation, gamble with their gold to pass away the time, quarrel with one another in obscene language, and sometimes wound or kill one another with knives or revolvers.

This unpleasant company did not prevent Mrs. Rankin, wife of the commander of Fort Buford [William Galloway Rankin] from taking passage on the *Guidon*. She is a pretty young woman, half French and half Spanish, and she is going to her family.[29] She spent last winter at Buford. She was there when the rumor spread that the fort had been attacked and captured by the savages, who, it was told, had massacred the whole garrison, consisting then of only one company. The newspapers gave strange details of that story. They told how Captain Rankin, seeing that all was lost, killed his wife himself to save her from worse treatment. The suspension of communications during the winter kept the friends and relatives of the supposed victims in terrible anxiety for weeks and even months. It was not until spring that news from Fort Buford revealed that all these reports were nothing but stories invented at someone's pleasure. It is true that hostile Indians had come around the fort frequently and for a time had contributed as much as the snow to the disruption of communications; but they had refrained from attacking the fort, which was protected by a closed palisade and was otherwise too well fortified to be in any real danger of redskin attack.[30]

---

his command in 1867. Department of Dakota, *General Orders*, 1867, General Field Orders no. 2, July 4, 1867.

[29] Captain Grant Marsh, who often visited Colonel and Mrs. Rankin on his trips up and down the Missouri River, says that Mrs. Rankin was "a beautiful Cuban lady." Hanson, *The Conquest of the Missouri*, p. 84.

[30] The report of the massacre of the garrison at Fort Buford first appeared in the *Army and Navy Journal*, April 6, 1867, when almost the entire front page was devoted to the recitation of details. It was not until May 18 that this journal could announce that Fort Buford was safe and that the rumor was false. The story appeared in the *Montana Post* on April 6 and in the *Helena Herald* on April 11. The story from the *Helena Herald* is quite typical of the comments that accompanied the report: "Some weeks since we saw and copied an article from our Eastern exchanges stating that this little garrison had been attacked by a large body of Indian savages, but who were repulsed with some loss. Col. Rankin had previously written to his superior officers whose headquarters were in princely dwellings within the confines of civilization, laying before them as before the War Department at Washington his perilous and beleagured situation, and strongly

The Indians never attack military posts to occupy them in force. They would lose too many warriors. They limit their efforts to drawing out a small detachment and then luring it into an ambush. Then, if they are at least ten to one, they will hurl themselves on this party drawn out on a false pursuit, and will massacre it if the soldiers do not fight back with intelligence and energy. That is what happened at Fort Philip Kearney [*sic*], where ninety men and three officers met this fate. They made the mistake of pursuing a band of marauders sent to draw them into an open ambush, and when they saw they were surrounded, they massed in a ravine where the odds were all against them.[31] If they had been better commanded, they probably would have escaped, as did a detachment of twenty-five men under the command of Major [Albert M.] Powell. They took shelter behind some wagons and not only held off a thousand Indians, but killed a hundred or so, wounded two or three times as many, and the rest fled when they caught sight of reinforcements.

Wednesday, August 21. An Indian subaltern came from Fort Berthold today. Since the departure of the company garrisoned there, he has been guarding the grain left in storage and has faithfully kept the women and children from stealing any of it. In payment for this service, he comes to ask for some provisions which are to be given to him and which will be renewed each month as long as the grain is under his care. As he is the first Indian I have seen at Stevenson, I shall briefly describe his costume, which is not without a certain character. It is composed of an antelope-skin tunic, striped transversely with blue on the sleeves, chest, and back. On the shoulders, two imitation braces in porcupine quills in different colors. No painting on the skirt of the tunic, but bordered with a fringe of animal hair, which decorates the forearms and hips, too. Hair braided from the front on each side of the face and tied behind the head, hanging down between his two shoulders like the tail of a horse. On his chest,

urging immediate reinforcements as necessary to enable him to hold out any length of time against the assaults he knew the great force of Indians threatening him were able to make. But the Department heeded not his repeated supplications and by dispatches to the *Post* of a late date . . . the sad and shocking story is told, of his entire annihilation—the Indians, coming upon the post in renewed force, succeeded after a most desperate battle in which the savages lost some 300 killed . . . in capturing the post and in barbarously butchering every officer, soldier and civilian connected therewith! It is stated that Col. Rankin shot his devoted wife to prevent her from falling captive to the savage fiends!"

31 This was the famous Fetterman Massacre. See 49 Congress, 2 session, *Senate Executive Document* no. 97.

a large, silver-plated medal of Washington given him by the government, and above that an oblong copper medal with a matching chain bearing the inscription "Immaculate Conception," a souvenir of some Catholic missionary. "Immaculate Conception" on the red chest of this savage! After all! Unfortunately, the costume is spoiled by a pair of gray trousers coming down on his moccasins. The horse is rigged out in a saddle of uncovered wood, very high pommel and cantle. No bridle. A long leather lasso passed through the mouth of the animal in a running noose is enough to guide him.

There are many French-Canadians here. The traders at Berthold are French with the exception of one. Their people are all of French-Canadian origin. French is their language. The interpreters speak it much better than they do English. The contractor and almost all the carpenters and masons are either French or Canadians. The half-breeds are all sons of Canadian fathers. My native tongue will certainly be a great help to me here.

The convoy of 110 wagons left yesterday for Devils Lake. With it went Lieutenant [R. Frank] Walborn, who is to hire about twenty half-breeds from the Red River for us. Their pay is the same as that of a soldier, sixteen dollars a month, rations, clothes, and a horse. If they do not take the uniform, they get an additional six and a half dollars a month in place of it; if they bring their own horse, forty cents more a day. They are used for reconnaissance around the post, herding cattle, carrying correspondence by horse in summer and fall, and by dog sleds when snow covers the land. In case of an expedition or a march on the plains, they serve as scouts.

Thursday, August 22. After acquainting myself sufficiently with what was going on, I took command of the district and the regiment today.[32] The officers of my general staff are: Captain [John Vincent] Furey (bt. major), quartermaster of the district and the post; Lieutenant Marshall, assistant adjutant general of the district and adjutant of the regiment; Lieutenant [Foster E.] Parson[s], quartermaster of the regiment and commissary of the post; Lieutenant Norwell, assistant inspector general of the district (gone right now);[33] Doctor [Charles C.] Gray, surgeon major. The post is commanded by Captain (bt. lt. col.) Powell. Among the officers, six are married, and

[32] Colonel Joseph Nelson Garland Whistler relinquished command of the Middle District on August 21 in General Orders no. 5. General Orders, 1867. Department of Dakota, War Records Division, National Archives.

[33] Throughout the journal, De Trobriand spells the name of Stevens T. Norvell as "Norwell."

five have their young wives with them, who, with their children, make our military colony lively and gay.

In the group I did not mention Major (bt. colonel) Whistler, who was here only temporarily, awaiting my arrival. He is going on leave in a few days, taking with him his wife and three children. When he returns, he will command the post at Devils Lake. Col. Whistler is an old soldier and a fine man. He has spent twenty-one years in the service, all of them on the western plains, except during the last year of the war when he commanded a volunteer regiment in the Army of the Potomac. He is waiting to take passage on the *Deer Lodge* when she comes back.

Every married officer eats with his own family. The others, all lieutenants, have mess together. I have my meals with Major Furey, quartermaster of the district. There is not much variety in the table fare: fresh beef (once or twice a week), ham, salt pork, kidney beans, tomatoes and other canned vegetables, preserves or fruit conserves. Most of the households have a cow and a few hens, which are a great resource. In the fall the most valuable things for us are venison and wild fowl, particularly the wild fowl. Right now there is an abundance of large woodcocks as well as young wild ducks; later, ducks, wild geese, plovers, and prairie chicken will come and will be here in number until the snow is too deep for hunting.

The heat is extreme. The mercury rises to $+$ 110 degrees F. in the shade during the day. However, I do not suffer as much as in a temperature of 85 to 90 degrees in New York. Why is that? It is not because of the light breeze that usually blows on the edge of the water. Rather, it must be because of the atmospheric condition. The air is very pure and dry; the sky is clear and spacious. There is always fair weather. Here it never rains from the month of June to the month of November. To make up for this, there are terrible windstorms from time to time. Last week the whole camp just missed being blown into the river. Almost all the tents were knocked down, the furniture was upset, the dishes were broken, and a sheet-iron stove was rolled up to the foot of the plateau by the storm. All that in the midst of terrible whirlwinds of dust, and not a drop of rain. Yesterday the weather was stormy; we thought there was going to be a deluge, but there is still nothing but violent wind. This time, at least, all the tents have held down.

Saturday, August 24. A man drowned this morning while bathing in the river. Although he was a good swimmer, he was dragged

49

into an eddy where his strength was quickly exhausted. When he called for help, they thought it was a joke, and he disappeared forever. His body has not been recovered; how can anything be found in that muddy current?

A beautiful night. How amazingly clear the air is! Never have I seen so many stars, in Europe or America, and never have they seemed to shine with such brilliance, either at the zenith or at the edge of the horizon. The feeling of the spaciousness of sky and earth is more striking here than in any other place I have been.

Sunday, August 25. When the wind blows here, it usually becomes a tempest. The fly then clacks furiously on the canvas roof. The tent itself is shaken almost to pieces and seems ready to blow away at any moment. And what miserable dust! Everything is contaminated with it. To compensate us for these conditions, the mosquitoes disappear immediately. Not a one shows up while the wind blows; but when the air is calm and the evening warm, they come back in swarms, and we get rest from them only when we are protected by mosquito netting.

Wolves are plentiful on the prairie. Every night they prowl around camp, especially when a beef has been slaughtered. Then we can hear them howling and yelping at the open air slaughter house outside the line of sentinels. Sometimes they even make their way within our lines. Last night three of them came up to the tents of the mess hall where there was some fresh meat. Driven by hunger, they tried to dig up the body of the wagoner who was killed by the Indians a few days ago. Measures have been taken to insure the safety of the soldier's tomb.

Monday, August 26. A party of Indians came in from Berthold this morning to sell the vegetables and corn they cultivated and harvested. They belong to the Ree and Gros Ventre tribes. I do not know why the Canadians gave them the name "Gros Ventres," for their stomachs are no bigger than the others; on the contrary, they are like all the other Indians, thin and generally tall.[34] Their real

[34] De Trobriand discovers later that the stomachs of the children are large until they reach the age of puberty. See below, p. 86.

The Ree Indians are called by various names, the most common of which is "Arikara." When French traders met them in 1776 and when Lewis and Clark saw them in 1804, they were friendly to the whites; however, they became hostile after encounters with rival traders. Smallpox and wars so decimated the tribe that they joined the Gros Ventres and the Mandan at Fort Berthold. They belong to

name in their own language is Hedanza [Hidatsa], which is decidedly more euphemistic and means "men of the willows," for the tribe has lived on the banks of the river from time immemorial.

A group of visitors came down the river in a bull boat. The bull boat is simply a buffalo skin stitched in the form of an almost cylindrical tub, without stem or stern. A light framework of wood holds it in shape. In this skin tub, a man is seated, shoulders here and legs there, behind two squaws squatted down near him. As usual, these two women do all the work and have the task of paddling, taking their lord and master wherever he wants to go. When they disembark at the destination, one of them takes the little boat on her shoulders, or rather on her head, and the other carries the provisions. The brave is always like the fourth at the burial of Marlborough: he carries nothing. If the skin is in poor condition and of no value, the boat is abandoned, for in that equipage one can float down the current easily but can never come back up. Thus the chief use of bull boats is in crossing the river from one bank to the other opposite the village of Berthold.

In the evening, the *Deer Lodge* returned. She could not get higher than Fort Buford. She brings from there a detachment of one hundred men sent to meet a big beef herd here and to drive it up to the post, a distance of about two hundred and fifty miles. But the herd has not showed up yet, and we do not know when it will arrive. The escort must wait for it, and they will provide a useful reinforcement of workers for our building until it comes.

Wednesday, August 28. For three days there has been fire on the prairies about twenty miles away in the direction of Berthold. During the day, the only evidence of its advance are the columns of smoke drifting in the air in the distance far above the horizon; but when night comes, a flaming line casts its ruddy reflection on that part of the sky. The fire is approaching us, and fanning out wider and wider. When it first appeared, it was nothing more than a distant glimmer showing up against the silhouette of the badlands; the following night, it was already a gleam of light shining at the edge of the sky

the Caddoan family. Hodge, *Handbook*, 1:83–86; Charles E. DeLand, "Aborigines of South Dakota," *South Dakota Historical Collections*, 3:271–584. De Trobriand spells the tribal name as "Ree" most often, but he also uses variations of "Arikara."

Two distinct tribes are called "Gros Ventres": the Atsina, or Gros Ventres of the Prairie, and the Hidatsa, or Gros Ventres of the Missouri. The latter tribe was the one residing with the Mandan and Arikara at Fort Berthold in 1867. Hodge, *Handbook*, 1:508.

and gradually losing itself in space. Yesterday the flames began to run along the crest of far away hills, driven southward by a north wind. Apparently the blaze is on the right bank of the river.

These fires are not uncommon. When the high grass is dried out by the sun, it takes very little to start the fire accidentally, and no matter how little the wind is blowing, the blaze spreads and fans out very rapidly. Quite often, too, the Indians themselves deliberately set the fires, because they believe that the cinders are a fertilizer which will stimulate the growth of grass next season and will thus make better pasture for the horses and buffalo. Since these animals form a great part of their food supply, they hope to attract them into their region by the lure of thick pasture, but I do not think the buffalo are very aware of this. They are as wandering and nomadic a beast as the Indians who hunt them. It is not unusual for them to disappear for two or three years from a certain region where they were plentiful before. They return or do not return according to whether or not they are disturbed. In any case, the sight of fire hasn't brought them back. They do not have a highly enough developed feeling for the beautiful to admire as we do that long band of fire lighting up the night, although it certainly is a wonderful spectacle.

Saturday, August 31. Three steamboats passed by today going down the Missouri: the *Miner,* which belongs to the fur company, the *Centralia,* and the *Only Chance.* The water is so low that none of them were able to get up to Fort Benton. It is getting late in the season, and in a country where it almost never rains before the beginning of winter, there is no reason for them to hope that the waters will rise. So they go back to St. Louis before the coming of cold weather. Others will pass during the months of September and October. Then nothing will ply the river until May of next year, not even our long boat, which will be hauled up on the bank at sight of the first ice. Once the river is frozen, we cross dry shod, and for the four winter months, it will be an open road for our teams.

The *Miner,* which, in spite of her name, does not take any miners on board, took away Bt. Col. Whistler and his whole family, which consists of Mrs. Whistler, two young girls ten to twelve years old or perhaps older, and a young boy six or seven years old. These children have come to the age when their education must be taken in hand, and this is absolutely impossible in the frontier posts where they have been with their father up to this time. Officers who have no fortune and who consequently have to stay in the service all their lives, find themselves in a most difficult position in raising their children, especially when they are girls. If they keep them with them in the military posts scattered around the desert, any instruction is impossible, and the rest of their education is completely lacking, too, unless the mother can undertake it, but it is seldom that she is capable of doing so. Generally she has enough to do when she manages the household and cares for the children, which is difficult and expensive so far from every resource. If, on the other hand, the children are sent away to be brought up in some educational institution, their mother will probably go with them, and then no matter what economies are practiced, almost the entire salary will be eaten up by the expenses. The whole family is in poverty, a poverty in which not even appearances can be kept up, if one can judge by this case. When will a family separated in this way be united again? Perhaps never. To bring the daughters back to the frontier post is almost equivalent to giving up an establishment in life for them, or at least it narrows down their chances to the possibility of entrapping some young officer. Even temporary reunions are rare and costly, for then the officer who travels has expenses and cannot cross such enormous distances without a considerable outlay. I believe that this is one reason why so many officers leave the service after a few years when they have a chance to live in their own home or elsewhere by some other means. Bt. Col. Whistler will probably ask for some post in detached service which will put him close to Georgetown near Washington, where he will leave his family. But he probably will not get it, for this type of work is very much sought after, and the old soldier who has spent his life on the plains far from the political world and sources of favor cannot exert enough influence to make his plans succeed. So at the end of his two months' leave, he will have to take the road back to the frontiers and rejoin his command at Fort Totten on Devils Lake.

The departure of Colonel Whistler gave me the two large hospital tents he used as quarters, a wall tent for my servant, and a kitchen, half plank and half canvas. My two tents are joined together and connected on the outside by a covering of slabs. Both are planked, and a good stove protects me already from the first frosts. It is lucky for me that Colonel Whistler wanted to get rid of most of his furniture when he left. Thanks to this circumstance, I have been able to furnish my two rooms adequately. In my ignorance of the ways and resources of the Upper Missouri, I had imagined that after my arrival at Fort Stevenson I should be able to order what I needed at St. Louis or Omaha and to get it before winter. If I had depended on doing this, I can imagine what a picture my fifteen-foot square rooms would have made with my camp bed, rocking chair, four bags, and nothing to go with them. Everything is for the best after all, and without sending anywhere for them, I now have a chest of drawers with a mirror, a washstand, some chairs, a table, a clothespress, and even a carpet. My table is now adorned with Col. Whistler's china and glassware.

So I am definitely established for the rest of the fall until we take up our winter quarters in the fort. My books are on the table, my lamps on the chest of drawers, my uniforms in the clothespress, and my sidearms on the rack. Here and there twenty familiar objects remind me of family and absent friends. These are like old companions that have followed me in my distant wanderings for a long time. This was given to me by such-and-such a person; that I bought in such-and-such a city. Three tobacco sacks come to me from Venice, Rennes, and from Brest. A cigar case reminds me of New York, a hand mirror of Boston, a cape of Rome, a portable writing case of Paris, a memorandum book of Tours, etc., etc. These are my most faithful companions, the confidants of joys and sorrows that are gone today, the things that are left to me from the vanished days that will never return. Of those whose memory is evoked by the things around me, some are roaming about the world, some have stayed home, where perhaps I shall see them again some day. Others are dead. The gifts of these have become as relics, bequests of hearts that beat no more. The hand that gave them to me lies far away under the earth, and how much of that youth, beauty, grace, talent, and even genius remains here on earth? Dear vanished souls, shall I see you after death in a better world? I do not know, but I hope so.

I should like to be one of those people who have been able to be convinced of the possibility of communication, improperly called supernatural, between those who have left this world and those who are still in it. I do not accept the term *supernatural* because if such communications do exist, it can only be by some *natural* law which we still do not understand. There is nothing *supernatural* but miracles, a believer will say; but I do not believe in these miracles, and what has been dignified by this term is nothing but the unexplained effect of a natural cause. How many miracles modern science has achieved by the pure and simple application of natural laws! What would a locomotive, a steamboat, an electric telegraph have been to the ancient Romans and Jews of the year I? They were just so many miracles so long as the mechanics were concealed. All Paris flocked to see the miracles of Robert Houdin, miracles for which you and I have never found an explanation; but we do not believe that there is anything *supernatural* about it because we cannot explain it.

[*Communication with the dead*] Whatever the term may be, how I wish I could communicate with those who live in another world! A few years ago I did everything in my power to accomplish this. For a whole winter in New York, I followed at the home of one of my friends the private seances of the most famous medium. I saw things there that were certainly extraordinary, but I am not convinced of the origin assigned to them. On the contrary, in several cases I positively identified some magnetic phenomena that I had tested a few years before myself. Neglecting nothing, I personally submitted to all the formulas, all the tests of direct evocations; nothing was manifested in visible, auditory, or tangible form.

There is now only one chance for me to unveil the mystery, to solve the enigma. There is in France a person whose life is bound to mine by mysterious and exceptional conditions in which magnetic phenomena have played a great role. It was in my first youth, more than thirty years ago; and I shall add that since then, although I have tried under all possible conditions, none of these phenomena have been reproduced for me with any other subject. Since that time, I have seen this person only at long intervals (three or four times in thirty years) and few letters have been exchanged between us. And yet neither time nor space has broken this mysterious bond. If this person happens to die before I do and there is any possibility of communication between the living and the dead, by virtue of a promise solemnly exchanged by us, she will tell me of it. If she does not come, I shall then die convinced that natural laws cannot be reconciled with such communications.

As for incorporeal influences which come to us from another world and have a positive effect on our life in this one, I should not refute them just because the origin and means of action are not obvious to us. On the contrary, I am strongly tempted to admit of them when I think of the vicissitudes of my past life. Circumstances can be such that our destiny is involved in their movement; but how many times we escape from the ones which seem most naturally to involve us, only to fall within the orbit of those whose evolutions seem far from us. It would be useless to call for the intervention of the free arbiter; for it is precisely by the neutralization of the free arbiter at certain times that these incorporeal influences transform into material effects. Our will responds to some inexplicable reverses

55

and ceases to function according to our predictions and well-laid plans. The decisive moment passes; the combinations have changed, and there we are launched on the new road ending in aims completely different from the ones we had planned on and really preferable to the one we had followed. How did all that happen? Through mysterious influences which, though independent of us, act on us and for us. From the beginning of time, popular belief has attributed them to stars. People said that one was born under a good star or a bad star, according to whether these influences proved to be good or evil. Peasants attribute them to the protection or enmity of the gods or of certain gods, the Christians to Providence, Catholics to the intercession of the Virgin or the saints, or to the evil power of the devil. And why not to those who loved us in this life and who still love us in the new world where they have gone ahead of us, or why not to those who carry beyond the tomb resentment of some evil that we have unjustly done to them?

I could write a long chapter on this subject without digressing from the memories of my life. It has been so varied and so fruitful in unforeseen events that for a long time I have been seeking an explanation for it, going back from effect to cause in the hope of finding an explanation there that would satisfy me. But let the past sleep now. Here I am following a new path I have not sought, for when the news of my transfer to the regular army reached me in France, it was the thing I had least expected. As usual, I complied with the fate that has made me; and as a result, I am set up in a tent in the heart of Dakota without the slightest idea of what the future has in store for me.

September 1. The first harsh signs of autumn are here already. The night was as cold as in November, and—a rare thing in this climate—the day began with a humid and gray sky. Some drops of rain sprinkled the dust. With the exception of a summer storm when I was coming up the Missouri, this light rain is the first I have seen since my return to the United States two months ago. Usually the weather here is consistently fair; the air is dry, and the atmosphere extraordinarily clear, which explains the deep blue of the sky during the day and the scintillating brilliance of the myriads of stars at night. Around noon everything changed; a violent wind came up, and sweeping across the plains, it rushed on the camp, driving before it whirlpools of dust. During the whole afternoon, it shook our tents furiously; it even ripped up some of them, and no matter what we did, we had to put up with the dust which seeped in everywhere, penetrating everything, particularly our eyes, ears, and lungs.

The wind died down considerably by sunset. At that hour two Indian scouts arrived, equipped and armed like our soldiers except for the boots or shoes which they have replaced with moccasins, although they are traveling horseback. This deerskin footwear is much softer on the feet, and there is nothing better for a long march. These Indians have been sent to us from Fort Rice.[35] They are bearers of a letter from Lt. Col. Otis who commands the post, a letter in which, according to the instructions of Gen. Stanley (Colonel of the 22nd inf.) commanding the Southeastern District, he tells me that a considerable band of Sioux Indians, now camped in the neighborhood of Fort Sully, is preparing for an expedition against the Ree Indians established with the Gros Ventres and Mandans around Fort Berthold.[36] These three tribes just named are peaceful and not very formidable, either in numbers or by inclination. Nevertheless, they have been at war with the Sioux of lower Dakota for a long time. From time to time, the latter make a raid on the former to steal horses, mules, or cattle, and as many scalps as they can get without running too great a risk. As both are friends of the United States, we have no business interfering in any of their quarrels, and we have nothing to lose if the redskins devour each other. However, I had to warn the three tribes immediately of the attack threatening them so they could be prepared for it.

Since Fort Berthold has been abandoned as a military post, it has again become a trading post, and three or four traders and agents of the Northwest Fur Company remain there. Mr. Wilkinson, Indian agent of the United States for the three tribes and others, re-

[35] On September 2 a letter from an officer at Fort Stevenson (probably De Trobriand) was written to the *Army and Navy Journal* after the issues of that weekly for August 3 and August 10 were received from the Indian scouts. He comments on the happenings at the fort, on the new divisions in the department, and on the efficiency of the communication system. His letter was prompted by the appearance in the *Army and Navy Journal* of a letter he had written while waiting for a boat to take him to his post on the Upper Missouri. In the letter, the writer had expressed a fear that Fort Stevenson would be cut off from communication with the rest of the world for the winter. *Army and Navy Journal*, August 10, 1867, p. 813; September 21, 1867, p. 73.

[36] The Mandan Indians are a Siouan tribe who, with the Gros Ventres and the Rees, made up the three tribes of Fort Berthold. Lewis and Clark estimated the tribe at 1,250 people in 1804, but after the smallpox epidemic of 1837, their numbers were reduced to 125 or 145. The tribe signed the treaties of July 30, 1825, of September 17, 1851, and the unratified treaty of July 27, 1866. Hodge, *Handbook*, 1:798. In the manuscript, De Trobriand spells the tribal name "Mandane." The editor has corrected the spelling to "Mandan" in this translation.

sides there, too.[37] As the Indians never attack any fort, although these forts are usually nothing more than an enclosure of palisades around the buildings, the whites are safe even without a military garrison. Moreover, Berthold is just fifteen miles from here, and I could lend them a hand if they needed it.

The Sioux Indians will bother us still less; but it is safer to be on guard so they do not have a chance to steal mules or cattle, a temptation that they never have been able to resist.

A few days ago twelve warriors of the three tribes went on the "warpath" down the river in four bull boats (four boats made of a buffalo skin stretched over sticks forming an inside skeleton) to steal from the Sioux some horses which they planned to ride back. We have had no news of them, and it might be that after going out to look for wool, they will come back clipped. Nevertheless, if they arrive without being discovered at the camp where the others have left their squaws and children, they will be able to do more harm than they anticipated and bring back more spoils and scalps than they hoped for.

The two scouts from Rice also brought a rather important packet of mail: business papers, newspapers, and personal letters. General rejoicing about this. They will leave tomorrow at daybreak.

Monday, September 2. In the afternoon, a steamboat coming up the river was sighted at the foot of the bluffs. All glasses were immediately pointed in that direction. She was a boat of considerable tonnage, and she must have a special cargo to go up the Missouri at this season of the year. Soon the name *Mary MacDonald* could be made out on the paddle box of her wheels, and after the customary blaring of the whistle, the steamer moored at our wharf. She was sent by the quartermaster general's department in St. Louis, and her whole cargo was for us. Among other things she brought us twenty complete teams of six mules each, with wagons, harnesses, a wooden storehouse, windows, doors, shingles, timberwork, planks, grain, tarpaulin, etc. In addition to these things, the officers found a number of things

[37] The relationship between Mahlon S. Wilkinson and Colonel de Trobriand revealed in this journal is an illuminating example of the relationship between the Indian Bureau and the Army in the 1860's. There is no evidence that Wilkinson participated in nefarious practices, but it is clear that he was too indolent to discharge properly the duties of his office. Letters to Wilkinson from the Office of Indian Affairs and letters from Wilkinson to the Office of Indian Affairs, 1867–1869. Natural Resources Division, National Archives; Charles Larpenteur, *Forty Years a Fur Trader on the Upper Missouri* (Elliot Coues, ed.), 2:418.

on board to buy: potatoes, onions, wines (bad quality), brushes, wax, lamp oil, etc. Thus everyone has provided for the completion of his outfit for winter, because it is probable that no other boat will come up here this season, unless, perhaps, it should be the *Deer Lodge*. As for myself, I have made sure of enough illumination to light up my long winter evenings and have provided myself with the means of occupying them by reading or writing by the light of a good lamp. The unloading of the cargo went on the greater part of the night by the light of pine knots fixed in iron holders, since the captain wished to get under way again as soon as possible. Mr. Shields, clerk.

Tuesday, September 3. Dined on board the steamer on fried ham, potatoes, corn, and a cup of coffee, after which we watched from the upper deck the comical spectacle of the unloading of one hundred and twenty mules on the loose; they hesitated at first, sometimes refused to go out on the gangway, up to which point the bravest or the most intelligent had gone with no trouble; then they all rushed out on it at the same time, or even jumped overboard by themselves. And such jumping! Such running and kicking when they found they were on land again. It must be delightful to roll in the dust after a steamboat trip; not one of them failed to do so. And such happy brayings! When the unloading was completed, goodbyes were said; the steamboat cast off, and turning her prow in the direction of the current, she followed it in a long turn, faded in the distance, and finally disappeared around a bend in the river, leaving the wharf loaded with building materials that will speed up the completion of the fort and make our establishment in permanent quarters much easier.

About nine o'clock, since the weather was agreeable, I went to hunt game on Douglas Creek, accompanied by the surgeon major and followed by my orderly carrying his carbine. When we returned between twelve and one o'clock, the heat was overpowering, and I was quite worn out. Soon the wind came up, and, increasing more and more, finally blew in a tempest from the northwest for the whole afternoon and most of the night. And the dust enveloped us worse than ever.

The fire still burns on the prairie to the west and south. When it seems about to die out, the wind fans it up again, and drives it in some new direction. At nine o'clock in the evening, it was stronger in the southeast, with another blaze on a hillside to the south which was farther away and weaker. The flames do not seem to be coming toward us very much. They are still invisible beyond the horizon, which in that direction is lighted up every night.

Wednesday, September 4. We were not prepared to accommodate the reinforcement of mules that arrived for us yesterday. Since there is no corral to put them in, they have been tied up as securely as possible with ropes in front of the camp where we keep our draft animals out of the reach of the Indians. During the night, eleven of them broke loose and made their escape. Instead of staying around camp, they dashed out onto the prairie, and two or three squads of men, sent out on horseback in different directions, have not been able to find them. I suspect that these men are afraid of Indians and did not dare to go out of our sight. They will beat the brush, more or less, up and down a few ravines, and they will not find them there; they will not venture out on the plains for fear of unpleasant encounters. We saw only one squad that was oblivious to the advantages of cover as they gazed across the plains from the top of the hills. Many of the new soldiers, thoroughly frightened by ridiculous reports and absurd commentaries on the Indians, have become accustomed to considering them so dangerous that they think more of avoiding them than of fighting them.

The truth is that the Indians are much less fearful than they are painted. If this were not true, how could we establish and maintain in the very heart of their country weak, isolated military posts of two or three companies, far from any help or support and sometimes even without communications with the outside world for the whole winter? Put white men in the place of the redskins, and all these posts would be seized and destroyed in a season.

I have here two hundred and fifty men camped in open country without any kind of fortification, entrenchment, or defense. A few tree trunks forming a crude palisade have been driven behind the tents where the officers' wives live to convince them that they are safe from Indian arrows—and that's all. The provisions, stacked up under a temporary shelter by the wharf a few hundred yards from camp, have no protection other than the rifles of three or four sentinels night or day. The cattle graze on the plains all day under the guard of three men and a corporal, and spend the night in a weak enclosure some distance from here. The front of our sawmill is not protected by the guardpost. Our buildings now being constructed are five or six hundred yards out on the wide open plain, where a band of Indians would meet no more opposition than the wind. Near there the sutler and ten civilians have their tents and are building their double cabin of logs. Finally, my two companies work by day and sleep by night in their tents without protection. How could there be a better chance of attack for an enemy who can marshal a thousand warriors when it wishes and who must be tempted by the booty of our herds and teams, to say nothing of our scalps? However, the hostile Indians do not dare come to attack us.

Once—it was a few days before we arrived—their "warpath" brought them into our immediate neighborhood. There were five or six hundred braves in the group, more than twice our number. During the night, they hid in the rolling ground near camp so they could surprise some workers out alone or steal mules, supreme objective of warrior ambition. The boldest took positions behind some piles of adobe near the foundations of the new fort. In spite of all this, they were detected at daybreak, and the men were put under arms.

However, a wagoner, an old dragoon, intimidated very little by the redskins, went out with his team without any escort, although he had received the orders. When he arrived at the foundations of the fort, he saw that he was surrounded by half a dozen Indians, who cut the traces of his animals and stole four mules. One of them shot an arrow at him point blank, and so the wagoner was killed through his own fault. He was unarmed and stupidly went out to throw himself into the jaws of the wolf.

Those who did the deed fled before the escort arrived or the garrison was able to find out what had happened. The whole band of warriors then began to circle on their horses two hundred yards away and to make all kinds of triumphant gestures. A rifled piece was immediately aimed at the main group. A shell came whistling at them and burst in their midst. One of them had his leg torn off, another was rather seriously wounded, and one of their horses was ripped open. It took no more than this to put six hundred warriors in flight, and the whole band galloped away, disappearing as fast as they could; they crossed the river in great haste twenty or thirty miles down. Since then, we have heard no more about it, and not a hostile Indian has appeared on the horizon.

The only real danger from them is that of isolated assassinations. They scatter in force in the environs of the forts where the woods or thick brush afford them a place to hide and lie in wait for lonely travelers. But if woodcutting is done by detachments, they will hardly risk an attack.

Opposite the camp and across the river from it, I have a small detachment of ten men commanded by a sergeant. They have with them a dozen oxen which drag to the edge of the river the few hundred logs they have cut from the woods. Their cabins are there, and they stay there night and day. However, not an Indian has showed up on that side. They are afraid of being discovered and of not being able to retreat safely, since the woods are on an alluvial terrain with the river on one side and a line of bare and rather sharp cliffs on the other. In addition to this they have great respect for our long-range cannon, especially after the experience they have had with them.

[*Indian warfare*] In order to give an account of how the Indians make war—the plains Indians in particular—one must understand their ideas about warrior bravery and their complete ignorance of what we call heroism. To them the highest good is in stealing and killing as much as they can with the least possible risk to themselves. Since they have no conception of the feeling that makes us scorn danger they, quite on the contrary, take it into serious consideration, and even a scalp or booty will not bring them to gamble their life on a fifty-fifty chance. They will not venture an engagement unless they hold all the winning cards. To risk as little as possible—such is their fundamental maxim. This explains the system of ambushes, sieges, and the traps which in their eyes constitute the whole art of warfare. Running away as fast as possible without fighting, even against quite an inferior force, seems more praiseworthy than reprehensible to them when it is justified by a certain number of risks that are avoided. Too, they never fight in the open unless they are at least ten to one, and in this way they recognize the superiority of the "Pale Faces" in spite of themselves. To appear unexpectedly, kill some poor unarmed devil, stampede a herd of cattle in order to steal them, and disappear before any forces can be deployed—this is invariably their strategy.

When they surprise a man isolated some distance from the forts, they first try to cut off his retreat by racing around him swiftly, making a circle, drawing in closer and closer. If the man gets frightened and runs without thinking of using his weapon, he is lost. The Indians, who are wonderful horsemen, close in together to chase him; and as they are very skillful in using the bow without stopping or reducing the speed of their horses, they will kill their victim by hitting him in the back. Almost all the men lost in the Department of the Platte River on the route of the Pacific Railroad have been killed in this way. But if, on the other hand, they are dealing with a resolute and cool man, he has every chance of getting away, and the danger is more apparent than real. To get out of such a predicament, he must beat a careful and deliberate retreat, arms ready, and the moment the enemy comes in range, draw a bead on him. The Indian who is thus threatened will immediately throw himself behind the neck and flank of his horse and get away as quickly as he can. By that simple demonstration and by playing his game, he will keep the whole band in awe, even if they are fifteen or twenty strong. Even if he does open fire on some horseman bolder than the rest, the others will not risk moving in on him, for they have already learned by experience about the rapid fire of our new arms, and they know that our carbines are reloaded as soon as they are fired—just time enough to take the cartridge and put it in the open breech.[38]

Experience has proved that a man with presence of mind can return to the fort safe and sound if he uses these tactics, even from quite a distance, unless the Indians galloping in the distance, shouting and crying, are able to get close enough to his carbine to shoot their arrows at him, although their range is only half that of the carbine. If they are armed with guns, they will not have any greater confidence, for they have old weapons of inferior quality which cannot be used with any greater effectiveness.

Last winter, hostile Indians remained almost the whole time around Fort Buford, then an insignificant post garrisoned by a single company from my regiment. They wearied and vexed the little garrison by increasing their duties, by forcing them to remain inside the palisade; but they never inflicted any loss on them, and did not prevent the weak detachments, which were sent out to fill the water barrels at the river, from going down and coming back unharmed.

So defense against the Indian is not the great difficulty; that is nothing. The problem is to pursue them and to get at them on the desert plains, their natural haven of escape from punishment for their depredations. This is the problem that has not yet been solved. "War parties" move around in groups of only two or three hundred in order to be more sure of getting a living. Each warrior carries with him a piece of buffalo meat that has been dried in the sun. This is all the food he needs for a few weeks. His horse eats no grain; he gets enough good nourishment by grazing on the prairie. His forage grows everywhere and does not have to be transported. Since his horse is not shod, forge apparatus is unnecessary. There is no equipment to carry. His saddle is nothing; his bridle just a lasso of buffalo

---

[38] Some breechloaders were being manufactured, but because rapid improvements made manufacture in quantity impractical, most of the troops were supplied with Springfields converted into breechloaders.

leather, and he hardly uses that. If he must go up a hill on the gallop while being pursued, he will run alongside his horse in order to spare him, helping himself along with the lasso when he needs it. On the summit, he will jump in the saddle without stopping and go down the opposite slope full speed, so confident is he of the sureness of his pony's legs. If, in spite of these advantages, the band is pressed too hard, the red warriors agree on a rallying place far away and spread out in every direction; then the pursuers are left with nothing more tangible to chase than men speeding away singly.

From these facts it follows:

1. That infantry is absolutely useless in pursuing Indians on the "warpath," and must be left in garrisons. The only use to which it can be put is to range far out during the winter to surprise the permanent villages where the tribes keep their women and children. The confessed aim is to exterminate everyone, for this is the only advantage of making the expedition; if extermination were not achieved, just another burden would be added—prisoners. To exterminate, the expedition must be very certain of the position of the villages and their character; for in so rigorous a climate as this, such privations, sufferings, and dangers for the soldier accompany an expedition across the ice and snow that it would be criminal to undertake it thoughtlessly and without being almost positive of the results.

2. That the cavalry is the only arm that can be used effectively in pursuing Indians. Unfortunately, nothing can be accomplished for a number of reasons: the superabundance of recruits who are not horsemen and are only awkward children in points of horsemanship when compared with the redskins, who are as much at home on the backs of their ponies as they are on their own legs; the task of transporting grain, shoeing equipment, and supplies to pursue an enemy who has no need of these *impedimenta;* the character of the horses which are almost as inferior as the men for this type of service on the plains. The Indian pony without stopping can cover a distance of from sixty to eighty miles between sunrise and sunset, while most of our horses are tired out at the end of thirty or forty miles. The Indian pony has no harnessings to load him down. If he is too tired, his master will usually jump on a fresh mount chosen from among those which usually accompany the war parties and will let him continue the trip unburdened. If one of our horses is exhausted, we have an unmounted horseman. In brief, the movement of Indian horsemen is lighter, swifter, and longer range than that of our cavalry, which means that they always get away from us. Certainly General

Custer is a good cavalry officer, brave, energetic, intelligent. He served brilliantly during the war and accomplished a good deal against the Confederate cavalry. What has he done against the Indians? Nothing. Vainly he exhausted men and horses, pursuing the Indians without making contact with them, and his best reports amount to four or five men killed to one of the enemy.[39]

What can be done to offset these disadvantages? First, modify the recruiting system for frontier cavalry by substituting as far as possible, perhaps by the attraction of high pay, men who are used to horses for men with no experience or worth who now encumber the ranks; by forming auxiliary squadrons composed of frontiersmen who know the Indians and who are able to fight them their own way; finally, by enrolling in volunteer companies the Indians themselves who are allies of the United States and who are at war with the hostile tribes, the line officers being taken exclusively from among the men of the plains who are familiar with the habits, ideas, and languages of the tribes. In this way, the red companies would render the same services to the government that the native tribes of Algeria rendered to France.[40]

This last system has recently been inaugurated by General Augur in the Department of the Platte River, and excellent results are still coming from the experiment. Two companies forming a squadron of two hundred men have been recruited from the Pawnee Indians,

39 After the Civil War, George Armstrong Custer was assigned to the 7th Cavalry on duty at Fort Riley, Kansas, where he led expeditions against the Cheyenne and Sioux. Their expert horsemanship and facile shifting defeated the strategy of the 7th Cavalry. Custer served against the Indians in Kansas, Dakota, and Montana before he died at the Battle of the Little Big Horn in 1876. Frederic F. Van de Water, *Glory-Hunter*, p. 169.

40 Joseph R. Brown, Minnesota trader and journalist, claimed the distinction of Americanizing the European system of using native troops. In 1866, he wrote of his plan to Henry Hastings Sibley: ". . . my Scouting system, the System I hang my coat, boots and pantaloons on, is quite a different affair. *It* does not propose to Employ Scouts as an appendage to an army, but to employ a force of Indian Scouts, with a *very few* whites as artillerists, and with this force, by a free use of physical or moral suasion . . . I *propose* to conquer a peace with the Savages occupying the vast prairies of the North West . . . This system I claim as peculiarly my own, *in name,* and no farther. In the Indies and Algiers the English and French have successfully adopted and pursued the same *system* under the name and style of arming *Native* troops. But in this free and Enlightened country a very grave and serious error might have crept into our institutions, by entrusting the safety of the frontier to *Native American* troops." Joseph R. Brown, Lac Traverse [Minn.] to Henry Hastings Sibley, September 19, 1866. Sibley Papers. Minnesota Historical Society; see also Régis de Trobriand, Fort Stevenson, D. T., to Bvt. Lt. Col. Chas. H. Graves, Fort Rice, D. T., June 3, 1863. Department of Dakota, War Records Division, National Archives.

and these two hundred are more effective than any regiment of one thousand to twelve hundred men in the regular cavalry.[41] The Pawnees are mounted on Indian horses, which are not shod and do not eat grain. They are dressed in campaign uniform like our men; wide-brimmed hat, blue tunic, and clear blue trousers. While they are doing regular guard and outpost duty, they keep their equipment, but as soon as they fall on the Sioux, they immediately throw off their saddles, their boots if they inconvenience them, even their uniforms if they have not become accustomed to them. They leap onto their horses, ride them bareback, and do wonders with them. In this way they have protected the cattle and draft animals, recaptured a good number of those which had been stolen, and brought back scalps with them. They are obedient, easily disciplined, sober, energetic, vigilant, brave, and the unanimous opinion of the officers who have seen them in action and whom I have consulted is that one of them is worth at least three or four of our regular cavalrymen. They are commanded by a plainsman who can do anything he wants with them: a white man, of course. He has the rank and pay of a major. Since these two companies and their officers are not officially recognized, they are paid by the quartermaster's department; the pay is the same as in the regular army.

We hope that custom will not triumph over experience and proved facts, and that this innovation will be developed to the extent necessary to get the best possible results from it. The results are of the greatest interest, especially if we are going to have a somewhat general war with the tribes of the plains.

Thursday, September 5. The mules which escaped from the corral have been found. When they came to the trail from Berthold, they followed it and were captured by the friendly tribes of the neighborhood. Three of them, accompanied by two white traders, brought them back to camp. As a reward, they received some salt pork, a barrel of biscuit, some coffee, and miscellaneous provisions. They left very happy and in great haste, fearing that they would meet on the way a detachment of Sioux, who left the neighborhood of Fort Sully to attack their tribes. But it is not probable that they will have that unpleasant encounter in the fifteen miles between us and their reserve. The three tribes are on their guard, and if the Sioux war-

41 The Pawnee belong to the Caddoan family and inhabited the valley of the Platte River, Nebraska. Throughout Indian hostilities on the plains, the Pawnee remained peaceful, serving as scouts in the United States Army. Hodge, *Handbook,* 2:213–216.

riors are not too superior in number, they will have their work cut
out for them. They assure me that they can fight equal numbers very
well, but that their disadvantage is in their great numerical in-
feriority. This is what makes them powerless and keeps them constantly on a cautious defensive.

Sunday, September 8. High winds still shake our tents and en-
velop the camp in whirlpools of dust. They have free play. There
are no barriers on any side, and they have a clean sweep in all directions across the flat plain bordering the river, the horizon of which
is defined only by low rolling hills and on which there is no vegetation other than short grass dried out by the sun. One night recently
was rainy, but in spite of the wind the days have continued to be
clear. But the sun has lost much of its power, and its rays now give
off little heat. It is the kind of weather they enjoy during October in
the state of New York.

The advance scouts of a train of one hundred wagons coming
from Fort Totten have just arrived. The convoy that they left twenty
and some miles behind, advancing slowly across the plains with the
majestic pace of oxen teams, will be here tomorrow. It is coming to
get the provisions left here for Fort Totten, a part of which had been
sent off the second day after my arrival.[42] With the party comes the
paymaster and his secretary, some traders, and agents of fur companies established at Berthold. The escort is commanded by Lieutenant [Benjamin Curtis] Lockwood. Lieutenant Walborn who went
to Devils Lake last month, took the lead and has just arrived at camp.
The news he brings of conditions at Fort Totten is bad. The paymaster will give me new and fuller information on this subject. We
shall see.

Monday, September 9. I have talked at length with Major
[George] Pomeroy, paymaster, and separately with Lieutenant Walborn and Lieutenant Lockwood. All information about the deplorable lack of discipline at Fort Totten caused, basically, by the habitual drunkenness of Samuel A. Wainwright, commandant of the post,

[42] Fort Totten was supplied both by the Missouri River route via Fort Stevenson and by the overland route from Minnesota. Although the Missouri River
route was considered cheaper, the overland route was more certain. Supplies arriving from St. Louis via Stevenson were loaded and unloaded as many as five
times, and the storage facilities at Fort Stevenson were never adequate to take care
of the goods for two posts. Inspection report of regular troops made at Fort Totten,
D. T., October 19, 1868, by Stevens Norvell. Department of Dakota, War Records
Division, National Archives; *North Dakota Historical Collections*, 3:186–187.

is in agreement. There are now only five officers on duty at Fort Totten: Captain Wainwright, a drunkard; Captain [John Henry] Piatt, another drunkard; Lieutenant [Charles Henry] Leonard, discharging the office of adjutant, who follows their example; and two good officers, lieutenants [Platte Marvin] Thorne and Lockwood. One can imagine the state of discipline and the condition of the service when authority is in such hands. When the commandant is drunk, which is almost every day, he gives himself over to his ridiculous or brutal eccentricities, which, of course, earn him the hatred and scorn of his men. One day he will take three or four men, ropes around their necks, to a wood where he pretends he is going to have them hanged. Of course the execution does not take place. On another day, for no reason at all, he puts a sergeant under arrest and has him paraded before the companies, all because this noncommissioned officer, who was under arms, had saluted the officer of the day in the usual way, while the captain contended on his own authority that the man was to take off his cap. Then, the next day, after the fumes of drunkenness had cleared away, he apologized to the injured sergeant because he feared the consequences of this flagrant injustice. One night the soldiers got into his [Wainwright's] tent and stole five or six gallons of whiskey he had stored there. Naturally the whole camp, or almost all of it, was drunk in the morning. The officers lost all control over the men and they committed flagrant acts of mutiny and insubordination. The commandant was hooted at, the usual result of his drunkenness, and the prisoners who were delivered by force from the guardhouse remained at large. No report of these events was sent to general headquarters. These occurrences, as well as the general demoralization of the garrison, have been kept a secret within the post, since the chief guilt rests on the commandant of the post. Now, for the first time in the three months that Captain Wainwright has had command of this new post, news of the deplorable state of affairs reached here.[43]

And now one can clearly see the great inconvenience of having our troops scattered around in little posts isolated from one another by long distances and the lack of regular communications. Here again are demonstrated the results of a system, which in the absence of a distinct general staff recruits all the officers from that branch of ser-

[43] Major Pomeroy declined to make an official report on the condition of the command at Fort Totten, and De Trobriand did not report the situation to the Department at this time. Régis de Trobriand, Fort Stevenson, D. T., to Bvt. Brig. Genl O. D. Greene, A. A. Genl, Department of Dakota, St. Paul, December 21, 1868. Department of Dakota, War Records Division, National Archives.

Fort Berthold, Dakota Territory, 1867–69

vice in the regiments where their absence leaves vacancies inimical to the general and particular interest of the service.

Without counting the new lieutenant colonel ([Andrew W.] Bowman), who hasn't had time to join the regiment and who will not arrive until spring, and also the major (Whistler), who is on leave and who, it seems, won't return any sooner and probably not before two years, half of my captains are missing, as follows:

Theodore Yates, Co. E. Sick in Milwaukee, and in all probability not able to serve again.

George W. Hill, Co. A. Detached as a member of the district court in Minnesota.

Charles J. Dickey, Co. B. Detached for recruiting.

William M. Wherry, Co. G. Detached to Richmond on the general staff of General [John M.] Schoffield [*sic*] (contrary to regulations).

George Meade, Co. I. Detached to Philadelphia on the general staff of General [George G.] Meade (contrary to regulations).

Five regimental captains remain for ten companies, distributed as follows:

Wm. G. Rankin, Co. C. Commanding Fort Buford, where five companies hold garrison.

Francis Clarke, Co. F. At Fort Buford.

Albert M. Powell, Co. H. Commanding Fort Stevenson.

Samuel A. Wainwright, Co. D. Commanding Fort Totten.

John H. Piatt, Co. K. At Fort Totten.

Among the lieutenants, there are three on vacation, two officers in detached service, and one on leave. Four out of the ten are left for the regiment. Of the second lieutenants, one is in detached service, one is on leave, and one has never joined the regiment since he was assigned to it. Seven remain.

In all, sixteen out of thirty-five officers are absent from their corps, which reduces to nineteen the number of those who are performing the duties of the three posts in the district, and this includes the commanding colonel, the adjutant, and the quartermaster. Among the regimental officers, fourteen are absent, sixteen present.

Under ordinary circumstances, the first measure to be taken to bring about justice and to put things back on good footing at Fort Totten would be to place Captain Wainwright under arrest with an accusation before a general court martial and to transfer the command to the first officer in rank after him. But it so happens that this officer is no better than his superior, and even worse, for in addition to being a drunkard he is afraid of his men, is incapable of commanding respect, and does not even dare to punish them. Things go from bad to worse, and after putting one under arrest and accusation, we should have to do the same to the other. Then who would be left to command the post and the three companies, to perform the duties of officer of the day, etc.? Three lieutenants, one of them not worth much. Impossible. And all this has happened because Captain Hill, who would be second in command if he were with the company, is detached for district court in Minnesota, and who, consequently, cannot replace Captain Wainwright if he is deprived of his command.

The exchange of two companies from one post to another would not improve the situation, for Captain Wainwright is first in rank, and in the absence of my two high-ranking officers, he would have to take command of the post where he was sent. Moreover, the garrisons of the three posts are busy doing work that cannot be delayed because of the lateness of the season. At Stevenson and at Totten new forts are being built, and at Buford new quarters and new storehouses are going up to take care of the garrison which has been increased from *one* to *five* companies. So no movement of troops across the plains can be ordered now, and winter will make it impossible for five or six months.

It is thus that a colonel finds himself with his hands tied in a situation that urgently demands prompt and vigorous action. In the present case, after looking at the question from all sides, I am reduced to the only measure possible: Ask the general headquarters of the Department for the return, as soon as possible, of Captain Hill to Fort Totten, so he will be there to assume command if the need arises;— and meanwhile to send by the train which is leaving day after tomorrow a sharp reprimand to Captain Wainwright, telling him peremptorily that I shall not tolerate the condition his command is in as the result of his habitual drunkenness; that he must act to put an end to it immediately; that if any of the acts that degrade his authority as an officer and his character as a gentleman occur again, I shall not hesitate to have recourse to the severe measures that military regulations put in my hands. This should tell him plainly that in such a case he will be called before a court-martial. A word to the wise is sufficient. We shall see what effect the warning will have.

Tuesday, September 10. The paymaster paid the troops today. We shall not see him again until May or June. So the soldiers will get quite an accumulation of back pay all at once, and they will have great temptations when they come into the possession of eight or nine months' pay, *one hundred and fifty dollars,* more or less.

In the afternoon, a band of Indians, fifty to sixty strong, appeared on the horizon near the river flats. After coming nearer, they sent one of their number to make themselves known. They belong to a branch of the Sioux nation, are coming from Fort Rice, and are going to Fort Berthold, where, it seems, they are going to settle down peacefully near the three tribes, who are already there. They camped near the river, below our wharf on low ground covered with good grass for their horses. Tomorrow at daybreak they will be on their way.

Wednesday, September 11. I was informed just today that no provision has yet been made to feed our cattle for the period of December to April, when snow covers the ground. A contract has been made between the quartermaster of the district and Mr. [D. W.] Marsh, trader and sutler, by which the latter, who is furnished with mowing machines, promises to gather and stack all the hay of suitable quality that he can get within a radius of ten miles around the fort for seventeen dollars a ton. But this contract provides forage for only the animals of the quartermaster, horses and mules, and does not include the cattle. Moreover, the reinforcement of one hundred and twenty mules which arrived from St. Louis the other day, although thirty of them have been transferred to Fort Totten, will use all the crop and will leave no surplus for the quartermaster to give to the cattle of the commissary. So it is urgent that we secure in advance subsistence for our cattle during the winter, for they are the principal food for our men, who, I fear, will be deprived of potatoes, onions, and other vegetables. To keep the cattle in the best possible condition so they can survive until spring is so much the more important since some cases of scurvy have already broken out in the garrison as a result of using salted meat and being without vegetables too long. Since all our men are busy working on the fort and the garrison cannot furnish any detachment to gather hay, I have taken it on myself to authorize the commissary to conclude a contract with the best possible terms for one hundred tons of hay to be stacked at the fort by October 11.

The contract was made with Mr. Pochler and Mr. [Joseph] Anderson who have undertaken the transportation of the provisions of Fort Totten with the convoy of one hundred wagons. Because they receive no assistance in machines or otherwise, and because they must bring the hay from a distance of twelve to fifteen miles, the price is set at thirty-three dollars a ton. Mr. Marsh offered to deliver it in stacks on the premises for twenty-six dollars, but it would have been necessary to go out on the prairie to get it, where it would have remained at the mercy of the Indians, in danger of being burned and without any protection at all for months. The risks were too great, and economy might be too disastrous. I have written to the quartermaster general of the department, where General Terry will approve the order and ratify the contract.

Thursday, September 12. The convoy from Fort Totten left today, taking with it all the supplies destined for that post, with the exception of a supply of grain for which they could find no room. Part of the wagons (about half) will come back again to take what had to be left behind on this trip. The escort drawn from the three companies garrisoned at Fort Totten is under the command of a lieutenant, Lockwood, an energetic and capable officer; but the lack of discipline which is prevalent at the post has spread a bad spirit among the men thus detached. Four deserted en route; two others tried to do so, and two struck and beat a lance corporal. As there is danger that they will escape the punishment due them when they return to Fort Totten, I had the four locked up under guard, and they will remain here as prisoners, assigned to heavy labor until they can answer summons before the military court.[44]

Friday, September 13. The proximity of the detachment from Fort Totten has brought its fruits. Last night nine men deserted, stealing from the corral as many mules, saddles, and bridles. As soon as their departure was discovered, Lieutenant [Martin E.] Hogan with a sergeant and four men got on their trail to give chase. He lost no time in following the route of the convoy for Fort Totten, overtook them, and chased them until fear of being captured forced them to spread out on the plains. A heavy fog then filled the air, and made it possible for eight of them to elude the pursuers. The ninth, whose

[44] In the *Army and Navy Journal*, the alarming rate of desertion from the army on the plains was frequently noted. The principal causes of desertion seem to be these: soldiers devoted most of their time to nonmilitary duties and received $16 a month plus about $6 extra-duty pay, while the civilian laborers working with them received $45 a month and board; mining and land speculation seemed more attractive than a military life; the barracks and food were inferior; the infrequent visits of the paymaster allowed as much as a year's pay to accumulate. *Army and Navy Journal*, August 29, 1868, p. 22; October 26, 1867, p. 157; December 28, 1867, p. 298.

mount was carrying the provisions of the little band, was made prisoner; and about one o'clock in the afternoon Lieutenant Hogan and his men came back to camp, bringing the prisoner, the provisions of the deserters, and their extra goods.

Immediately Lieutenant Walborn received the order to ride out with eight men and a sergeant to take up the pursuit again. The deserters, who are spread out on the prairie, will waste the rest of the day in getting together again. Their mules are worn out from a twenty-mile flight on the gallop and can hardly take them farther without resting. They will scarcely dare travel by day, knowing they are closely pursued, and they will be forced to remain hidden in some ravine until night. Since they do not have any compass or provisions, they will have to follow the trail of the convoy, and Lieutenant Walborn has every chance of by-passing them, waiting in some ambush and gathering them in with a cast of the net. Otherwise he will push on to Fort Totten with the order he carries for Captain Wainwright to furnish him with fresh horses and every assistance in his power to help him capture the fugitives, whether they arrive mixed in with the convoy or not.[45]

The band of Medicine Bear, as this petty Indian chief is called, came back today from Berthold, where apparently it had gone to pay a few days' visit. However, some of them must have stayed there, for they do not seem to be as numerous as they were when they went. They camped near the constructions, and during the afternoon a number of them, men and women, came to beg for provisions, which were given to them. They are accompanied by about a dozen Rees, who will leave them here and return to Berthold tomorrow when the wandering band gets under way for Fort Rice.

Sunday, September 15. Almost all day the wind blew in a gale, and after coming up in the southeast, it shifted to the south, then to the southwest, and finally to the west, where it calmed down at sunset. It carried in its impetuous course thick clouds of fine sand from the wide banks bordering the river above and below the camp. The air was so darkened by it that the rays of the sun could hardly get through. Spirals of dust were flying through the air wherever the

45 On October 29 a deserter from Fort Stevenson gave himself up at Fort Snelling. He reported that several deserters from Fort Totten and other posts were in the Red River country in the employ of the Hudson's Bay Company. These deserters had Colonel Whistler's horse with them. E. B. Alexander, Fort Snelling, Minnesota, to Bvt. Col. J. N. G. Whistler, Fort Stevenson, October 29, 1867. Department of Dakota, War Records Division, National Archives.

wind swept up the bare ground, around the new buildings, in the camp, and in particular in the field where the adobe is being made. The men were not working; they rest on Sunday. Any other day, work would have been forcibly suspended. This is our "Simoon." Everyone remained in his tent, which was closed carefully, but no one was able to shut out the dust which, in a time like this, seeps inside in quantity, no matter what is done for protection against it.

This situation does not exist because of any lack of care in setting up the officers' tents, for they have a covering of planks on the outside, and, in addition to this, a "fly" nailed on a framework covering the roof in such a way that the wind cannot slip in between the two. These precautions were taken when the change of weather and the end of heat presaged the coming of winter. Everyone then protected himself against the cold in advance with a bulwark of planks and the installation of stoves. The officers who did not have any large hospital tents had small double houses built, and these are more spacious and comfortable than their wall tents. The sides and gable ends are of boards, and the roof, composed of a thick tarpaulin, is of sailcloth and lets in light. Moreover, some doors with glass sections have been found, and these complete the lighting very satisfactorily.

Even the private kitchens have been protected against the wind and cold by a shell of boards called "slabs." A slab is the first slice that the sawmill cuts off a log intended for construction, and consequently it is rounded on the bark side. Necessity makes men ingenious, and all our preparation for autumn proves it. We have at our disposal nothing but boards and sailcloth, and with these two materials we are succeeding in getting installed in rather comfortable shelters where we can brave the rigors of the season. There is not one of us who doesn't look on his rough cottonwood floor, shrunken by the dry air, with as much satisfaction as he would the most beautiful oak or walnut floor in a brick or stone house. A man can get used to anything; no saying is truer than this. The straps of the tent are buckled when the wind blows, just as the door of a country house would be shut, and when the unleashed tempest on the plains shakes the frail building furiously, and it bangs, rattles, shudders, but holds fast, we sleep as soundly in a camp bed as if the roaring of the wind were rocking us to sleep in a curtained bed under the roof of a marble house. However, if there is rain mixed in with it, I do not think that this will be the case; but, thank God, we are spared the test, and we have not had to deal with humidity in the air. We are so far from the two oceans that the wind can blow from any direction;

the clouds formed by the evaporation of great masses of water get
to us only after discharging their liquid load elsewhere, and what
is left is hardly enough to veil the sun for a few hours, and it disappears without leaving any traces on our sandy soil. The atmosphere
has been like this for three months. The melting of the snows in the
spring causes some great seasonal rains, and on the plains this is
enough to support the growth of short and crisp grass; it is higher
and straighter on the lowlands where there is humidity for a longer
time, but where there is not enough of it for the growth of trees.
This is what invariably limits the growth of woods to the immediate
neighborhood of river courses, which are rare and far apart, or to
the hollows of ravines where ponds can form. The alluvial lands that
the Missouri forms and then destroys in the caprices of its course are
more favorable to the growth of forests. It is on these low banks that
are found the large trees which furnish building material now being
used in our construction. There is nothing like this on the high plateaus, and when one climbs to the top of the hills which overlook the
river, he can look out over immense horizons and see nothing but
the plain, the undulations of which are like the waves of the great
ocean. Our vast prairies are an immobile ocean.

Two steamers, which are known to be on the upper river either
near Benton or Buford, have been expected here for a week or two,
but have not appeared. Another steamer chartered by the government
to bring us building materials, the *Amanda,* was already on her way
when the *Mary MacDonald* passed her. That was sixteen days ago,
and the *Amanda* still has not appeared on the horizon. Evidently
these different boats have run aground on some sand bar or are held
up by shallow water, which makes navigation most difficult if not
impossible. It is this prospect much more than the fear of ice that
puts an end to the navigation of the Upper Missouri each year at the
beginning of September. Steamers which could carry a profitable
cargo at this time of year seldom dare to undertake it, although there
are still two months left before the river freezes over. But the dryness
in this whole region during the entire summer and the lack of any
important tributaries below the Stone River [Yellowstone] cause the
river to go down gradually from the first days of July. Navigation,
which is easy (comparatively) in the month of June, is less so in July,
and still less in August. A number of sand banks which can be easily
passed over at the beginning of summer are high and dry in September and narrow down the channel everywhere, and it becomes shallower and shallower until it finally is less than two feet deep over

bars. If the steamboat is loaded to displace three or three and a half feet of water, there she is stopped. If the bar is narrow and shifting, a passage can be successfully forced through by steampower and cranes; but if it is more solid and so wide that it cannot be forced, the boat will stay there, compelled to wait for an unexpected rise of a few inches, which cannot be depended on, or to back out in order not to have retreat cut off, or finally, if she is at some post, to lighten the load by discharging part of the cargo, or all of the cargo if she is giving up the trip.

This explains why not one of the three steamboats expected for two weeks has showed up and why we are deprived of the letters that the *Amanda* is undoubtedly bringing us. The water is already so low that it is doubtful if she will be able to get here, and as for the *Deer Lodge,* from now on it seems almost fantastic to hope to see her back this year.

Wednesday, September 18. The abundance of waterfowl is a great and valuable resource for our table. Without it our fare would be limited to a steady diet of beef and ham. But it takes only a few hours to furnish the larder with wild geese and ducks, a kind of jacksnipe as heavy as the woodcock or perhaps the prairie chicken, the heaviest known partridge. The ones found in the neighborhood stand as tall as a European pheasant. Major Furey has made two hunting expeditions, bringing back six ducks on his first trip and six ducks and two geese on his second. In the evening, Captain Powell (Bt. Lt. Col.) brought back nine ducks and two geese. One can easily get an idea of the abundance of this kind of game from these figures. At the approach of winter, the wild geese, which went farther north to lay eggs and hatch them, return south with their families. Night and morning they can be heard passing over in flocks, honking, and many alight on the banks of the Missouri or on the two little streams near camp, Douglas Creek and Snake Creek. They stay there for quite a long time with the ducks, which are plentiful in the willows where they make their nests. As these birds of the solitude hardly know man, they are much tamer than in populated regions, and one can approach them much more easily than in France, for example. Thus the sight of the camp and its activity does not turn them from their course, even when their flight brings them very low over it. I have seen some crossing or going up the river skimming the water to land on the flat ground stretching out below us and feeding in full sight of the men who come and go on the escarpment where our tents are located. A shot from a carbine fired at them from here just drives them two or three hundred feet away, where they alight again. As they are fired on, the geese, like the ducks, become more wild; but although they take alarm more quickly, they are still easy enough to get because of the lay of the land and the willow underbrush in the favorite places where they stay within a radius of five or six miles from the fort.

Thursday, September 19. The sled dogs which will carry our letters to Fort Totten during the winter arrived today with their harness, the sleds, and their drivers. The latter are half-breeds of a Canadian father and an Indian mother. They are young and vigorous; the Indian type is notably dominant in them: dark eyes, long, dark, straight, stiff hair the color of burnt earth. From their father they get a heavier build and dark sparse mustaches. The Indians, as you know, naturally have little beard, and they pull out hair by hair the little they do have when it appears at the age of puberty. Men and women 'let no hair grow but that on their head; one wonders why they, who more than any civilized race live according to the natural laws, go contrary to nature in this particular. The half-breeds dress in the American manner, but the Indian instinct shows up in some detail, as for example a variegated sash of gaudy colors.

The breed of dogs used to drag the sleds is tall on its legs, very close coupled, covered with thick hair, half dog and half wolf in appearance. Their ears are short and half drooping at the tips; their muzzles are long and pointed; their yellow, almond-shaped eyes have some resemblance to those of the Asiatic races. They are generally whitish in color, but crossbreeding has introduced some notable varieties among them. Of the nine dogs which make up our three teams, one is black and white, positively a griffon because of the length and stiffness of its hair; another of blackish color looks like a mastiff. They seem to be taciturn in temperament, as if they bore the imprint of the principal Indian characteristics. They are unsociable, undemonstrative, seem surprised at nothing, and look on things that happen around them with a lordly indifference. Don't pet them if you are tempted to; you may not be able to get away with it. If the attempt bores them, they move away with an expression that shows how they feel; if it displeases them, they draw back their lips and show their long fangs without changing position or growling. Apparently they scorn useless words and are satisfied with that mimic demonstration which is always enough to drive away the unwelcome.

They are fed only once a day, in the evening. The prospect of supper at the end of the trail gives them an ardor that they would not otherwise show. Experience has proved that they work much better on an empty stomach than they do after they eat. For supper, they are fed pemmican, buffalo meat chopped up fine and held together by grease; this keeps for years when it is dried in the sun and pressed into hard molds. The transport of it in sacks of buffalo skin is so much the easier since it seems that this concoction contains more nutriment in a small volume than any other.

The Indian quadrupeds do not love work any more than the Indian bipeds. One need but see their resigned and suffering faces when they are put in the harness. They try to get out of work by feigning illness, but once on their way, they make their fifty miles briskly if they must do so to get their supper. Their trips for us will not be over thirty-five to forty miles on the days they are on the trail.

Their harness is composed of a padded collar the shape of a large band, which is worn on the front of their shoulders. To this collar two traces are attached. The ends of the traces are hooked to the whiffletree of the sled and held up by the loops of a small variegated blanket, which is decorated with bells sewn in the collar and which covers the back of the animal. This harness seems rather heavy, but they assure me that it does not tire the dog that wears it.

As for the vehicle itself, usually it is simply a long straight board curved at the front end in the form of a reverse "C." A pack is fastened on the sled and serves as a seat for the driver, the whole thing weighing about two hundred and fifty pounds. However, we use a more commodious and more perfected form of the sled than the usual one; it has the exact form of a shoe whose sole, flat and extended out behind, replaces the heel. The driver, wrapped with buffalo skin, gets on. His legs and the lower part of his body are doubly protected from the cold, and if all the load of the sled cannot be put in the shoe, there is no difficulty fastening it on the back. This extremely light sled is made of buffalo skin stretched over a light frame, like the bull boats.

French is the language of the half-breeds, although they speak English and some Indian dialects (Sioux generally) as well. Like their masters, the dogs have a marked preference for French; they have been brought up, trained, and commanded in French, and the easiest way to get acquainted with them is to talk to them in French. I suppose it is because of this fact that I had the privilege of petting them at our first meeting near the wagons which they accompany and stay near. Although they are perfectly free, they never come among the tents. They are philosophically contented to sleep under the carts near the corral, and if Alexander were to come to ask them what he could do for them, no doubt they would answer (if they could talk) "Get out of my sun."

Saturday, September 21. I leave today for Fort Berthold, where I am going to visit the Indians of the three tribes who are there and make a hunting trip in the neighborhood where I am promised an abundance of game.

Monday, September 23. The day before yesterday, between one and two o'clock in the afternoon, we got under way. An ambulance drawn by four mules constituted our turnout. I took my place there with Major Furey, quartermaster, Lieutenant [Mott] Hooton, and the assistant surgeon, Mat[t]hews.[46] MacDonald, one of our scouts, took the lead, armed with his Henry carbine, and two orderlies, one of whom was leading my horse, escorted the carriage; we had our hunting rifles and everyone wore his revolver in his belt.

It is six leagues, fifteen miles, between Fort Stevenson and Fort Berthold. It is a two-hour trip. After crossing Douglas Creek on the bridge we had built there, we are out on a vast, level plain, bordered on the north by the hills in a bare chain stretching up behind the fort and on the south by the sinuous course of the Missouri. Nothing grows on this plateau but a short crisp grass, completely dried out in this season of the year. The buffalo have frequented this place, for here and there heads bleached by the sun show where a number of them have been killed by the Indians. Five or six miles from the fort, the plains become narrower, and soon end in the badlands, the name generally given to all alkali lands where no vegetation grows and where the rain washes deep rivulets in the sides of the heights. These lands are desolate looking, and there is something sinister about them. Here the trail winds across three or four miles of mountains, which are low but very sharp where their slopes have been corroded by the rains; at a distance, some look like a dome supported by fluted and superimposed columns. In these places the sides are sheer. Between these arid mountains there are valleys which are almost as arid;

46 Dr. Washington Matthews was born in Ireland. He became assistant surgeon in 1868 and surgeon major in 1889. One of the best informed men on the Upper Missouri, Dr. Matthews gave assistance to many writers and editors preparing material about that region. He wrote the descriptions of forts Rice and Stevenson in *Report on Barracks and Hospitals*. F. B. Heitman, *Historical Register of the United States Army*, 1:697.

the spring rains and the thawing of the snow temporarily form small streams of water in them, but they are completely dry this season of the year. On the banks of their twisted beds grow bushes and some trees, the only vegetation in these parts. The country is far from being without character; on the contrary, it has a very distinct stamp, but somber, inexorable, it grips the soul much more than it pleases the eye.

The plains are not like this. They give quite a different impression. More than anything else, it is an impression of immensity, of open space, and of an individual left to his own resources in the midst of nature where nothing belongs to anyone and everything belongs to everyone. Nothing here suggests limitation or division of the common land. It belongs to whoever crosses it, the white man as well as the red man, the buffalo, the wolf, the bear. Against personal dangers, the protection of government is a myth; the only real protection is in a steady heart and a good carbine. But although these badlands have a bad reputation because of the facilities they provide for an Indian ambush, the danger is but an uncertain eventuality and does not change at all the feeling of freedom under the sky that almost always exults one.

Although the great sea spreads out before the eyes a still more vast and unlimited horizon than the plain, the impression is not the same. At sea, one is aboard a ship where men are gathered in a structure where everything, even the smallest objects, is the work of civilization, and the living testimony of its arts, sciences, and laws.

There is none of this on the plains. No houses, no cultivation, no people. Wild nature and solitude surround one, absorb one. Even the wagon which carries us is little more than a vehicle adapted to wild life in a country where there is still no kind of pleasure carriage. Had the way been shorter, and especially the sun less hot, all of us would have been on horseback, in spite of the necessity of carrying our arms in our hands while passing through these "insecure" mountains whose blackish peaks fade away on the banks of the Missouri.

On coming out of the badlands where no living thing noticed us, except a red fox which was busy with his own hunting and which stopped his race for a moment to watch us pass, we came to a second plain, similar in every way to the one we first crossed. The region of the mountainous badlands rises up like a barrier between the two at equal distances from Fort Berthold and Fort Stevenson.

The first human being whom we met we saw first in the distance as a black speck, which little by little took the form of a man traveling on foot. He was a French-Canadian trapper by the name of Beau-champ, about whom I shall have more to say in the near future.[47] Naturally, he was armed with his carbine and was carrying a sack of bullets and a powder horn over his shoulder. But the thing in his accoutrements that struck me first was a heavy chain which would have recalled the galley slaves if it had been fastened to his leg in-stead of at the belt, and if it had ended in a ball instead of a heavy iron trap that our man carried on his shoulder. Beauchamp was going to set traps near a beaver lodge he had discovered not far from here and where he hoped to catch one of these industrious animals.

A little after this single encounter, Fort Berthold began to loom in the distance, and the nearness of the Indian village was soon re-vealed by strange silhouettes which appear rather bizarre to one who does not know the meaning of them; the open-air tombs of the red-skins and the stakes used for the tortures that they inflict on them-selves to obtain from the Great Spirit what they most desire: success in hunting or in war, deliverance from sickness or misfortunes, victory over their enemies, the chance to kill and scalp as many of them as they can and still escape from harm, robust health, a good harvest of corn, etc. Nothing has induced them to give up these voluntary, horrible tortures, in which they seem to have faith. Today as in the past there is expiation by blood, a vague semblance of Golgotha.

The torture stakes are trunks of dead trees divided into two parts at the top and stripped of bark. When a young warrior has decided on his own torture, he goes to the stake accompanied by his relatives in the midst of a gathering of the tribe. Usually he passes an iron arrow in his flesh or under his arm in a seton. Many inflict themselves with a wound on the stomach. They pass into it the end of a cord that they then knot firmly, and they are hoisted up by the cord and are suspended, singing continuously an improvised religious chant. They remain thus, bloody sacrifices, hung on the stake until the cord snaps or their skin breaks, or, if both resist, until the loss of blood and the pain make them lose consciousness. Then, if one of their relatives is willing to throw at the foot of the stake a buffalo skin, a blanket, some corn, or any other offering to divinity, they are taken down, unless they die victims of that horrible ordeal. I have seen some who proudly carry these terrible scars. Others impose less

[47] Not much is known about Peter, or Pierre, Beauchamp, beaver hunter, trader, and Arikara interpreter for the American Fur Company. It can be ascer-tained that he was at Fort Berthold by 1848 and that he died there about 1870. The material about him given by this journal is probably the most extensive in existence. *North Dakota Historical Collections,* 1:356.

bloody punishments on themselves, but nevertheless very rough; for example, dragging five or six buffalo heads in the thorns, brush, and stones until the rope breaks, which comes only after tremendous effort and crushing weariness. The youngest train themselves in physical pain, which is considered a meritorious act or one of expiation, by slashing the flesh with the point of a sharp knife. The scars left on their chests are considered marks of distinction.

The last kind of voluntary torture is the women's ordeal of mourning. When their father or husband has died, especially when he is killed by an enemy tribe, they go to the upper platform of their lodges and give themselves up to lamentations, while they stab themselves in their arms, legs, and all the fleshy parts of their body. This generally lasts a year, unless an enemy is killed before then to pay the price of the blood. A death for a death, and the mourning stops immediately.

In combat, the Indians attach infinite importance to bringing away their dead and wounded; because of this, it is difficult to figure their losses exactly. As soon as one of their men falls, the others immediately rush to carry him away, which is much easier for them since they fight at a great distance and never in formation. The body is brought back to the village if distance and circumstances permit it, unless he is buried in the Indian manner on some height from which he seems to dominate the solitude he roamed during his life.

To get to Berthold, the cemetery must be crossed. It is in a corner of the plain on the outskirts of the village, with no enclosure or line of demarcation where the dead are placed up on their final resting places. The families wrap them in blankets and animal skins and bind them from head to foot with strips of leather; then they fasten them in the same way on screens raised up from eight to ten feet and supported by four round poles driven into the ground. The Indians of Berthold, a little more civilized, sometimes close up their dead, especially the children, in boxes, which is infinitely less picturesque. Evidently this custom originated from the anxiety to preserve the dead from the depredations of carnivorous animals. The wolves which live in packs on the prairies dig up the corpses and eat them; but it seems that the vultures cannot get to the dead when they are bundled up in the open air this way. Although the bodies of the three warriors recently killed by the Sioux were there, I did not notice any emanation spreading about in the air. The heat of the sun and the dryness of the air, they tell me, dries up the bodies in their wrapping; in winter the cold freezes them; and when the inclemencies of the sky finally break the bonds and rip open the wrappings, in place of white bones, mummified members are exposed and stay that way if they are not covered up again.

[*Fort Berthold*] Behind the field of the dead, Fort Berthold appears. It was built first as a trading post by Northeastern Fur Company, occupied for two or three years by a company of infantry, and finally abandoned by the government to its original owners in June of this year.[48] It is simply a square of buildings constructed of squared logs, which open on an interior court. The two high, massive doors that give access to it close on hinges and are strongly barred on the inside. For the defense of the outside walls, two blockhouses jut out at two of the angles opposite each other. They are pierced with loopholes from which one can fire from the outside along the ramparts, and they have an upper floor overhanging the ground floor for protection. The location is perfectly chosen. It is on the tip of a point of high ground where the water is always deep enough to afford a landing for steamboats. The river hems in one side of it, and on the other, beyond the Indian village, the level plain stretches for several miles and one can see far enough to catch sight of any enemy in time to get the animals in and to stand on defense.

The traders live in the interior, I mean those who are agents of the fur company which owns the fort. The principal one, a Frenchman (from France) named Gustave Cagnat, invited us into his four room lodging: the first [room], which is his office, served us as a dining room. In the evening, they made a bed for me on the floor there, with a mattress, a buffalo robe, and a double blanket, just taken out of the storehouse, I suppose. Each of us had a pair of sheets and a pillow, consequently a complete bed. The second room is Gustave's; the third and fourth were assigned to my traveling companions. There is no kind of furnishing. For the occasion, a chair and a washbasin were all that were necessary. Another side of the square court is inhabited by the Indian wives of two other employees, each of whom has her family in a separate dwelling. On this side, near the stables, the lesser employees live, too. The third side is taken up by the storehouses of the company, the fourth by other storehouses where is stored the government grain, for which we still have no place at Stevenson. The interior of all the dwellings is simply whitewashed; the roof is made of narrow boards covered over with grass and a layer

48 The American Fur Company, not the Northwestern, built old Fort Berthold. See above, p. 22.

of earth a few inches thick. This covering, which forms the ceiling of the building, keeps out the dampness. In the winter, the cold is too severe; in the summer, the sun is too hot, and the rains do not last long enough in this essentially dry climate.

There are no white women at Berthold, or in any other nonmilitary post in the country. Here every white man takes an Indian wife with whom he lives and who keeps his house and bears him children. These children almost never speak any language but that of the mother, and stay in the tribe if the father leaves the country, which is rare. In a savage country where the Indians' mores fully acknowledge polygamy, the whites like anyone else can have several wives if they so wish, but they cannot take advantage of it unless they have some reason for sending the one they are supporting back to her family. It seemed to me that such a case was rare. The great ambition of a young "squaw" is to be the wife of a white man, for she is infinitely better treated than if she were the wife of any Indian, no matter which one. She is not subjected to exhausting work, which in Indian life makes women real beasts of burden, cultivating the soil, carrying the loads, caring for the horses, etc. With a white man, they are better dressed, better cared for, better fed. They would hardly risk losing all these advantages since, elevated by the choice of a white man, their return to a redskin would be a real comedown from any point of view. So they are submissive, attentive, diligent, taking care of their children and the father of their children. And the latter, who is contented and well taken care of in his home, devotes himself to his business without feeling a need for a change or without yielding to it. Perhaps in time he will take a second companion who is younger than the first, but he will not send back the latter, and the household will go along as it always has with no internal discord to disturb the customary peace.

The children of the whites carry the stamp of their origin in the lighter color of their skin and in the character of their faces. Some resemble their father almost entirely. These children are better cared for than many, the girls especially, who dress like their mothers in Indian garments as they do in our regions. Several traders who are more attached to their children send them to St. Louis to some school or convent where they learn English or receive a primary education; after this they return to the desert, the girls to live like their mothers, if they get a chance, the boys to serve as interpreters or to throw themselves into an adventurous nomadic life as most of the half-breeds do, working for the company, or the government, hunting or warring with the Indians. It is notable that the French language is a good deal more common among them in these parts than English, which is a result of a great infusion of Canadian blood in the tribes.

[*Marriage among the Indians*] Although these households I have just spoken of have not received religious or civil sanction to regularize their marriages, one can say, nevertheless, that these unions are recognized as such in the tribes where no other kind is known. According to Indian ideas, the wife, inferior and subordinate to the man, is an object of commerce which they buy and sell permanently or temporarily, almost as they buy or hire a horse. So the father (the mother has no voice in the matter) finds it very simple to give his daughter to a passing stranger for some small present, and if a child is born from the union, it is far from being a disgrace; rather, the addition to the family will be a distinction in that it will remain a living testimony of the preference of a white man. The young girls themselves anticipate these transactions in which they have their share of profit, and when their fathers have no hand in it or when they are orphans, they seek out themselves what they consider a distinction and an advancement. After they have become mothers under these conditions, they are not less sought after by the young Indians. The one who buys her in marriage will be proud rather than embarrassed to adopt the little half-breed as his own child and to give him the same place in his family as the ones who come after him.

This manner of doing things proceeds logically from a whole set of ideas, completely different from the ones on which our civilized mores are based. From our point of view, we cry immorality, but any Indian whom we tried to make understand what we mean by this would be very surprised. Everything in this world is relative; nothing is absolute but mathematical truth, which has nothing in common with philosophical truth. One need not cross the seas and go deep into solitudes of the New World beyond the limits of civilization to prove how little this is short of the truth. But here one can really see the sharp contradiction of its aphorisms. The subject of Indian customs when studied firsthand is fertile in new suggestions. It is a field that cannot be explored without opening visions of great scope for the curious mind which can go back from effect to cause and meditate on the relation between the two. The field is too extensive to dwell on here. I shall get back to my story.

My visit had been announced at Fort Berthold. A number of Indians were grouped near the entrance; others had squatted down along the houses in the interior of the court; some were standing erect and silent, wrapped in their blankets or their buffalo robes near Gustave's door where our carriage stopped. The most important was Crow Belly, chief of the Gros Ventre tribe.[49] In another place I told about how this name was given to them by the Canadians; now I shall add that the name is explained by the shape of a good many of their children who really do have bellies like pumpkins, but this unusual roundness invariably disappears at the approach of puberty. Their young people are like all Indians, thin rather than fat, erect in stature, with legs like those of a deer. Their true name is Hedanza, [Hidatsa] which means "men of the willows."

[*Crow Belly, Gros Ventre chief*] The chief was naked to the waist, where his blanket was carelessly knotted. He was wearing a chain from which hung a large medallion of the President. His hair was drawn from each side of his forehead through a sort of thin copper sheath and was plaited behind in six or eight braids which hung down his back. He had one or two copper bracelets formed from a heavy brass [copper] wire rolled in a spiral about two inches wide, and some earrings. His trouser legs (that's all there is to the garment for an Indian) were curiously worked in bright colors in which yellow dominated and decorated on the outside seam by a fringe of multicolored leather. The same type of ornamentation on his moccasins. Unfortunately, his otherwise picturesque costume was spoiled by a shabby hat of common straw, which had as its only decoration a band of animal or vegetable fiber around the crown. This incongruous hat spoils my Crow Belly for me. Our first interview was the least complicated. The interpreter was not there. We shook hands silently and with great gravity. The other followers pressed around the door and even entered the room, where they either stood leaning against the wall, squatted down, not on their heels in the fashion of Orientals, but with their feet together, a position they can hold for hours at the time: all of them motionless, grave, and silent. The chief himself had not entered. When I went out at the end of a few minutes, I found him where I had left him, looking unperturbed, fanning himself gently with an eagle wing embellished with sweet grass. He is tall, straight, sturdily built. At the age of fifty, he hasn't a gray hair. His eldest son, whom I have met since, is the handsomest man I have seen among the Indians, not because of his stature, which

49 Crow Belly signed treaties for the Gros Ventres as "Crow Breast." De Trobriand himself labelled his sketch of the chief "Crow Breast," although he calls him "Crow Belly" in the journal. Kappler, *Indian Laws and Treaties*, 2:1056.

is not above average, but because of the wonderful proportions of his figure, the shape of his limbs, the development of his chest, the breadth of his shoulders, and the easy vigor of his manner.

I asked first of all to visit the village, and my host suggested that we begin the tour by a visit to Pierre Gareau or Garaut, the indispensable man *par excellence*. So we went to Pierre Gareau.[50]

The first buildings facing the north side of the fort are the dwellings and storehouses of the traders who do not belong to the fur company. These are long cabins of logs and earth (log houses) separated into different rooms. The principal one, which belongs to Mr. Marsh, has the shape of a building with four sides forming a long square around an interior court on which dwellings and storehouses open, with the exception of one part near the entrance. Mr. Marsh has moved his residence to Fort Stevenson, where he has opened a store for the garrison, leaving at Berthold the Indian trade goods under the management of an agent. Another French trader, Mr. Gerard,[51]

---

[50] The name is spelled "Garreau" by most authorities. The Garreau family had lived on the Missouri for many years when De Trobriand met Pierre. Lewis and Clark, wintering at the mouth of the Missouri, noted that "Mr. Garrou's boat loaded with provisions passed up for Prairie du chien to trade." In 1805, they again mentioned "Mr. Garrow, a Frenchman who has lived many years with the Ricaras & Mandans." This was probably the father of the Pierre Garreau of this journal. In *The Journal at Fort Clark 1834–1839*, Pierre Garreau is mentioned frequently, and Annie Heloise Abel, the editor, says that it is evident from the *Fort Pierre Letter Book* that Pierre Garreau had charge of affairs at Fort Berthold as early as May 9, 1848. He died in 1881 when his hut at Fort Berthold caught fire in the night. Reuben Gold Thwaites, ed., *Original Journal of the Lewis and Clark Expeditions*, 1:272, 5:355; Annie Heloise Abel, ed., *The Journal at Fort Clark 1834–1839*, p. 270, 283; Larpenteur, *Forty Years a Fur Trader on the Upper Missouri*, 1:124–126; *North Dakota Historical Collections*, 3:48.

[51] There is some disagreement about the birth date of Frederic Gerard, one of the best-known traders on the Upper Missouri. The *North Dakota Historical Collections*, 1:344, states that he was born in St. Louis November 14, 1829, while the date given in the register of baptisms, St. Louis Cathedral, is August 30, 1833.

Gerard hïred out to the American Fur Company at Fort Pierre about 1848. In 1855 he went to Fort Berthold where the American Fur Company had a post, and he remained in the employ of fur companies until he became an independent trader in 1872.

It was rumored about the West that Gerard had taken gold from the boat of some miners who were killed below Fort Berthold in 1863 or 1864. The story appears in the biography of "Soldier" (*North Dakota Historical Collections*, 6:183–184), in "The Pioneer Experiences of Horatio H. Larned" (*North Dakota Historical Collections*, 7:49–51), and in a manuscript letter of Harry P. Stanford to the Montana Historical Society, May 23, 1928. The three stories vary in detail, but they all agree that Gerard got the gold.

In 1872, after his venture as an independent trader proved to be a failure, Gerard became a government interpreter. He was with Reno at the Little Big Horn as leader of the Ree scouts. In 1883 he opened a store in Mandan, and in 1890 he had done the same thing, and has transferred the greater part of his affairs and goods to us. Now both have their log houses behind the new fort.

[*The Indian village*] Behind the dwellings of the traders rises the Indian village. I can think of nothing to which I can compare it. It is a collection of great domes of earth built close to each other in no particular order, and between the buildings there are light scaffolds loaded with corn drying in the sun. The streets are merely twisted passages left between the lodges. Right now, the most prominent objects are the husks and leaves of corn which are scattered around everywhere; women in garments of heavy cotton cloth busy with their work, naked children, heavy and fat, running and frisking around before the doorways, and thin dogs resembling famished wolves wandering sadly through the village in quest of some morsel that is impossible to find. Here and there a red man wrapped in his blanket silently crosses the scene, indifferent to what is going on, and carefully hiding his curiosity to see "the great white chief," as if the presence of this person was nothing unusual.

[*Interior of a lodge*] Here we are in front of the lodge of Pierre Gareau. It is the same as all the others. On the outside, it is, as I have said, a vast mound of earth, flattened on the top in a kind of terrace in the middle of which a round hole gives passage to the smoke. A single opening gives access to it; it is a narrow and low entry cut in the thickness of the wall and protected on the outside by a kind of projecting vestibule made of the edges of trees squared with the axe. No door; the entry is always open. The upper platform, a sort of observatory from where the Indians can scan the plains for a distance, is often ornamented with some trophy of arms or rare feathers shining in the sun, the armory of the family.

On the threshold, a hanging of skins or a blanket blocks the view of the interior. Between that hanging and the entry, two wooden bars as high as the elbow go along the vestibule, leaving to the right and to the left a free space where the horses are brought in each evening and from where they are led to pasture each morning. The

---

moved to Minneapolis where he was employed by the Pillsbury Mills. He died in 1913 and is buried in St. Joseph, Minnesota. *North Dakota Historical Collections,* 1:344–348; Van de Water, The *Glory-Hunter,* p. 323; *Mississippi Valley Lumberman,* 13:3; Sister Anastasia, Gerard's daughter, has four letters from her father, dated March 8, 1876, May 1, 1876, July 6, 1876, and March 28, 1876, telling of events both before and after the Custer Massacre. She also has two pictures of Gerard.

two bars inclining to the left and right of the hanging lead into the sanctuary of the Indian family. Here the mode of construction is easily discernible. A strong quadrangular framework, ten or twelve feet high, is supported by four posts made of logs which are squared or merely stripped of their bark. On this skeleton, which holds the whole edifice, strong round logs are placed like the spokes of a wheel to form a roof, on which rests a layer of brush and on top of that a thick layer of earth. The light comes through the single opening left in the top to give passage to the smoke from the hearth which is in the center of the lodge. This hearth consists of a circular excavation about four feet in diameter and six to eight inches deep. The fire is kept up in the center by poking it with hardwood sticks. Above is usually hung a kind of primitive pothanger or iron chain hanging from a wooden crossbar and ending in a hook.

The beds are ranged along the inside wall of the lodge, leaving around the hearth a large space where the members of the family or their visitors move about, sit down, or stretch out on the beaten earth. There are no seats other than a few boxes. In the absence of boxes, people sit on the ground on animal skins; the women who are not busy are more than willing just to sit on their beds. These beds of boards on which a mattress or dry grass is laid, are quite similar to ours in form. They even have a frame supporting a curtain of skins, blankets, or mats, which, when they are closed, give them the appearance of high oblong boxes. They are always open during the day. In the spaces between them are stacked or hung the saddles, the straps which serve as bridles, the arms, and different utensils of Indian life.

Pierre was outside when I entered his lodge; one of his wives (he has two or three, I believe) got up immediately to go and fetch him, giving me time to examine the lodge at my leisure. Three squaws were seated on the ground; one was keeping up the fire, another cooking some corn in a frying pan, and the third working at those pieces of Indian handicraft that strangers especially look for. A man was stretched out on a sort of low couch set against the hanging; a girl twelve or thirteen years old was pounding corn in a mortar; some children and young girls were grouped at the edge of a bed.

That whole gathering just raised their heads when we entered and went back to their positions or occupations immediately with no other sign of interest or curiosity, as if nothing had happened. Those who had their backs turned toward me did not look around once. Two or three women said a few words to Gustave or spoke among themselves as calmly as they did before our arrival, and that was all. I could have belonged to the lodge for ten years and things would not have happened in any other way.

[*Pierre Gareau*] Soon Pierre Gareau arrived. He is a half-breed who is past sixty, but whose vigor and energy belie his age. Nothing about him indicates the savage. He is dressed completely in the American style, except for the moccasins which are in general use in this country anyway, even among the whites. These soft shoes, soft on the feet and warm in the winter, are so comfortable to wear that one gets used to them right away and then has trouble in putting on our hard footwear again. Trousers, overcoat, woolen shirt, black tie, and cloth cap, such was and still is the outfit of Gareau. His black hair, worn the ordinary length, is sprinkled with threads of gray. His brick-red complexion could be attributed to the effects of the sun and is seen everywhere among our European country people. It is that of the country folk in southern France. His features are striking, his eyes dark and intelligent, and his wide mouth, well supplied with small, closely set teeth, has some resemblance to that of a bulldog.

He came to me, hand stretched out cordially, knowing that I was French and that he would not have to talk to me in English. His father was Canadian, and French is his natural language (Canadian-French, of course). Although he learned English, he speaks it badly and with difficulty. To him it is a task, but to speak French is a pleasure. They are all like this; the blood and the language always stay with them: French blood, French language. Neither the English nor the Americans succeed in this. After the customary civilities proper to the occasion, I proposed that he show me the village and be my guide, which he accepted as a matter of course, and we started out talking away. First he took me to a second lodge which belongs to him and which he calls his "council lodge," because it is there he receives the Indians who want to congregate. Nevertheless, there were some beds, and he introduced two old squaws who are his sisters and some young ones who are his nieces. And as I questioned him about his family, he told me with a gloomy look that he had had three sons, three warriors, who some years before were all surprised and killed by the Sioux while they were out with a hunting expedition. But immediately, as if to console himself for it, he enumerated for me the Sioux that the three tribes had killed, and told me in detail of one of his recent exploits.

[*Gareau's story*] (The fight took place during the winter. The tribes had left the village and had sent only forty warriors with the women to get corn in the lodges. There were sixteen whites in the fort, among whom were Gerard, G. Cagnat, Paquenaud, etc.[52] A Gros Ventre had a broken leg; two or three were wounded; but the whites, after furnishing the savages with some double-barreled guns, withdrew to the fort; the Sioux had eighteen or twenty men killed. Gerard himself killed seven of them, Paquenaud three. Part of the lodges were burned, quite an amount of corn was lost. From the fort to the outside they apostrophized like Homeric heroes. "Paquenaud, you can't fly away in the air or bury yourself in the earth; your last day has come, etc." Paquenaud paternally urged them to go away after each Sioux was killed along the palisades.)[53]

"Some years ago," he tells me, "the people from down below (the Sioux) came back to the north to take part in the Minnesota Massacres, and as our people did not want to have a hand in it, they came back this way to attack and destroy the village. They were seven hundred strong at least; we numbered scarcely two hundred warriors; all the rest were old men, women, and children. The Sioux appeared on all sides at the same time. They wanted to surround us, making flight impossible, and to massacre us to the last man. The women and children were hurried into the fort pell-mell, and preparations were made to defend ourselves to the death; but we were not able to do very much. The men were poorly armed. They had only their bows and arrows. Some white traders and I had nothing but guns.

"The Sioux came in closer and closer on the plain and drew up in a semicircle with their flanks resting on the river. When they got near the lodges, they began to gallop in all directions, whooping, yelling, and abusing us to make us come out; but our people restrained themselves very well and kept themselves in ambush on different sides waiting for the moment when the enemy would get mixed up among the lodges where surely more than one of them would have been killed. But they were suspicious and would not come into the village.

"At that time, there was a small wooden fort, a square log house as you might call it, in front of the village near which they put a guard. The Sioux massed to attack it, that is, to burn it, and as the wind blowing from the north was carrying the smoke onto the village,

---

[52] Charles Patineaude, also spelled Packeneau and Pacquenaud, came to the Missouri River in the 1840's. He was interpreter for the American Fur Company with the Gros Ventres at Fort Berthold. He died around 1872. *North Dakota Historical Collections*, 1:376. De Trobriand sometimes spells the name "Paquenaud."

[53] The material in parentheses is a marginal note in the French manuscript, with no mark indicating where it belongs. This editor has inserted it in the most logical place.

those who were inside could escape; but the smoke screen blinded us, and as we could no longer see what the others were doing, they said to themselves: It's better that everyone withdraw to the big fort for fear that some will find themselves cut off without knowing it. They did this.

"The Sioux, burning everything they could before them, thus entered the village, and, sheltered by this smoke screen, they came up to the big fort. They had torn down the log houses to burn the wood, and because of this, we could not see twenty feet in front of us. I was on the blockhouse (bastion) to the northwest. I said to the others, 'Now is the time to keep your eyes open and stop any of these vermin from setting fire to the fort, for with that wind, everything would go up in flames, and that would be the last of us. So if we have to die, at least we can first kill all those who come with firebrands.'

"As I speak Sioux, I could hear everything they were saying on the other side of the smoke, and I immediately learned in this way that one of them had crawled under the smoke screen up to the foot of the blockhouse, and by looking down through the opening in the floor of the bastion, I saw him glued against the wall between the loopholes in such a way that our people below could neither see him nor get at him. But from above, it was another thing. I poked the barrel of my gun through the opening in the floor, and as he was rummaging in the clay between the logs to lodge his firebrand, I fired a bullet at him that smashed his skull, and the loophole was all splattered with his blood and brains. Then I shouted in triumph, and the enemy knew that their man was killed.

"He had fallen in a sitting position against the blockhouse, and I thought that he still might be able to escape if he were only wounded, because, you see, these people often make a pretense of being dead so you don't finish them off. But in order to make sure of the thing, Man-Chief, whom you know, the same one who guards the government grain here, and to whom you give rations for his trouble,—this Man-Chief passed his long lance through the opening and buried it in the neck of the victim. But the Sioux didn't budge. Then we both shouted again, and I said to the enemy in their native tongue: 'Pack of thieves and scoundrels, if there are any among you who are men, let them come and gather up their dead. Come then, come carry away your carcass if you aren't cowards and dogs.' But they didn't dare to come, even through the smoke.

"Then I said to Man-Chief: 'We'll hang him up and take his scalp and we'll string him up high from the top window. So we let down a lasso in which we caught his neck; the head lopped over on his shoulder, and we hoisted him up. At this moment, the good God favored us with his grace: The wind changed and the Sioux saw their man hung up like a dog and his firebrand extinguished. Then the wind blew so much of the smoke on them that they now had no way to get to the fort; so now it was the Sioux who were afraid of being caught among the lodges, and they left the village and went back to the lower country."[54]

During this recitation, Gareau had approached the fort, and as a peroration showed me the exact place where he had killed his Sioux and the top window from which he had hung him. "The mark of blood remained on the wall a long time," he told me with a sigh of regret, "but finally the wind, the rain, the cold, and the heat have erased it."

"That's too bad," I said seriously.

"Alas! What can we expect?" he said, shrugging his shoulders like a man who has finally resigned himself to the inevitable.

For some time discordant cries, sounding like a kind of monotonous chant and accompanied by strange noises, had been heard in the village, and as I listened, looking in the direction from which these strange sounds came, Gareau told me that it was a band of Rees rehearsing the evening performance before the medicine lodge. We went toward it, and I soon witnessed a most curious spectacle.

[*The medicine lodge*] In the center of the village and in front of the "medicine lodge" there is a circular place of considerable dimensions, surrounded by separate lodges, and in the middle of this there stands a young tree so carelessly planted that it died before it took root. It is directly opposite the entrance of the "medicine lodge," which is distinguished from the others only in that it is bigger. It is there that the Indians make their medicine; that is, the simples, the juice of boiled plants or dried herbs which they use to dress wounds, and especially the charms with which they ward off evil powers, keep from the path of dangers, and assure themselves of health and success in their enterprises. No one but the initiated is admitted to the lodge during the day when the operations are carried on; but in the evening, everyone can attend the daily productions that the troupe of Rees gives in this season of the year. It is the playhouse of the village, and there is a different program every evening. I had already heard of

[54] The story of how the fort was saved from the Sioux appears commonly in the lore of the Upper Missouri. In the *North Dakota Historical Collections* (1:345, 7:44–48) there are some variations on the story as it is told in this journal.

these performances, and I was to attend one in the evening. However, I was curious to see that part of the performance which is given in the open air and which includes only the musical and vocal part in costume.

This is how it goes:

[*Musical performance*] A squad of seven or eight Indians leaves the lodge and ranges itself in line near the dead tree. Almost all of them wear no clothing but the loincloth, a piece of cloth about a foot wide and three feet long at the most. They fix one end of it in front to a belt of leather or something else and, passing the cloth between their legs, bring it up behind under the belt so that the end falls outside. The loincloth fully satisfies all that modesty demands of them, and often it does not even have the full dimensions that I have assigned to it. So see what the color of the skin can do. Had it been white, it is probable that I should have found the exhibition a little indecent; but the skin was red, and it did not occur to me that there was anything to criticize. So, dressed in a loincloth, shod in moccasins, body painted with red, blue, white, black; streaked, striped, speckled, decorated with bracelets and necklaces, head ornamented with one or several feathers, hair braided on the sides from the forehead and from the back or brought up in tufts or hanging in long black locks down the back, the savages came forward, carrying in their hands a dry gourd containing some small pebbles and decorated to suit their fancy. Forming in a line, they sing their chant while beating time with their gourds, moving their body, stamping first on one leg and then another. Then by going around on the right side of the tree, the band retires still stamping in time, and the last sounds of the chant are lost as they enter the lodge. Immediately a second squad, painted and decorated differently, comes out, ranges itself the same way, sings another chant, which, however, closely resembles the first one, with the same accompaniment, the same stamping, the same evolutions, retiring in its turn, only to be replaced by another, and this goes on for hours.

The four squads relieve each other successively, with no concern about what is happening on the grounds, where, it must be admitted, no one but me seemed to be paying the least bit of attention to their exercises. The women came and went, taking care of their work; the children ran around or rolled on the ground with or without their loincloths; the dogs stretched out on their thin backbones. But neither bipeds nor quadrupeds worried about the artists. I can understand this, for it was not long before I had enough of it myself, and I did not wait until all the squads had passed before I relieved Gareau from the resigned guard he was mounting near me.

[*White Parefleche, chief of the Rees*] We returned to the fort where dinner hour called us and where the chief of the Rees was presented to me. "White Parefleche" is not handsome.[55] He has long, black hair, despite the rather advanced age which shows in his face. His eyes are small but keen; his nose is strongly aquiline; his large, thin mouth has scarcely any lips, and his protruding chin juts up before his nose. He is of average height, thin and nervous. He has a lined face; his body is painted blue with white and red stripes which twist on his chest and go down the length of his arms. He was wrapped in his blanket, which covered his left shoulder and left his right hand free, which he stretched out in greeting. With the handshake, we exchanged only the word "How," which is the general expression of greeting, of welcome, and of approbation. The moment for the negotiations had not yet come. White Parefleche seems to scorn ornaments as adding nothing to his dignity. He had neither necklaces, bracelets, plumes, nor shells in his hair. He is what he is, and that is enough for him. He goes out as he came in, with impassive dignity.

The tribe of Rees of which he is chief is the most important of the three; numerically it is as strong as the other two put together. It also seems to me that it has become the most enterprising and the most warlike; this is easily explained by its number of warriors, which enables it to do what the others cannot undertake alone.

Dinner consisted of game: buffalo meat, prairie chicken, and wild duck; no vegetables and no wine; for dessert, some preserves and coffee without milk. At Fort Berthold there is (for the time being at least) neither cow nor fowl. Everyone ate heartily, and after we crowned the repast with the indispensable pipe, we started out for the assembly room where seats were reserved for us.

[*Dramatic performance*] These seats consisted of a small, rough bench resting on four legs six to eight inches high; the only furniture of this kind it was possible to get in the village. It was placed to the right in the first row of the place reserved for spectators and took in the space between the entrance and a line marked by the first two of the four great posts which held up the edifice. The middle zone and the one opposite the audience were reserved exclusively for the

55 White Parefleche is more commonly known as "White Shield." He signed his name "White Shield" to the treaty of 1866, and the traders at Fort Berthold called him by that name. Kappler, *Indian Laws and Treaties*, 2:1056; F. F. Gerard, Fort Berthold, to Rev. P. J. de Smet [n.p.], February 2, 1868. Office of Indian Affairs, Natural Resources Division, National Archives.

Philippe Régis de Trobriand

performers. In the center of the building under the opening in the roof where the star-studded vault can be seen through the smoke-blackened roof, the circular hearth held a brilliant fire of little dry branches. The flame which rises up from it furnished the only light for the spectacle. I noticed that on the side where the artists make their rounds, a little edge incline was raised so that a dim light was projected on the point of ground where they perform. An Indian was especially charged with keeping up the fire with small armfuls of dry wood. His talent seemed to be in lighting up the scene brightly in the interlude and dimming it at the critical moment in the performance.

[*Vocal and instrumental music*] When we took our places, the first part of the program had begun. It consisted of pieces of vocal and instrumental music executed simultaneously by the four bands of actors. The members of each of them were grouped separately, seated on mats around a sort of big drum that the leader of the orchestra struck in time with the accompaniment of the gourds each musician (!) was equipped with. This rhythmic noise was blended with a barbarous chant in which one could distinguish a solo from time to time, invariably taken up again by the chorus. I tried in vain to make out a melody. The four diabolic orchestras, howling and shrieking at the same time, each on a different measure, as if it wanted to drown out the others with the uproar of its vociferations, made the most abominable charivari that one can imagine, and in all this the only appreciable thing was a dissonance that set the teeth on edge. Gareau explained to me that the subject of these ferocious cries was an invocation to the Great Spirit to obtain from him the usual things: health, no diseases, success in the hunt and in war. Very few of the spectators attended this "overture," which usually lasts half an hour. A rather curious observation: this invocation is the only subject on which the Indian devotes his chants. His ideas about women preclude any notion of extolling love. Neither heaven nor earth causes a poetic fiber to vibrate in him, for he has none, and the lack of all sentiments of this kind in him is so marked that he does not even sing about the great deeds of the hunt or of war, and is ignorant of the art of inflaming the ardor or the ambition of young warriors and of preserving the memory of his heroes. Impossible to be more prosaic.[56] Oh, Chateaubriand, where is your noble savage!

[56] De Trobriand's statement on Indian music is true only for the early period. See Frances Densmore, *The American Indians and Their Music*, p. 84–90, 62–66.

Finally the hubbub subsided and died out in lugubrious lamenting and suppressed mumbling. When it was quiet, the performance began. It was quite simple, consisting of legerdemain and tricks accompanied by dances and chants. Since in such a case each group went through these musical exercises by turns, I could recognize their general character, and I shall try to describe them. Each chant is just a phrase which opens with the highest notes sung out in a shrill voice, changing to *diminuendo* on the middle notes and ending in a *moriendo* on the lowest notes in a sort of guttural and muffled groaning. The most complicated of the chants have an answer of piercing notes cried out by the orchestra leader, and then the chorus immediately takes up the first motif. The minor mode generally prevails in these jerky phrases, and six-eight time is the most common rhythm. There is not a suspicion of harmony; no attempt at a second part; always, all the way through, unison in the form of crude ejaculations.

The first band came forward between the two posts in the rear in the same costume that they were wearing at the rehearsal; that is, nothing but a loincloth and ornaments. They sang their song standing in a line, with no drum, but still using the gourds, and during this time, the first Indian on the right began to run around the hearth with a sort of half pause to the left and right, accompanied by a shaking of the fist in the air and a similar movement with the foot. The second time around, another Indian joins the first; the third time, a third Indian, and so on, until seven or eight members of the band had completed the circular course together, singing all the while.

[*Legerdemain*] Then a buffalo skin was laid out behind the posts, a good distance from the spectators. A gourd was placed on it, then covered over with a piece of fur, so that the outline of the gourd was discernible. A fellow then came out from among the spectators and pretended to smash the gourd under his heels, stamping on the spot from which the gourd had been withdrawn by a string. This done, the band pressed around the buffalo skin to lift it up and show the spectators the pieces of the broken gourd, and then they covered it up again. The trick was in putting the gourd back together again. The chants and the circling around the hearth began again; then the band again grouped around to lift up the skin in such a way as to hide what was going on behind, and then one of them came out, triumphantly holding in his hand the gourd that he had put there in the first place. Magic could not be performed in a more naïve way.

The second band came out, sang and ran around like the first;

then one of them came forward holding an ear of corn in his hand, struck himself in the pit of the stomach with it, and pretended to be making a great effort to sink it into his body. When he finally let go, the ear stuck to his skin at a horizontal angle. The round was over.

The third band spilled a cup of corn kernels on a buffalo skin and pretended to eat them; that is, the kernels disappeared as the Indians went across. It was not very wonderful.

Most of the other rounds were of the same quality. A little doll driven into the ground grasped in both hands the stem of a pipe they gave her to smoke; a squaw wrapped in a buffalo robe had on her chest a heavy collar which was fixed there with no apparent means of support; a bunch of dry grass that she wore on her neck made a little crying sound when they pressed it, like the toy dogs that amuse children.

The only thing that was a little less banal was the perfect imitation of the groaning of bears in a semidarkness purposely arranged. The actors wore on their heads the heads of bears or wolves and hung their skins down over their shoulders, so that a sort of bracelet of bear claws and paws was arranged as a band on the wrists and ankles.

We did not wait for the end of the performance, although we were told about Indians who swallow arrows as our sword swallowers cause wooden sabers to disappear and who leap into the fire like the incombustible Spaniard. The heat had become suffocating and the dust intolerable. While going through the crowd to get out, I noticed that it was composed principally of women and children. The few men kept near the entrance and did not seem to be taking part in the entertainment. I don't believe that there were any Gros Ventres or Mandans among them. These two tribes furnish no actors for such performances, and it is very seldom that they are spectators. Lantern in hand, Gareau took us back to the door of the fort which was closed again behind us, and everyone went to fortify himself with a good night's sleep for the hunting party planned the next day at daybreak.

Sunday, September 22. But daybreak found us all in bed sleeping like logs. Jean Brazot, the old white-haired Negro who serves Gustave, was slow in preparing breakfast.[57] The sun was already high on the horizon when we mounted our horses and terribly hot when

[57] The Jean Brazot here mentioned is probably John Brazeau, a Negro who for many years was employed by the American Fur Company and its successors.

we arrived at the hunting ground. The Indians, who had gone before us to pasture their horses there, already had some game. Very few ducks remained on the lake; the geese couldn't be approached, and the prairie chicken had taken refuge in the thickets. Briefly, after trying for an hour without any great success, we voted unanimously to return, and the hunt changed into a horseback ride, the pleasures of which were greatly diminished by the heat of the sun.

The Indians of Berthold complain that the Sioux often steal their horses from them. I am not very surprised, considering the negligence with which they guard them. This morning some of them brought their horses near the pond three or four miles from the village and left them in good pasture to come back for them later. I saw no guards other than a few children, and yet they feel so insecure that they will not lead their horses to pasture and bring them back without being armed with their bows and arrows, which they carry crosswise on their two forearms and not on their shoulders, for some reason I don't understand.

Their dogs never go with them outside the village. These animals are not good for hunting or for protection. When the Rees have anything to fatten them with, they eat them, and they actually enjoy such a feast. However, almost all of them are very thin, and they are used to drag loads proportionate to their strength. The outfit is rather curious. It consists of two poles crossed at one end in the form of an "A." The acute angle thus formed is covered with a piece of skin, the fur of which is worn on the back of the dog, where it is fastened by a strap which forms a collar. In the middle, the two poles are connected by a circle composed of a web of strings or thongs which support the load that is fastened to it. The other two ends of the poles drag on the ground behind the harnessed dog. The burden cannot be heavy, but it lightens the load that the wife would have to carry without this help. The Canadians call this vehicle the "travois."

During dinner, which was served at one o'clock at Berthold as it is everywhere in this country where people dine at seven or eight o'clock in the morning and where they have supper at seven o'clock in the evening, I was forewarned that the three chiefs, accompanied by the principal personages of their tribes, would soon come to have

He spoke both French and Sioux fluently. Dr. Matthews says that when the fur company employing him in 1868 sold out, he was discharged. Dr. Matthews took him to Fort Stevenson, where he died. Larpenteur, *Forty Years a Fur Trader on the Upper Missouri*, 1:12.

"powwow"; that is, an assembly in which they deal with business matters and which in English is called a "solemn talk."

[*Powwow*] In fact, when the table had been cleared, Crow Belly entered the room, gave me the greeting, and went to sit down against the wall, or rather against a box which was there. The second chief of the Gros Ventres, Poor Wolf, soon followed him, and after saying "How," he, too, went to squat down against the wall. The chief of the Mandans, Red Cow, soon did likewise. Red Cow had killed a female buffalo of that color—a very rare thing. Therefore his name. He was accompanied by his lieutenant, Eagle Who Pursues the Eagle.[58] The former had no ornament; the latter wore a dark neckerchief hanging down on his chest, and his hair drawn up and knotted in bunches on the left side of his head: regular features; aquiline nose, large and well-moulded mouth; indifferent air; keen eye. Eagle Who Pursues the Eagle carried a long pipe, the bowl of which was made of red stone [catlinite], rare and curious, and which had a flat and profusely ornamented stem. Poor Wolf had his war hatchet of good workmanship. I forgot to mention that the chief of the Gros Ventres had added to his bracelets, rings, and a straw hat a many-strand necklace of Indian workmanship, decorated with beads of all colors and with many pendants that hung down on his chest.

Some time passed in waiting for the chief of the Rees; not a word was spoken by anyone, and from time to time warriors arrived alone, and squatted down silently along the wall in the order of their importance. White Shield had gone to look for the interpreter, Pierre Gareau. They arrived together, accompanied by the second chief of the Rees, Star Man. Among the warriors were: Long Bone, whose great height can be imagined—in shell necklace and earrings; Man-Chief and Four Times Four. The chief of the Rees had but one ornament, a shining white piece of stone, bone, or shell fastened on the front of his neck in the form of a necklace. Some warriors had woolen shirts of gaudy, variegated colors; two or three had trousers of colored, fringed skins; none had weapons except Poor Wolf.

[*The peace pipe*] When everyone was squatted down along the walls, the second chief of the Mandans drew out an ornamented

---

[58] Poor Wolf, also known as "Lean Wolf," lived with the Gros Ventres in their villages on the Knife River, then moved to Fort Berthold when he was twenty-four. He signed the treaty of 1866 as "Poor Wolf." He was still with the three tribes when interviewed by C. L. Hall in 1906. *North Dakota Historical Collections*, 1:439–443; Kappler, *Indian Laws and Treaties*, 2:1056.

Eagle Who Pursues the Eagle signed the treaty of 1866 as "Running Eagle." Kappler, *Indian Laws and Treaties*, 2:1056.

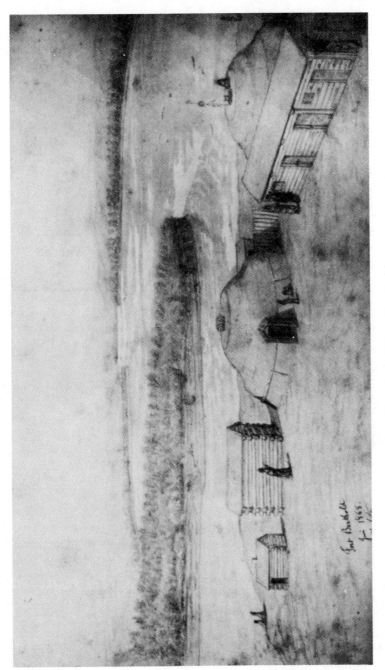

Interior of Fort Berthold

purse containing a handful of killikinnick, inside bark of a plant that the Indians use for tobacco. This dried and crushed bark doesn't taste bad in a pipe. I don't believe it is a narcotic.[59] So, Eagle Who Pursues the Eagle filled his pipe, lighted it, and after inhaling a few puffs, passed it on to Crow Belly, who was to be the principal orator of the conference. He, after inhaling a few puffs too, passed it on to Pierre Gareau; he to his nearest neighbor; and the pipe made the round of the assembly going from mouth to mouth.

I remained seated near the table, with the interpreter at my right and a little farther down Major Furey, Lieutenant Hooton, and Doctor Matthews; but as the conference took place in French and seemed likely to last for some time, my three officers soon disappeared among the warriors who were standing crowded around the entrance of the room. Through politeness, the pipe was not offered to me, because I smoke only tobacco and I had just put mine on the table. While theirs was circulating, no one said a word, and it seemed that we were gathered there just to look at each other.

Finally Crow Belly got up, crossed the room with a slow and dignified step, shook hands with me solemnly as a sign of friendship and good faith; then he walked back to sit down at the same pace, and after some silence, spoke in these terms:

[*The chief of the He-dan-zas*] "My father is welcome among us; we are happy that he has come to pay us a visit. We know that he is the great chief among the Pale Faces. I wanted to go to pay him a visit over there when I learned of his arrival; but I was detained in the village until today. I wanted to visit you, but I have not been able to yet. Since my father is here, his Indian children want to ask him if he will allow them to trade for powder, which they need very much for defense against their enemies and for hunting furs and meat. We have been deprived of powder for some time; why? What have we done to be punished by our Great Father, the chief of the Pale Faces (the President)? What does he have to reproach us for? Quite a few years ago, our Great Father ordered us to make peace and to live in peace with the Pale Faces and with the redskins with whom we were at war. Some lands were assigned to us, and we have lived on them; and when those who made the treaty died, we who succeeded them remained faithful and we observed all that was commanded

---

59 Kinnikinnick was made from a species of dogwood or from the inner bark of red willow. This was either ground up alone or mixed with tobacco. De Trobriand's spelling, "Killikinnick," is one of the accepted variants. Hodge, *Handbook*, 1:692.

us.[60] We used to be powerful; our warriors covered the plains and returned from the hunt with much meat and many skins; when they went on the warpath, they brought back many scalps. But we have become weak, and our enemies attack and harass us. They steal our horses, and when they meet our young braves on the hunt, they kill them if they can; and because we are weak, we need powder to defend ourselves. We cultivate the earth, and we live in lodges on the lands that we have left. We trade with the corn that we can spare; but that is not enough for our needs. The hunting season has come; the buffalo are becoming more rare and more difficult to kill; our bows and arrows are not enough, and we ask our father if he will permit us to buy powder as we did in the past."

This discourse, recited in a musical language in which there are many vowels (the language of the Men of the Willows) and with measured gestures, was frequently interrupted with exclamations of "How" by the assistants, sometimes one alone, sometimes all together —in the manner of our parliamentary debates, where "Hear, Hear" accompanies truths spoken by an orator. Crow Belly was silent, the interpreter translated his speech, and, taking my turn to speak, I answered:

[*The reply*] "I am happy to pay this visit to my children of the three tribes, because since my arrival in this country, I have had nothing but good reports about them—and I am very interested in them because I can praise them for their good conduct, and have nothing to reproach them for. (How! How!) So first I want to say that if trade in powder has been suspended for a time, it is not a punishment which has been inflicted on them, for they have deserved no punishment; it is just a general measure which has applied to them at a time when in order to punish the bad Indians, the Sioux, the Cheyennes, and other liars and thieves, it was necessary to forbid the trade of munitions.[61] Our Great Father in Washington is very

60 The three tribes signed the O'Fallon treaties of 1825, which were treaties of peace and friendship, the Laramie treaties of 1851, in which their lands were defined, an unratified treaty of 1866, and an agreement of 1866. Kappler, *Indian Laws and Treaties*, 2:242, 594, 1052; Royce, *Indian Land Cessions in the United States*, 2:726; Hodge, *Handbook*, 1:798.

61 The Cheyenne, people of Algonquian stock, were forced westward onto the plains by pressure from the Sioux. These Indians mingled with western Sioux, adopted many of their customs, and joined them in warfare against the whites on the northern plains. The tribe was greatly reduced by cholera in 1849 and by the war with the whites. The northern band took part in the battle with Custer in 1876, and the southern band took a leading part in the general outbreak of the southern tribes in 1874–75. Hodge, *Handbook*, 1:250–256.

far from Dakota where the Missouri flows; but the good conduct of his children who live among the willows was reported to him, and he then ordered that powder be sold to them. (How!) I am happy to tell this to you, and to announce that I have already given orders which will assure you of a good hunt and will enable you to fight your enemies with better luck.

"I did not wait until today to find out about your history and to learn what I could do for you in order to reward you for your good faith and good conduct. If you have become weak after having been powerful, it is not through your own fault, or because you have been good friends with the Pale Faces and with their government. The Great Spirit permitted a horrible sickness (smallpox) to spread more death among you than all your enemies could have done, and as you did not know of medicines with which to combat the scourge or the method of prevention, three-fourths of your warriors, your women, and your children perished, and you were left weak.[62] But because you are weak, our Great Father will give you greater protection, and I shall do everything I can for you—I know that there has been a custom of trading a keg of powder (twenty-five pounds) with each of the three tribes at the opening of the season of the hunts when you left for your winter quarters in the low, wooded lands. That time has now come. You can have this amount of powder, not in a single lot, but distributed in different portions according to what each is able to buy, with the provision that no man can go into the country with more than a pound at once."

This conclusion, and the rest of the address, was received with marked favor when Pierre Gareau, delighted to have some French to translate, repeated it first in the language of the Gros Ventres, which the Mandans understood, too, and then in the language of the Rees for the benefit of the latter. Then, after another period of silence, Crow Belly took the floor again:

"My father has spoken truly. He is right in all he has said. His red children thank him; but the powder he allows us to buy will be used up before winter is half gone. So I ask him, I beg him, not to leave us without ammunition for part of the cold moons, when the snow covers the plains and when most of the game goes into the low lands, but to grant us two kegs to each tribe. We must have two kegs

62 Chittenden says that after the smallpox epidemic of 1837 there were only thirty Mandans left. One of the best accounts of the progress and horrors of the disease is Abel, *The Journal at Fort Clark, 1834–1839*, p. 121; Hiram M. Chittenden, *The American Fur Trade of the Upper Missouri*, 2:615.

to be sure of a good hunt, to feed our families, and to bring back the peltries which are our principal resource when the grain does not grow in the earth."

I should mention here that the quantity of powder requested by the chief in the name of the three tribes was still much less than what the existing orders allowed me to grant them.[63] They asked for 250 pounds of powder for the winter, and they can have that amount every month, for the three tribes together number 250 warriors, and the limit is one pound of powder a month for each of them. Nevertheless, since I found that the orders regulating this which were given before my arrival had been more liberal than necessary, I pretended to calculate and meditate on the scope of the request, and addressing the chief of the Gros Ventres:

"How many warriors among the Men of the Willows?"

The chief thought it over, and answered: "One hundred."

Then to the chief of the Rees: "How many warriors among the Rees?"

The chief pondered and said, counting on his fingers: "One hundred and eighty."

And finally to the chief of the Mandans: "How many Mandan warriors?"

"Seventy," he answered with a resigned expression.

I began my apparent meditation again, and I had not answered when White Shield got up, came over to clasp my hand, returned to his place, squatted down on the floor, and expressed himself in this way:

[*The chief of the Rees*] "Why does my father hesitate to grant his children of the three tribes the powder necessary to live? Are they not the faithful friends of the Pale Faces? And didn't my father himself say that he has nothing to reproach them about? Must they suffer for their good conduct and their submission to the commands of our Great Father? The Dakotas of the lower plains (the Sioux) have sent us messengers who have said to us: 'What profit for you is there in remaining friends of the Pale Faces? You are weak, poor, and the white men scorn you. But we who steal their mules and their

---

[63] This refers to the order issued by General Terry January 29, 1867, which permitted traders to sell ammunition to the Indians under the supervision of the post commanders. The maximum amount that could be sold to an Indian each month was to be fixed, and the trader was to keep a record of his sales. The record was to be inspected each month by the post commander. *Army and Navy Journal*, February 16, 1867, p. 406; Department of Dakota, *General Orders*, General Orders no. 3, January 29, 1867.

horses, we who kill their warriors and attack their camps on the prairies, they are afraid of us; they ask for peace, and to keep us peaceful, they give us presents and do not avenge their dead. What we have taken from them will remain ours, and they will give us still more, for fear that we shall take more from them. Do as we do, and you will have more booty, and more presents, and you will be stronger and richer.' This is the message that the Dakotas from the low country have brought us. Did we believe their words? No. Were we tempted by their promises? No. Did we act according to their advice? No. Between the Sioux and us there is no score but the score of blood. And so, since they were unable to induce us to join them, they made war more vindictively than ever, and in the field of the dead are stretched three of our warriors on whom the rain has not yet fallen since they were surprised and killed on our hunting grounds.

"Our enemies are the enemies of my father and the enemies of the white men. They are the dogs who make war for booty and presents and who make treaties to violate them. We make war only for a just cause, to defend ourselves, and we remain faithful to the treaties that we make. Yet, this year's presents have not reached us, and the guns with which we were furnished and which were very useful to us have been taken away. Why? We don't know, for we have made only good use of them, and not one has escaped from our hands.

"Let my father listen to justice, and let him grant what is just to his red children as well as to his white children. The color of the skin makes no difference; what is good and just for one is good and just for the others, and the Great Spirit has made all men brothers. As for me (pinching the skin of his chest where a horrible scar perpetuates the mark of the torture stake), I have a red skin, but my grandfather was a white man. What does it matter? It is not the color of the skin that makes me good or bad. My father, you can grant us the powder we ask and fear nothing from us. It will not leave the three tribes and will be used only to kill game that the Great Spirit sends us or to defend ourselves from our enemies, from whom we ask no other protection."

The language of the Rees is unlike that of the Gros Ventres or the Mandans. There is an abundance of guttural emissions which remind one of Welsh or low Breton of Celtic origin, while the other two have a certain connection in sounds with Spanish and Italian of Latin origin.[64] The chief's speech, accompanied by naturally elo-

64 It is the Mandan, rather than the Arikara, that have caused the speculations about Welsh origins. As early as 1823, a member with the Long expedition

quent gestures, had provoked a number of "How-Hows!" When he
stopped talking, he resumed his impassive attitude and expression of
silent gravity to listen to my answer, *intentique ora tenebant.*

[*The ammunition question settled*] "The chief of the Rees has
spoken well," I said then. "He recalled things which I already knew,
but which I like to hear repeated. My children of the three tribes
were wise when they closed their ears to the lying words of the Sioux;
if they had listened to them, they would have drawn on themselves
the unhappiness and ruin which will surely be the punishment of
the bad Indians of the lower plains. For the Dakotas from the low
lands lied when they said that the white men were afraid of them.
The white men live in vast territories in the direction of the rising
sun, and they number more warriors than there are buffalo on the
prairies. What are the Sioux in comparison? Already they have been
defeated in several combats and the blood of a number of their
warriors has paid for the blood of white workers whom they killed.
Soon they will be driven from their hunting grounds and will themselves be forced to ask for peace, which will not be purchased from
them by any present. And if they do not submit to the orders of our
Great Father and continue to make war on the Pale Faces, they will
be destroyed and their race will be annihilated and the great plains
will no longer know their name. And you, faithful friends of the
white men and submissive children of our Great Father, from day
to day you will become richer and more powerful by cultivating your
fields in peace during the summer and by hunting in the winter with
no fear of the ambuscades of your enemies. (How! How!)

"White Shield spoke of two things which he does not understand and which I want to explain to him and to my children of the
three tribes. This year's presents have not been distributed; but they
have arrived and are held here in the storehouse. Mr. Wilkinson, the
agent of our Great Father for Indian affairs of this section, wanted
to begin distributing first the presents of the tribes who are farthest
away. He has gone to Fort Buford, pressed by the lateness of the
season, and afraid that he could not get there if he were to stop here
first. The steamboats have hardly enough water to go down river

---

reported: "There has been a long-standing report that the Mandans speak the
Welch [*sic*] language; the thing has been pushed by the Welch, proverbially per-
tinacious genealogists." Charles DeLand submits all the evidence then available
on this problem in "The Mandan Indians," but still leaves the question open for
further investigation. Colhoun Diary, copy, Minnesota Historical Society, typescript p. 58; *South Dakota Historical Collections,* 4:651–726.

now, and we haven't seen any of them for weeks; but the first one which arrives will probably bring Mr. Wilkinson here where he must spend the winter, and he will immediately distribute the presents. (How! How!)

"As for the guns loaned to you, if they were taken back, it was not because the three tribes made bad use of them, nor because our Great Father had less confidence in them, or wished them less well. It is simply because the guns had to be fixed for loading by the breech with a new kind of cartridge, and when we received the new arms with this change made, we had to return all the old guns we had so they could be changed too.

"And now, in conclusion: I grant to my children the request for powder they have made me. They can trade for a quantity equal to two kegs a tribe, but in such a way that no warrior has more than a pound at one time, and moreover, if their munitions are exhausted before the end of winter, I shall permit them to restock in just proportion to their needs."

This conclusion, as can well be imagined, caused complete and unanimous satisfaction. There was a redoubling of "How!" And the pipe circulated more actively than ever. The chief of the Mandans, who had not yet had his turn to speak, did not want the conference to end before he expressed his sentiments. He complimented me and thanked me in very flattering terms. "We have known great chiefs sent by our Great Father," he told me. "Many have spoken to us; but none have told us as good things as has my father; none have showed us justice and right so clearly and have gladdened the heart of his children so much. We are contented and grateful."

This simply proved that Pierre Gareau spoke French a great deal better and to greater advantage than he did English; perhaps, too, my predecessors had troubled themselves less than I about the condition of the three tribes. Whatever it was, the effect was excellent, and when I rose to close the meeting, which had lasted fully two hours, the chief of the Gros Ventres, who had consulted with the others, announced that they would not leave for their winter encampments without visiting me at Fort Stevenson, as evidence of their respect and affection. So we shall have a solemn visit and, Pierre Gareau tells me, each chief will be accompanied by forty warriors. This will mean the distribution of a few pounds of sugar and coffee and boxes of crackers, but the spectacle is well worth that.

[*Indian billiards*] I left the chiefs and the warriors, not one of whom—and this was remarkable—had said a word in the "Powwow," to talk among themselves, and I went outside the fort to get some air. Four young Indians near the cemetery were busy playing a favorite game which I wanted to learn about, and I approached them with Gustave Cagnat. Each of the players had a pole about six feet long, the bark of which had been taken off in all but three places: this formed three large six-inch bands, separated by equal intervals. The players were divided into two couples. One of them had in his hand a round, flat stone, pierced in the center like a wheel. This player, his opponent beside him, threw the wheel before him. Both followed the course of the wheel until its first impetus had slackened, and then, still running, each threw his pole toward the point where it seemed that the wheel ought to stop. The winner of the point was the one whose pole was so thrown that the middle band lay nearer the wheel. The other two players then went on with the game in a contrary direction so that the game progressed back and forth over the same ground. I understand that the two partners who first made a certain number of points won the game. The players seemed to take great pleasure in this game which they call "billiards" and at which they are very skillful. Their poles thrown from quite a distance rarely miss reaching the moving wheel, so that it stops between the two, which were lying so close together that it often leaned against one of them when it came to a stop.

As I was returning from the outdoor billiard game, Beauchamp the trapper came out of his log house, and invited me to come in to see a beautiful beaver which he had caught in the trap the night before, and which he had not yet skinned so he could show it to me as if it were alive. I accepted the invitation with pleasure and we went in.

[*Trapper's cabin*] Beauchamp's cabin is roomy, as clean and comfortable as this kind of building can be, where beaten earth replaces the floor. Beauchamp does not live like an Indian, although he has spent his life among them, differing in this from Gareau, who, with the exception of his costume, has adopted all their ways. Beauchamp's room has only one bed; the fire is made in a fireplace there, and people sit down on seats. All the hunting and fishing equipment is hung on the walls, and—what struck me most forcibly—in the corner there is a little library of five or six shelves stocked with books which have obviously been used. I am sorry that I did not look over the type of books that made up this little assortment; but the beaver absorbed our attention first, and then Beauchamp's stories made me forget the books.

The animal, which he caught this morning, was stretched out on a board, belly up; I leisurely examined his four terrible teeth which make him the most formidable of the rodents and with which he fells the heaviest trees; his paws, short and armed with formidable claws to dig the soil; his tail, flat and scaly, a veritable trowel with which he beats and strengthens the earth of his buildings; his head, round like a cat's except for the jaws; and his heavy body covered with the most velvety of fur.

Beauchamp, in raptures because he had a chance to speak French, indulged himself to his heart's content. If he must speak English, he is taciturn, satisfied to answer questions or to translate laboriously, for he is in the service of the trader Gerard as interpreter; but speak to him in French, and he does not hold back; he tells stories, and his accounts, as you will see, lack neither interest nor originality. French blood always rebels against the English language!

[*The beaver*] First the trapper gave us some curious information on the ways of the beaver, his habits, his work, and the way he is trapped. He is, as everyone knows, the most industrious of animals, the most skillful builder—I was about to say engineer—and in truth, the word "instinct," which man's vanity applies loosely to the intelligence of all the quadrupeds, is absolutely void of meaning when applied to the beaver. It must be admitted that he is "reasonable." He lives in a society and in families, gets his nourishment from roots and different plants, makes provision for winter, and builds for himself dwelling places that are marvels of their kind. His habits are inoffensive; his ways are those of work, not individual work but community effort. He could be cited as the model of the patient, laborious, honest, and intelligent worker.

When they find on the bank of a small, isolated river a favorable place for their colony, protected by thick underbrush and bordered by trees suitable for their work—and they are never wrong about these things—the first thing they do is provide against the shallowness of the water by blocking up the river with a permanent dam. To accomplish this, they go to work building an embankment. If the stream is not very wide or very deep, and if the current is not very swift, they are satisfied with damming it in a straight line with a mixture of mud and brush, larger at its base than at the top, a solid and compact work nevertheless, which holds up when a man walks over it with no particular care. But if their difficulties are greater, their intelligence will be revealed in their astonishing ingenuity. Their construction will become proportionately more resistant by adding logs, and instead of stemming the current directly, they will run it out obliquely in such a way as to break the shock of the water, by leaving a freer outlet at the base of the dam. And if the extent of the dam is too great to be secure, they will build a salient which juts out, cutting the current in the middle and throwing it back on both sides. In his book on frontier life, Colonel Marcy tells of seeing a real masterpiece of this type.[65] Some beavers choose two large trees across from each other on opposite banks of a river which they want to dam up before the lowering of the water in the dry season. Each tree is in length more than half the width of the stream. They go to work felling them, managing their work so they fall into the water simultaneously, and then leaping into the water, they make them float to the place they have chosen by so guiding them that the end of the trunks come to rest on the two banks, while the intertwined branches form an angle against the current. As soon as this first foundation seems to them firm enough, they cut off all the little leafy branches, using them in the embankment to finish off their work, which will soon assure them of a water level protected from any eventuality resulting from seasonal changes. Who taught them that the resisting force of a dam broken by a salient is a great deal more than that of a dam built straight across? Is this instinct? I do not believe it is.

If the beaver insists on always having a constant water level, there is a real reason for it. It is to hide under water the entrance to their lodges which have no direct access to the bank on which they are placed. To go in or come out, the beaver must dive to a certain depth and come back up through a passage under the water which leads him to his lodge. The room is circular; the ceiling is a kind of dome, usually supported by logs cut to the desired length and placed in such a way that they strengthen the edifice. The ground and walls of beaten earth are irreproachably clean. The size varies with the number of the members in the family which live in the lodge, from two to six or seven. Each has his bed made of grass and little twigs; the beds are always along the walls to leave the center free. Near the outside entry, the boughs, roots, or plants that the beaver uses for food are gathered; in the winter when he is hungry, he dives and gets the repast of the day from the pantry, and goes to sleep at peace with his conscience and digestion.

Man who makes war on all creation, himself included, naturally makes war on the beaver to use his fur and to eat his flesh, which, it

[65] Randolph Barnes Marcy, *Thirty Years of Army Life on the Border,* p. 347-349.

seems, tastes good, especially the tail, which the trappers claim is a most delicate morsel. As the beaver very rarely shows himself, and, moreover, as the fur is spoiled if he is shot, they must depend on the trap to catch him. This trap, which we call a wolf trap, is a strong iron one, equipped with a chain. The trapper goes to the lodges in the evening and sets his trap in four inches of water, the chain under water too and fastened securely to some tree trunk. The bait is a very peculiar kind.

Inside the beaver, in his posterior part, there are two glands full of an odorous secretion which for a time, I believe, was widely used as a medicine. This secretion, dried and pulverized, retains its strong odor, which, however, is not disagreeable. The trapper rubs a little stick with it, and places it in the water in such a way that the animal he wishes to trap must put his foot on the pan of the trap in order to smell the bait. When the beaver has smelled it, he is lost. The odor has an attraction for him, and it draws him into the trap where he is soon caught. The skill of the trapper lies in placing his trap in such a way that the animal catches one of his hind legs, which are the strongest. If he is caught by a foreleg, there is a chance that by twisting and turning in attempts to get free, he will finally leave his paw gnawed off by the trap, and will get out of it at the price of a foot and a wound, which will heal. The trapper, finding the animal captured when he visits his traps at daybreak, beats him over the head with a stick, and the poor worker dies his ignominious death.

The beaver is singular in that its sexual organs are not visible on the outside. They are internal, and a single opening is visible under the large tail, which makes it very difficult even for the most practiced eye to distinguish between the male and the female, unless the animal is opened up.

[*Mores and ideas of the trapper*] While Beauchamp was talking to us about the habits and peculiarities of the beaver, I had noticed through a door opening into a second room three or four Indian women, seated on mats, at work decorating moccasins. "Is that your family?" I asked him. "Oh, no!" he answered. "One of them is my wife; the others are her friends who come to work with her. I have but one wife, the daughter of the chief of the Rees. She is good-humored, a good housekeeper, and takes care of the house well. I do not ask for more, and for around twenty years I have had no desire to take others, although it is the custom among the savages, with whom I have, so to speak, lived all my life. I was born in French Canada near the state of New York when there were still some savages down there. I got a taste of their life early."

(Beauchamp is fifty-eight years old, not a white hair in his thick crop of hair, and he is as strong and vigorous as a man of forty. The result of an active outdoor life. His only son, who is fifteen or sixteen years old, speaks English, and learned to read and write in a boarding school, but he has forgotten everything since he returned to the savages.)[66]

"Roaming the forests and prairies like them came to me by instinct. I believe that the good God put this in my nature, for as soon as I was of age, I got a job with the fur company, at first not attaching myself to any particular tribe. Later, I went down to St. Louis, where I was employed by Mr. Chouteau; but cities do not agree with me. It isn't in my nature. I was miserable there, so I didn't stay, and I shall never return. I shall die on the prairie where I have lived. Since I took a wife in the Ree tribe, I have always stayed with them, and I shall probably stay up to the end, for I have no other family, and I think they are permanently settled on the reserve, where I am employed by Mr. Gerard. You see, my general, everyone has his lot in this world. There are some who stay in cities and villages and carry on business all their lives. Some are rich, others are poor; some are happy, others are miserable. It suits them, and that is good. That would not suit me even if I were rich. I understand nothing of their laws and their taxes, of their differences and their machinery of government. Houses piled on one another so you can't breathe, streets where everyone pushes you into gutters; farms where fences keep you from going here, or hunting there; this is Pierre's and that is Jacques', and nothing for the simple creatures of the good God. My God, no! Here, the plains, mountains, woods, river, and everything belong to Beauchamp and to everyone, with no injustice to anyone. I set my traps where I wish, no one has anything to say to me. With my gun or my carbine, I go where I please, and the buffalo or antelope or beaver that I kill belong to me, and I live according to my taste and in my own way, troubling no one, and with no one troubling me."

The supper hour having arrived, I left Beauchamp, promising to come back to talk to him in the evening, which he assured me would please him very much. So I went back and, taking up the conversation where we had left off, I reminded him of his last phrase

---

[66] The material within the parentheses was written as a marginal note in the original French manuscript, with no indication of where it was to be inserted.

in which he boasted of living the way he pleased, with no one troubling him. Then I added by way of objection:

"And the Sioux?" I wanted to get him to tell stories, and I succeeded admirably.

[*Beauchamp's story*] "Ah! As for the Sioux," he said, "that's another thing. The score is even between them and me. It is to the death. They have already lodged three bullets in my body, and I am no worse off for it today, although they give me some bad times. They know me, and I know them. I have knocked over quite a few in my life, and it is not so long ago that I killed three in the same morning."

"Really," I said. "Tell me about it."

"Gladly," he said. "One time we had been on a good hunt in the 'bottoms' (alluvial land) and we were on our way back to this village. I had my wagon full of skins and meat. A beautiful lot! (With a sigh) And a fine wagon drawn by two good horses. I was with the Rees, for as you know, their chief is my father-in-law. A good savage; White Shield, they call him. But that isn't what we are talking about. As we were coming near the lake, the same one where you made a trip this morning, those vermin Sioux appeared on all sides on the hills and in front and behind to surround us, as is their custom when they are the stronger. And they were really the stronger, the bandits, three against one, I would stake my life on it! This meant booty and scalps from us, as you can imagine. But our men said: 'That's not the way it's going to be, and if we are weaker, at least we'll kill as many as we can.' This meant that instead of scattering into the bushes to escape to the village, every man for himself, we began the battle immediately. They came galloping in on us by fives or sixes, or by the dozen or twenties, so it looked as if they were going to swallow us up. But we fired our rifles at them. What else was there to do? And our fire was so brisk that they turned tail and retreated, and others took their places. Of course some of our men were falling too. When it was a Sioux, they dashed out to prevent us from taking him away or from 'lifting the scalp.' When it was a Ree, we were the ones who ran out to bring him back, and they tried to exterminate us with bullets and arrows.

"In the meantime, there were some of the party who were leading horses loaded with meat or skins through the thickets where severe fighting was also going on whenever they met some of the Sioux separately. It was either good or bad luck. There were some who reached the village; there were some who remained en route;

but most of the outfit was still around my wagon, burdened with a load heavy enough for six horses, which we could not get into the brush, let alone the two good beasts drawing it. Then my companions drew in as close as they could. The ones who were on horses and had bows and arrows dashed out one after another, advancing or retreating. Those who had guns had put their horses in the brush and stayed with me behind the wagon which we used as a rampart, as one would say, and when they (Sioux) came too near, we shot from behind the shelter as long as we could, and there were some who went down. It was then that I, for without boasting I can say that I shoot better than the savages, killed, or almost killed, three of them; but they were carried away before I could take their scalps. And it was then that two of our wounded were stretched out on the ground, having fallen from their horses, and I ran to them, and lifted them up on my back, one after the other, still holding my gun to keep the scoundrels at a distance. And they cried out, 'Coups! Fine. Fine.' I shouted to them from my side, 'Howl like the dogs you are; but keep your distance or you are as good as dead.'

"The two wounded men who are still living in the village said to me then, 'Beauchamp, there isn't another white man who would have done what you did for us.' 'You're wrong,' I told them, 'the whites stand by their friends no matter what the color of their skin, and another would have done the same'."

"I am not so sure," I interrupted.

"Anyway, it was still better to tell them that, wasn't it?"

"Briefly, to finish up, as they were the stronger and we finally didn't have time to reload, they got up to the wagon, cut the traces of the horses, and chopped up the spokes of my wheels on the side opposite from the one where we were holding out; and so the horses, the wagon, and everything inside, were lost. Since the good God willed it, one must console himself, isn't that right? But since that time, whenever I lay a Sioux low, I say: 'Good! There's another one for the wagon.' I know what I mean."

And there was nothing mild about Beauchamp's expression.

"How many must you have to square the account?" I asked.

"As many as come within range of my gun," he said.

"And have some already come?"

"Ah, not as many as I wish; but the last time we wiped out seven of them at a blow."

He threw down an armful of dry wood on the fire, and went on with a happy expression in which I clearly read the satisfaction of revenge:

"It was last spring. They were returning from the Knife River, or somewhere near there where they had gone to trade for powder and arms with the half-breeds from the Red River. As they had to pass near here to get back to the low country, they thought it was a good chance to steal some of our horses out to pasture or to kill some of our young men. But since there were scarcely thirty of them, they had to make their coup on the sly; so they came like thieves in the night to lie in ambush behind the heights that you saw over there, and in the morning, when the horses went out to pasture, they dashed out, and stole eight or ten of them. But the savage who was leading the horses saw them coming in time to escape, and he streaked back to the village to tell what had happened. Some had already seen the Sioux from a distance, and our young men were already mounting their horses to pursue the scoundrels.

"Of course, it took scarcely no time to get them together, and we dashed out after the Sioux as fast as we could go. They knew they were discovered and ran; but the horses were tired, having already made a long trip, and we gained on them so fast that the trail was as visible as buffalo on the snow, and there was no danger of taking the wrong route. In spite of everything, they kept some distance ahead of us for twenty-five miles, when we at last caught up with them. Finally we had them, the bandits. At first they fought in a group, but seeing they weren't the stronger, they began to run, every man for himself, into the ravines and coulees, our young men after them until they had taken back half again as many horses as they had stolen, and with them, seven of those vermin who remained dead on the ground. They couldn't carry them away, and so when we returned to the village, we brought with us seven scalps, seven pairs of hands, and seven pairs of feet. The rest was for the wolves."

"And how many of your people were killed?"

"Three; but they were brought back with their hair, and their bodies were hoisted up, wrapped in skin and blankets, as is the custom of burying people among the savages."

As a corollary to his story, Beauchamp insisted that a distinction be made between the good and bad savages and that one is unjustly confused with the other. He himself was not without personal grievance against the government, for last winter a general order on the whole frontier had barred all white men among the three tribes from entering the military post, on which they were dependent.[67] Whether it was distrust of their conduct or solicitude for their security, I do not know, but Beauchamp had obeyed, perhaps to the satisfaction of his conscience, but certainly to the great detriment of his purse. "For," he said, "during the winter months, I could easily have cut and piled three hundred cords of wood on the banks of the river where we were cutting, and in the spring, I would have sold that to the steamboats like white bread; it would have netted me two thousand dollars if it brought me a cent. And that is how they treat us. You need not be surprised if I prefer savages. You see, general, if people knew how things happen, they would see that savages are often better than civilized people. Just think, everything that the good God gave them is taken from them, and three-fourths of the presents or the 'annuities,' as they are called, will be stolen by those who have the responsibility of distributing them. And if they come in to complain, they will then get nothing at all but abuse or blows. I myself have seen in this village people who have died of starvation, and there would have been many others if it weren't for a captain who took it on himself, at his own risk, to have food distributed to the old and infirm, not knowing whether or not he would have to pay for this out of his own pocket. And yet you see they have no malice or revenge, happy to observe the treaties and acknowledging the little that is done for them. They shoot down or exterminate those who have no more patience with injustice and who fight to defend themselves. Father Smith [De Smet] says that everything happens because the good God wills it; but I do not see it that way."

"But," I said to him by way of explanation, "when these things happen, it is the fault of the bad savages like the Sioux who steal and kill, and the others have had to suffer through no evil intention on the part of the government, which, quite on the contrary, strives to protect them."

"Yes," he said, "when the soldiers are commanded by leaders like you. But most of the time, the generals, the colonels, and the captains make a game of the savages. Some among them get drunk, not in your case, more often than they should, and nothing more is needed for a tribe to be massacred, as happened to the Cheyennes when a drunken

[67] The traders were forbidden to establish themselves on military reservations by General Orders no. 9, Department of the Platte, July 24, 1866. The order as it applied to posts within the Department of Dakota in 1867, was revoked by General Terry on January 28, 1867. Department of Dakota, *General Orders*, General Orders no. 2, January 28, 1867.

colonel fell on them without warning, massacring the women and children at the very gates of the fort where they had put their arms and where they had received rations to nourish themselves and even some little flags of the United States, supposed protection. There were some, I have been told, who were killed with the flag in their hands. A good deal of trouble grew out of this in the low country, but whose fault was it?"

"Beauchamp," I said to him, "the deed that you speak of is a crime that I should not think of justifying or excusing; but you must remember too the massacre of the whites in Minnesota."[68]

"That is true," he said, "but who was responsible for the Minnesota Massacre? The Sioux. And why did others join them? Because they bore in their hearts the injustices and injuries that had been done to them for years, and they had said nothing about it. A great many of them were killed, and forty or fifty were hanged; but did they hang Covington [Chivington], or was he even tried? The relatives of those he had massacred could not obtain justice or reparation and wanted to avenge their dead in the Indian manner. So they killed as many whites as they could. That is how the trouble came. They say the Indians do this and the Indians do that; but one must see the reasons for things. As for the rest, I leave the Sioux to you. You can exterminate them as you will, the harm done will not be great; but it is necessary, too, to protect the good savages, like these, general; and you will never have any trouble with them."

The evening wore on, and we were to return to Fort Stevenson early the next day. I thanked Beauchamp for the pleasure that his conversation on beaver and Indians had given me. He excused himself for his frankness, hoping that it had not displeased me. "With you, general, I can speak with an open heart, because you speak French; when I must speak English, it is another thing, and I don't know what happens, but then I have nothing to say. Ideas don't come to me."

I took leave of the trapper with a handshake, and when I was outside, his last word from his doorway was: "And remember, general, what I told you is the real truth; the Sioux are bad people, confirmed bandits, *republicans in their souls!*"

And he closed the door.

I was very glad he did, for I don't know how I could have hidden

---

[68] For the report of the official investigating committee on the Chivington Massacre, see 39 Congress, 2 session, *Senate Executive Document* no. 26. The Chivington Massacre took place in 1864 and the Minnesota Massacre in 1862.

from him the irrepressible laughter that seized me at that unexpected qualification made as the supreme expression of hate and scorn of the Sioux. The word seemed magnificent to me. It paints with one stroke the true French-Canadian from Lower Canada. *Republican!* This is the supreme insult. To say Republican is to say a Robespierre, a Marat—a ferocious beast of the Reign of Terror. This man has been privileged to live thirty or forty years in the American Republic, in contact with its institutions and government, but that does not alter his first impression of a Republican. He is always the enemy of the throne and the altar, the *bête noire,* the monster stained with the blood of the past! Note that Beauchamp hasn't a shade of royalism or imperialism in him. His social ideas are extremely radical, but that matters little. Worse than a liar, worse than a thief, worse than a bandit, the Sioux is more than these: Republican!

Monday, September 23. We left Berthold this morning at eight o'clock. At ten, we were back at Fort Stevenson, with no incident worth mentioning. But here we found that the steamboat *Amanda* had arrived yesterday, and had unloaded two hundred and some barrels of lime, a new steam engine for the sawmill, some lumber, and other articles she had for us. She brought four personal letters for me, two from Madame de T——— and two from my eldest daughter. The steamboat was now waiting only until the quartermaster arrived to sign the official receipts, and she left almost immediately after our return from Berthold, not at all anxious to prolong her stay in our country in this season of low water. The same evening, at nightfall, floating lights told us of the approach of another steamboat coming down the river. It was the *Only Chance,* fully loaded with miners from Montana. As this sort of people are blusterers and quite undisciplined, and as men attached to the steamers have no scruples about selling whiskey to the soldiers or about helping them to desert on board, infractions that are made easier by the darkness and in spite of the sentinels, an order has been given to the captain of the *Only Chance* to cast off and tie up for the night farther down stream. The latter did not take it very well and at first refused to obey without a written order, accompanying his demand with impertinent remarks. This made it necessary for the officer of the day to tell him that if he did not cast off immediately, his hawser would be cut with an axe and his boat set adrift. So he was forced to obey, and he departed, taking his whiskey and bad humor farther away.

Note—I brought from Berthold a double-barreled shotgun for hunting this fall, and hunting paraphernalia, powder flask, and bullet sack that I found for sale at Gustave's. The weapon seemed to me a good one, although it didn't cost very much, but the traders have no market with the Indians, to whom it is forbidden to sell guns, and I suspect that this is an English weapon which paid no duty at the frontier.

I also acquired some savage curiosities of unquestionable authenticity. The Mandan chief sold me one of his bows and ten arrows with sheath and quiver of deerskin, everything but the arrows carrying marks of use. I got these for the price of a buffalo robe; that is, six dollars in provisions of his choice at the trader's (sugar, coffee, tobacco, biscuit, etc.). For the same price, Four Times Four sold me his necklace of bear claws. A tobacco pouch of good workmanship, and a pair of moccasins made by Gustave's wife complete the souvenirs of this first visit to my redskin children. In this way, I shall gradually be able to make quite a collection of curios.

Wednesday, September 25. Summer heat. Sky always blue, sun scorching. The thermometer went up to ninety-three degrees F. in the shade.

Thursday, September 26. Great agitation among the canine tribe around ten o'clock in the evening. A furious baying, like a hunt in camp. A wolf had come in among the tents, looking for adventure. The sled dogs got his scent and attacked. The enemy took flight, rather badly mauled by our Indian quadrupeds who are used to warring against the prairie wolves.

Monday, September 30. Last Tuesday I went out to try my gun in the willows at the edge of the water. At the end of two hours I came back with a duck, a prairie chicken, and two snipes of the large breed. I definitely made a good buy. I have no dog yet; but my orderly goes with me everywhere and spares me the trouble of carrying my game. The great heat last week prevented me from trying again; but today, since the weather was cloudy and the hay carts were sent out five or six miles from here to gather forage on the banks of Snake Creek, the quartermaster and I took the lead on horseback, followed by two mounted orderlies, and we hunted there in the morning. Never in my life have I seen so many wild geese. On the big sand bank at the mouth of the creek, there must have been no less than a hundred of them. Unfortunately, we could not come up to them from under cover on any side, and having only small-size shot, we were unable to fire on them. We made up for it with ducks, prairie chickens, etc. Total: twenty birds for the larder, ten each.

In the evening, the last steamboat of the season, the *Huntsville*, passed Fort Stevenson going back to St. Louis. We shall see no more steamboats until next year. There are still two or three up river by forts Benton and Buford; but they are hopelessly stuck on sand bars where the shallowness of the water has left them almost high and dry. These will never be seen again. The engine will be dismantled and saved. The winter and ice will demolish the hull, and there will be hardly enough left for firewood.

Tuesday, October 1. Finally, after three full months of blue sky and dry weather, the rain came last night. It fell all day today. As a change it is not unpleasant. Unfortunately, it delays our building, for no one can work, and we have no time to lose.

The moistened adobe becomes soft on the outside and really cannot be used before the sun dries it up again, which will take a full day of sunshine. The trees have put on their yellow and red autumn livery. After this rain and the cold that will probably follow, it won't take them long to lose their leaves, which are already getting bright. This will be a change for the banks of the river. On the prairie, the appearance of the countryside won't change, except that the snow will make the plain all white in the winter, as it is all green in the spring, and all yellow in the summer.

Wednesday, October 2. Beautiful weather, clear sky, cold air. Went out with my gun for an hour or two; brought back two geese and a wild duck. This simply shows how abundant the game is; now I won't bring up the subject again. Today a convoy arrived from Devils Lake (Fort Totten). It is the same one that has already made one trip here. It will leave the day after tomorrow, taking with it the complement of provisions needed by the three companies garrisoned at the post. It is the last one of the season we shall see. Newspapers received up to September 13. Everything is news for us.

Thursday, October 3. The convoy of cattle which we have been expecting for a month for the winter provisioning of my three posts finally arrived this morning under an escort of one hundred men and two officers of the 10th infantry, forming a part of the garrison of Fort Wadsworth in the District of Minnesota.[69] Part of the cattle were left at Fort Totten. About sixty head are left for us, and the others are going on to Fort Buford under the direction of one hundred men who came for the herd in the last days of September and who stayed here to wait for them until today. But this reinforcement has been useful in helping us with our work. These hundred men are under the command of Lieutenant [George] Mitchell, a good officer, well trained and intelligent. They are detached from the five companies at Fort Buford, twenty men from a company. Piercing cold all day; icy rain in the evening.

Today the prairie around us presents the most animated sight that I have yet seen. The camp situated on the edge of the plateau above the river; the workshops, the sawmill, and the corral behind. Some hundred yards to the west, the buildings of the fort in construction. On the opposite side, the wharf and the provisions piled under temporary shelters; behind the wharf, the line of tents belonging to the detachment which came from Fort Buford for the cattle. A little farther, the mounted escort which brought it here, with its conical tents (Sibley), its forges, and its horses out to pasture. Not far from there, the convoy from Fort Totten with its yokes of oxen and shelter tents. Finally, two hundred head of cattle graze lazily on the yellow grass, sometimes on the plateau, sometimes on the slopes of the hills, and sometimes in the depressions in the land. They are guarded by horsemen who gallop after those which try to run away from the herd. The guards on foot would look like motionless stakes planted around on the surrounding heights if it were not for the barrels of their carbines shining in the sun. There is continual coming and going among these groups, giving the scene an unusual animation which is in striking contrast to the silent immobility of the far away solitudes which form a frame for it.

Friday, October 4. The convoy from Devils Lake left with its load. The officer who commanded it, Lieutenant Leonard, appointed because of two promotions in the regiment (second lieutenants [Philip Howard] Ellis and Hogan advanced to first lieutenants) in company "B" in the garrison of Fort Buford, stayed here to go to his post with the escort for the cattle.

[*Submission of Indian tribes*] Patenaud or Paquenaud, the

69 Fort Wadsworth was established near the head of the Coteau des Prairies (Highland of the Prairies) July, 1864, because of the outbreak of hostilities on the northwest frontier. It was abandoned in 1888. *Report on Barracks and Hospitals*, p. 377–380.

guide and interpreter, paid me a long visit in my tent, and furnished me with new information about the Indians of this region. Coming from Fort Totten with the convoy, he met a great many of them. Some of the chiefs came to talk with him; one or two less trusting bands did not want to come near. Almost all are going to Fort Totten to make their submission. Somewhat compromised by their participation in the Minnesota Massacres four years ago, they found they had to leave their lands near Devils Lake and go onto the great plains, where they found no comparable hunting grounds, and where they lived so miserably and underwent such privations that they came back in despair to put themselves under the protection of the government by a treaty of peace. They will winter in the locality of Devils Lake where the woods, game, and fish are abundant. Furthermore, we shall see to it that they stay there with their families, whose presence is an assurance of their good behavior in the future.

During the winter, some hostile tribes in the direction of Fort Buford, the Unkpapas, the Cheyennes, and part of the Blackfeet[70] and Spotted Tails, go to the Knife River to get munitions, where the half-breeds from the Red River of the North come to trade with them. Last winter these half-breeds, all sons of French-Canadians, carried on this profitable commerce with impunity on the river of the White Lands, but this time, it is not going to be this way, and we are going to put an end to it by destroying the establishment they are now building to store the munitions and Indian whiskey they have for the savages.[71] If they offer resistance, we shall make an example of them. Indian whiskey is nothing but alcohol mixed with water. Is there any reason to be surprised about the terrible effects it has on the unhappy redskins whom it poisons?

This evening, the accidental discharge of a loaded rifle in the hands of a corporal caused the death of a soldier in the detachment ready to leave for Fort Buford. The victim was an excellent soldier—naturally. These misfortunes never happen to the good-for-nothings about whom one could say "good riddance."

Saturday, October 5. The cold persists, and the river is getting

70 The Sihasapa (Blackfeet Sioux) are a small division of the Teton Sioux who were not mentioned in the travel journals until Catlin. They acted with the Hunkpapa and Sans Arcs in hostilities against the whites. Hodge, *Handbook,* 2:568–569.

71 A year later, Lieutenant Hogan did lead a company of the 31st infantry from Fort Buford and destroyed a camp of half-breeds on the Little Muddy River. 40 Congress, 3 session, *Executive Document* no. 1, p. 34.

lower and lower. However, the newspapers from St. Louis which we have received announce the departure of a steamboat for Fort Buford and the intermediary posts on September 5. So this boat can arrive almost any day now. Probably the department of the quartermaster loaded it with vegetables. It is possible that it is bringing the assortment of furniture I ordered in Omaha.

The escort of the cattle which came from Fort Wadsworth left this morning to return to its post. One of the two officers commanding it, Major (brevet) [Jesse A.] Hampson of the 10th infantry, carries with him a letter from me for Colonel [Samuel S.] Hayman, old companion in arms of Kearny's division in the Army of the Potomac. I am asking him to engage for me fifteen Indian scouts, whom we cannot find here since our three tribes are afraid of weakening themselves and since the men, being at war with the Sioux, consider detached service too dangerous. In these trips across the plains, the detachments find an abundance of game of all kinds and for the most part live on deer and buffalo meat; but the nights are cold, and it is really too late in the season for these expeditions to be an unmitigated pleasure.

Sunday, October 6. The hundred and some head of cattle destined for Fort Buford left this morning under escort of one hundred men brought here for that purpose by Lieutenant Mitchel[1]. To help him in his command, he has another officer, Lieutenant Leonard. The latter, because of the promotions of two second lieutenants to first lieutenants, is assigned to company "B" at Fort Buford. He came from Fort Totten as commander of the escort for the last convoy, and in this way he was able to report to his new post. The detachment from Fort Buford which arrived here by steamboat five or six weeks ago had no wagons with it, and (Bt. Colonel) Captain Rankin who sent it made the mistake of furnishing the men with only their blankets and a change of underclothes. So I had to lend them two wagons for the transportation of their rations. Moreover, as Lieutenant Hogan (promoted) was going to Fort Buford too, I furnished him with an ambulance for Mrs. Hogan, who is taking her bed, blankets, and furs in it, and will be as comfortable as circumstances permit. A wagon carries their baggage and their furniture, as well as Lieutenant Leonard's baggage. These three wagons and the ambulance must be returned to general headquarters immediately. Twelve men and a sergeant left with the detachment to bring them back. Lieutenant Ellis, because of his promotion, goes to Company "H," which is garrisoned at Fort Stevenson, and he will make use of this opportunity to command the returning escort on his way to general headquarters. It will take the convoy eleven or twelve days to get to Fort Buford. In returning from there, the escort will ride in the empty wagons, and the trip made in this way will take only seven or eight days. So in twenty days they will be back.

Around eight o'clock in the morning, the detachment got under way, preceded by an advance guard, followed by the bellowing herd walking with a slow and dignified step. The mounted cowboys galloped on the flanks, and the rear guard on foot finished up the procession. They passed behind the camp near the sawmill, then behind the fort in construction, then little by little disappeared on the far away plain, after crossing Douglas Creek. They were lost on the horizon; we were left to our own devices for seven or eight months. No other convoy will put in an appearance until next year. The prairie, so teeming with life three days ago, because of the presence of three convoys or detachments, has taken on its deserted and silent look again, and from now on movement is concentrated in a very restricted area, the camp and outbuildings its center on one side, and the fort in construction and the two log houses of the sutlers on the other.

Monday, October 7. Hunting party eight or nine miles from here with the quartermaster and two mounted orderlies. That long ride across the rolling prairies, rolling prairies where not a tree grows, where not a human being is visible, those endless, narrow ravines, those low hills, those valleys where at long intervals the now dry bed of some river twines; those plateaus where the eye finds no object upon which to rest; those far away horizons where the lines formed by the changing character of the terrain are lost in the uniformity of yellow grass dried by the summer sun; this dreary and lonely solitude, which the day illuminates but does not give life, where everything seems asleep, where no movement shows life, where the storm itself can run wild without awakening anything but an imperceptible ripple in the grass; all this has something impressive about it. Sometimes the desert absorbs one and man is nothing but a small particle lost in this immensity; sometimes one takes possession of this space, and the fever of liberty intoxicates as this limitless course opens everywhere to the horseman's gallop.

[*Douglas Creek in fall*] We dismounted at the edge of a stream of water which winds through the desert, the steep banks of which are usually sheltered by slender reeds. This is the same small stream which, after a thousand twists and turns, empties into the Missouri below Fort Stevenson. In this season of the year, it no longer flows toward its mouth; its course resembles a huge serpent cut up into a multitude of segments. Now it is a series of long and narrow stretches of water, separated here and there by a thin thread of water hidden under the grass or by strips of sand or by a slimy crust completely dried up. Sometimes the stream is thirty or forty feet wide and stretches on to the foot of the hills in the distance; then it suddenly stops on a bar of small pebbles. Sometimes it is only a pond settled in the elbow of one of its banks. And sometimes it shrinks to a little creek five or six feet wide, half hidden by the reeds. Wild geese and ducks are plentiful here, and only rarely are they disturbed in this retreat. Today the geese were gone, due no doubt to the return of the heat which has made the south wind stifling for two days and to an October sun whose rays are not dimmed by a cloud. To make up for this, the ducks were very numerous. We brought back eleven of them (the major six and I five). If we had been better shots and had hunted more carefully, we could have brought back around twenty.

Three or four years ago, General Sully crossed this country with a rather considerable column of troops. The tracks made by the wheels of his wagons and the trampling of his teams are still very evident, and the double line on the prairie is visible for quite a distance.[72]

These excursions are rather tiring because of the necessity of carrying a rifle in one hand and guiding the horse with the other all during the trip.

Both of the orderlies are armed with Sharp's carbines and hang the game on their saddle horns. It is always necessary to go armed when venturing out on the prairie, and since the hunting gun is loaded at the muzzle—the breechloaders would be useless if we exhausted the supply of cartridges, which are impossible to replenish for months—prudence demands that a revolver be carried in the belt. These precautions are necessary because we might meet hostile Indians. It is always essential to have means of keeping them at a dis-

[72] In 1864, General Sully led an expedition against the Sioux through this country. He came up the Missouri to the Cannon Ball River, up the valley of the Cannon Ball and northward to the Heart River. After leaving most of his baggage on the Heart, he moved forward to attack an Indian encampment on the Knife River. He then returned to the Heart River and marched westward to the Yellowstone. The return march was down the left bank of the Yellowstone, and down the left bank of the Missouri to Fort Rice. Folwell, *A History of Minnesota*, 2:295–299.

tance by the rapidity of fire, which would be impossible with a simple rifle, slow and awkward as it is and impossible to reload in such a situation. Indians plotting evil could slip up the coulees, and remain concealed until they were but a short distance away, surrounding the hunters, whom they had spotted from a distance, without themselves being seen. This possibility adds to the pleasure of the hunt— the peculiar feeling that it can end in a fight. This is not probable, but it is certainly possible, and this possibility cannot be put out of mind. This is why we always keep some bullets ready to slip in the rifle barrels, and why we never cross a ridge of land without scanning the horizon, or why we never go into a ravine without looking as far as we can. So here the hunt has more spice than where there is no salt of danger.

The buffalo have been seen twelve or fifteen miles away; but we do not believe that they will come near the fort this year because of the two shots of cannon that are fired every day at dawn and sunset by higher orders. These detonations carry far and will probably keep the buffalo at a distance, as will the sounds of the bugle and drums which are repeated often during the day. Many have been killed in this neighborhood; the prairie around camp and in every direction is strewn with horned heads dried and bleached in the sun, and with bones that the wolves have cleaned with rare perfection. Still, we haven't seen a trace of them today.

Tuesday, October 8. Today the Indians of Berthold came to take leave of me before departing for their winter camp. Each tribe was represented by its chief and its deputy chief, plus four of its principal personages, except for the Gros Ventres, whose chief did not come. I don't know why he didn't. Nevertheless, six members of the tribe were present; this made eighteen in all. Forewarned of their arrival, I had arranged my tent to receive them by laying carpets on three sides and sitting down at a table with the officers behind me in the second tent which I use as a bedroom. The deputations took their places, sitting down on the carpets. Since the weather was cold and a gale was blowing, all of them were wrapped in their buffalo robes, hair on the inside, tied in at the waist with a leather belt. Almost all of them let this wrapping fall down on their legs when they entered my tent where the stove kept the temperature high.

[*Indian costumes*] The chief of the Rees, White Shield, was wearing a soldier's jacket underneath; another had a Zouave jacket with a braid, to which he had added some ornaments. The most picturesque was undoubtedly an old Mandan chief whose antelope-skin shirt was ornamented with many colored porcupine quills. Several had necklaces of various kinds, and others earrings or bracelets either on their bare arms or on the sleeves of a woolen shirt. All of their trouser legs were of deerskin, fringed on the outside seam and decorated with porcupine quills. The Mandan chief, Red Cow, was naked to the waist under his buffalo robe. Their headdress consisted of either a Madras or a silk handkerchief, usually knotted in a band around the head. Some had only their thick black hair, cut at the forehead, or rather above the eyes, braided at the temples, and falling down their backs in long braids, partly painted, white especially, or in a long tail as the chief of the Mandans wore his.

The powwow resembled the first one in every detail. I commended them for not selling a single grain of powder to the other Indians and for not letting any that they were permitted to buy from the traders leave the three tribes, which they have solemnly promised. The question came up of a visit which eleven Miniconjous[73] and three Unkpapahs had just made to trade horses and buffalo skins for corn. These tribes are hostile. The different bands have made peace, or rather a truce, for a few days to trade, after which they set out for the plains. Those who came to visit the tribes of Berthold will not hesitate to resume hostilities against them, if they have a good chance to do so. It is one of the hallowed practices among the savages, who, as a result, are sometimes at war, sometimes at peace, depending on whether or not they find some advantage in it; unless a permanent treaty of peace binds them by ties of good friendship. I recommended to them that they never buy horses or mules stolen from the government and bearing the mark U.S., nor any animals that have been shod, and, consequently, stolen from whites, but to acquire only Indian ponies. They could easily understand this. They agreed to it without hesitation. They confirmed for me the reports already received on the traffic carried on by the half-breeds from the Red River of the North in powder and munitions with the hostile Sioux and Cheyennes, protesting vigorously that they have never taken part in it, which I know to be true, for the hostile Indians have more munitions than the three tribes, and would be in a better position to sell to them than to buy from them. The rest of the confer-

[73] The Miniconjou, "those who plant beside the stream," are a division of the Teton Sioux. Known as the most troublesome and wild of the Teton bands, they made war on the other Indians and committed depredations against the whites. They signed both the treaty at Fort Sully in 1865 and that at Fort Laramie in 1868. Hodge, *Handbook,* 1:868.

ence was spent in denunciations of the Sioux who make war on them
and in compliments and thanks to me and to my officers. Finally, to
close the meeting, I announced that I had given orders to have distributed to them salt pork, biscuit, coffee, sugar, and beans. Upon
which, they naturally proclaimed that I was a great chief and that
their Great Father in Washington had been really inspired to send
to them *an old man* whose head was white because of the wisdom
and understanding under his gray hair, and that I was a more just
and generous man than the younger men who had been indifferent
to them. And after calling the favor of the Great Spirit on my ven-
erable head, they went to receive their rations, to which I myself
added half a pound of tobacco for each chief.

Since the day was already far along and the sun was setting, they
will spend the night around the log houses of the sutlers and will
return to Berthold tomorrow morning, happy and satisfied.

Wednesday, October 9. The days are speeding by, winter is
approaching, and our buildings are coming along slowly. The pleasant plans we had made to get into our winter quarters by December
1st are gradually disappearing in the face of reality. The work already completed gives us an exact measure of the time required to
complete it, and it is now evident that it cannot be completed this
year. So the work must be limited as much as possible to the strictly
essential, and we must be satisfied with procuring adequate protection against the extreme rigors of this climate during the winter.
The program has been modified to accomplish this. Of the five houses
making up the officers' quarters only three will be built, and they
will not even be finished on the inside. Two will house the families
of the four married officers. In mine, which is double, I shall take
in two unmarried officers, and three others will live on the second
floor in the attic. They are going to build for the latter a log house
with a dining room and kitchen where they will take their meals.
The guardhouse and the prison will be built temporarily in the same
fashion, and probably the offices. This kind of building can be thrown
together quickly, and except for its lack of elegance, it is as warm
and comfortable as any other. But even with these modifications, the
work will not be ready until the month of December; and so the men
who work like beavers every day have nothing but unheated edge
tents to shelter them from the wind, the snow, and the cold at night.
God grant that the months of October and November be not too
severe.

This is the present state of the buildings:

Storehouse: walls finished, roof almost completed.

Hospital, companies' barracks, house of the district commandant: walls finished, rafters in place, no floors or roof.

Officers' house for two families: stone foundation finished for
both; framework up for one; the walls not begun yet; a row of foundations dug for the rest of the buildings, the palisade, and the outside corral.

Construction was begun in July. A few days less than three
months have passed, and half of the work to be done is not completed. We shall postpone until next year all of the second storehouse
and the two officers' storehouses, not to mention the offices, which
will be built temporarily of logs or slabs like the guardhouse and
the prison, and the work of finishing all the buildings on the inside.

Today the wind died down and the weather became mild enough
for us to hope for the advent of Saint Martin's summer (Indian
summer).

Thursday, October 10. The Mackinaw boats, as they are called,
are now coming down the river, since the shallowness of the water
holds up the only two steamboats still in this country between Buford
and Benton. Six of them came today. They stopped at the wharf
around noon to buy from the commissariat some provisions needed
by the men on them. Then they got under way again. They are flatboats, each carrying six, eight, or ten men, and up to fifteen; the
lightest ones take the usual form, a bow and a stern, and resemble all
rudimentary craft; but the heaviest are shaped just like a large
oblong box, squared bow and squared stern. One that passed by today had added a kind of semicylindrical covering of planks over two-
thirds of its length. All such craft are worked by oars, usually two
on each side; sometimes four, but very rarely. Another stern oar serves
as a rudder. To this must be added a small mast on which a square
sail is hoisted when the wind is blowing astern.[74]

It is in these boats that the miners from Montana return to the
States at the approach of winter, when their season has been poor
and they do not have enough to pay a passage of $100 to $120 on board
the steamboats. Moreover, this price is exorbitant when one thinks
of the way they are packed in berths or in temporary bunks made
of planks and built one above the other on the lower deck of the

[74] Mackinaws were usually forty to fifty feet long, with a twelve-foot beam
and a three- or four-foot hold. They could carry up to fifteen tons and travel up to
a hundred miles a day. This was the cheapest kind of transportation down river.

steamers. Those who were unlucky in the search for gold naturally
stay in the gold fields longer than the others, spurred on by the hope
of finally making some rich find; and even if they have that luck, the
steamboats are all gone by that time, and there is left only the
Mackinaw to bring them down to winter with us.

A few days ago, eight poor devils came to the fort this way, not
to buy, but to beg for some provisions, which were given to them
so they could go on their way. Among the eight—to use the expression
of one of them—you could not have found enough money to pay for
a small glass of whiskey apiece. Those who came today were not in
this condition, but whatever were the contents of their purses, they
looked more like bandits than honest Christians. In general, all
miners have that look when they return from the mines. Their clothes
are worn threadbare; their heavy boots are down at the heel or split
open; their trousers patched; their beards long and dirty; their hair
idem; they have no underwear; they just wear shirts or heavy flannel
under an ordinary greatcoat or a jacket fringed with antelope skin,
all more or less tattered. Their old soft felt hats have a seedy look, and
if they wear a cap of buffalo or fox skin, their appearance is not
improved by it. Probably they prefer to keep this poor appearance
in order to conceal better their profits if they have any; they are then
able to outfit themselves in new clothes from head to foot when they
get back to civilization.

All or almost all are armed with rifles, carbines, or revolvers;
this goes without saying, for their personal safety demands it in their
adventurous life. In the absence of law, justice, and courts, every
man protects his wealth and person by force, or by a mutual compact
among a number of individuals in a common cause, in an association of revolvers, carbines, and bowie knives. It is because of this
that the eight Mackinaws that visited us today travel together, for
mutual protection against the Indians. The precaution is well taken,
but it isn't always effective. Thus, on this side of Buford, they had
to pass by a camp of Sioux who signaled them to land. Of course they
were on their guard. The Sioux fired on them and killed a man on
board one of the boats. The miners retaliated as well as they could.
What was the effect of their fire? They do not know, but they have the
consolation of believing that they killed or wounded some redskins.

[*Three Indians attempt murder*] We ourselves are not safe
from isolated attacks, or, to express it better, from attempts to murder the men who go out from their post without arms. Just today
we had a sad experience with this sort of thing. I have said before

that we had a post of a dozen men with some teams of mules and oxen on the other side of the river, across from camp. The men had just returned and were bringing up the teams used during the day to drag to the edge of the water the logs cut for the construction of the fort. Bt. Colonel Powell and Lieutenant Walborn, returning from a hunting party on this side, had just crossed the river in the longboat, and were scarcely in their tents when cries rang out from the opposite bank. The sentinel at the wharf called the corporal of the guard, and an instant later my orderly half opened my tent and said: "Colonel, a man killed by the Indians." I dashed outside and made out two or three men on the other side of the river running up and down the bank crying: "Send the boat—hurry." Someone answered: "What's wrong?" And the reply came to me distinctly: "A man killed or wounded (shot) by the Indians." I ran to the tent of the commandant of the post to have him send a detachment immediately, and a few minutes later, he himself, armed with his carbine, led fifteen men to the boat on the run. The detachment, pulling hard at the oars, arrived promptly on the other bank, where they saw the men of the post grouped in front of their log houses. The fifteen reinforcements joined them immediately, and everyone disappeared into the thicket, except some left to carry the victim to the boat. This is what had happened:

Since no hostile Indian had showed up around the camp for more than two months, the men had gradually relaxed their precautions against any surprise attack and frequently went out some distance from the post without being armed. One of them, back from work, had gone out into the woods to gather some wild plums before his supper. He was unarmed and was going along a narrow path when he suddenly found himself face to face with three Indians decorated with feathers and dark paint, their war costumes. The soldier, surprised and surmising their sinister intentions, tried at least to ward off the danger or delay the attack by a friendly greeting. He gave them the "How" of welcome, offering his hand to them; but the three bandits threw themselves on him, striking him on the head with the wood of their bows. Our man took flight immediately, running as fast as his legs would carry him, crying: "Murder!" to warn his comrades. He had not gone twenty steps when he was pierced with three arrows: one in his shoulder, another in his arm, the third through his neck. Nevertheless, he went on until one of his companions ran to meet him, and both gained the cabins, but the irresolute corporal there did not dare pursue the murderers for fear of falling into some ambush with his men. By the time Colonel Powell arrived, the Indians, who had disappeared after making the coup, must have had a good head start. In vain the detachment beat the woods in skirmish line. They found neither redskins nor any trace of them in this underbrush which is so thick that a hundred of them could have dispersed into it without a chance of being discovered before nightfall, which was coming on rapidly. The detachment returned as the moon was coming up, after unfortunately wasting its time and trouble.

The wounded man was carried to our hospital immediately, where Dr. Grey [*sic*] proceeded to extract the arrows. For one of them in particular, the operation was difficult, since the iron struck the bone of the arm and bent. An incision was necessary. Arrows, as you know, cannot be drawn out where they came in; they must be drawn in, the iron first. The patient, under the influence of chloroform, came through the operation without feeling the pain. Nevertheless, he has suffered a great deal since then. The doctor is still confident that he will come through it without being a cripple. He had a narrow escape.

Friday, October 11. It was noon. Wonderful weather; the sun shining. When I left my tent a little before dinner, my attention was attracted by some Indians on horseback on the crest of the cliffs overlooking the wooded lands on the other side of the river where we arc still cutting trees for the construction of the fort. This sight soon attracted the attention of the other officers, the ladies, and the men in from work for dinner. The number of redskins increased from one minute to the next. They appeared at several points at the same time, by twos, threes, fours, and soon a dozen of them were plainly seen coming down the slope of the cliffs and going into the underbrush. One of them came out a little later, galloped through the leafy growth up to the bank of the river, and waved in the air a thing we took to be a white flag, but which was in reality only a war shield. Mr. Marsh, the trader, long familiar with the ways of the Indians, could see nothing good in this performance; but the officers, whom I credited with better judgment because of their experience with life in the territories, were unanimously of the opinion that it was just a matter of having a peace conference with us. Being still new to Indian ways, I left Colonel Powel[1], commandant of the post, full freedom to take whatever measure he deemed appropriate. The result was that at first he didn't take any.

Fort Douglas, Utah Territory

The Indian began to gallop right and left in the clearing, singing at the top of his voice. Mr. Marsh said, shaking his head: "It's his war song." But they answered: "It's to attract attention in order to get an answer." When Mr. Pease, agent for the Fur Company of the N. E. and trader at Buford and Berthold, arrived unexpectedly, Colonel Powell requested that he ask the Indian what he wanted.[75] To Mr. Pease's particular cry of summons, the Indian answered with a like cry and took up his war chant more fervently than ever. "They are hostile Indians," said Mr. Pease, "and they have come to do mischief."

The eighteen men of the guard who were relieved this morning were immediately recalled and received the order to cross the river in the longboat under the command of Lieutenant [George S.] Ward. While they were being assembled, all eyes were turned to the part of the distant woods where a detachment of seven men were at work with six mules and two oxen. The mules, we now knew, were the booty that the Indians had promised themselves and that they were going to try to carry off. We had counted a dozen Indians on horseback in the brush through which ran the road that must be followed by the men in returning to the corral. Three men left at the log houses were posted on the highest roof with their guns and were keeping on the lookout expecting an attack. The longboat carrying the reinforcement of eighteen men left the wharf at the same moment that the mule teams, the two oxen, and the escort of five men (not including the two wagoners) were emerging from the brush where the work was being done into a clearing bordering the river which had to be crossed by following along the exposed bank. Would they get there? Would it be in time? This was the question that everyone was asking, as they looked from the boat crossing the river to the team crossing the clearing. The driver was hurrying too much; the men had to run to keep up with him; a bad sign. Fear was spurring them on. I wanted to see them come on resolutely, without hurrying, the escort covering the wagon and ready to open fire; but nothing resembled this less.

The Indian who had come to make his boasts and sing his war chant across from us began to gallop back to get out of the way of the team, but did not get out of rifle range; however, not a shot was

[75] David Pease was a partner in the firm of Hubbell and Hawley, later the Northwest Fur Company. When General Sully marched by Fort Berthold, he arrested Pease on a charge of selling liquor to the Indians and took him to Fort Pierre for trial. *North Dakota Historical Collections*, 1:376. See also, Diary of William L. Larned, p. 52. Typescript in the Minnesota Historical Society.

fired at him. What were those imbeciles thinking of? We shall see. It should be noted that they were now armed with excellent rifled breechloaders, so rapid and easy to fire that in the hands of a resolute man a weapon of this kind would easily get rid of half a dozen Indians, especially Indians on horseback.

[*The coup de main*] Between the corral near the cabins and the big clearing stretches a band of woods full of underbrush. The road crosses it without going back more than twenty or thirty paces from the bank, a space filled with dense brush and some higher trees. It was at the edge of this wood, which was not more than one hundred or one hundred and fifty yards wide, that the Indians had ambushed. There were hardly a dozen of them and only seven dashed out toward the mules. Just one volley, and the red scoundrels would disappear; but on seeing them appear—just seeing them appear—the corporal (an abominable coward named George E. Wilson) and the four men—without firing a shot, without putting up a show of resistance, abandoned the mules and cowardly ran to hide themselves like sheep behind the slope of the bank—the worst place, by the way, that they could choose to take shelter. One of the drivers (they were unarmed) jumped to the ground; the other one still urged the mules on; but the oxen tied on behind slowed down the pace. The Indians dashed through the brush crying "How! How!" to deceive them about their intentions. But the driver was not taken in, and when they were fifteen or twenty paces away, he jumped down and slipped into the brush at the edge of the water, where he disappeared. The thieves asked for nothing more. In another minute we saw them throw themselves at the mules, cut the traces, slash off the harness, and prepare to carry away their booty. One of the animals, however, ran toward the cabins, and was saved.

All this happened before our very eyes, and we could do nothing but level one of our cannon, and throw some ineffectual shells above the woods where the action was taking place. And during this time, Lieutenant Ward finally disembarked, lost some precious moments in getting the men lined up on the bank according to the manual and in deploying them in skirmish line to go through the impenetrable underbrush which could not harbor anyone, instead of running straight to the aid of the team and its contemptible escort. However, Mr. Pease, Mr. Howell, the clerk of the quartermaster, and a few others with carbines of long-range precision, did their best by opening fire on the redskins from across the river. They had noticed that in order to lead the captured mules out of the underbrush, the savages would have to take the road, the route which passed twenty or thirty paces from the point where our five cowards had taken refuge. With one voice everyone called on them to climb up the bank and fire on the thieves.

"Fire on them! Charge them!" And other encouragements to make them blush for their cowardice.

Finally, they decided to climb the slope, but slowly and without spirit; the first two into the bushes fired their guns. No more was needed to make the Indians break into a gallop, fleeing pell-mell through the brush. But it was too late; they had gained the edge of the woods and were taking the five mules away with them. Our men, seeing the danger past, came out for the charge, and the shots that they had not dared to fire at the redskins when they were coming on them they now shot when they saw them run away. No more would have been needed to save the mules, if they had only had the resolution to fire when they should have instead of shamefully running away.

Our shells followed the fugitives up to the top of the cliffs, and our skirmishers scoured the flat terrain in vain. When they reached the heights, the Indians had disappeared in the direction of Berthold. However, they must not have gone too far away if they stayed near the fires they lighted. For they were still blazing on the heights at nine o'clock in the evening.

The detachment returned. The ten men on duty on the other side of the river will be withdrawn tomorrow, and the last logs that were still to be dragged to the edge of the water will come over on the ice when the river is frozen, if we need them. The rest of the wood that we need will be taken from this bank under the protection of twenty men and an officer, in place of ten.

Corporal Wilson will be reduced from his rank for cowardice before the enemy, and his four men withdrawn from the quartermaster's department, where they were receiving an increase in pay. The only thing such cowards are good for is making mud for adobe.[76]

The Indians who made this attack this morning are Unkpapahs, a hostile tribe addicted to theft and brigandage. Pray Heaven that I

[76] G. E. T. Wilson was tried at the court-martial meeting February 4, 1868. He was sentenced to be paraded before the troops with a placard, bearing the word "coward" on his back, to be dishonorably discharged, and to be confined at hard labor for ten years. He was sent to Stillwater, Minnesota, for imprisonment. Department of Dakota, *General Orders,* 1868, General Orders no. 22, July 23, 1868; Hanson, *Conquest of the Missouri,* p. 121–123.

never get the chance to settle with them the account that they have just opened with me today!

[*Indian trickery*] P. S. I have just learned that four of these Indians came up to the men when they were still working in the woods. They had pretended to be friends; they had exchanged some "Hows!" and handshakes with them at the very moment that their companions were preparing the ambush where our mules were stolen. They were there to count the men, to see how they were armed, etc., and to give to the others the signal when they approached. Such are the redskins, and such is the confidence that they can inspire by their demonstrations of friendship! It goes without saying that the three assassins of yesterday evening were of that band. They came to scout out the land for today's surprise attack. This is the situation in which we are placed by our lack of horses and scouts. They give them to us on paper; actually we are still waiting for them.

Another band of Indians is sighted from this side of the river in the badlands halfway from Berthold. This must be a part of the band that insulted us today, for they crossed the river at that place yesterday. The fires burning during the day and this evening are probably signals between them. If they only would attack the camp!

The soldiers detached as skirmishers on the other side of the river are sure that they saw the Indians load on a horse the body of one of their men who was killed or wounded. I hope with all my heart that they have made no mistake. They say another one was shot from his horse. There is nothing certain about it.

Saturday, October 12. Eight Mackinaws arrived at nightfall to spend the night near the wharf where the men on board are now having their supper cooked. They bought various provisions and report that the season has been good in general for the gold hunters in Montana. This company looks better than the last. The men in it look more prosperous. It is noticeable that they are all vigorous fellows, tall, broad shouldered, and usually young. They act very decently and seem very different in their manners from the insolent blusterers who came down on board the steamboats.

Monday, October 14. Beauchamp arrived here Saturday with his beaver traps to make war on those which have their lodges in the creek near us. The following night he had a very good catch. Yesterday I went with him to the willow grove to see him set his traps. He puts them under the water, about four inches from the surface, as I have explained elsewhere. I have said that in order to attract the beaver from this side, he makes a small breach in their dam so that the water can get through. As these industrious masons never fail to inspect their constructions, and after they finish them, to keep them in a constant state of repair, they must, of course, get to work closing the breach, and in so doing they smell the stick rubbed with castoreum, put there to attract one or another of them into the trap. This is what happened, and this morning Beauchamp made a new catch, not counting the two muskrats caught in the two other traps.

[*Muskrat*] The muskrat is the beaver in miniature, except for the tail, which is proportionately longer and of a different shape. The head is the same, the incisors are alike, the body and the paws have the same shape. The front ones are shorter and more slender, equipped with claws to scratch and dig in the earth; the back ones are stronger and longer and have toes with a membrane, which, however, does not connect them, while the back feet of the beaver are completely webbed. The fur of the muskrat is much browner than that of the beaver. It is the size of a fat rabbit. It, too, digs little lodges at the edge of the water, but makes no pretense of erecting dams. The beaver works on a large scale on the trees; the muskrat works on a small scale on willows and small roots. The muskrat does not have the peculiarity in sexual organs that I noticed in the beaver.

[*Heron*] My walk with Beauchamp gave me the chance to kill a very tall heron (blue crane). He measured five feet, less two inches, wing spread, and four feet from his beak to his feet.

[*Swan*] This morning the first swan of the season was killed. It is a wonderful bird, not differing from the tame swans in Central Park in New York, except that its beak does not have a ring of black —perhaps this one was still too young, probably from last spring. The day before yesterday, three of these birds stopped on the opposite bank of the river not far from camp. After staying there about an hour, they continued their flight, and no one tried to approach them. These are the first we have seen this year. They are numerous around Devils Lake, as is every other kind of game, large or small.

Tusday, October 15. Mr. Pease leaves today for the States. He will go to New York and carry a letter to Kinney from me. In two or three months, he will bring back my French hunting rifle, a carbine, and my paint box, on which I depend very much to take up part of my time pleasantly. Bought from Beauchamp three beaver skins for a winter cap, a collar, and a pair of fur gauntlets.

The hostile Indians who committed depredations in the Department of the Plat[t]e during the summer are now coming north, and are establishing their winter camp on the banks of the Missouri: the Cheyennes above Fort Buford, near the Milk River; the Rappahoes,[77] Unkpapahs, and a part of the Blackfeet on this side of Buford, in the neighborhood of the Knife River. The Crows are uncertain, but have committed no act of hostility against the whites as yet, and neither have the Assiniboin, although some of the latter have stolen horses from Mr. Pease, who had some supplies to deliver to Col. Rankin.[78]

The absence of any cavalry in Dakota, and the lack of horses at our posts, which have not yet been furnished with them, will force us to remain on the defensive during the winter, whereas with two squadrons we could sweep clean all the bands wintering on the river, destroy their lodges, capture part of their animals, etc., all the things that are not possible with infantry.

Anniversary of the birth of Lina, who is twenty-two today.[79]

Wednesday, October 16. MacDonald and one of the half-breeds came back from Fort Totten today, bringing the mail. The trip was not without dangers. Dog Den is a bad place to travel across any time. There the terrain is broken by sharp hills and narrow ravines, very favorable to ambuscades. This time the danger was greatly increased by the presence of the Unkpapahs (Error: It was the band of Medicine Bear. See October 18.), hostile Indians who stole five mules from us last week. It seems they lost one of them, for they now have only four. They have there ten or twelve lodges, which means about fifty redskins. This is the band of Black Moon, Four Horns, Red

---

[77] The Arapaho belong to the Algonquian family and are closely associated with the Cheyenne. They are divided into a northern and southern group, but the division is largely geographic. According to tradition, their early home was in the neighborhood of the Red River of the North. Hodge, *Handbook*, 1:72–73. De Trobriand spells the tribal name in a number of ways, usually as "Arrapahoes."

[78] The Crow or Absaroke are a Siouan tribe forming part of the Hidatsa group. They were the traditional enemies of the Dakota. Hodge, *Handbook*, 1:367–368.

Hodge interprets "Assiniboin" as "one who cooks by the use of stones," while Dodge calls them "pot boilers." A Siouan tribe, they were originally a part of the Yanktonai, but they separated early, probably before 1640. When the buffalo were plentiful, their chief occupation was making robes and pemmican. Hodge, *Handbook*, 1:102–104; Richard Irving Dodge. *The Plains of the Great West*, p. xxi. De Trobriand often called them "Assiniboine" and "Assiniboines."

[79] "Lina" is De Trobriand's daughter, Marie Caroline, later Mrs. Charles A. Post.

Horn, and others who have left the band of Bear's Rib to live by plundering and robbing.[80] Now they are hunting in this region, going toward Buford on their way to their winter quarters. Not far from their camp was another camp of Santees, who are allied with the whites and from whom there is nothing to fear. Among the savages were some half-breeds who were selling them Indian whiskey. When, during the night, our two men passed between the two camps, the Unkpapahs were celebrating; that is, drunk, beating the drum, and shaking their gourds, dancing and singing around their fires. If Mac-Donald had had about twenty men with him, it would have been a fine opportunity. The Unkpapahs would have paid dearly for their attack of the other day. But the only use our men could make of the night was to hide their movements from their enemies and get away with the third horse which was carrying the mail. Nevertheless, they talked with the half-breeds, and learned from them that the hostile Unkpapahs had announced their intention of killing on sight anyone they met carrying the mail of the whites, whether they were whites or half-breeds. This threat seemed to make a certain impression on our scouts, so in order to ward off the dangers that threaten our communications with Devils Lake, we are going to transfer our line farther to the west. The advantages of the change are obvious, for we can shift the mail route between Totten and Buford to a station established on the Mouse River, only sixty miles from here. This is half the distance separating us from Fort Totten, and since the country is frequented by hunters from the three tribes and the Assiniboin, it is much safer than the narrow passes of Dog Den.

The plan for the winter was to send from here and from Totten two dog sleds which were to meet halfway and exchange their mail sacks. In adopting the new route, we shall send only one sled from here to the station, and the dogs which are at Fort Totten with their drivers will be transferred here to relieve the worn-out teams or

80 Four Horns, Sitting Bull's uncle, was chosen as one of the four Hunkpapa chiefs in 1850. He was wounded in 1864 when General Sully attacked the Indians at Killdeer mountain. After the Battle of the Little Big Horn, he escaped to Canada, where he remained until he surrendered in 1881. He was a prisoner at Fort Randall until 1883. Stanley Vestal, *New Sources of Indian History*, p. 194.

When Father de Smet went on his mission to the hostile Sioux in 1868, he met Black Moon, Red Horn, and Sitting Bull, the leaders in the hostilities around the posts under De Trobriand's command. In their speeches, and in that of Running Antelope who replied to them, one can see the reasons for the hostilities of this time. Father de Smet includes these speeches in his report to the peace commissioners on this visit to the hostile Sioux. There is a copy of De Smet's report in the papers of John B. Sanborn, Minnesota Historical Society.

to replace the animals which are missing for one reason or another.

Next Monday, MacDonald will leave with three half-breeds to explore the new route, to ascertain the exact position of the station, and to go by there to Devils Lake, from where he will once more bring the mail by the route followed up to now. The Yanktonnas [*sic*], Santees, and Cut Heads are around Totten, camped near the lake and on good terms with the garrison, which has no complaint against them.[81]

In the afternoon, two chiefs came to pay me a visit. One, well known in these regions for his constant attachment to the whites, is Running Antelope, or Cabri Who Runs; the other, who has not yet earned his name, is the last son of Bear's Rib and the chief of the friendly Unkpapahs. Cabri Who Runs is his uncle. (Note: The Canadian-French generally call the antelope "cabri" although the two animals are very different.)

The two Indians were dressed in new blankets and colored woolen shirts, having received their annual presents from Fort Rice, near which their usual residence is located. The uncle had a sort of brown hunting coat, a red silk handkerchief around his neck, and large copper earrings. The nephew had around his shoulders a wide band of red cloth, the ends of which fell almost to the ground, symbol of his dignity, I suppose. His trousers were of blue cloth with a red band decorated with copper buttons in the form of balls sewed transversely three by three. Both had their hair parted in the middle of the forehead and tied on each side from the face in sausages ending, in the case of the nephew, with what seemed to be a marten fur, the same shape as a fox or wolf tail. Both wore on the top of their heads an eagle feather fixed in a little *chignon* that formed their scalp lock.

Bear's Rib, whom the Canadians call in their language Flat Rib of the Bear, has left a great reputation on the Upper Missouri. He was a man of great courage and implacable resolution, faithful to his word, which could be counted on in any circumstance. Old General [William S.] Harney won him over to the whites, and from that time on no ordeal shook his devotion, which finally cost him his life. First he left a part of his tribe (the Unkpapahs) which refused to follow the same line of conduct and persisted in its hostility toward the government. Those who followed him found him to be a harsh judge up to the end. For him, there were no gradations of punishment, and all violations of his orders were punished by death, he

81 The Cut Heads are a small band of Sioux. They signed the treaty of April 29, 1868. Kappler, *Indian Laws and Treaties*, 2:998.

himself performing the execution with a revolver which he always carried in his belt.

Singular examples of this summary justice are related in stories of the undisciplined young people of his band around the military posts, which at this time extended hardly north of Nebraska. At that time there was a bell at Fort Pierre to sound the alarm.[82] One of his men, who was received at the fort with him, got the idea of firing on the bell, and he sent a bullet at it. Old Bear's Rib marched straight to the culprit and, firing his revolver, laid him out dead at his feet. The suppression of theft was no less energetic; indeed it was so vigorous that the stamping out of this activity so dear to all Indians, among whom theft is in good repute, created a hatred in the hearts of some of his warriors which was suppressed only by the fear he inspired.

[*Death of Bear's Rib*] The chief was not unaware of it, and he so fully realized the danger his life was in among his own people that his wives kept a constant watch around his tent, relieving each other in the night like sentinels. He himself never went out without his revolver and a short double-barreled gun; but nothing could shake his inexorable will to make respected the word he had given to the whites, who, in turn, treated him generously, distributing to him provisions, blankets, and munitions. When his young redskins dealt with the traders, they often saw him come to sit near their counter, legs crossed, his head in his hand, not saying a word to anyone, and absorbed in meditative silence. There were neither protests nor disputes. The exchanges were made easily and promptly under the dark eye of the old chief whose anger no one dared provoke. He had killed eight or nine of his people when he finally fell victim to the vengeance he had kindled against himself. It seems that the officers' table had just been served when eight or ten warriors dashed into the room, grabbed the plates, and plundered the dinner. Bear's Rib rushed up, and, forcing his way into the midst of the marauders, stretched one of them out on the floor. Then all of them flew at him and murdered him, but not, however, until he had killed a second and wounded a few.[83]

[82] Fort Pierre, named for Pierre Chouteau, was the chief post of the American Fur Company until 1855. Because of its position in the Sioux country, it controlled the fur trade of the Black Hills and much from the valley of the upper Platte. Bought by the government as a military post, it was rendered useless when Fort Randall was established by General Harney in 1856. *North Dakota Historical Collections*, 1:423.

[83] There is another version of the death of Bear's Rib, chief appointed by General Harney in 1856. It is said that the Sioux became discontented when the government did not carry out the promises made by General Harney and that

Such was the end of Bear's Rib. His murderers fled, I believe, and went to rejoin the hostile part of their tribe. He was buried with full military honors, and since his band left the choice of his successor up to the commandant of the fort, his eldest son was designated and commanded for a time, contrary to Indian custom, by which the choice of a chief is made by election. The eldest son of Bear's Rib died with sickness, and it was then that the young brother of the dead man was called to the command. This is the young chief who paid me a visit today with his uncle, Running Antelope, who exercises over the band an authority analogous to that of a regent, although his nephew is twenty-five years old. But the Indians consider age a guarantee of wisdom and capability; to them youth is ardent and giddy, and this is why guardianship of a young chief sometimes lasts until full maturity.

Beauchamp, who is still here, detained by his beaver hunt, (he caught five and lost two, each of which left a front paw in the trap) knew Bear's Rib very well. He told me a story which illustrates the character of the chief before he made so terrible a reputation as a judge.

[*Beauchamp and Bear's Rib*] Beauchamp had two horses stolen on the prairie while he was in a thicket setting traps at the edge of a stream frequented by beaver. He soon learned beyond a doubt that the animals were in an encampment of Unkpapahs hunting not far from there. He was very attached to his horses, and to him the loss of them was of considerable material importance. So, in spite of the obvious risk he would run in going to get them, in spite of the urgent advice of the Rees to keep him from going, he resolved to take the chance and to go to the Unkpapahs. He got into the camp without any difficulty, and it did not take him long to spot his two horses tied to the door of a lodge. The first thing he did was to put the saddle, which was lying on the ground, on the back of the better of the two horses. The Indian bridle, as you know, is nothing more than a long strip of leather ending in a loop. During these preparations, the thief came up and began to yell. Beauchamp, determined to get back his property at any cost, straddled the animal and cocked his carbine. Other Indians ran up, naturally siding with the thief, and encouraged each other to kill the Pale Face on the spot. That

they murdered Bear's Rib because he was a government appointee. *North Dakota Historical Collections,* 1:426–427; Kingsbury, *History of the Dakota Territory,* 1:255–256.

is probably what would have happened if Bear's Rib, attracted by the noise, had not come up to ask the cause of the uproar. Beauchamp was claiming his horses; the Indian did not want to give them up. The dispute was particularly centered around the second horse, which the chief then took by the bridle and fastened to the door of his own lodge until the facts were further clarified. The thief seized his knife, cut the bridle, and took the horse back to where he had put him first. The chief, calm but menacing, went to unfasten him for the second time and brought him back to his lodge. "Beware," he said to the young Indian, "of touching this horse again."

But the delinquent did not heed the injunction and cut the bridle a second time. Then Bear's Rib reached for his gun, killed the unfortunate animal, the innocent cause of the conflict, and put an end to the strife. Then, falling on the undisciplined warrior, he beat him with a club until he was three-fourths dead, while Beauchamp, taking advantage of the commotion, stole away at full speed, only too happy to withdraw from the squabble with at least his better horse and his own skin.

Such was the man whose last son came today to sit down in my tent. He is a tall young man with a face more melancholy than martial, and with a soft voice that is somewhat of a contrast to his wide shoulders and great height. His uncle, Running Antelope, spoke first in approximately these words:

[*Speech of Running Antelope*] "My father, we have come today from the village of the three tribes to visit the great white chief whom we have heard talked about on the banks of the Missouri, to listen to his words, and to give him our hand as a sign of submission and fidelity. My heart rejoices to see in this country a great chief who commands other chiefs from the rising sun to the setting sun, and to bring him such words of peace and friendship, as the other chiefs before him since the time of White Beard (General Harney) have heard from me. These words are not deceitful; all who have passed on the banks of the Missouri know this. My mouth has never uttered a lie, and my hands have never been stained. Since the day we made an alliance with the Pale Faces, I have always been faithful to them at all times and in all places. The skin of my body is red, but my flesh is white; because for some years, I have eaten the bread of the whites, I have received my nourishment from them, and I have become accustomed to living like them. Others have made treaties and have violated them; one day they have been whites to receive presents, and another day they have stolen their horses or have stained their hands with the blood of travelers on the prairies. But my tongue is pure, and my hands are clean.

"And what I say for myself, I say too for this young son of my brother, Bear's Rib, who lost his life in the cause of the whites.

"All the services I have been able to render to the great chiefs that our Great Father has sent among us I have rendered to them since the days when White Beard, after taking me with him into the upper and lower country, said to me: 'Go among the redskins and carry my words to them, or go among my soldiers and take them my writings.' I have faithfully carried the written word to the blue uniform. To the redskins I have spoken as my father had commanded. Some have made peace and have kept it; others have remained on the plains and have not wanted to listen to my counsels; but still I shall continue to speak to them, if my father so wishes, to lead them to what is just and to observe the peace."

Running Antelope is very intelligent, as his face indicates, and he expresses himself with clarity, accompanying his words with eloquent gestures, as do most of the Indians. I answered with praises for his past conduct which I already knew (this was true), for I had heard of him when I arrived on the Missouri, and I received his visit with so much the more pleasure since I knew him by reputation. In a few words, I made my feelings known to him:

[*Reply*] "I want what is just, and the right will always be the rule of my conduct, constant protection and encouragement to the friendly Indians who keep their word and live in peace and friendship with us, war to the death and exemplary punishment to those who attack us and play a game of deceit and betrayal. For those, punishment can be delayed. Perhaps it will not fall on them in a week, in a month, in a year; but they will not escape it, and I shall settle my accounts with them, without fail, when the forts are built and when the time comes. But the good and honest men, whether they have white skins or red, can count on me to do everything in my power for them, for such is the will of our Great Father, and such is my own inclination."

I need not remark that my comments were received with repeated approving "Hows!" Then I gave the conference the character of a dialogue by asking a series of questions about the hostile faction of the Unkpapahs, about the wintering plans of those in the other band, the number of their lodges (90), and the approach of the Cheyennes, Arrapahoes, and Blackfeet from the direction of Buford.

When this part of the conference was finished, the young chief, who until this time had remained motionless and silent, got up and came over to clasp my hand and to present to me, as his uncle had, the papers he carries, which are certificates of loyalty to the whites, recommendations to the commanders of the military posts, and even orders sent to Bear's Rib by different generals. When I had looked over these different documents, the young chief addressed these words to me:

[*Speech of the young chief*] "My father will listen to my words with indulgence, for I am young and without experience; I have not yet taken a place in the councils among those whom age has made wise or valor has made illustrious. But I have in my heart the feelings that my father, Bear's Rib, put there, and I have in my head the words that he often repeated to me when I was younger. He said to me: 'Whether I live or whether I die, always be a friend of the whites; protect the traveler who crosses the prairies, and our Great Father will protect you. The Great Spirit who has made the white men as numerous in the land of the rising sun as the stars in the sky at night willed that they spread over the plains to live with his red children. It is his will; we must obey him, for he is the father of all men, whatever the color of their skin. The white men will have pity on the red men who live in peace with them. They are generous to your father and to all those who like him have made an alliance with them. They will be generous to you, to your brother, and to your tribe if you remain faithful.' My father died carrying out his own words; my brother died without changing his feelings or conduct. And as for myself, I have never had any other thought. What Bear's Rib has taught me, I shall practice, always following the example he left me. I wanted to assure my father of this, to hear his good words and to feel my heart grow stronger when the great chief spoke."

One can guess what my answer was. It was all laid out. Eulogy to the memory of Bear's Rib, honest and good man, faithful to his word, and devoted to the whites. His merits were reflected in his son, and everything that had not been done to repay him during his too-short life is a debt which will be paid to his son who can always count on our friendship and protection, according to the will of our Great Father.

After renewed thanks on the part of the two Indians and renewed assurances from me, I closed the conference with something more substantial by sending for the commissary of the post. Lieutenant Parsons was an old acquaintance of Running Antelope, and there was a warm exchange of "Hows" and handshakes. I announced to my visitors that the lieutenant had ordered that provisions be given them, and that they could follow him to get them, and as the young chief had asked the interpreter Paquenaud in a low voice if he could not get some pipes of tobacco instead, I added to the provisions two twists of tobacco that I had bought for myself at the sutler's. My two redskin children withdrew, delighted with their new father, of course, and resolved to try new measures during the winter to bring about the submission of the hostile tribes, to whom they will repeat these words.

At the close of the conference, they left for Berthold with Gustave Cagnat and Paquenaud, who had accompanied them here.

[*Indian children*] While I am on the subject of Indians, I might mention a peculiarity of Indian women which should have had a place in the account of my visit to Berthold: the extraordinary way in which they bring their children into the world. The fact will seem unbelievable to our civilized ladies, but it is strictly and absolutely true. The Indian women, burdened, as we have seen, with all the rough work that among other peoples is left to the men, do not stop any of their activities during their period of pregnancy. Up to the last moment, they go after wood, carry the burdens, and take care of the horses. When the pains come, they stop and give birth to their child wherever they are, wash themselves and the baby if there is water near by, and return to the lodge, carrying their papoose upon their load. The next day they take up their work again as if nothing had happened. If the thing happens in the winter, they will break the ice to proceed with the washing of the child and themselves in ice water, and the mother and the child seem to be only the better for it! The fact is so well known, so well authenticated, that there can be no doubt of it. This is what mother nature does for her children. Let us compare this with what civilization does for hers: long torture, medical attendance, intervention of chloroform, puerperal fever, two weeks in bed, thirty days in the bedroom, and such precautions. And the indispensable cares! We have made for ourselves in society not only a conventional life, but an artificial constitution. Physically and morally, we have corrupted the work of nature, and our women sometimes die in childbirth and are always martyrized. The Indian woman gathers up her baby on the prairie and goes on her way.

The children do not seem to be affected by it, for they are generally robust and well formed. It can even be contended with some degree of certainty that infirm or crippled children are much more rare among the Indians than among us. Some years ago, a child of repulsive ugliness lived among the Gros Ventres. I do not believe that Indian women are very susceptible to feeling violent emotions during their pregnancy, but for one reason or another, one of them had brought into the world a boy whose round and wild eyes were placed on the sides of his head like those of a hare. The unfortunate one had no nose of human form, but a sort of cavity divided in the middle of his face—in a word, the head of a monster. Otherwise he was well formed physically, and his intelligence was not inferior to that of other children. He grew to the age of thirteen or fourteen under the burden of general revulsion, and repeated manifestations of which made him aware that his horrible ugliness made everyone look upon him as an object of antipathy and scorn. Life became a burden to him at an age when such feeling is usually unknown, and he hated it as an evil that he wished to be rid of as soon as possible. The chance for deliverance that he seemed to have been waiting for came one day, and he did not let it slip away.

He had gone with some other children of his age to take horses to the pasture when hostile Sioux ambushed in the neighborhood suddenly appeared. His companions immediately hid in the brush to get back to the village, and, as he made no move to follow them, they cried to him, "Hurry up. Hide or they will see you and kill you for sure." And he, straightening himself up to his full height, said: "It is what I want. Run and leave me here. I am too ugly to live. I can do nothing with life for myself or for others. It is good that I die and I am waiting for them to come to kill me."

They did not fail to do so. While most of the plunderers took possession of the horses, some ran toward the child who stalwartly awaited them, and whether his monstrous ugliness increased their natural ferocity or whether they attached some superstitious idea to it, instead of killing him on the spot, they took him out on the prairie some distance away, and there cut him up in pieces while he still lived. Those who saw that horrible execution from a distance heard no cry, and the child endured the torture to the end without complaint or struggle, like certain tribal heroes whose memories live on in the tribes. Finally death delivered the soul from its odious prison, and the body, hacked up by the butchers, was buried by those who pitied him, but who did not mourn him. His physical ugliness was a shame to the tribe, but there was a valiant heart and a proud courage under that monstrous exterior.

147

Friday, October 18. The band of Medicine Bear went by camp today on their way to Berthold. This is the band which MacDonald and the scout noticed near Dog Den, and which they took for the Unkpapahs. These savage simpletons had a good hunt. They had a number of buffalo skins and a quantity of meat when they were unfortunate enough to meet the half-breeds and their horrible whiskey. They did not fail to get drunk, and they had a night of debauchery; but while they were drunk, their furs passed into the hands of the half-breeds who got them for a few bottles of poison. So they have little left, and they go crestfallen back to Berthold to get some munitions and to take up the hunt again.

Right now there are hostile Indians at Berthold who have come to trade horses for corn and probably powder, if they find a way to get it. They have come in great numbers, crossing the river by swimming with their horses or with bull boats. Mr. Pease sent us warning that they intended to cross the river in force to attack us. Let them come, and they will get a good reception. We are on our guard, and we are keeping watch on the teams sent to bring in the timber, for an Indian attack means a surprise move to steal mules or cattle. As for attacking the camp, that would be the greatest pleasure they could give us; but unless they have lost their senses, they will not be so stupid. They must have been successful in their stealing this summer, for according to reports arriving from Berthold, they are well armed with guns or carbines, and fully supplied with ammunition, horses, and mules.

The wagon escort is reinforced every day by men relieved from guard duty at eight o'clock in the morning, which brings the total force of the escort to more than fifty men.

Saturday, October 19. Foggy day. Cold, penetrating wind from the N.E. Mr. Wilkinson, government agent for the friendly tribes of this district, came back from Buford, where he had gone to begin the distribution of the annual presents to the tribes. The steamboats are not coming down any more, and he had to embark on a Mackinaw to get back to Berthold, his residence. There he made the distribution to the three tribes, who, having received their presents, will leave for their winter encampment one of these days.

[*Indian corn storage*] One would expect that they would leave their provision of corn in storage under guard of some of their people. They do not do this. Their way of keeping the grain they intend for trade is much more original and completely Indian. After each family has harvested and husked its corn, the men go at night beyond the limits of the village to dig a hiding place, a location that they choose with care. This hiding place, of course, is usually in a thicket and always in dry ground where the rise of the water and the rain cannot damage the contents. The hole is round and as narrow as possible. The inside capacity is measured by the amount of grain to be buried. The inner sides as well as the bottom are very clean and lined with hay woven into mats. So it is here that they come as secretly as possible to hide their grain without being seen. They close the opening carefully and cover it with earth, leaves, and grass with such cleverness that nothing betrays the location to the eye. When they leave the village for their winter encampment, they leave the corn in these hiding places which are very hard to find.

However, it often happens, accidentally or otherwise, that they find someone else's hiding place, and the result is that they steal from each other. If the thief is caught in the act, he runs a serious risk of being killed on the spot by the owner, for such thefts take place only in the night; but if the theft is discovered after it is done, the family arranges to make full amends for the theft, *damages and interest*. Among the Indians, there are only two punishments, death or damages. The alternative is resorted to in every possible case, including murder. Gradation consists only in the importance of the damage. So much for stolen corn; so much for a horse stolen or crippled; so much for a man killed. Only, in the last case, the damages go to the family rather than to the victim.

When Running Antelope saved the lives of Gerard, Paquenaud, and two other whites, there was a fight between those who wanted to kill them and those who wanted to protect them. The latter were the stronger, since they killed two or three of their adversaries. On the basis of this, it seemed just that Gerard give two good American horses, not to those who had saved him, but to the ones who had attacked him, to pay for the lives of those who had perished. Their blood being thus atoned for, all idea of vengeance vanished, and there was no more question of a difficulty among the survivors.

Sunday, October 20. The steamboat *Amaranth* arrived today on her way to Buford. Since she had no freight for us, she stopped only a minute to unload the mail and four officers rejoining the regiment: Captain and Mrs. Hill and lieutenants [Oskaloosa M.] Smith and [William E.] Hoffmann [Hofman] going to Fort Totten where their companies are stationed, and Lieutenant Stevens F. Norvell, who remains at general headquarters as assistant inspector general of the district. The mail brought by the *Amaranth* is the best we have had. For my share, I received a batch of twenty-two personal letters and four numbers of the *Army and Navy Journal.* My afternoon was pleasantly passed in going through that correspondence, among which are some letters dated two months back.

Monday, October 21. First real freeze of the season. The pond, which is formed by Douglas Creek near camp, was completely frozen this morning. It is still cold this evening. If the wind stays in the north, it is possible that we can begin the skating season in a few days.

Tuesday, October 22. The *Deer Lodge* has returned as she said she would. She came to Berthold loaded with the annual presents for the allied tribes. She should have brought me the rest of my furniture. Unfortunately, the person entrusted with buying it and sending it to me was gone from Omaha when the *Deer Lodge* passed there. This mishap postpones until next spring the arrival of the furniture I was expecting. The delay is not important, since my quarters will not be finished this winter and since I shall extend the hospitality of my unfinished quarters to several unmarried officers, who will furnish them themselves.

The Mackinaws are still coming down the river. Four or five passed today.

Three Rees from Berthold came in a bull boat. More of their horses were stolen by the Sioux and so these three have gone on the warpath to do the same to their enemies and to steal from them what horses they can, not by main force, but in the night and through trickery. Of course they are risking their hides, or more precisely, their scalps, if they are discovered. So they are armed, two with guns, and one with bow and arrows, not to mention knives. I had some provisions given to them, and in the night they re-embarked in their buffalo skin, going down the river to the hunting district where there are some bands of Sioux now. If they succeed, they will come back riding across the prairies where they will find plenty of game. If they fail, the odds are strong that they will never come back.

Wednesday, October 23. The *Deer Lodge* went by here returning to St. Louis.[84] She brought some potatoes and onions which we

[84] On November 15 the *St. Paul Daily Pioneer* reported that the steamer *Deer Lodge* was bringing from Fort Benton $2,000,000 in gold dust.

have been without for some time. Also two armchairs for which the captain and the clerk refused to take any payment. Forced gift.

Thursday, October 24. Steamboats have come one after another since we stopped expecting them. This morning the *Lady Grace* arrived, loaded with grain for the winter feeding of our cattle and those of Fort Totten. In addition, she brought us ample reserves of biscuits, from which the Indians will profit more than we, for we are well provided with flour, and our men eat very good bread. Yesterday, in the afternoon, the men from the steamboat, noticing a band of from one hundred to one hundred and fifty antelope on a point where it was easy to cut off their retreat, landed and spread out across the peninsula with their carbines. In this way, they killed twelve of these animals, a good bag and one from which I profited, for the captain offered me for my table one of these antelope all dressed and ready to cook. This is a very welcome provision, and one that came just in time.

[*False alarm*] Speaking of antelope, we had a comic alert today because of these animals. A number of them coming down a ravine to feed on the rolling plain were sighted by some of our men, who in the distance took them for hostile Indians. Since their report was confirmed by some officers who were also deceived when they saw these animals follow one by one the bottom of the ravine like Indians on the march, the camp was under arms in a minute. The cannon were turned to the points where they expected to see the redskins emerge, and as we had at this moment five or six wagons loaded with hay coming from the haystack, the men relieved from guard this morning were sent on foot under the command of the officer of the day to reinforce the escort. The half-breed scouts left on the gallop; the detachment deployed themselves in skirmish line as they approached the first rise of ground, behind which their enemies were supposed to be gathered. The cattle were immediately herded into the corral, and the ladies took their places near one of the pieces to help in the fight. However, I had trained my spyglass over all the corners and ravines of the chain of hills and the plain without seeing anything suspicious there. I then followed the course of one of our scouts who galloped straight to the ridge, reached the crest, disappeared on the flat land behind, and soon emerged on the flank of a second hill, disappeared again, and finally, still on the gallop and going in the same direction, gained the summit of the highest hills. If there were Indians around there, he would have to conceal himself well or be quickly surrounded. Finally the scout dismounted, and we saw him holding his horse by the bridle, advancing cautiously, and almost crawling in order not to be seen. What did he intend to do? It was soon explained to us, and the whole mystery was solved by the reappearance of the antelope, which, having noticed our man, reappeared, escaping along the ravines and over the ridges of the distant horizon. Everyone began to laugh and returned to his tent more or less disappointed.

The wagons and ambulance, which were sent to Fort Buford the sixth of this month with lieutenants Hogan and Leonard in company with the escort of the cattle, returned today. Since Lieutenant Ellis is a member of a court-martial, he was not able to return with them. He will report to his new post at Fort Stevenson by steamboat, if he gets a chance to do so before he is relieved of his temporary functions, or by land with an escort which will be furnished to him for that purpose.

Friday, October 25. The *Lady Grace,* having unloaded her freight at the wharf, left again this morning, but to our great surprise, to go up the river instead of down. Either she is going to cut a supply of wood in the direction of Berthold or she is going to meet the *Imperial,* whose coming was announced. In fact, toward the middle of the day she returned to moor at our wharf, and a quarter of an hour later the *Imperial* was doing likewise. The latter is a big, heavy steamboat which left Fort Benton more than two months ago and which a hundred delays have kept en route all this time. She is overloaded with passengers and carries more than three hundred miners from Montana. The water is so low that she has been stopped twenty times by sand bars through which it took days to force a passage. During this time, the provisions were giving out. Then she had to stop at points where game was plentiful and land a party of passengers armed with carbines who came back on board only after they had killed a number of buffalo, deer, and antelope. She got under way once more and stopped again when the provisions were exhausted, without ever being sure that the hunt would be successful. They bought what they could at Fort Buford; but for three hundred men it was little or nothing, and thus, with delay and trouble, they got to Fort Stevenson after a trip of nine weeks, whereas they ought to have been en route only two or three weeks. The *Lady Grace,* knowing how things were on board the *Imperial,* waited for her to take on those passengers who did not mind the additional expense and who would give up their passage paid in advance on the *Imperial* to take another on the *Lady Grace* under quite different conditions of comfort and speed. This is, in effect, what happened, but for only a small number. After a two- or three-hour stop, the two boats got under way again.

Scarcely had they disappeared around the bend of the river when the smoke of the *Benton* was sighted in that direction. This is a steamboat loaded with merchandise for the sutlers and traders. She was announced so long ago and did not show up that her coming this season was given up. Finally, she has arrived. She brings nothing for the garrison directly, but a good deal indirectly by completely restocking the stores of Mr. Marsh, where we shall find much more to buy from now on. She left this morning for Berthold where she will leave what he couldn't find a place for here in this new and limited establishment.

Saturday, October 26. Captain Hill and his wife with their servant, and lieutenants Smith and Hoffman, left this morning for Devils Lake, going to their post with an escort of twelve men and a sergeant. They took along seven wagons and an ambulance which are transferred to Fort Totten from where we shall soon receive a new convoy sent to transport the grain left here for that post by the *Lady Grace.*

Sunday, October 27. I have abandoned my two big tents which have become too cold for the season, especially during the night when the fire in the stove goes out. In place of this, I have had built a small house of boards with a door and a window and two tarpaulins for roofing, superimposed, but separated by a space of four or five inches. The whole thing is held up by rafters. With a floor and a stove, I am completely sheltered from the cold and wind. I do not mention rain, which is a rare thing in this fine climate. Today, for example, it was splendid, and the air was so agreeably warmed by the rays of the sun that not a fire has been lighted all day. With a slight variation of temperature, the days have been much alike for two or three weeks. The fact is that the month of October has been as fair and agreeable as in any other part of the United States where it is the most charming month in the year.

Monday, October 28. The days follow one another, but are always different. Yesterday, superb weather, warm and brilliant sun. Today, disagreeable and glacial. We awakened to snow that the north

wind carried through the air and swept onto the prairie. The countryside was covered with its white shroud. It isn't winter yet, but this
is the forerunner of it. In the afternoon, the sky brightened up; but
the cold became more intense. The wind stays in the north, which is
far from forecasting a modification of temperature.

(Birth of Marco and Zampa!)[85]

Tuesday, October 29. The *Amaranth* passed by here, returning
from Fort Buford. The steamboat stopped only a few minutes at the
wharf to unload the baggage that Lieut. Norwell had left at his post
when he went on leave. Now his post is at general headquarters as
assistant inspector general of the district.

[*Trouble at Fort Buford*] A very serious affair occurred at Fort
Buford, where Captain (Bt. Colonel) Rankin is commanding the post
in the absence of the lieutenant colonel. It seems that while Lieutenant (Bt. Major) Little was drunk, he gravely insulted his superior,
and went so far as to strike him and knock him down. The charges
and specifications have been addressed immediately in order that
General Terry, who commands the Department, can order a court-
martial. I am going to send on the papers with the recommendation
that the trial be held as soon as possible. This is the outcome of
drunkenness, too common among the officers of the army. But I shall
eradicate this vice from my regiment, or I shall not be able to do
a thing.

Thursday, October 31. The steamboat *Zeffa* finally arrived from
up river. She is the last of the steamboats which went up the river at
the beginning of summer. Her trip has been as endless as the series
of her accidents. It seems that there is no sand bar on which she has
not been stuck. At one time, she and the *Imperial* found themselves
in such a position that it was believed that there was no way to get
them out. Nevertheless, in one way or another, they dug a passage to
the channel, and now they will be able to get to St. Louis before the
river is closed by ice. Above Fort Stevenson, there is now only the
Benton, which has gone to carry some provisions to Buford for the
sutler and will be back a few days from now. After that we shall not
see the smoke of any steamer on the horizon until spring.

[*The Rankin–Little affair*] Lieutenant Ellis arrived on the *Zeffa.*
The scene between Bt. Col. Rankin and Bt. Major Little did not occur in his presence, but in a neighboring tent. Consequently he was

able to hear the noise of the dispute which had no witness other than Captain Clark[e], in whose tent it took place, and Lieutenant Hogan, officer of the day. Both Rankin and Little were drunk. With Rankin it is habitual; with Little it is occasional. Both of them had wine, or rather, bad whiskey, and were quarrelsome. They had met half an hour before in this condition, and Lieutenant Little reproached Captain Rankin for certain illegal transactions, such as the sale for his own profit of rations to the Mackinaws. Upon which Rankin ordered Little to go to his tent, under arrest, to which the latter replied that he would rather be damned than go. Rankin sent out for the officer of the day (Hogan), and gave him the order to inform Little that he was under arrest. In half an hour, he himself went to see if his order had been carried out, and he found that Little had gone to Captain Clarke's quarters and had not obeyed the orders of the officer of the day any better than he had those of the commandant of the post. The scene took place there; the dispute between the two officers led to blows, and Captain Rankin sent his charges and specifications against his subordinate: 1. For disobeying orders; 2. For conduct unbecoming to an officer and a gentleman in treating him, Rankin, as a thief stealing from the government and as a damned scoundrel; 3. For violating article nine of the articles of war which says that "any officer or soldier who strikes his superior officer or who draws or lifts an arm against him or who does him violence in the execution of his duty under any pretext, or who disobeys a legal order of his superior officer will be punished by death, or whatever other penalty, according to the nature of the offense, will be inflicted on him by the sentence of a court-martial."

From another quarter I have learned that Lieutenant Little has signed and sent charges and specifications against Captain Rankin for appropriating government funds and other crimes of this sort. If these facts are true, the abuse of whiskey will at least have had the advantage of ridding the regiment of two unworthy officers, provided that the court-martial does its duty and that the President of the United States does not intervene unwarrantedly to turn aside the course of justice.

Today the garrison mustered for pay.

Friday, November 1. Beauchamp came from Berthold to bring me two beaver skins that I had ordered from him. I learned through him that the Indians of the three tribes had been scandalously robbed by the agent charged with distributing the annual presents to them. This is nothing unusual, and it can even be said that it is the general custom on all frontiers. If one were to go to the heart of the matter, he would find that the hostilities of most of the tribes and the troubles that result from them are hardly more than the result of the notorious bad faith with which the agents steal from them the greatest part of the annuities sent by the government. In regard to the three tribes, this is what happened, according to Beauchamp:

[*Robbery by Indian agents*] The agent Wilkinson had kept the presents to be distributed in storage for some months, and it was difficult for the poor redskins, who had no access to the storehouse, to feel assured that the merchandise was still intact. But they posted a guard outside at night, and several times their sentinels are sure they heard the noise of hammers and the opening of boxes at an hour when it might be supposed that everyone in the village was asleep. Then when some of the employees of the traders of the fort appeared in new flannel shirts, they said: "You can subtract those shirts from our annuity." Perhaps they were mistaken, but it is improbable.

Then one of the steamboats (the *Deer Lodge*) came to Berthold with the rest of the annuities, consisting of provisions, dried meat, hams, sacks of flour, blankets, cutlery. The merchandise was unloaded under the eyes of the Indians who flocked to the bank. They themselves could state the number of boxes or sacks of different kinds, and they decided that the distribution would be made right there. Nothing could be more convenient; but, in spite of their entreaties and protests, the agent ordered that all the merchandise should first be carried to the fort and there be put in storage, where he guarded it two nights and a day. When the time for the distribution finally came, the boxes had been opened and a great many were only half full. The boxes of knives, which were full when they arrived, had lost a third of their contents. Some blue shirts trimmed in red had disappeared; some sacks of flour marked "U.S." with the government stamp had been replaced by sacks without a mark containing scrapings, residue from the traders' stores. The number of blankets was greatly reduced. In this case, White Shield, chief of the Rees, refused to sign or recognize a receipt in full for the presents sent by the Great Father from Washington. The agent was furious, and on his own authority declared him deposed from the dignity of chief, and replaced him with a young man of the tribe, without even paying him his annuity, amounting to two hundred dollars.

[*Complicity of the traders*] Now, if you ask me what has become of the merchandise stolen from the Indians, I can give but one answer: The day before yesterday, an eight- or ten-wagon convoy left Berthold for Devils Lake where the merchandise they carry is intended to be sold to the Indians who frequent that post.

Question: Where does this merchandise come from? And if it legitimately belongs to the Berthold traders, agents of the Northwest Fur Company, why this transfer to Fort Totten? Aren't there tribes at Berthold that they could trade with as well as elsewhere? Especially considering that Mr. Pease, one of them, must bring a convoy of merchandise to Totten from St. Paul where he has gone for this purpose. All this seems very transparent to me and fully confirms what has been told me and repeated everywhere on the Indian frontier and elsewhere; that is: the agents of the Indian Bureau are nothing more than members of a vast association of thieves who make their fortune at the expense of the redskins and to the detriment of the government. They accept an annual salary of fifteen hundred dollars, and at the end of a few years they return to the States, having done their business. You know what that means.[86]

[*The Indian Bureau*] There is only one remedy for this evil: transfer all the administration of Indian affairs to the War Department; replace the agents with quartermasters from the frontier posts under control of higher authorities, and then the government will save millions and will easily live in peace with the Indians. But when will they adopt this remedy? It has been proposed and strongly recommended and supported in Congress and elsewhere. But the whole interested association of plunderers combined made a fuss, and using every means, legal or illegal, has been able to keep themselves in, despite every effort and all the proofs gathered about their malfeasance. Living by corruption, the Indian Bureau maintains itself by corruption, and God only knows when Congress will shake loose from its venal influence and put an end to its career of spoliation.

Saturday, November 2. Around noon, the snow began to fall; it fell continuously all the rest of the day; it is still falling while I am writing these lines before retiring.

85 Marco and Zampa are De Trobriand's dogs.

86 Bishop Henry B. Whipple, in his report of 1868 to the Board of Missions, said that a salary of $1,500 was not enough to support a family in the Indian country far from supply centers; that the government selects the agent to reward him for political work and then sends him into the Indian country "knowing he will & must steal." Whipple Papers. Minnesota Historical Society.

Monday, November 4. Winter has definitely made its entry on the scene. Yesterday, the weather cleared up; but the cold was very keen, and by evening the snow had enveloped the whole country in its white shroud of sparkling crystals, which it has kept since. Last night was still colder. This morning the thermometer went down to fourteen degrees Fahrenheit (ten degrees below zero centigrade).

Douglas Creek is frozen; but the Missouri is not filled with drift ice yet.

This afternoon, the *Benton* came back from Fort Buford and stopped only a minute to deliver some mail and take on board the masons and some other civilian workmen whom the quartermaster dismissed for the winter. This time she is absolutely and irrevocably the last steamboat of the season. There are no others on the upper river now, and there are none starting the trip up. This one was hurrying, pressed by the fear of being caught by the ice; and in fact, if the weather continues, she hasn't an hour to lose.

The mail she brought us from Fort Buford contains five charges and twenty-one specifications signed by Lieutenant Little against Captain Rankin. They include conduct inimical to good order and military discipline; conduct unworthy of an officer and a gentleman; misappropriation of government funds; violation of such and such an article of war, etc. There are in the specifications a number of deeds of indecency and rascality, and, according to certain details, it seems that Little acted in self-defense when he knocked down the drunken Rankin who insulted him and struck him only because he, Rankin, was drunk. The court-martial will decide the case. In the meantime, I am sending an order which puts Captain Rankin under arrest and relieves him of his command. By seniority, Captain Clarke will take his place. He is a good officer, and very strict and attentive to the details of service. The change will be all for the good. He will name a quartermaster for the post, because Rankin, for a very obvious reason, arranged things in such a way that he held both the positions of quartermaster of the post and commandant, which, moreover, is permitted by military rules.[87]

Tuesday, November 5. The cold is increasing. This morning at seven o'clock, the thermometer had gone down to four degrees Fahrenheit (a little more than fifteen degrees below zero centigrade). We

[87] The charges and specifications are listed in a letter from De Trobriand to Lt. Col. Ed. W. Smith, Department of Dakota, St. Paul, November 5, 1867. Department of Dakota, War Records Division, National Archives.

went to look at the ice in Douglas Creek, and we decided to wait a day or two yet before going out there with our skates.

A mile and a half from camp we have a rich coal mine which is easily accessible. Literally, it is only a matter of stooping down to gather it up, the top beds being even with the ground on the slope of the ravine. This coal, which is extracted in hunks with a pick, is of excellent quality and very pure. It burns easily and is all consumed into cinders. It is providentially fortunate for us and is used in all our stoves. The fuel is ten times easier to get this way than if we had to send out people to cut green wood or to gather dead wood on the sand bars four or five miles from here or on the other side of the river. Economy of time, workmen, and steadier and longer lasting fires. This is what we gain by it. Such a coal mine in the States would be an enormous fortune for the lucky owner or owners. Here, it belongs to everyone, and since it is located on the reserve of the fort, the garrison takes possession of it, and exploits it for its own use without a cent of cost to the government for which, on the contrary, it is a saving of a considerable sum.[88]

Wednesday, November 6. The ice is strong enough on the pond formed by Douglas Creek below the fort. So we have inaugurated the skating season in superb weather and moderate cold.

Thursday, November 7. The cold is becoming much less severe, but not enough to harm the skating, which is excellent. Those of us who indulge in this exercise devoted the whole morning to it.

[*The annuities affair*] In the afternoon, Gustave Cagnat came to see me. Gerard had already paid me a visit yesterday. Both, you remember, are traders at Fort Berthold. Gerard confirmed for me, in general, the report of Beauchamp, although with some remarkable variations in his details. Now, Gustave, questioned by me, affirmed that there are some gross exaggerations. He declares that in his presence, the agent Wilkinson asked explicitly and repeatedly the old chief of the Rees not for a receipt in full but for a receipt to account for the goods he had received, taking care to explain the difference

[88] On his trip up the Missouri in 1872, Thomas P. Roberts, assistant engineer for the Northern Pacific Railroad, noted the coal bluffs about eight miles above the Big Knife River. Above this point, he reported that they were quite common and that coal for Fort Stevenson was being mined about ten miles up. Dr. Matthews says that the coal mined for Fort Stevenson was good fuel, but that it burned rapidly and disintegrated when exposed to the air. Thomas P. Roberts, *Report of a Reconnaissance up the Missouri River in 1872*, p. 12; *Report on Barracks and Hospitals*, p. 397.

to him through the interpreter Pierre Gareau. He explains the deficit of part of the presents in this way: the first steamboat which was loaded with them in the spring accidentally foundered in the river; the sugar was dissolved; provisions were spoiled; others were lost. The agent had to make a new requisition to replace them. That was only partially filled, as the letter of advice that Wilkinson showed Gustave proves. Thus, instead of two boxes of hunting knives, only one arrived; the same with the blankets. The old chief, ill-advised and urged on (according to Gustave) by whites who have a bad influence over him, (Beauchamp and Gerard, I suppose) obstinately refused to give a receipt even for the said merchandise, and would have consented of himself to give his position to the second chief, Son of the Star, who was replaced by the chief of the warriors, Iron Bear. The following dialogue was exchanged between White Shield and the agent:

Agent: "My friend, you are getting too old; age troubles the brain, and you speak and act like an old fool."

Chief: "I am old, it is true; but not old enough to fail to see things as they are. And even, as you say, if I am now just an old fool, I should still prefer a hundred times to be an honest red fool than a thieving white scamp like you."

Not bad for a savage.

Only in his anger, old White Shield seemed to have declared that the command caused him more trouble and weariness than satisfaction and that he was willing to resign it, or something like this, and Wilkinson would have taken him at his word.

All this seems very involved to me, and I see only two things clearly: first, that as a result of commercial competition, Gerard and Cagnat are enemies, the former having the Rees as special clients, and the latter the Gros Ventres and Mandans; second, Cagnat makes common cause with the agent Wilkinson, and Gerard has Beauchamp as an employee, who, being the son-in-law of the old Ree chief, backs up his interests and prejudices.

However it may be, the business is not under military jurisdiction. A report has been addressed in the name of the Rees to Father de Smith [Smet], Catholic priest who is very influential among these native tribes with whom he lived for a long time. The Father is now in Washington and is prepared to bring the report to the attention of the Secretary of the Interior in whose department the Indian Bureau operates, and even to the attention of the President. I am rather curious to see what will come of it.

The wind from the northwest which had come up in the afternoon grew stronger and stronger toward evening. It was mixed with squalls of hail, snow, and rain during part of the night.

Friday, November 8. This morning the weather had cleared up; but the wind still blew in a gale. Its violence increased rather than diminished toward midday; the temperature continued to fall, the sky darkened, and soon the atmosphere was filled with a fine snow driven violently by the wind. The little flakes got thicker and thicker, and the storm raged all the rest of the day. This evening it is roaring outside, shaking my canvas roof, and blowing down tents in its fury. The snow is gathering in drifts wherever it is pushed by a whirlwind into the shelter of any obstacle which stands against the wind from the north. So the doors of our cabins facing south are blocked with it, and probably tomorrow the ravines will be filled. But my stove is roaring; my lamp burns steadily; and my warm plank cabin seems twice as comfortable to me. On the other hand, in such weather our work does not progress, and the soldier suffers in his none-too-snug tent. That's the other side of the medal.

Saturday, November 9. Bitter cold; violent wind. Today I saw at the sutler's a magnificent eagle killed by one of his people with a carbine. His wingspread measured seven feet and one inch. His claws are extraordinarily long and powerful. When he was killed out on the prairie near the badlands, he was fighting savagely with another eagle the same size. This is not a white-headed eagle; his head is brown like the upper part of his body and his powerful wings. The tail feathers are white and dark at the ends.[89] These are the feathers that are especially sought after by the Indians for head decoration. To them, the tail of an eagle killed is worth three buffalo robes.

Sunday, November 10. During a very cold night, the Missouri has become covered with blocks of ice. It drifted all day and completely froze in the shallow water where the current is not so swift. The weather is clear, the air calm; but the thermometer is not rising very much.

Monday, November 11. Part of the Black Catfish band of the Yanktonah tribe has arrived here.[90] They came from Fort Rice where they found but little game, and this induced them to go back up

89 This bird is the golden eagle.
90 The depredations of Black Cat Fish and his band in the vicinity of Fort Rice (1864–1866) are recounted in the diary of William L. Larned, p. 49, 51, 52.

north to winter near the buffalo range. They have their women and children with them, and they have put up their lodges for two or three days near Douglas Creek on the edge of the woods. In all, there are hardly more than twenty-five or thirty of them.

Tuesday, November 12. The promised thaw has arrived, not with fog and rain as in New York, but under a clear sky and a brilliant sun. Under the power of its rays, the ice began to melt everywhere, and on the river it is shrinking noticeably in thickness and quantity.

[*Mail stations*] Yesterday morning, in accordance with my orders of the evening before, a group of six soldiers under a sergeant and four half-breed scouts left with two wagons filled with rations, forage, and necessary implements to build log cabins. These cabins are to be located at indicated points, and will serve the mail carriers between Totten and Stevenson as shelters during the night, or in case of a snowstorm, during the day. They are to be constructed: 1. At Cold Water; 2. At Dog Den; 3. At Bass Island. This last station will be halfway. It is here that the two couriers who start from the two extremities of the line will meet the evening of the next day following their departure; they will set out on the route regularly on the first, tenth, and twentieth of each month. While my six men and two of the scouts start building the first station, the two other scouts, loaded with the mail, will go on to Fort Totten, with my orders. The day after they arrive, the commandant of the fort will send out a party of ten men and a sergeant who with the scouts of the fort will go to work building an intermediary station—two, perhaps—between Bass Island and Totten. The work will be finished before the end of the month, and the regular service which will bring us letters and papers three times a month will begin December 1.

Thursday, November 14. The Yanktonahs want to winter near the fort on the edge of Douglas Creek; they offered to scout the neighborhood and inform us of the approach of any hostile band, if such should be the case. They will scour the country in all directions on their hunting expeditions, and they can be of some use to us. In return, all they want are some provisions from time to time, which is easy to grant them since they are so few. Two of them have been given the job of going to Fort Rice to bring back the letters and papers which must have been there for us since the passage of the last steamboat and which came by way of forts Abercrombie and Wadsworth or by Sioux City, Randall, and Sully. They left this morning with a mule to carry their provisions and a sack for the letters.

The plan for the officers to move into their permanent lodgings this winter has been definitely given up. It would take too long to make the two unfinished houses habitable; the others have nothing finished but their stone foundations. So we are going to build log houses as temporary lodgings for the officers and offices for the different branches of the service as well as for the musicians. The two quarters for the company, the hospital, and the storehouse are the only ones far enough along to be definitely occupied next month.

Wednesday, November 20. Anniversary of the birth of Beatrice.[91] She is seventeen years old today. How time flies!

Monday, the day before yesterday, a band of Yanktonahs arrived here. It is the band of Black Eyes, a chief known for his fidelity to the whites and the services he has rendered on various occasions. Thus— some years ago, I believe—several whites had just been captured by a party of hostile Santees when Black Eyes, who was near there with warriors, attacked the Santees, defeated them, and rescued the prisoners, perhaps saved their lives. He even furnished one of them with a horse to get back to St. Paul and get the necessary assistance there.

[*Yanktonahs in camp*] Black Eyes is accompanied by about twenty braves and ten women and children. As they approached the camp, they arranged themselves in battle lines on the plain, all mounted, and rode forward singing in chorus a song of peace. Then they filed one by one behind the tents to go into camp on Douglas Creek, near the lodges of the little band of Big Hand who belongs to the same tribe. There is nothing more picturesque on the prairie than these bands of mounted Indians. A genre painter would find in them a series of striking pictures, without changing anything, modifying, diminishing, or adding to nature. The vigorous manner of the redskins, their dark, thick hair falling down on their shoulders, their varied head ornaments, the bright and sometimes violent colors of their striped blankets, their buffalo skins, the ornamentation of their saddles and arms, the appearance of their lean ponies—all these form on the immense level perspective of the prairie picturesque groups which are far removed from the subjects furnished by the life of civilized countries.

Yesterday, Tuesday, on going into the sutler's cabin to make some little purchases, I found about fifteen Indians gathered there,

91 Beatrice is De Trobriand's second daughter.

among whom were Black Eyes, his brother, Howkah, and the leader of his warriors whose name means "The One Who Wears Beautiful Things." Among these beautiful things, I immediately noticed a certain jacket ornamented profusely with little copper buttons which had attracted my attention when I came up the Missouri to my post. I had noticed it on the back of the owner, who at that time had no other clothing but a flimsy loincloth. Today he was completely dressed, with necklaces, head ornaments of porcupine quills, and copper rings. The chief (Black Eyes) had an antelope-skin jacket worked in porcupine quills of different colors. Howkah (The One Around Whom They Sing) was notable only for a soldier's hat decorated in the front with a copper bugle and a pair of blue glasses set in a frame of the same color, such as are worn by people who have bad eyes to keep them from contact with the air or from the effect of light. Moreover, these glasses are a great help to the eyes in winter when the sun shines on the snow-covered plains. But the idea of wearing them as decoration for a hat was an original touch that was completely Indian.

[*Accidental interview*] After I had spoken a few words to the sutler, Black Eyes asked one of the people who understood Sioux who I was, and when he found out that I was the great chief who commands other chiefs, there was a commotion among his followers, and Black Eyes came forward, offered me his hand, and greeted me with the indispensable "How!" Howkah did likewise, and The Man Who Wears Beautiful Things, who is also called Black Cat, then greeted me in the same way. There followed a short, broken conversation, rather badly interpreted by one of the employees of the quartermaster named Leblanc, a young Canadian who understands and speaks Sioux, but not enough to fill the office of interpreter. Nevertheless, one by one the three Indians presented me with their papers, commissions, and the certificates of their virtues and of their character as faithful allies. We discussed nothing else, but the chief, Black Eyes, merely announced his intention of paying me a visit with his warriors as soon as we had a satisfactory interpreter. Pierre Gareau, best known of them all, is expected in a few days; moreover, two half-breeds arrived a few hours later, bringing the mail from Fort Totten. But we did not need to call on them.

[*The powwow*] This morning, after breakfast, MacDonald, the guide of the half-breed couriers, came to tell me that the Yanktonahs had found among the Canadians employed by the quartermaster a man named Martin who spoke Sioux very well and that they wanted

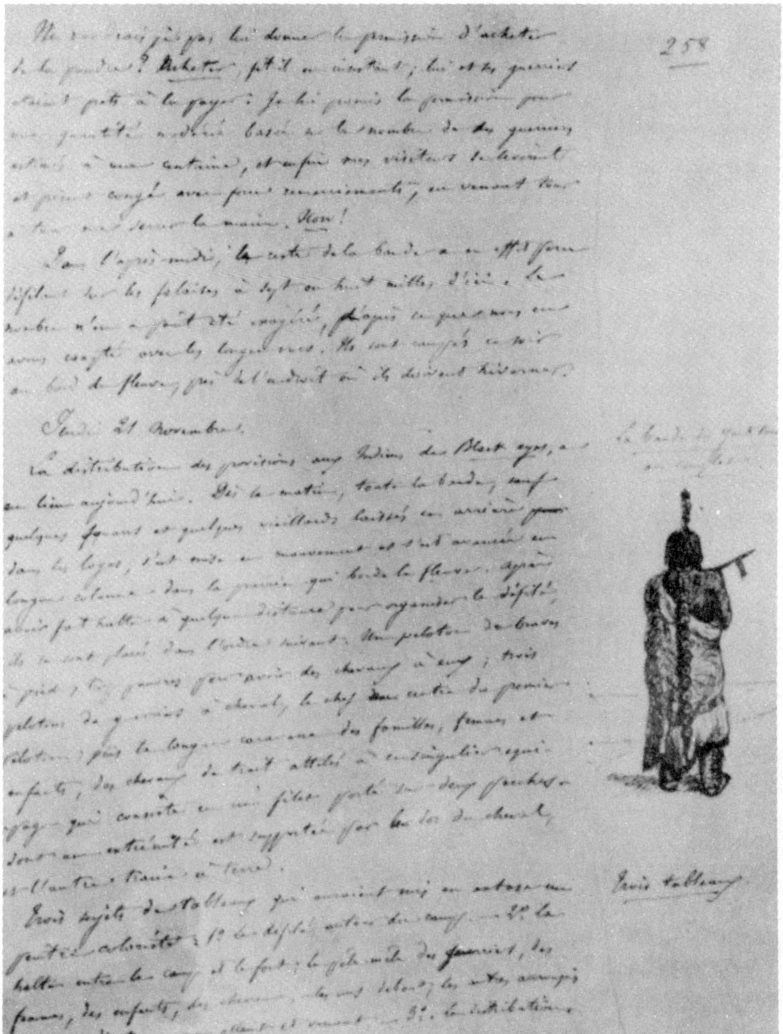

A page of the Journal

to pay me a visit and have a powwow with me. Having nothing better to do at the moment, I had them informed that I was ready to receive them. Then they presented themselves, Black Eyes (in Sioux Yah-Psah-Ta-Pah [Ishta-Sapah]), Howkah, and Black Cat leading around twenty braves or warriors in their customary garb, most of them in checked flannel shirts, everyone wrapped in a buffalo robe or brown blanket. Old Big Hand, with his oddly shaped hatchet and a bunch of red and white feathers on the back of his head, was with them, although he did not belong to the same band.

Black Eyes (I don't know why they named him Black Eyes, for all Indians have jet-colored eyes) is my height, but thinner than I, of course. I have not met a single fat man among the redskins. Their diet is no more conducive to stoutness than it is to gout. The chief has small, half-closed eyes, which make him look as if he is winking; nose very aquiline, mouth rather large, thin lips, pointed chin; his expression is shrewd, but not malicious. His straight hair, parted in the middle of his head, falls on his shoulders and covers his two cheeks in such a way that his face seems longer than it really is. He wears on his head only an eagle feather fixed vertically in his scalp lock. Howkah and Black Cat, on the contrary, have round faces, prominent cheek bones, round and flat noses, big mouths, and thick lips. None of them was painted any color but red.

Everyone sat down; the chiefs on the chairs, the others on the floor, the last arrivals outside the open door; they lighted the calumet, I lighted my pipe, and the silence lasted for some minutes, the calumet going from mouth to mouth. Then again the ceremony of papers and certificates that I had already read yesterday, but which they begged me to read to them again for greater security. That done, another pause preceded the opening of the conference, after which Black Eyes, having exchanged a preliminary handclasp with me, then with Martin, the interpreter, began to speak. It was the usual preface spoken in such cases.

"I [De Trobriand] am a great chief; I command a great many warriors, and the Indians of the plains, having learned that our Great Father in Washington had sent me to them, felt their hearts rejoice. That is why the Yanktonahs of the Upper Missouri said: 'We shall go to visit our father, the great chief who had not come to us yet, and we shall be happy to know him, for his renown is great among the white men and is already spreading afar among the tribes of Dakota.' (How!)"

[*Profession of faith*] And then the customary answer: "After the great war between the white men in which we, the men from the North, defeated the men from the South and recaptured all their immense territory that they intended to take from us, our Great Father in Washington sent me to his children of Dakota, not to make more war, but to keep peace. What I want is justice for all. In my eyes, all men are the children of the Great Spirit, whatever be the color of their skin, and in my command, I shall do what is just and reasonable for everyone, for the redskins as well as the Pale Faces (How! in chorus). So, the Indians who are honest and faithful friends of the whites will always find in me a man ready to protect them and to do everything in my power to help them. And the Indians who lie and are the enemies of the whites, those who steal and kill, they will not have in Dakota an enemy more determined and more persevering in waging war against them and in punishing them." (Prolonged assent).

[*A question of ownership*] "When I was a child," went on the black-eyed chief, "the Indians freely roamed the plains, *which belonged to them,* without meeting any white men; but today the Pale Faces are everywhere as they are in *their own land,* and their soldiers are established on the whole course of the great Missouri from the lands where it rises to those where it loses its name."

(Pause. The chief looked at me with his half-closed eyes. I had really pricked up my ears at the assertion of the right of ownership on the plains; but I remained immobile and silent, awaiting with an impassive face for what the crafty Indian was leading up to.)

"And as my father with his warriors occupies a part of our hunting lands, I wanted to come and wish him welcome and visit him with the feelings and the faith of a friend." (How!)

But to be thus placed in the supposed position of the guest of the Yanktonahs did not suit me, and I hastened to reverse the roles.

"A great many things have happened since the chief was a child," I said in a little more animated voice and looking at him a little more directly. "If he has a good enough memory to recall the times when the Pale Faces were not on the plains, he undoubtedly remembers, too, that formerly there were, in the direction of the rising sun, numerous and warlike tribes of Indians who undertook to make war on the Pale Faces, and who have been so completely destroyed that neither plain nor mountain knows their name today." (Deep silence. People talk a great deal about the impassiveness and dissimulation of Indians, but only Black Eyes and Howkah remained impassive. All the others, eyes fixed on me, heads bent slightly forward, showed unreservedly a close attention to and an almost avid interest in each one of the sentences that Martin translated into their language.) I went on:

"And why have these tribes been annihilated or dispersed? Because after having made treaties with the whites, they violated them; because after having sold great hunting lands to the Pale Faces, they tried to keep them from settling on them; because after promising them alliance and friendship, instead of living in peace with those who came first to cultivate the land, these tribes stole their animals from them, burned their farms, killed or maltreated them, and took their women captives. That is why the Great Spirit, seeing that they were liars, thieves, and murderers, permitted their tribe to be destroyed, and not only have they failed to recover the lands which they sold, but they lost forever those remaining to them. So, the white men, whose race is so numerous on the earth that no Indian could count them, have advanced toward the setting sun and have come up the Missouri. But the Indians who kept faith and remained the friends of the whites have received payment for the lands sold and have kept the ones where they wanted to settle, and today they cultivate the land, are rich and happy, and live in peace and great friendship with the whites who live around them. The bad Indians who broke their word during the great war between the whites, and who, being at peace with the Pale Faces, surprised and massacred those they could get at in Minnesota, those Indians lost the right of ownership of their lands. Many were killed in the fighting; some died on the gallows, hanged ignominiously by the neck; the others abandoned their lands which now belong to our Great Father, and when they submit and ask for peace, it is to obtain the protection of the whites and their help in keeping them from starvation when they have no game."

The chief hastened to assure me that he and his band were entirely innocent of everything that had happened in Minnesota, that none of them had taken part in the massacre, and, moreover, that he could not have violated any treaty, because he had never made any and had never sold any lands.[92]

"If you have made no treaty and sold no lands," I went on,

[92] The Yanktonai signed the treaty of peace and friendship at Fort Lookout, June 22, 1825 and the treaty at Fort Sully, October, 1865. The treaty of 1865 provided that the Yanktonai withdraw from the overland routes in exchange for annuities. By 1867 the lands between Minnesota and the Missouri had been ceded by the Chippewa, the Sisseton, and Wahpeton. Kappler, *Indian Laws and Treaties*, 2:227–230, 903–904; Royce, *Indian Land Cessions*, map number 11.

addressing him directly, using the singular, for it is an invariable rule in Indian languages in which the plural is never addressed to one person, "the great Yanktonah chiefs have made some and have sold great lands between Minnesota and the Missouri."

"That is true," he said, "but these are lower Yanktonahs, and the lands of the Upper Yanktonahs extend (making a circle with his hand) everywhere here, far up into the north."

"No," I continued, "the lands of the Yanktonah do not extend so far; you told me that I was here on land belonging to them; you are mistaken. This land never belonged to them. Before belonging to us, it belonged to the Pa-Na-Ni (the Rees), the Hidatsa (Gros Ventres), and the Mandans, whose preserve took in all this part of the plains. They are the ones who are now settled at Fort Berthold where they live in peace and cultivate corn, in good faith and friendship with the whites."

The chief smiled and shook his head in the negative.

[*Argumentum ad hominem*] "If you have made no treaty," I went on, "why do you live at Fort Rice in the summer under the protection of the whites? If you have sold no lands, why do you receive annual presents from the Great Father for yourself and your people? Who gave you the shirt that you are wearing and those of your warriors, and their clothes with the same buttons as our soldiers, and the blankets that I see here on their shoulders? You have sold no lands; however, you receive payment for them."

For a few minutes the warriors showed an obvious uneasiness at the turn that the conference was taking. They exchanged some remarks in an undertone, the sense of which I guessed from the way in which they were looking at the chief who was not doing so well in the discussion which was the principal reason for their visit. Finally, Howkah, making himself their spokesman, addressed a few words to his brother, and offered me his hand.

"We think," he said, "that enough words have been spoken on this subject, and we should like to talk about other things that the chief wants to tell you."

"Let him speak," I answered shortly.

[*The real objective*] The chief with the black eyes understood fully that he had put himself on insecure ground and hurried to get off it by repeating his protestations of devotion to the whites and by appealing to his right to their friendship because of his past conduct, as the papers he had showed me proved. Then, giving up all pretense of welcoming me to his lands, he humbly asked me for permission to establish his winter camp in our neighborhood, in such a place as I should name. I made no objection, and left the choice up to him, reserving only the immediate neighborhood of the fort and the wooded lands from which our men were getting building materials. Then he proposed the woods bordering the river six or seven miles from here, near Snake Creek. "For," he said, "the chief at Fort Rice told me: 'Go to the north where you will find a chief more powerful than I, who will welcome you because of your conduct and faithfulness to the whites. You will be his friend, he will protect you and *give you provisions for you and your people*'." (The final remark of the conference was shameful.) "The buffalo are scarce and the game far away," he added, "but my father, who is a great chief, will help us out."

[*Indian beggars*] I had been warned that Black Eyes was an inveterate beggar, even among the Indians with whom begging is a favorite vice. So I was not in any hurry to grant the request, although my instructions from General Sherman are to be liberal with the friendly Indians in these matters. I asked the chief how many tepees or lodges there were in his band. He has one hundred and fifty-three, with an average of five or six people in each, including the women and children. He told me that the band which he had preceded by two days would arrive this very day and asked me if I would not give him some provisions before its arrival. No, I would give them to him when his band came.

Then, in order to have the greatest possible assurance, he told me that what I should grant him would be received with gratitude, convinced as he was that I would give enough *in order that each could have his small share,* so that jealousies would not be stirred up. And, as I remained silent, he enumerated on his fingers what he was requesting: sugar, coffee, biscuits, salt pork, and corn. I promised only that I would see what I could give him now, for, I told him, "when the end of winter comes, if game has not been plentiful, you and your people will not have enough to eat, and I must keep enough to help you then, because you will need it then more than now."

Then, there was another thing: he asked me for some hats for his warriors, and, in addition to this, what I could give them in the way of clothing. As for this, I politely sent him on about his business by reminding him that he had received his presents at Fort Rice and that it was the Indian agents, not the officers, who were in charge of giving the redskins articles of clothing. I was going to close the session, when he held me for a last request.

Wouldn't I give him permission to buy powder? *Buy,* he insisted; he and his warriors were ready to pay for it. I promised him permission for a moderate quantity based on the number of his warriors estimated at about one hundred. Finally my visitors got up and left with very constrained thanks, coming one by one to clasp my hand. *How!*

In the afternoon, the rest of the band appeared, filing along the cliffs seven or eight miles from here. The number was not exaggerated, according to those we counted with field glasses. This evening they are camped at the edge of the river, near the place where they are to winter.

Thursday, November 21. The distribution of the provisions to Black Eyes' Indians took place today. Beginning in the morning, the whole band, except for some squaws and old people who were left behind in the lodges, started to move and advanced in a long line on the prairie bordering the river. After halting some distance away to organize the procession, they placed themselves in the following order: a group of braves on foot, too poor to have horses of their own; three groups of warriors on horseback, the chief in the middle of the first group; then the long caravan of families, women, and children, draft horses hitched to that singular contraption which consists of a net carried on two poles, one end of which is supported on the back of the horse and the other drags on the ground.

[*Three tableaux*] Three subjects for pictures which would have put a color artist in ecstasy: 1. The file around the camp; 2. The halt between the camp and the fort, the pell-mell of warriors, women, children, horses, some standing up, others squatted down on the ground, still others coming and going; 3. The distribution. The interior circle of warriors and heads of families were seated on the ground; the outside circle of women and children seated in like manner. In the center the provisions: four barrels of salt pork, four barrels of salt herring, four barrels of corn meal, a barrel of hominy, a barrel of rice, ten boxes of biscuits, a sack of sugar, and a sack of coffee. Near by, a group of officers and soldiers. The wagon which brought the provisions, the camp in the background, and the prairie stretching away to the hills on the horizon. In the three pictures, a torrent of color under a cloudless sky and brilliant sun.

The Indians, under the direction of the chief and their leaders, made the distribution themselves, and the whole band took the road

again in groups for their encampment, and this time without order
or ceremony.

[*Unexpected couriers*] While I was attending this picturesque
spectacle, two employees of the mail service arrived as couriers from
Fort Buford. While coming by the Knife River route, they were captured by a band of Indians and taken as prisoners to an encampment of Tetons and hostile Yanktonahs. They pretended they were,
or were taken for, half-breeds from the Red River, thanks to their
half Indian costumes, although they are white and English. They
understood enough Sioux to get the meaning of a deliberation in
council which was to determine their fate. The Yanktonahs wanted
to put them to death. It was the band of a chief called Two Dogs.
The Tetons, on the contrary, insisted that their lives be spared. Their
chief, whose name I forget, spoke at length and eloquently, it seems,
in favor of the captives, and in the end his opinion carried. They
were set free, after taking from them their Henry carbines and ammunition with the following warning: "We are letting you pass,"
the savages told them, "and you can return from Fort Buford. But
once you are back, return to your homes and stop carrying the papers
of the Americans. If the Americans wish to communicate with each
other, let them carry their correspondence themselves, for then we
shall know *whom we must kill.*" This was explained to them by a
Teton who spoke passable English.

The courier whom I questioned is of the opinion that it will
be impossible to keep up communications between Totten and Buford by the route now followed. Not only is it infested with hostile
Indians, but it is without any possible protection against the winter
storms on a great part of its course. It crosses the plains, and in such
a region it runs for a hundred miles without passing a tree. So, it is
just about decided that in the future the service will be made by
Fort Stevenson, for between Stevenson and Buford, the route follows
the river, and consequently goes through the wooded lands, which
offer shelter from the storms, refuge from Indians, and firewood.

And even by this route communications will not be free from
exposure to great dangers. The courier counted between Buford and
Berthold six encampments of Indians, most of them hostile, and
still others in considerable numbers are said to be in this region.
Coming from Buford, the two couriers traveled only at night, resting
and sleeping during the day, hidden in the brush with their horses.
If they are captured, it means their life.

At Buford, a wagon sent out for wood was attacked two miles

from the fort. It had an escort of only five men. One of them was killed; his body was found horribly mutilated, according to the report. Another was seriously wounded by an arrow in the body. The four mules were stolen. No savage was reported as killed or wounded.

[*Rankin–Little again*] The Rankin–Little affair has entered a new phase. By the mail from Fort Buford this evening, I received two strange documents: In one Captain (Bt. Lt. Col.) Rankin asks that the charges and specifications he has made against Lieutenant (Bt. Major) Little be withdrawn; in the other Lt. Little makes the same request in regard to Captain Rankin. While sending these papers on to the general headquarters of the Department, I added the following endorsement:

"Respectfully forwarded *disapproved*. I respectfully and earnestly request that such a strange application be rejected. Nothing could be more detrimental to the military discipline than the scandalous comedy of these officers under specified charges of the most serious character being allowed to secure to each other impunity, in adjusting their past differences over a bottle of whiskey or otherwise. The application in itself proves that neither of these officers has in him any sense of justice or self dignity."[93]

Later in the evening Marshal, the adjutant, brought me the papers to tell me about the things he had noticed while looking them over, and there are strong indications that lead one to suspect that the document signed *Thomas Little* is a forgery. On closer examination, I shared Lt. Marshal's opinion, and the comparison of writing of the document with Captain Rankin's, as well as the inexactness of Lt. Little's signature and certain other attendant circumstances revealed to me rather clearly who the author of the forgery was. I am

[93] This endorsement appeared in the French manuscript in English. Rankin's letter addressed to the Department was dated October 27, 1867. Department of Dakota, War Records Division, National Archives.

De Trobriand took vigorous action to clarify the situation at Fort Buford. On November 21, J. M. Marshall, A.A.A. General, Fort Stevenson, wrote to Major Little at Fort Buford asking him why they had asked that the charges and specifications be withdrawn. De Trobriand had already, on November 7, asked headquarters that the leave granted to Rankin be suspended. On November 6, the same day that De Trobriand received orders for Rankin's leave, Marshall issued special orders no. 29 from Fort Stevenson, placing Rankin under arrest and instructing Rankin to "turn over all property and funds in his possession pertaining to the Quartermaster and Subsistence Departments . . ." Régis de Trobriand, Fort Stevenson, Dakota Territory, to Bvt. Lt. Col. Ed. W. Smith, A.A. Genl, Department of Dakota, November 7, 1867; Special Orders no. 29, Headquarters, Middle District, November 6, 1867. Department of Dakota, War Records Division, National Archives.

sending the two documents with the above endorsement; but I am sending with them the following communication addressed to Bt. Lt. Col. Edw. W. Smith, assistant adjutant general of the Department:

"Sir, — I have the honor to report *privately* for the information of the Bt. Major General commanding, that since I wrote my endorsement on the applications of Bt. Lt. Col. Rankin and Bt. Major Little for the withdrawal of the charges and specifications preferred by each of these officers against the other, several circumstances induce me to doubt very much whether the application signed *Thos. Little* is a genuine one. Without expressing what my suspicions may be as to the author of the forgery, (if forgery it is) I will content myself to call your close attention to the handwriting of the document, to the date which is anterior to the one in which the charges preferred by Bt. Major Little were forwarded, and to the signature of this officer which seems more a counterfeit than anything else.

"I may add that a letter dated November 3ᵈ from Fort Buford has been received today at this post, requesting in the name of Bt. Maj. Little, that an affidavit supporting certain charges against Bt. Lt. Col. Rankin may be taken from a woman supposed to be at this time at Fort Stevenson. Also that when the mail left Fort Buford, Bt. Maj. Little was still in close arrest by order of Bt. Lt. Col. Rankin.

"I will ascertain as soon as possible whether Bt. Maj. Little has really written and signed the document or not. I have the honor to be, etc."[94]

It seems to me that this Rankin is getting himself in deeper and deeper, and that little by little he has become a drunkard, a thief, and a forger, if the charges against him are proved; and if he is, as I am sure he is, the author of the forgery—*Cui prodest.*

Friday, November 22. A special mail pouch arrived today from Fort Rice, brought by five men, a sergeant, and four Indian scouts accompanied by the two Yanktonahs whom we had sent. As for me, I received two letters from France and three from the United States, somewhat delayed, as well as the papers for the month of October. Lieutenant Colonel Otis, who commands Fort Rice, proposes that we exchange papers and despatches twice a month by sending at a fixed day from each fort a party of a few men who will meet halfway. This arrangement, which we eagerly accept, will start the first Monday of December, every two weeks. So we are now assured of two

94 In the French manuscript this letter appeared in English.

routes of regular communication. One by forts Totten, Ransom, and Abercrombie, the other by forts Rice, Sully, and Randall.

Received a letter from Lieutenant Colonel Hayman, promoted in the 17th infantry, which is stationed in Texas. Between the yellow fever which is raging there, conflicts which are still going on between the authorities and the ex-rebels, the politics of the President on one hand and those of the Congress on the other, Hayman foresees great trouble, which puts a certain dash of absinthe in the ambrosia of his promotion. At least he gets a few months' leave out of it. He sends me word that he cannot recruit scouts for me among the tribes near Fort Wadsworth because they are still at war with several tribes of our region, with the result that none of their young men want to enlist to come to the Missouri. So we are going to try to find our scouts among the Yanktonahs of the chief with the black eyes.

Saturday, November 23. The last smile of autumn vanished yesterday with the last rays of the setting sun. After twelve days of magnificent weather, during which we had only a frost at night that disappeared early each morning, the sky was overcast in the evening, and the temperature dropped because of a wind from the northwest. This morning we had a light snowfall, after which the thermometer kept going down rapidly. Around noon, it registered twenty degrees Fahrenheit. At four o'clock, it had gone down to sixteen. Now (eight o'clock in the evening) it is fourteen (ten degrees below zero centigrade), and everything points toward a very cold night.

We made good use of the twelve days of fair weather to finish covering the company quarters; but the log houses intended as lodgings for the officers could not be begun until the day before yesterday, and if the cold weather does not let up, the work will suffer and new delays will result. *Speriamo pur!*

Tuesday, November 26. The thermometer is still ranging between twenty and twenty-five degrees Fahrenheit. Snow has been falling steadily since morning.

Yesterday evening, around eight o'clock, when it was pitch dark, some shots on the other side of the river brought everyone out. It was the marauding Indians who had come under cover of darkness to try stealing the mules used to drag the felled logs. But the post has a sentinel night and day whose watch tower is a turret on the roof of the log house. The sentinel, noticing the marauders, fired from above, and the men rushed outside, pursued them up to the brush, where the redskins disappeared for good. The animals are in a palisaded corral contiguous to the post. So the thieves have little chance of getting at them. Moreover, the reception they got yesterday evening will probably discourage them from trying the adventure again.

[*Emigration of waterfowl*] NOTE: The waterfowl have emigrated *en masse* since the first days of the month. As soon as Douglas Creek froze over, geese, ducks, and snipes disappeared as if by magic. The blackbirds, those pretty black birds with the golden eyes, followed them. They lived with us familiarly, well fed by the grain scattered on the ground around the corral and the forage storehouse. They swooped down in swarms near camp among the cattle and even lighted on the backs of the mules. One day, returning from an unsuccessful hunt, I yielded to the temptation of numbers, and I killed twenty-two of them with one shot. They are very good to eat roasted. They are the size of the thrush or robin. Now, we have for the winter only the grouse or prairie chicken, which are numerous and easier to kill in this season, for the snow and cold make them slow in flying away, and they perch in the sun on the trees where it is easy enough to approach them and shoot them sitting still. But if we have no more waterfowl, we are compensated by the fur-bearing animals which gather in the thickets on the banks of the river; more and more buffalo are showing up in the neighborhood; deer are more numerous in the wooded places; and the antelope are easier to approach and are slower in their flight.

The magpie stays with us: Isn't it strange that we must come to the banks of the Missouri to find in America this bird that is so common throughout Europe? Still it is true that I did not see a one in the many years spent in the Eastern States, and the first which I saw flying across the river above Omaha filled me with great joy (childhood memory). It is the same bird as in France. Same plumage, same behavior, and same habits.

Wednesday, November 27. Snow last night; snow all day; and nothing indicates that it will stop tonight, although it has been falling for thirty-six hours. Impossible to skate. The wind is changing, shifting from the northwest to the northeast and to the east; but the temperature remains low, and the thermometer goes up a few degrees during the day, only to go back down at night. Those of us who have plank cabins have not suffered so far. Those who are in tents are less fortunate. And the work on our winter quarters progresses little in such weather. How many precious days we lost in putting up the walls and framework of two houses that will be of no use to us until next summer!

Thursday, November 28. A prisoner in my cabin. Still the snow; still the wind from the north; and the thermometer below zero Fahrenheit!

Friday, November 29. The Missouri, which for days was becoming more and more filled with drift ice, is completely frozen over from one side to the other. Nothing moves on the frozen countryside. This morning at seven o'clock the thermometer was thirteen degrees below, Fahrenheit; that is, forty-five degrees below the freezing point. During the day, which was very fair if one disregards the cold, it went up to nine degrees above zero, a difference of twenty-two degrees in six hours; but this evening it is falling again, and in all probability it will go down to twenty below during the night. And we are still in the month of November. That is promising for the months of January and February.

Thursday, December 5. The band of Black Eyes stayed in its encampment only a few days. Whether the buffalo in the neighborhood are more scarce than they figured or the wandering nature of the Indian got the upper hand, they lost little time in coming back by the camp, crossing Douglas Creek, and camping above us in the woods from which we got much of our building timber. Then they came to inform us that their sojourn on this land was for just a few days while waiting for the ice on the river to be solid enough so they could cross it with their animals and baggage. Since Sunday (December 1st) several of our men have crossed from one bank to the other. Tuesday (the day before yesterday) their musical band composed of three small drums and twenty-four singers, joined by five or six squaws, came on horseback in great pomp and full dress to give me a goodbye performance; that is, under the pretext of dancing and music, to get some more provisions from us. Nevertheless, I am not complaining about it, for the spectacle was worth seeing.

[*Yanktonah concert*] After advancing abreast on horseback, singing a song of peace, which ended in a sort of baying in falsetto voices, the company dismounted, and leaving the horses to the care of the many women and children who followed in great number, they formed a circle and began their musical presentation. What I wrote elsewhere about the music of the Rees applies in every detail to the music of the Sioux, except that the latter have no gourds with little pebbles in them and use only drums for all accompaniment. On these drums (there were three of them in the band) they beat the time, holding the instrument with the left hand and striking it with the right hand with a stick lightly padded at one of its ends. To their song they soon added a spiritless dance consisting of balancing themselves in time first with one foot, then the other. So the music was rather insignificant; but the costumes were worthy of notice, or at least *some of the costumes*. The orchestra leader and two others had on their heads a simple headdress of eagle feathers sewed on a canvas band. The feathers were bound together by an iron wire or by a withe, and held in place this way. The front of the canvas band, beginning at the place where the feathers were sewed, was covered with ermine tails or threads of wool curled in fringes, looking like what is called chenille in needlework. The face was painted in two colors, applied in different ways; for example, temples, jaws, and both lips black, the eyes, nose, and part of the lips red. Black and red are their two colors. It didn't seem to me that they use white or blue like the Rees or Gros Ventres. Two of the Indians crowned with eagle feathers had in their hands a ceremonial baton six or seven feet long, covered with a spiral of bear or buffalo skin, and ending in an eagle feather, below which two or three others hang like tassels.

The warrior who was on guard to keep a free space around the musicians and to hold the crowd of women and children at a distance wore a brown fur cap resembling marten (probably a kind of marten that the Canadians call *foutreau*) around which six or eight eagle feathers were fixed. Above a jacket with infantry buttons, he wore a double necklace with pendants of ermine tails on his shoulders, back, and chest. Because of the sharp cold, all the others were wrapped in buffalo robes which covered the rest of their costume, from which I concluded that they had decorated only their heads and necks.

One of them, who had remained on his horse near the musicians, was showing off a white pony which was painted fantastically a yellow saffron color around the eyes, on the head, around the nose, and on the shoulders and haunches. On the rump was a design which seemed to me a poor imitation of the government mark, "U.S."

Naturally the presentation ended with a distribution of rations to the actors. It had no other real purpose, although the pretext was to bid us farewell before the departure of the entire band which was announced for the next day, Wednesday.

[*Importunity of Ishta-Sa-pah*] Wednesday (yesterday) the band had not left. They said they were going to break camp. That would be this morning. Now this morning a gale was blowing, and they thought they couldn't get under way in such weather. Had I made a bet that they would come begging before they started on their journey, I should have won it. First Ishta-Sa-pah came by himself requesting an audience with me to find out if I had received an answer to a letter that he had begged me to write to Lt. Col. Otis, commander at Fort Rice, about some provisions which arrived there for him after his departure. The answer had arrived and was very satisfactory. Then he asked that the provisions which he had left in storage at the warehouse be delivered to him and his family. Nothing could be more fair. But I took advantage of the occasion to lodge a vigorous complaint about the attempts made by his young men and their women to steal from us. Whoever says Indian says thief. These same redskins who are positively friends of the whites, who receive annual presents at Fort Rice and incidental provisions at the different posts they visit in their travels, do not hesitate when they are in the neighborhood of a fort or post to seek out every means of stealing what they can. Here the temptation is irresistible, for, since the fort is not finished, all the provisions are in the tents of the commissariat; the grain, especially the corn, of which they are very fond, is piled in sacks under the sheds, and these days the harnesses still hang on pegs inside a temporary corral, easily accessible. Indeed, nothing in camp is enclosed with palisades. The result has been that these last nights the sentinels fired several times on marauding Indians who took advantage of the darkness to come to commit their thefts. Although they knew by experience that the guards were watching and that they were running the risk of being killed by gunfire, they nevertheless succeeded in stealing a few sacks of corn, in cutting some harnesses to take off the leather thongs, and, finally, in carrying off two saddles.

[*Incorrigible thieves*] During the day, they sent their women and children, if they didn't come themselves, to prowl around the storehouses and to find out how they could steal most easily, and after this reconnaissance, they would make, or try to make, their coup in the night, until the "Who goes there?" of a sentinel, followed by a shot, put them to flight for a few hours or until the following night. One of the quartermaster's men, Martin, whom I use as interpreter, even surprised one of the squaws cutting one of his harnesses in broad daylight. Familiar with Indian behavior, as with their language, he thrashed the woman soundly and conducted her outside the limits of camp with kicks in the rear. Since we cannot adopt this Sioux treatment as a rule, we must forbid all Indians, without exception, and especially the women who swarmed the place, from entering the camp and approaching the storehouse and corral. As the ground is covered with snow, and since we have even had the first quarter of the moon for three nights, one would think that the difficulty of escaping the notice of the guards would keep the Indians at a distance; but that is not the situation, and the temptation to steal is stronger in them than the fear of danger.

The chief seemed to be very humiliated when I reproached him about this. He protested his ignorance of these misdeeds, and in fact, I believe that the principal men are not involved. He expressed all his regrets for the bad conduct of some of his young people, of whom he said he felt ashamed. And he withdrew, promising to make a search of his lodges and to bring back everything he could find belonging to us.

[*Red Horn*] Toward the middle of the day, I went to the sutler's, Mr. Marsh, having received the information that a hostile Indian had been among Black Eyes' Yanktonahs yesterday; he had even gone into the sutler's store where his conduct had aroused such suspicions that one of the employees, revolver in hand, had put him out. These suspicions were confirmed by Black Eyes, for when he was questioned about it by Captain Powell, he revealed that he had, in fact, been visited at his camp by a warrior of the unsubdued Unkpapahs named Red Horn who has been reported to us from Rice as an incorrigible thief, murderer on occasion, and whom we suspect of having taken part in the theft of mules here and at Buford. Jack and Junot, the two employees of the sutler, gave me an account of the details that aroused their suspicion; how they had seen the unknown Indian sneak some crackers when a soldier was buying some, and how the passive attitude and withdrawal of Black Eyes, who was present, had brought them to the conclusion that this man must not belong to his band. During this time, Howkah (The One Around Whom They Sing) the leader of the soldiers (The One Who Wears Beautiful Things, and he certainly isn't wearing them today) and two or three others dropped in. When I found out that Red Horn had left yesterday evening for Berthold on his way back to his camp where he had tried to bring the Yanktonahs to add them to the hostile bands, the subject was closed. Howkah offered me his hand, and, since one of the half-breeds was there, he began his little request, always with exactly the same introduction: Friend of the whites, obedient to his Great Father, faithful to his word, he is ashamed and his heart is troubled to learn that *wicked little deeds* were done in the night by some of the young people. Foregone conclusion: He was going to leave tomorrow with the others and his family had nothing to eat. He wanted to get a few provisions, only enough for five persons. I refused. We have already given too much to people who sought to steal from us; not that I accuse Howkah of it, but as second chief he ought to have more authority over these young people, and since they acted badly, I wouldn't give anything more to anyone.

I was curious to see if, after that, they would try by another means to get some provisions from us. Not much time passed before my curiosity was satisfied.

Around four o'clock, I was reading in my cabin when Indian singing broke out loudly in the direction of the fort. I inquired the reason for it and was told that about twenty Indians were approaching, singing, bringing back the two saddles stolen the other night. That was all that Black Eyes' search had uncovered. Naturally the corn could not be identified now, and the pieces of harness were too easy to hide. Still singing, the Indians under the leadership of Howkah and the leader of the soldiers filed across the camp carrying the two saddles that they put before my door. Then they squatted down in a circle to await my good pleasure. And what could possibly be my good pleasure save to take the saddles and to have provisions distributed to those who brought them back as a reward for the restitution and an encouragement to follow the path of virtue? So, once again, whether you will or no, these red devils succeed in getting some provisions out of us.

[*Recidive*] Between eight and nine o'clock in the evening, three shots fired from the post on the other side of the river told us that these determined thieves, despite the snow, despite the moonlight, were still prowling around the post to steal something from it and thus use to good advantage their last night in our neighborhood. A quarter of an hour later, Captain Powell brought me the sergeant of the post. The sergeant crossed on the ice to report that the Indians had swarmed around the post all day, in spite of the efforts to send them away. This evening, several came back again to prowl around and succeeded in stealing two sacks of corn from the little corral adjoining the log house. Our men fired above the heads of the thieves, knowing that they belonged to a *friendly* band; and they have fled for the moment; but since they escaped punishment, they will probably return in the night. The sergeant asked if they still could do nothing more than frighten them.

"Are they armed?" I asked.

"Yes, we could see their bows and quivers."

"Well, if they return, order the sentinel to take good aim; try to kill one of them; it is the only way we can have peace with such inveterate thieves."

The sergeant withdrew, evidently satisfied with the order he had received. Tomorrow we shall see what comes of it. If the marauders do not come back, it will have no effect; if they do come back, so much the worse for them. Patience has its limits, beyond which it degenerates into weakness, and especially when dealing with these Indians, it is necessary to guard against weakness, for they scorn the weak and respect only the strong.[95]

So tomorrow I hope to be rid of these *friends*, the most troublesome that one can have in the neighborhood.

Friday, December 6. Disappointment. I have not finished with the Indians yet. First, the Yanktonahs still have not gone. They assure me that they are decamping and that a part of the band has got under way. But I notice a number of horses in the distance on the prairie, which proves that a great part of them still remain.

Furthermore, the old chief of the Rees, White Shield, the same one deposed by the agent Wilkinson, arrived yesterday with about twenty of his warriors. He spent the night in the log house of Gerard, one of the traders, and this morning he asked me for an audience through Beauchamp, who came with him to serve as interpreter. So around ten o'clock, I admitted the old chief and three of his principal warriors, but when I opened my door for them, whom do I see but Black Eyes, Howkah, and the leader of the warriors! I thought that by admitting the Rees without inviting the Sioux, the latter would stay outside, but with the unceremoniousness of a child of nature, foreign to everything that civilized men call discretion, my three intruders followed the four other Indians in. Through Beauchamp, who speaks a little Sioux, I gave them to understand that I had to talk business with the Rees. "How!" they answered in com-

[95] In his letters to Department headquarters, De Trobriand frequently warned his superiors against countenancing any manifestation of weakness in dealings with the Indians. In one letter, he wrote: "With them as with all barbarian tribes, *force* is the real superiority; the strongest dictates the law; the weakest submits to it. This point decided, one rules, the other obeys, *and there is peace.* Otherwise no. Hence, the practical truth well acknowledged on these frontiers, all the philanthropic theories notwithstanding, that to have peace with the Indians, the first condition is to whip them." Régis de Trobriand, Fort Stevenson, to Bvt. Brig. Gen. O. D. Greene, A.A. Genl, Department of Dakota, St. Paul, September 6, 1868. Department of Dakota, War Records Division, National Archives.

mon agreement. That's fine. And not imagining that they could be
intruding, they sat down. I had either to tolerate their presence or
put them out. I did not know whether in their minds it might not
be an insult for which they would try to take vengeance on the Rees.
In order not to disturb the peace concluded between the two tribes,
and considering, moreover, that as they speak a different language,
they could understand nothing of what was said, I decided to let them
attend the conference. So the calumet passed from mouth to mouth
between the Sioux and *Pahlanis,* and I smoked my pipe, everyone
keeping the most profound silence. This pause which invariably pre-
cedes all powwows is undoubtedly designed to give the one who is
going to speak time to think over his words, and everyone must respect his meditation or meditate himself; but I very much doubt that
those playing a secondary role and the assistants do anything but
enjoy themselves when their turn comes to inhale the kinnikinick,
and the rest of the time to think nothing.

The silence was longer than usual and lasted fully a quarter of
an hour. The chief of the Rees was, I suppose, embarrassed or an-
noyed to discuss his affairs in front of strangers; but finally, resigning
himself to the inevitable, he decided to break the silence.

[*Indian character*] The conference lasted two hours and taught
me more than any other about Indian character and customs. The
chief had come to complain about having been deposed and not receiving all the presents sent out for him and his band by the Great
Father in Washington; and for two hours, no matter how explicit
or urgent I was in my direct questions, I was not able to get a single
answer of yes or no to anything. He stuck to generalities with great
circumspection and craft, refusing to talk about any definite fact. He
supposes, he thinks, he believes, but he never affirms a fact, even an
undeniable one. For example: Was the merchandise unloaded on the
bank of the river when the steamboat left—yes or no? In answer, a
long story about the steamboat going up the river to Fort Buford, the
agent on board. What things are missing? Answer: The boxes were
broken and everything seemed mixed up and some articles of clothing similar to those of the Indians were worn by the whites at the fort.

Impossible to get out of him whether or not he consented to be
replaced as chief by his son who was previously second chief. Impossible to make him tell why he refused to sign the receipt for the merchandise delivered. "The red man raises his hand to the sky and
calls on the Great Spirit to be witness." Finally, the question: What
does the chief ask me to do for him? Sentences about how his heart

is rejoiced to see me, for I am good and just to my red children. Categorical question: Does the chief want me to report his words to Washington? This time I thought I had him. Ask him *yes* or *no,* I told Beauchamp. Neither yes nor no: I can do so if I want to, but he won't be at all happy about that!

Then I explained to him how useless a report would be since he could not or did not wish to speak about any definite fact: how the whites manage the sending and receiving of merchandise. I was prepared to state that our Great Father and we, the leaders of his soldiers, thought that the Indians were not receiving all that was given to them, and that someone often stole part of it; but if our Great Father could not do justice, it was only through the fault of the Indians themselves, who weren't keeping track of what was sent to them and therefore couldn't prove that anything was missing, although they might be convinced of it. The chief listened to me religiously, but he was evidently more impressed by the friendly intention that inspired my words than by any practical sense that they might carry. He withdrew, shaking my hand cordially and declaring to me that his heart was satisfied and that he was going away happy.

After the Rees left, the three Sioux sat down again as if nothing had happened. This time my patience was at an end. I opened the door, and calling them outside, made them understand by signs and a few words in Sioux that last night some of their people had gone to the post located on the other side of the river to steal grain, and that I had given the order that they were to shoot *to kill* the thieves. Upon which Howkah very clearly answered that I had done well, and that it was too bad for them. Black Eyes assured me that it was Unkpapahs, which was not true. Upon which, I turned my back on them to go to eat. And there were my three beggars marching behind me in hopes of grabbing something more. Then I turned around and pointing out the direction I was going, I said to Ishta-Sapah, adding gestures to words: I go there, and putting my finger on his chest and stretching my hand in the opposite direction toward his camp, I said: You go there! He could equivocate no longer, and finally my three *bores* took the road for their lodges, empty-handed.

I must mention here in passing that today I began to study the Sioux language. In the evening from time to time Martin will come to spend an hour in my cabin and will give me a lesson in the following way: I ask him the name of things in common use among the Indians, and then I write the word with the French spelling as it is pronounced. And in the same manner, the adjectives, adverbs, and verbs. Since the Indian language does not have any syntax, it is a matter of memory. When I have enough words in my head, the phraseology will come very easily, for it is most elementary. The verbs have no tense. For: I have come yesterday; *I to come yesterday.* Where did you come from? *From where you to come?* For: You would go if I wished; *You to go if I to wish.* I concluded from this that I can hope to speak Sioux fluently next summer if I apply myself to it with some diligence this winter.[96]

Saturday, December 7. This morning, on leaving my cabin to go to breakfast, the first thing I did was to take a look at the plain beyond Douglas Creek to assure myself that the Yanktonahs had left. The plain was empty. Only a few horses were there, undoubtedly belonging to the nine lodges of Unkpapahs camped on this side at the edge of the woods. I was still rejoicing after breakfast when to my great surprise I looked through the window behind my cabin and once more saw my intolerable beggar Black Eyes with his inseparable Howkah and four or five of his warriors coming toward my door.

"What else do you want?" I asked him in a tone of voice to show him that I was tired of his visits.

"To tell you some news."

I sent for the interpreter and resigned myself to listening to news which was simply that the band had left; that part of them had gone to join the Rees and the other half had left to go up north to hunt between the Knife River and Devils Lake. Good! But six lodges remain here, and in these six lodges, the present company and their families. On this subject endless sentences about their friendship for the whites and their past history that I already know by heart, all of which, of course, led to a request for provisions. I refused point-blank; but I took the trouble to explain to them that I had to feed my soldiers for six moons before any steamboat would bring other provisions, that I had to save the little surplus I did have in order to be able to help my Indian children during the rest of the winter and in the spring, if they had no game and if they were hungry, that the Yanktonahs belonged to Fort Rice, where they got their clothes and provisions, and that I had already done enough for them by giving them a feast and twice adding to it provisions for a number of them. Now I had to think of the three tribes, our always faithful

96 While De Trobriand was learning Sioux, he compiled a Sioux-French vocabulary of two hundred words and expressions. This manuscript, called "Vocabulaire Sioux" is in the possession of Waldron Kintzing Post of New York City. The editor has a filmcopy of the vocabulary.

friends, who, although they lived in my neighborhood most of the time, did not come to bother me with their requests as did Black Eyes and his people. Furthermore, I was tired of this sort of thing, and in place of trying to live on the whites like this during the winter without doing anything, he would do much better to show some pride and energy and go out on a hunt with his young men to get meat. Finally, I was disgusted with the conduct of his young people, who, after being well received and well treated by us, sought only to steal from us or induce their women to do so.

[*The end of patience*] The pipe passed from mouth to mouth, and now Ishta-Sapah, now Howkah, spoke to tell me again what they had already told me ten times. Finally, seeing that my resolution was unshakable, they humbly entreated that their women be allowed to gather up the kernels of corn scattered on the ground and lost when the sacks of feed for the cattle were loaded or unloaded, promising that they would be under the surveillance of one of their people who would see that they did no damage. In order to get rid of them, after two hours of conversation, I granted them the permission on condition that the women be constantly under the surveillance of the first soldier of the band whom the chief pointed out to me. And do you know what came of it? This afternoon they came to gather the corn that was left, and at sunset, the chief wagoner reported twelve sacks of corn cut open with knives and their contents considerably lightened, of course. That's an Indian, and especially Sioux! Black Eyes, his band, and his women can be considered as typical. I need not add that the concession granted this morning was withdrawn this evening. They are forbidden to approach the camp, and they can go hang out somewhere else.

Sunday, December 8. Today I received my promotion by brevet to the grade of brigadier general in the regular army, effective from last March 2, 1867, when I was still at Brest. If I had known it, I could have spared myself the expense of the complete outfit of a colonel; but understand that I am not sorry.

The weather is fair, but cold. The Missouri is solid ice and the plain an unbroken expanse of snow. The thermometer has not gone above 20 degrees Fahrenheit since November 26. It fluctuates between 15 above in the day and 15 below at night, a difference of 30 degrees in 12 hours. It averages around zero (18 degrees centigrade below freezing). We can stand this temperature much better than one would suppose, knowing we are under canvas.

It is evident that the atmospheric condition is such that we feel the heat and cold much less here than in more humid regions, by the sea, for example. The sky is clear, the air bracing; the nights are splendid and when the air is calm, there is nothing to complain about. But when the wind blows! Watch your nose and ears! The air is full of razors then.

Hunting is easy and plentiful. The prairie chicken gather on the trees where they can be shot easily, especially with a carbine, for then they don't fly away when one misses them, and in this way several can be killed on one tree. With bird shot, it is necessary to get closer to them, and one runs a greater risk of frightening them away. Whether with shotgun or carbine, the larder is always well stocked with game.

Wednesday, December 11. Between six and eight o'clock in the evening, two prisoners escaped and deserted. One of them had a ball and chain on his foot, which he will probably get rid of with a file. For their escape, they went into one of the stables and took two mules on which they fled, despite the cold, the snow which fell all morning, and the deserts which they must cross. The full moon will favor them in their journey, but what route will they take? Of course, they had to gather some provisions, but their mounts, lacking forage, cannot take them very fast or far. Tomorrow morning we shall go out to look for their tracks. If they have gone toward Berthold, there is a good chance that they will be picked up. If they have taken the direction of Devils Lake—before they get to British possessions, they have a chance of dying from starvation and freezing, being killed by Indians, or being captured at Fort Totten. Dark outlook. However, they have gone.

Saturday, December 14. The weather has been a good deal milder for four or five days. During the day, the thermometer approaches freezing point, and does not go below ten or twelve above Fahrenheit at night. The sky has remained quite overcast. This softening of temperature has enabled us to push the work on the log houses energetically. The one in which I shall be quartered is walled up with mud; the roof is finished, and the frames for the doors and windows are in place. The weather was encouraging for the officers who like to hunt. We have taken advantage of it to replenish our larder with prairie chicken. Mine now contains more than thirty; they can be kept for a few months in this season of the year. We are certain that we shall not lack game for the holidays of Christmas and the New Year.

[*Winter hunting*] But outside of getting food, this hunting is not very engrossing. It is too easy and plentiful to offer much sport. When the snow covers the ground, the prairie chicken perch in flocks in the trees, where they pick at the buds and warm themselves in the sun, getting into the snow only around midday, to feed in the bushes where various little red and brown berries furnish them an ample food supply. (All of them are fat and do not seem to be suffering from hunger at all.) A bird of that size can be seen from a distance in the leafless trees. Because of the underbrush, they can be approached without too much difficulty, and they can be shot down at about fifty feet. By choosing those on the remote or lower branches first, five or six of them can be killed, one after another, without hurrying to reload the gun, before the rest become frightened and fly away. I do not know whether the cold makes them lazy or dull, or their unaccustomed elevation (they never roost in the months when there is no snow) gives them a feeling of stupid security. Nevertheless, if one follows them from tree to tree after they have once flown away, they are more difficult to approach and, when they are fired on several times, they finally become unapproachable. The officers who have precision carbines use them in preference to an ordinary shotgun, for they can fire at game from a greater distance and repeat the shooting for a much longer time, the bullet frightening them much less than the fine shot. I have seen a poor hunter fire about twenty shots on a flock of prairie chicken perched on a big tree in the open and get within twenty or thirty feet of the tree before the birds decided to fly away. On the other hand, a good shot can bring them down one by one in this way until finally the successive disappearance of most of them alarms the last ones left. The big woods, which border the river across from camp, has hundreds of them; we have only to cross on the ice to reach a hunting ground from which we can always bring back a load of game.

This evening snow fell in thick flurries with a northwest wind. The prairie chicken are going to have a few days' respite. But, whatever the number slaughtered here and at Berthold, the decrease will not be noticeable next summer, for they are plentiful in all the woods bordering the Missouri, and the few places where they are hunted are insignificant in comparison with the vast regions where in the winter they enjoy a peace devoid of all danger.

The buffalo have not yet appeared. The building of the fort, the movement which accompanied it, the coming and going of convoys, detachments, and couriers seem to have turned them away from this locality where last year they were numerous. However, they must not be far away, for the wolves have completely disappeared from the outskirts of the camp, and their tracks have become very rare in the woods. Undoubtedly they have left to follow some herds of buffalo, for they do this in order to attack singly the old ones who stay behind or the young ones who stray out on the prairie alone.

The deer are wild, and although their tracks are seen on the snow everywhere, they can be neither approached nor surprised. The antelope haven't appeared. This is not the case with those big rabbits, the size of our European hare, which in winter are as white as the snow on which they run and frisk about, especially at night in the moon-light. The day before yesterday, at nine o'clock in the evening, we were at our doorways watching five of them sixty or eighty feet away playing with each other on the snow, not worrying about the sentinel who was walking up and down, gun on arm. An end was put to the spectacle by a hunt started by some sled dogs, and at the speed with which they left, the hunt was probably a success.

[*Exit Black Eyes*] *Ishta-Sapah* appeared once more. This morn-ing he asked for an audience for just himself and showed up in full feathers with his headdress of eagle feathers, his mantle embroidered with yellow and red porcupine quills on the chest and on the arms, all sprinkled with little tufts of horse hair, and to complete the outfit, his eyes were hidden by a pair of eyeglasses decorated with cloth, and his forehead was covered with small bands of rabbit skin ending in a tuft of dark hair in imitation of an ermine tail. In this solemn garb, he came to say his goodbyes; that is, to request still more provisions. But first, he had to put me in a favorable frame of mind. That is why he began his harangue by assuring me that I was a great chief whose name was already celebrated among the Indians of the plains. I cut this exordium short by asking pointedly what he had come to do and what more he wanted. "Alas! He and his family had nothing to eat. His son-in-law had accidentally broken his gun. He was the only one of those remaining with him who could hunt; the others had only bows and arrows, and there weren't any buffalo. Would I let them die of hunger?" Peremptory and justified refusal from me to give anything more. Why didn't he go back to Fort Rice where he lives and where he has some provisions in reserve? All he asks is to leave, but how can they travel when they have nothing to eat? The prospect of getting rid of him once and for all modified my first resolution a little. I am sure that the wily redskin counted on that. "If I give you some provisions for travel," I asked him, "when will you leave?" "I am ready," he answered. "I should like to leave today; but I can get under way tomorrow morning." It was then expressly agreed that I should give him and his relatives something to eat on the condition that they leave for Fort Rice immediately and that I should not hear of them again. This was done. Soon afterwards they returned to their camp carrying salt pork and condemned rice, and this time I hope to be rid of *Ishta-Sapah* and his band, at least until next year.

A mail pouch has just arrived. From now on, our postal communications by way of Totten and Rice are regular and assured.

Monday, December 16. The weather is horrible, literally. All day yesterday snow fell almost continuously. The sky did not clear up, and snow was still falling last night. But the worst is the wind which began to blow in a tempest and swept the fine and icy snow along in violent gusts. Drifts of snow formed before our cabins, and this morning we were blocked so completely that it was necessary to use shovel and spade to make a passage. Toward nine o'clock, the sun came out for almost half an hour, but soon the storm began blowing again from the northwest, the air again filled with whirlpools of snow and the sun disappeared behind this opaque veil. Since then we have not known whether it was snowing or not; that is, whether the flakes which are small and thick like diamond dust were coming from the sky or the plain. Clearing away paths in camp has been given up, for no sooner are they made than they disappear under new drifts blown by the wind. In some places, the snow is three feet deep; in others, it is scarcely three inches. These drifts piled up by the storm are leveled off at its caprice; it carries them to other places, as the Missouri does the banks of sand; but only a few minutes are required to do the work while it takes the river days and weeks. And during all this time, we can scarcely see in front of us. Sometimes the view opens and then closes, and at times all that can be seen are objects within a radius of about twenty feet. Everyone has read the description of a simoon in the great deserts of Africa. For the Sahara, substitute the plains; for the sand, the snow; for the caravan, the garrison of the camp, and you have the same effect under different conditions. The detachment sent out to get wood was able to bring back but a small portion of the daily provision. Instead, it brought back three men with frozen noses or ears. Fortunately, we have some coal to help us out until tomorrow. But remember that since the mines were discovered after the establishment of the fort, our stoves are not made for coal, and we can burn it only with an equal quantity of wood. So, if we have no wood . . . Let us hope, however, that after two days and three nights of snow and storm, the weather will calm down again tomorrow and will permit us to keep our fires burning under our canvas roofs in this freezing cold. Useless to mention how much we wish to move into our log houses as soon as possible.

Tuesday, December 17. And, in fact, the wind had died down; the air is calm and the sun is shining, but with no warmth. Yesterday evening the thermometer registered three below; this morning at seven o'clock, ten below; and at ten o'clock, five below. Poor sun! It has tried in vain to put on a good face; for us it is the pale face of a convalescent. It shows life, but no strength and energy. Its daily course seems to match its lack of vigor. It comes up late in the S.E., makes its brief journey across the sky with languid resignation, and sets early in the S.W. as if ashamed of its impotence. In contrast, the stars shine twice as brightly, clear, sparkling like the lights of a festive sky.

However, justice should be done this poor sun which certainly isn't the one that Plouvier and Nadar sang of, the one of which they said:

> *Pour tout répandre en abondance,*
> *Pour faire éclore sous nos yeux,*
> *Amour, chansons, joie, espérance,*
> *Il n'a qu'à traverser les cieux.*

[*Parhelion*] Today the pale and cold sun of Dakota gave us a very strange sight. As if in its weakness it tried to make up for quality by quantity, it presented us with three suns at the same time, itself and its double reflection at equal distances away, one in the east and the other in the west. It is the phenomenon that astronomers call parhelion. It seems that it is produced only in very high latitudes toward the north. It is an effect of refraction, which I cannot explain now because I haven't the means. Moreover, observation of the actual event is enough for me. Of course the two false suns were much less brilliant than the real one. Nevertheless, each formed a nucleus of white light shining with a pretty effect. The sky, or to be more exact, the air was slightly vaporous, cloudless, but not without mists. Since everything is covered with snow, the brightness of the real sun was dazzling; but by shutting it out with the hands or any other opaque object, its doubles, which one could look at easily with the naked eye, shone in all their luster. The phenomenon took place from noon to one o'clock, and for us this day might really be called "the day of the three suns."

Wednesday, December 18. The thermometer is still going down! Yesterday evening at nine o'clock it was twenty-two below (F.), and this morning at seven o'clock twenty-six below; that is, fifty-eight degrees below freezing point. In truth, the Arctic itself can produce nothing much better than this, and I am surprised not to see the white bears one finds in the polar seas. The phenomenon of the three suns was repeated today, but an hour later in the afternoon. The effect of the refraction was more colorful and more brilliant than yesterday.

Thursday, December 19. We have the snowstorm back again. The day was terrible. A repetition of Monday.

Friday, December 20. Clear weather; stubborn cold. Even during the day, the thermometer does not go up to zero Fahrenheit anymore. Today it fluctuated between six below and twelve below in spite of the sun. The prairie has a very curious look. As the storm kept beating and sweeping the snow all day yesterday, driven by the wind, it formed banks or waves everywhere, which at a distance, and especially when the sun rose a little above the horizon, bear a striking resemblance to the waves of a vast lake stirred by the breeze. The color is close to that of water reflecting a white sky, and if it were not for the stillness, the illusion would be striking.

And our men are still working in this arctic cold. It is a necessity, for it is essential that we get ourselves housed as quickly as possible. They really understand it, and thus do their share stoutly and cheerfully. If there are complaints, which I doubt, they have never reached me.

As for what are called the pleasures of winter, the excessive cold prohibits them. To go sleighing (if we had suitable sleighs) would not compensate for the discomfort of getting a frozen nose or of rubbing the face with snow every quarter of an hour. Skating on ice covered with two feet of snow is out of the question. As for hunting, this isn't a pleasure any more; it has become a Herculean labor. One must open a road in the drifted snow, get his legs plastered with ice, get numb fingers if he takes off his fur mittens, even if it is for only two minutes to reload his gun. It is lucky that we got our stock of game for Christmas and the New Year in advance. If we had to hunt for it now, we should much prefer getting along without it.

NOTE: We have lost four cattle from the herd; four cattle frozen to death these last nights. They were found in the morning frozen stiff for lack of some shelter to protect them. But what can be done about it? The men must come before the animals, and the only thing we have been able to do for the latter has been to build some closed stables for the mules.

Tuesday, December 24. A mail pouch arrived from Buford today; probably the last one we shall receive this winter from that post. It was brought by three men who had four horses with them. The little detachment was under the leadership of a half-breed from the Red River named Gardepie.

[*The misfortune of Gardepie*] His name is enough to tell that his father is Canadian. His mother belongs to the savage nation of the Crees established in the British possessions.[97] Gardepie himself came from Berthold bringing the packet of letters for Fort Stevenson in order to tell me about the incidents of his trip. Like Brown,[98] one of the couriers who preceded him, he was captured by hostile Indians one day's travel on this side of the Yellowstone.[99] The band that captured him did not number more than twenty to twenty-five lodges situated on the bank of the river. The chief is named, as he understood, Marhpiaskat, which means *White Cloud.* Most of the savages were rather drunk, which proves that a half-breed trader was there with a supply of Indian whiskey (alcohol cut with water) and ammunition. They told Gardepie again that they were determined to intercept all mail from Fort Buford and to kill the American carriers. Don't complain, the chief told him, and consider yourself lucky that your life was spared. You are allowed to go because we all know you, but don't come back again or you will be treated like an

[97] The Cree are an Algonquian tribe of British America closely related to the Chippewa. Hodge, *Handbook,* 1:359.

[98] The Brown mentioned in this journal is John George Brown, an Irishman and an interpreter at Fort Stevenson. It is said that he had formerly been an officer in the British Army, and that at the time of the first Riel Rebellion, General Riel asked him to organize a band of frontiersmen along the Missouri to come to his aid. Joseph H. Taylor, *Sketches of Frontier and Indian Life,* p. 36.

[99] A correspondent of the *St. Louis Republican* at Fort Berthold wrote on December 23 the particulars of the attack on Gardepie's detachment. He says that the men were in the employ of Major Charles A. Ruffee. *St. Paul Daily Pioneer,* March 1, 1868.

American. For what difference is there between you and the Long Knives if you carry their messages and if you are paid by them for services? Do you know what you are doing? It is not our life that you are working for; it is our death, the destruction of the redskins, of our warriors, of our women, and of our children. Wherever the white men establish themselves, the buffalo go, and when the buffalo are gone, the red hunters of the prairie must die of hunger. Just a few years ago, the buffalo were grazing on both banks of the Missouri in countless herds; the prairie was often black with them, and living was easy for the Indian and his family, for they always had meat to eat and fur to trade. But the white men have advanced up the great river, and their warriors are building a great many forts on the banks of the river. They cross the prairies to the north and to the rising sun, and all the game retreats before them. On this side of the fork of the Missouri (the Yellowstone), there are hardly enough buffalo left to feed a part of us, and we have to depend on deer and antelope, and we have nothing to eat if we don't have them. That is why the white men must go away before all the game has left. You, to get new trousers, you help them and you are their friend; so you want to die for new trousers. You are well covered and warmly clothed. *I* am a chief. But look, you can see that I have nothing but old cast-off clothes to keep me from the cold. The white men are the cause of all this; if they had not come here, we all should have enough to eat and enough to clothe ourselves. We shall be able to live on our lands only when they have gone from them."

Gardepie exhausted all his eloquence; but this time he was able to save only the packet of despatches and three of his horses. The fourth had to be abandoned to the savages; but the two men who accompanied him were able to get away with him. The outcome is that communications with Fort Buford will be cut off until spring, unless hunger forces the hostile savages to abandon their encampments to try their luck on the other side of the Yellowstone.[100]

[*News from Buford*] The letters from Buford prove that my orders of last month have had effect. Captain Rankin has handed over the command to Captain Clarke. Lieutenant John Norwell commands the company; Rankin is named quartermaster and commissary of the post. From this I conclude that Rankin has suspended the arrests.

100 Both the *Army and Navy Journal* and the *St. Paul Daily Pioneer* carried stories on this interruption of communications. Both reports were sent out from Fort Berthold on December 23 and appeared on February 29.

Probably in the hope of finding a way to escape court-martial, he has asked for a leave based on a certificate of the surgeon who says he is suffering from gastritis, and that a change of climate would be very beneficial for a cure. I have transmitted the request—disapproved. Rankin, having nothing else to do, can devote all his time to taking care of his health until communications by water are open again, when he can expect that his trial will be held. *After* his trial, if some change of climate is beneficial to him, it is certain that in one way or another nothing will stand in the way of his having complete benefit of it.[101]

Christmas Eve! No Christmas supper for us. Everyone stays in his hut, probably dreaming of past memories that this date recalls. Outside, after a stormy day, the night is clear; the stars twinkle. Inside, the lonely lamp burns until the customary hour of retiring. Nothing marks this night from all the others, and if the calendar did not indicate that today is the twenty-fourth of December, no sign in heaven or on earth would reveal to us here that tonight the Christian world is festive, and that in families everywhere, the children, little and big, are rejoicing around the Christmas tree! And midnight mass! And the religious hymn of Victor Adam:

> *Minuit, chrétiens, c'est l'heure solennelle*
> *Où l'Homme-Dieu descendit jusqu' à nous . . .*

And the organ "with the sustained chords," and the whole rosary of awakened memories! How far away they are in time and distance! *O Tempo passato, perche non ritorni?*

Thursday, December 26. Finally, finally, I have moved into my log house. Yesterday, Christmas, passed like the others in my cabin, except that in the evening I dined with Mr. and Mrs. Marshal. Lieutenants Norwell and Ellis were in the party. Food plentiful, conversation banal and uninteresting. I finished the evening with Dr. and Mrs. Gray who had Major Furey and Lieutenant Hooton to dinner.

[101] The application of Rankin for a leave of absence was forwarded by De Trobriand on December 21. Since Rankin had disobeyed or suppressed the order for his arrest on November 7, a duplicate of the order was forwarded to Major Clarke. De Trobriand wrote: "This application for a leave of absence, seems to me but another step connected with the suspicious and unexplained application for the withdrawal of the charges & specifications in order to elude at any risk, the trial by a General Court-Martial. It will not be by any fault of mine, if ever the ends of justice are frustrated in this . . ." Régis de Trobriand, Fort Stevenson, Dakota Territory, to Bvt. Lt. Col. Ed. W. Smith, AA Genl, Department of Dakota, St. Paul, Dec. 21, 1867. Department of Dakota, War Records Division, National Archives.

This morning, moving began immediately after breakfast. A wagon came to take away first the kitchen utensils and the cook in order to assure us of dinner in our new lodging; then another wagon moved my baggage and furniture. And so it was with Major Furey, quartermaster, Dr. and Mrs. Gray, and Lieutenant Norwell. We are the only *tenants* whose quarters are finished, for we live in the same building.

[*The new houses*] The building is composed of seven rooms, on the same floor, of course; it is built entirely of logs eight to ten inches in diameter, laid one on the other and chinked with mud and large chips of wood, the whole forming the thick wall. The roof is composed of split poles, one end of which rests on a big log forming the roof tree and the other on the walls, since there are walls. Over these split poles, a layer of hay; over the layer of hay, a layer of earth; over the earth, the frozen snow. Since the roof is almost flat, seven logs form the height of the wall, which is consequently about eight feet high, including a last log thinner than the others which goes up to the edge of the roof, an entablature holding up the poles, hay, and earth. Each room is fifteen feet square, has a door, two little windows with six panes of glass (real windows), floor of fir, and a monumental stove with a drum, which almost doubles the heat. The rooms are separated by walls of logs and mud similar to the outside walls. These are cut by a door between the kitchen of each household and the room which serves as salon, bedroom, and dining room, if one prefers not to eat in the kitchen.

These log houses, humble structures of all the clearings in the solitudes of North America, are built in summer, so that the mud, which is the integral part of them, has time to dry before the frosts; in them one can endure the severest winters. But it must be remembered that ours was not begun until after the coming of winter, and that the building went on through frigid temperatures, snowstorms, and weather cold enough to crack the stones. To cement them with mud, we had to keep up great fires to heat the water used to mix with the earth. No sooner was the primitive mud in place than the cold seized it, penetrated it, and changed it into a hard mass, half earth and half ice. Then when the snowstorms came before the doors and windows were put in, the snow swept inside, burst into whirlwinds, got into the inside crevices of the roof, and stuck all over the rough bark. They swept out all they could, and since the stoves were put in this morning, we entered joyfully.

The interior of my room was like a chapel of the Virgin in the

month of May, minus the altar and statue. There the snow and frost
flowered everywhere in arabesque, in alabaster foam, and in fantastic whorls, all that in a dazzling whiteness with little warmth.
The stove was lighted, but the door was kept open in below zero
(Fahrenheit) weather to let the baggage and furniture in, so that in
this first battle between the fire and ice, the fire was defeated. It soon
had its victory. Once the door was closed, the temperature began to
go up with a surprising suddenness, and the stove asserted itself to
the fullest. At this, the ice and snow, knowing that they were really
defeated, began to break into tears. The thaw turned the mud back
into the state it was in before it froze; it softened it, weakened it,
liquefied it, and this revolution on the inside is still going through
the following phases: 1. Chunks of mud come loose from the walls
and ceiling; they are constantly falling and spotting everything exposed to this new kind of coating; 2. Hail of little pebbles, which,
released from the mud which held them, quickly take advantage of
their independence and obey the laws of gravity; 3. Holes, unnoticed
at first, show up; cracks are formed, and the gusts outside blow the
snow in winnows which powder my floor. It is snowing in my room;
4. The heat reaches the snow and ice in the chinks in the walls, in
the openings in the roof and in the bottom of the little grottos where
it was hidden. It comes out in little cascades which run on all sides.
It rains in my new lodging; rain, draughts, and little avalanches of
earth give me welcome. Is this going to last long?

Thompson (my orderly, an Englishman turned Yankee) spent
his afternoon in stopping up the chinks, holes, fissures, crevices, as
they showed up, going out, coming in, working on the outside, putty-
ing on the inside, crawling on the roof, and he did not have too
much time. George (my Negro servant) is bewildered. He leaves the
broom only to take the dust cloth, and then stops dusting to sweep
again, hardly finding time to put my things in order, make my bed,
and shake out my blankets. I asked him if he had ever heard of the
rock of Sisyphus. "Never." So I can't make him see the similarity between his work which he constantly does over again and that of
Sisyphus or the daughters of Danaüs whose whole story I don't know
either. Finally evening came. The holes are stopped up; the snow is
not coming into my house any more, and the trickling has changed
to dripping, which is becoming less and less frequent. Its source, it
seems, is almost exhausted. But here and there little avalanches come
down from time to time, and the silence of my cabin is broken by
the sharp sound of a little pebble tumbling down and bouncing on

Log houses at Fort Stevenson

the floor. My table, commode, chairs, and bed are spotted with little bits of earth, which make me eye my ceiling suspiciously. However, it is bedtime. So I shall go to bed and take care to cover my head with the buffalo robe and its thick fur will serve as both a blanket and a shield. After all, bear in mind that the temperature of the room is easily kept at the most comfortable point and that in the plank and canvas lodging I left this morning it was only by dint of firing that we could get far less satisfactory results. When the fire went out, the cold ruled absolutely and most tyrannically. In the night, one could feel his nose freezing at the edge of the blanket, and if it were necessary to get out of bed before the rekindled fire had roared for a quarter of an hour, one shivered as if he were in open air. Then, too, there were cracks made by the contraction of the porous cottonwood planks. In order to protect ourselves against the cutting draughts and blasts of snow, we had to caulk the cracks with tarred oakum, like an old ship which leaks in all its seams. So, everything considered, in spite of this first day of trial, I am still convinced that my new turtle shell, although it looks more primitive and less pleasing than the first, will none the less be infinitely more comfortable in which to brave the rigors of a long winter, a winter such as the heavens inflict on the icy plains of Dakota.

Friday, December 27. And there was a good reason for eyeing my ceiling suspiciously yesterday before I went to bed. During the night, I was awakened from a sound sleep by a plaster of earth which fell on my nose. So, the first thing I did when I got up was to get hold of as many of the old tents not in use as I could so I could make a tapestry on the interior. As a preliminary operation, I equipped my orderly with a trowel and set him to work replastering the mud all over, which cannot be done without discovering and stopping up still more new holes in my walls. After this we started to hang the tapestry, my servant and orderly under my direction.

Sunday, December 29. The work of cutting up the old tents for the best pieces, of fitting them to their new use, of putting them in place and nailing them up to the best possible advantage took three full days. Everything was mixed up with the endless moving of furniture, sweeping, and dusting. Finally the job is done; mud walls and ceiling or rather roof with chinks have all disappeared under a covering of canvas which is more or less white, or really more or less clean, but much more pleasant to look at. With a good imagination and poor eyes, one could imagine that he was in a plastered room, were there not two big crossed logs supporting the roof, which preserves the purely rustic-military character of the lodging. And what a wonderful stove! With three chunks of wood, one can't come near it, and it sends one to the other end of the apartment. With six chunks, I believe it would heat a theater all by itself. By doubling the amount, my room would become a sweating room, and I should go out and roll in the snow like the Russian peasants taking their national bath. Now the fire can go out at ten o'clock in the evening. After nine or ten hours, winter will not have come into my house, and I no longer depend on the punctuality of my Negro, George, to get me up at seven o'clock in the morning.

What a terrible contrast outside! The snow has piled up so high on the plains that our communications with both Fort Rice and Fort Totten have become very precarious. As for Fort Buford, since the hostile Indians are interfering with the communications, we cannot count on them for the rest of the winter.

[*Couriers in the snow*] On the sixteenth of this month, Bismorin, surnamed *La Bombarde* (he is a Canadian half-breed) left here with two Yanktonah Indians hired to carry our correspondence to Fort Rice. On the seventeenth, they were to meet halfway another party coming from Fort Rice. At the station recently built for this purpose, they were to exchange despatches and both be back the evening of the third day, or the fourth at the latest. The fourth day and the following ones went by without bringing us news of them, and not until the twenty-seventh did La Bombarde appear, alone and with no mail. The story of the trip is a real Odyssey. Although the snow fell often and in great quantities during the month, they did not expect to find it so high on the plains. Not having any dog sleds with them, they had great difficulties from the first. Not only was the snow deep everywhere, four or five feet in ravines, but the severe cold had frozen the surface into an icy crust, which cracked under the feet of the horses, injured their legs, tore off their skin, and in this way weakened them considerably. Nevertheless, they arrived at the meeting place. The other party had got there first and had waited in the cabin built for this purpose, but since no one came, they had turned back without pushing on farther, in spite of the orders which they had received. The fire they had lit was not out yet when our men arrived. They realized they would have to go on to Fort Rice. During the night, two of the horses were frightened, probably by the approach of some wolves. One broke his halter, the other succeeded in sliding his over his ears, and both disappeared into the woods, the station being on the edge of the river. In the morning, they had to run after them in the snow. One of the two Indians got frozen feet, and the other, the only one still with a mount, pushed on with the letters for Fort Rice. "I shall wait for you four days," La Bombarde told him. "By that time I'll have my horse and I'll have left your partner with some of your people, so that we'll return together without losing more time." The Indian left, and after unheard of hardships the half-breed finally found the two horses in the possession of *Ishta-Sapah,* who found them on his return to Fort Rice with his followers. He made no trouble about giving them back immediately and hurried with the others to the station to their man with the frozen feet. They took him with them, and it is probable that with their empiric treatment they will succeed in giving him back the use of his two legs.

La Bombarde, left alone, waited in vain beyond the appointed time for his other companion. His matches were lost or wet, and he had no more fire. His provisions had been exhausted during all these delays; he had nothing left to eat. Scouting around, he learned from some Indians hunting in the woods that the one he was waiting for had gone back to Fort Rice and that they had met him on his return. The half-breed got from them a little food to give him strength to get back to Fort Stevenson as quickly as possible. He got under way, bringing with him the horse of the crippled Indian and his own (both belonging to the government). Despite the cold and hunger which pressed him on, he could not get back in less than three days— three more days of misery, hardship, and suffering. He did not meet the Indian, and we have no news of him yet.

Such is the story of our last postal expedition to Fort Rice, which will not prevent another from leaving tomorrow, Monday; this one is composed of a soldier, a carter employed by the quartermaster, (Martin, my teacher of Sioux) and the invincible La Bombarde. This La Bombarde is amazing. He endures devilish ordeals with a stoic *sang-froid* and with what might be called a philosophy discouraged by nothing. He must have been through many other trials to come to the point where he looks upon his last trip as a very natural thing and to start out again in three days.

Monday, December 30. All our communications are more or less disrupted. The men with the mail from Buford to Totten who left the day before yesterday for Devils Lake returned discouraged by the obstacles, although they had a sled drawn by four dogs. They are going to reinforce their team at Fort Berthold where they have been stationed since two of their posts have been abandoned for the Mouse River route. Then they will leave tomorrow or the next day to try it again. We sent a courier in the same direction the twentieth of this month. Between Stevenson and Totten, remember, there are five stations or cabins where our men can at least find shelter every night. At the halfway station, (the third), they ought to have met the courier from Totten the evening of the third day; that is, the twenty-second, and be back here the evening of the twenty-fifth. To-day, the thirtieth, at ten o'clock in the evening, they still haven't appeared. So, there is already a delay of five days. If they fail to arrive tomorrow, our new courier will leave the day after tomorrow before we receive the letters and papers that the courier sent out the twentieth ought to have brought us. This is the benevolence of a winter in Dakota.

Tuesday, December 31. The year 1867 has come to its last moments. In two hours, it will have ceased to be and will join in the abyss of the past some millions of other years of which only a few thousand have left on us their distinct marks and of which scarcely forty—a nothing—have their place in my memory. I have neither family nor friends around me to bid it goodbye. For me no clock will strike the twelve strokes of midnight at its passing. No familiar sound, no family celebration will mark the portentous moment when 1868 succeeds 1867.

As I take leave of the dying year and welcome its successor, I am alone in a log house in the heart of the deserts of the American continent, dreaming of my dear absent ones, and looking back on bygone days. And what a variety of places and experiences are in the succession of those first days of the year!

1840—Tours, by the sickbed of my father, dead ten days later.

1841—Paris, life of a young man.

1842—New York, life of a gentleman traveler.

1843—Paris, twenty-five days before my marriage. Period of *grande monde de Paris.*

1845–1846–1847—Venice. Gold and silk. Painting, music, some studies in history; all the pleasures of society; no regret for the past; no worry about the future; enjoying the days as they come.

1848—New York, painting, music, and journalism, all as an amateur and in my leisure time.

1849—Charle[s]ton, traveling, en route for the island of Cuba.

1850—New York, *La Revue du Nouveau Monde*. Serious occupation.

1852—Tours, drawing family ties closer and reviving childhood memories.

1853—*Chateau de la Fourgeraie,* life of a country gentleman.

1854—Paris, life of leisure and freedom.

1855—New York, six years of journalism as a regular occupation. The children are growing up.

1862—Colonel, in a tent near Washington facing the enemy.

1863—In the field before Fredericksburg.

1864—In New York in the interval between two commands as a general officer.

1865—In the lines before Petersburg.

1866—New York. *Otium cum dignitate.*

1867—Brest, waiting between military adventures.

1868—Fort Stevenson, Dakota.

1869—????—Who knows?

And in going back over the thread of these dates, how many happenings, great and small, I find there! How many revolutions in the life of nations; how many sudden changes in my life! How pleasure is mixed with grief, light with darkness! How many clouds passed over the sun which seemed to be lasting shadows and which disappeared without leaving a mark! How many people met, how many things seen, how many thoughts provoked, how many ideas acquired in these trips from one world to the other; on one side across France, England, Italy, Belgium, Switzerland, Austria, and on the other across the United States, Canada, and the island of Cuba! And what a school in philosophy is four years in a gigantic war to crown the experience and knowledge of a nomadic life of twenty years. But what do I know? After all that, in comparison to what I should still be able to learn, if life were not too short and if one did not forget with the years half of what is learned. The little Greek that I knew I have forgotten, I do not know when, since I never had a chance to use it. Latin—I lost it the day I learned Italian. I should have forgotten Italian while studying Spanish if I had not stopped myself in time. And now I am learning Sioux, which will make me forget nothing.

How many things have I forgotten about history, mathematics, and ancient literature! So much that I sometimes wonder if the total of my knowledge acquired in thirty years is much greater than that which I have lost in the same period of time. In any case, what I remembered is a good deal more important and practical. This is what causes progress and improvement. Youth dreams about life; age achieves the practical. Age knows life thoroughly; youth hardly suspects it. With what a feeling of pity I take myself back today to that phase of my first youth and to those trivial things and vain illusions which then took up my time and fascinated me.

But after all, is it in those things which in fifty years we call serious, which we dignify by pompous names—noble ambitions, glorious works, *exemplary* life, *high* knowledge—that life is revealed to us with the most intensity in its hope, joy, or disappointment? Where is the most intense realm of the heart, the soul, the faculties? In passion or in reason? Everything is logical in this world. Age of passions first; the age of reason next. He who has not gone through these two phases has only half lived. The person who has had only passions knows but one side of life; he who has had only reason is no better off; and he who upsets the natural order of the two periods has been nothing but a fool from beginning to end.

At least, I need not reproach myself on this score, and I have not done things out of season. Too, in spite of the stormy days, how many fair days there were in my springtime, my summer, and my autumn. If I had to begin life again, I should still take it day by day as it has gone up to now.

And I should see you again as I saw you, and I should love you again as I loved you, you of whom I try in vain to say nothing here, although my thoughts are all filled with you—you who brighten my past when I look back, a past which is bright because of you and which would be dark without you—you who appear to me still young and beautiful and charming as in other days and who today are only a phantom carried off to other spheres, where faithful hearts are still attached to this world. Across the tomb as across space, my soul soars up and my thoughts unite with you.

1867. Goodbye! No other will give back to me what you have taken—unless in another life.

The night is half clouded; the stars glimmer uncertainly, half disappearing behind the floating mist as if they were afraid of revealing the secret I am asking them. But when there is doubt, there is still room for hope—and hope which slumbers before death awakens after.

Wednesday, January 1. The Dakota sky was uncordial in its welcome to the year 1868. The cold abated a good deal, so much so that the thermometer has been going up for a few hours, almost to the freezing point; but a mixture of snow and a most disagreeable sleet has been falling. However, the sun has tried to come out. Like a good prince it showed itself for a few minutes, after which the day ended without it. But what would it have seen that was unusual at Fort Stevenson? The officers came to pay me the usual visit in the morning, and following their example, I went to offer the wishes of the occasion to the four ladies who are here with their husbands and who moved into their new quarters yesterday and the day before. The compliments of the day exchanged, refreshments consumed, everyone went back to his quarters. Those of the officers who were still at camp dined with Lt. Colonel Powell who must spend another night in his tent. The men worked as much and more than usual, in order that everyone here might be provided for by tomorrow night.

Thursday, January 2. Which, in fact, has taken place. All day was spent in completing the moving. The sick have been carried to the new hospital. The 1st company took possession of its new quarters. The band did, too. All the officers are in their log houses this evening. All the provisions of the quartermaster and the commissary were transported to the large store some hours ago. The bakery is busy; the powder house is ready; the offices are functioning and the prison—I forgot to mention that yesterday, on the occasion of the New Year, I sent back to their companies all the prisoners awaiting either court-martial proceedings or the confirmation of their sentences, of which, after some months, they still have not been notified. I had been authorized by Gen¹ Terry to take this measure, in consideration of the long delays that the dossiers and settlement of courts martial must go through because of his absence. Gen¹ Terry belongs to the commission on Indian Affairs, and he was forced to leave his command four months ago to go out to conclude treaties with the hostile Indians on the Plat[t]e River and on the Pacific Railroad. This absence and the slowness of communications in this season of the year made the temporary liberation of the prisoners desirable from every point of view—for there are among them some who have already undergone a preventive imprisonment which is probably longer than the court will give to them. I hope that this will be taken into consideration. So today there are just four prisoners who are kept because of the more serious nature of their offense, theft or insubordination, or because of the recent date of their entry into jail.

You understand that "prisoner" means an arrested man who works all day at hard labor in the camp under the eyes of the guard and who sleeps under the same surveillance at night, a man with a ball and chain on his foot.

No news from Fort Rice, and no news from Fort Totten. A new mail packet was sent to Fort Rice December 30th (last Monday), and another to Fort Totten yesterday, January 1st. Let us hope that these have better luck than the two before.

Friday, January 3. At last we received a courier from Fort Rice. The three men sent December 30 met those sent from Fort Rice the same day right on time. Our two Indians were with them, the one who had frozen feet almost completely recovered.

Few letters come to us by this route. However, I received two from France, but dated earlier than those I received two weeks ago by way of Fort Totten. Papers in particular come to us by Fort Rice. We see by the ones we received today that all the regiments of infantry and artillery are going to be gradually reduced to the minimum of fifty men a company as eventualities reduce the ranks.[102] The result will probably be, if peace is not concluded next spring with the hostile Indians of Dakota, that the government will have to increase the number of regiments on the Upper Missouri. It is fortunate for us that this cannot go into effect here until the forts under my command are finished. Reading the papers, I consider myself fortunate to be far from the circles of political agitation. What is happening back there is disgusting, and in the South, in the states that formerly were in revolt, the military commanders can say to one another, as the Inca chief said to his minister, both on thorns: "And I, am I on a bed of roses here?"

Sunday, January 5. For the first time in a long while our men have not worked on Sunday. Now that we are provided for after a fashion in our winter quarters, their work will be much lighter, and they will have their Sunday rest regularly again and the suspension of work Saturday afternoon to prepare for the weekly inspection of the next day. Furthermore, even if they still had urgent work to do, it would be impossible today, at least outside. The day was the most

---

[102] Orders for this reduction were issued November, 1867. The *Army and Navy Journal* commented on this untimely reduction: "The war on the plains has been patched up by a hollow truce. . . . Everywhere on the frontier is life unsafe and the Indians unpunished and insolent, for the want of more troops. And this is the time chosen to reduce a force before confessedly insufficient." The *Army and Navy Journal;* 40 Congress, 3 session, *Executive Document* no. 1, p. 1.

terrible that can be imagined. The wind kept blowing violently from the north, carrying with it thick clouds of fine, icy snow. Was some of it coming from the sky, too, or had the storm really picked it all up on the plains to fill the air with these whirlwinds, airy billows which run wild like those of the ocean under the furious lash of the tempest? We don't know. What we do know is that objects can scarcely be made out at the shortest distance—and not facing the wind, for then the snow made it almost impossible for one to keep his eyes open and scourged the face as if an invisible hand had whipped it with sharp lashes. Imagine, if you can, what such weather is in a cold of fourteen degrees *below* zero Fahrenheit. So no one has put his nose out today. Everyone remained a prisoner in his cabin. We must put up with it. From now on, this is our lot for most of the winter days.

In our enforced captivity, we do not have even the diversion of looking outside. Our windows are covered with a thick layer of ice which cuts off vision and intercepts part of the light. A sharp cold usually covers the windows of dwellings heated on the inside with a layer of ice covered with sparkling points, which shine, at least in the daytime. But here the case is different; I suppose it is caused by the great humidity coming from the mud as it dries. It always forms on our panes a layer of *snow* instead of ice, which sometimes gets to be more than half an inch thick. When it reaches the point where it shuts out the daylight, one can easily scrape it off with a knife blade, except for a thin layer inside which sticks to the windows in the form of ice, but through which the light passes easily. We do not see any more on the outside, but we do see much better on the inside. Isn't it strange that the comparatively high temperature of the room does not melt this frost which would finally put us in darkness if it weren't taken off every day?

In contrast, when the snow accumulates outside on the windows, they remain perfectly transparent. One of my casements is half buried under a pile of snow which divided it diagonally: all the covered part was unchanged; all the part exposed to the air was clouded by the crystallization. But when my orderly had dug out and swept away the pile outside, the panes were clouded in a few minutes with the same opaque veil as the others.

As the back of the log house is exposed to the winds from the northeast and the re-entrant angle formed by the kitchen faces that direction, the snow piles up in that sort of cul-de-sac and it has already reached the height of the roof; that is, about eight feet high.

It is the warm side of the building. It is protected by this winter bulwark which will remain against it until spring.

This evening the storm seemed to grow rather than abate. The wind sings a sad song as it hurls itself against the chimney of the stove and shakes the roof of the cabin. Undoubtedly our couriers have remained at one of the stations all day. The arrival of the letters we are impatiently awaiting from Fort Totten is thus delayed.

Monday, January 6. If the day yesterday was as I wrote above "the most terrible that can be imagined," today surpasses what imagination can picture—for unquestionably the weather found a way of getting worse.

[*Luctantes ventos tempestates que sonoras*] I had believed it was impossible before seeing it and going through it. Yesterday evening when I had gone to sleep, the wind sang its laments in the chimney of my stove, making a pipe organ of it. This morning when I woke up, it was like a furious concert of whizzings and modulated curses in the most vehement tone. The storm has not abated during the night, I thought. Soon my servant opened my door, as reveille had just sounded. Only he leaped inside rather than entered and closed the door behind him with obvious haste. I opened my eyes to find out about this *ex abrupto* invasion, and to my great surprise I saw my man all white from head to foot—a real snow statue—all the more so since the frost gave his greatcoat a sculptured stiffness. "Where in the devil did you come from?" I asked him. "From my room." (George's room is separated from mine only by the dining room, forming the angle of the building, and the kitchen beyond—a distance of twenty-five to thirty feet at the most). "And I thought I'd never find the door. The building is half buried under the snow, and it's impossible to see in front of you." Continuation of yesterday, I thought to myself, and I was half on my way back to sleep while George, who has the great virtue of speaking only when questioned, was lighting the fire and brushing my clothes without any other explanation. When he went out, I got up slowly, and then I dressed leisurely, waiting for breakfast time. The hour for breakfast passed, and still another, and no George to announce to me that I was served. Surprised by this unusual delay, I resolved to find out the reason for it, and I opened my door. At the same instant, the air from the outside rushed inside in the form of a thick cloud of steam, a swirl of snow struck me right in the face and powdered me white from head to foot. Somewhat stunned, I hesitated on the sill and looked out.

Nothing was visible but a white opaque veil that the wind carried along in a mass without parting it and behind which the buildings only a few feet from my door were concealed. I looked down at my feet, and I saw the imprint of the panels molded on the wall of a pile of snow three feet high, on one side leaning against the door frame and on the other side slanting down to about two feet. It is there that George had made his passage and where the eddy of air kept digging a sort of furrow. I wanted to see more of it, and closing the door, not without some difficulty, I was at the entry of the dining room in two or three strides. It was open; I sprang inside. The snow had penetrated everywhere: the floor, table, chairs, furniture, and even the walls which were ornamented by a white decoration. To produce this effect in one night all that was needed was a chink as thick as a finger carelessly left at the top of the door which opened outward. Through here, the snow, driven by the storm, came in a sheet to cover everything with an icy dust. My orderly, my servant, and Major Furey's, all three battled together with broom and shovel, but it was lost effort. They had to open the door to throw out the snow; when the door was open, as much came in as was thrown out. The three workers looked like three good snowmen, and finally gave up the task, confining their work to clearing out the doorway so the door could be closed.

But how would we have breakfast? I looked into the kitchen through the small window opened in the wall for the convenience of service. The kitchen resembled a miniature opera setting. The long needles of ice that were hanging from the roof gave it the appearance of a grotto of stalactites which the caprices of the snow made appear entirely fantastic with its clusters, whorls, and waves. In the midst of this strange setting, the captive cook was watching the cooking of a beefsteak, which was then brought to me in my room half frozen. The cook could not get out all day. He is blocked in his kitchen by a solid bank of snow under which the door, because of its position, remains completely buried. But he made use of his captivity by energetically blocking up all the holes, slits, and chinks, which until now he hadn't bothered about. It's an ill wind that blows no one good. I can imagine the surprise of the culinary artist when this morning he came out from under his covers where he had slept very well to find his lodging changed like this. He must have imagined that he was still dreaming.

The whole day passed without the slightest variation in the weather. The thermometer still between twenty-two and twenty-three below zero; the snow still lashed by the storm through the opaque air; the wind from the north still shrieking and whistling—and the mournful concert still in the chimney of my stove. No one could get to the wood or coal. Those who like me find they have a sufficient supply for two whole days are fortunate. But how can we keep warm tomorrow if the storm does not let up tonight?

Needless to say, I have seen no one but my servant all day. To open the door was quite an undertaking, for if the wall of snow rolled inside, it was absolutely necessary to throw it out or the door wouldn't close. And during this time, the air rushed in with clouds of steam, and the snow swirled in.

However, it was quite necessary to open the door for dinner; second beefsteak, second cup of coffee with milk; but there was a dessert: a slice of peach pie. After this, I doubly barricaded myself, went back to my reading, writing, and by way of diversion, examining thoroughly all the problems of the knight on the chessboard. The hours passed with the same swiftness as they would have in the finest weather in the world: nothing hurries them or slows them down, although it sometimes pleases us to reproach them with being too rapid or slow, because of our pleasures or our troubles, our fears or our desires.

This evening I am going to go to sleep again to the song of the wind which still keeps up its melody. One of my windows is completely under snow. I hope that at least the other one will let me see light or else the sun when I wake up. Forty-eight hours of such a storm is more than enough to appreciate fully the rigors of a winter sky in Dakota.

Tuesday, January 7. Waking up this morning from a very clear and distinct dream in which I talked with the souls who are no longer of this world, I noticed the reflection of the first light of day on the red calico curtains at my window. At least this one wasn't under snow yet. I cocked my ear. The song of the wind was now almost an imperceptible murmur, and I concluded that good weather had finally returned. However, the deep silence that reigned outside set me to thinking. The hour slipped away, and George didn't show up. The best thing to do was to get up without waiting for him. So I lit the fire in my stove myself with some sticks of dry wood put in the house for this purpose; I finished my toilette leisurely, and I waited until nine o'clock without seeing anything or hearing anyone come. George must be blocked in his room and not able to get out unless someone comes to help him. So I decided to open my door in spite of the difficulty I should have in getting it closed again. I found myself face to face with a wall of snow four feet high, above which I saw nothing but the same white veil. The upper part of the entry, which formed a small window, let in the same cloud, and the same blast of snow struck me in the face. It was a continuation of yesterday with no variation, except that for one reason or another, the wind had stopped its concert in the chimney of my stove. This glance outside was enough to start a small landslide of snow. My door would not shut. I had to get my hunting knife with the large blade, hurriedly scrape the door jamb and the door frame, clean out the grooves, and when the bolt finally went back into its slot, a pretty carpet of snow stretched *diminuendo* from my door halfway across my room. Philosophically, I armed myself with the broom, gathered the snow into a pile on two or three feet of floor which is left without a rug where the door opens, then with a small board, for lack of a shovel, I scooped the pile of snow into a zinc tub which came in handy, although it was not intended for this purpose. I went through this domestic task seven or eight times during the day for every person who came in and, consequently, left my lodging. I shall even add here that I had to make my bed, get my lamp ready, and in a word, be as in *Le Ménage de Garçon*, "my chamber woman, my servant, and my janitor," for the simple reason that my servant and orderly could get to me only as snow men under greatcoats powdered white and frozen so stiff that they could hardly get out of them without ripping them, unless they waited until the frost with which they are impregnated melted into water by my stove. I prefer to take care of myself.

> *La neige a des rigueurs à nulle autres pareilles*
>
> . . . .
>
> *L'Indien dans son tipi qui couvre un toit de terre*
> *Est sujet au drift hivernal*
> *Et la garde qui veille au poste militaire*
> *N'en défend pas le géneral.*

My door closed again, I waited patiently for them to release me, which took place an hour and a half later. George opened a trench and made a passage up to my door, advising me not to open it before he let me know that I could do so with no fear of letting in a landslide.

The news that he brought was far from pleasant. An immense bank of snow had formed in the angle of the building and extended, sloping off gradually, forty or fifty feet in a S. E. direction. The dining room had completely disappeared, buried under the snow which passed over the roof without an obstacle. The kitchen was in the same condition. To get to the cook and to have him pass wood and provisions, we had to cut out a passage five feet deep. The closed lean-to, which houses our milk cow, was under snow, too. We were afraid that the poor beast was suffocated or dead with the cold. I was the only one in the building blockaded by the snow, which passed before my neighbors' door without stopping, except in back of the main part of the lodging where the bank of snow was as high as the roof everywhere. He couldn't tell me anything about the rest of the fort, for it was impossible to see that far and no one would go there if they didn't have to. Twenty-two degrees below zero and a storm from the north; this was more than enough to chill any curiosity. At least I should have some breakfast—breakfast such as it is—and George had come to ask me to be patient about that good news. Meanwhile, he was going to look for some pieces of wood. Soon he brought back an armful, getting the sticks from a log that he had cut up with an axe; but the poor fellow also brought back two frozen ears because he believed he could safely expose them to this sharp cold for less than a quarter of an hour. He rubbed them with snow repeatedly, but it did not have any effect, or at least had only a partial effect on one of them, which, at dinner time, half disappeared under an enormous blister. George had not thought it proper to talk to me about this accident before evening; the doctor to whom I sent him will probably send him back with his ear in *statu quo ante*.

[*The battle against the snow*] It was my orderly's turn to take the shovel to clear out the trench and keep the way to my door open. And it wasn't a sinecure. The snow blown by the wind and sliding in from both banks piled up at the rate of about a foot an hour. But Dupont—today he was an alert and vigorous Frenchman who was of some use—was spurred on rather than discouraged when faced with these difficulties. For two whole hours, I heard his shovel at work; I asked him for news about the weather through the door. Always the same thing. Only once did Dupont announce a favorable change: the sun came out and the wind seemed to be dying down. Attracted by this, I opened my door. The sun looked like a paper lantern; but apparently the snow was still just as thick. As for my orderly, nothing but his nose and cheek bones showed through the thick layer of snow that enveloped him. His fur cap was an iced cheese, and his face was masked by the ice which covered his mustaches, his beard, and up to his eyebrows, so that one guessed where his eyes were rather than saw them. In spite of all this, he said he wasn't cold; warm in fact. The vigorous exercise he was getting took the place of a stove.

When I stepped outside, I succeeded in closing the door quickly behind me, for I thought that since the sun had come out, I was quite able to do as much, and I walked out far enough to see how my lodging looked on the outside. It was just a mountain of snow with two openings; one to the east before my door; the other to the south was scarcely more than a large, oblique hole to get into the kitchen. The dining room had disappeared under the snow like Herculaneum under the lava. It looked to me as if this was the fate of most of the buildings like ours that lodged the officers and were located on the other side of the fort. I ran up to the servants' cabin. I glanced around in vain for the cow stable that I knew was there, and coming back, I understood perfectly well why George preferred to come to my room *by walking over the roof*. He had only to climb up the drift on one side and come down on the other, while going around it, he had to detour about one hundred paces, at the risk of getting lost, which had happened to Major Furey's servant in the evening.

Back from my short trip, I had just got at the sweeping and necessary scraping when two officers visited me: Lts. Parsons and Ward. The first, who is commissary of supplies, came to find out if I had enough to eat; it seems several officers who had just a servant and no orderly were forced to fast all morning before they were able to re-establish their communications with the earth's surface. My visitors informed me that the wind and the snow had shown unexplainable caprices. Some buildings are as accessible as they would be if no snow had fallen; others are literally buried. The latter was the condition of the three married officers' lodging, which is in about the same state as my dining room. Next to them, I am the one who is most badly treated. If they are worse off than I, married as they all are, they must not *be enjoying themselves*.

The hospital is in a deplorable state; the snow came in everywhere through cracks made by the settling of the adobe at the edge of the framework. The pharmacy is in exactly the same state as my kitchen was yesterday morning; a grotto of stalactites, decorated with arabesques of snow and with a carpet *idem*. Almost everyone, officers and soldiers, is without wood to burn. The officers kept up their fires with everything they could sacrifice: boxes and boards. The men laid hands on everything of this kind they could find. Finally, they were given the sutler's wood supply, which they will replace when good weather comes back. The worst is that an enormous drift has formed around the corral, which is half buried by it. We hope that the cattle have escaped under the canvas cover stretched on frames to protect them; but they haven't been reached yet, and they have nothing to eat.

The storm makes it impossible to carry hay from the stacks to the corral, and, moreover, the path to the shelters is not open yet.

The quartermaster himself came around four o'clock to tell me what he saw. The drift is fourteen feet high, and by an unexplained oddity, extends in a semicircle from the old storehouses to the corral, which it surrounds. The mules are in their stables, which the snow has invaded, but they do not seem to have suffered because of it. Some are frisking around outside; all of them have a surplus of forage to keep them in good condition. This is the situation we are in at the end of the third day of this terrible storm.

From beefsteaks, I have come down to the simple slice of fried ham. That is something to make a face about, but when one is hungry, it isn't hard to eat. But it is quite an abuse of language to call that a *dinner*. By way of this, the other day I was reading in one of the New York reviews (*The Galaxy*) the following passage: "Salt pork—that abounding curse of American civilization, a dish so abominable that even the impostor Mohammed denied it to his followers, and which certainly would have been interdicted to Christians had it been supposed they would ever relapse so far into Barbarism as to use it."[103]

After *dinner,* since dinner there is, I closed the door behind George and for the last time got on with the above mentioned cleaning; I then shut myself up to write these notes before going to bed. Is the weather going to get any better? I don't know a thing about it, and I can forebear going out to see. I shall know tomorrow when Dupont's shovel and George's step sound on the snow. For this evening, having a good supply of wood and some books, I am happy with a well-heated room and a well-lighted table, and I can easily forget the miseries and all that is going on outdoors.

Wednesday, January 8. When I woke up, daylight was coming into my room through a little more than a pane and a half. All the rest was under snow. Following the line of the drift, I believed that it must have completely covered my door; but I was mistaken. Dupont soon informed me from outside that it was only *four feet high* in the trench. When he gave me light by clearing away my window and

[103] The quotation from the *Galaxy* appeared in the French manuscript in English.

freedom by clearing away my door, I was happy to learn and to see with my own eyes that the sun was shining and that the storm seemed to be over. However, the air was still full of that terrible sparkling dust, the form that snow takes when it is whipped by the wind in extreme cold. The thermometer had gone up very little. It was still eighteen below. During the night, it had gone down to twenty-four below. Dupont assured me that "it didn't amount to anything now." It was hard for me to take his word for it, and I resolved to find out for myself after breakfast (another slice of fried ham and some codfish. Alas!) Protected against the cold from head to foot, eyes and nose scarcely outside of my furs, I went out.

The drift under which my dining room was buried had grown a good deal, if not in height, certainly in breadth. Its base had enlarged so much that it had taken the shape of a mountain flanked by a hill. I knew then that although the violence of the wind had diminished, it had still kept on blowing. Only it had shifted to the S. W. It was this change of direction that now protected the entrance to my lodging and made the snow which was blowing in at the rate of a foot an hour yesterday pile up at the rate of only an inch an hour today. But for the same reason, things became worse in other places. On the other side of the mountain, nothing was visible. The wind carried back from the banks of the river the snow which it had driven there. It lashed every obstacle facing south, sweeping over the kitchen, drifting along the roof and on this side and making the place untenable. So I directed my steps to the other side and went to visit the hospital and one of the company quarters. The sick room is habitable, but no more, and in spite of the two stoves around which the patients are grouped in a circle, more than a day's work will have to be done to make it a little more comfortable. The pharmacy is as they pictured it to me: a grotto of snow. They do not dare to make a fire before sweeping it out, for everything would be deluged by the thaw.

January 8, 1868 (*Continued*). There is nothing unusual about the company quarters. They are about what one would expect in their unfinished condition. At least the drifts did not get to them, and their doors and windows are free. This is true also of the band quarters, which are built of boards with all the openings to the south.

During my tour, the violence of the wind kept increasing. The improvement in the weather had been only a lull; now the storm came back full force. So, I could push on no farther, but before going back into my dugout, I looked around carefully at what I could see.

A long drift, starting with my future house in construction, went across the parallelogram in two almost equal parts in a crest of snow about five feet high. It inclined slightly to the south, up the hospital front where it straightened out again, twice as high, and spread out three times as wide behind the guardhouse, which it enveloped up to the roof. In the northeast angle, the lodging inhabited by Asst. Adj't. Gen'l Mr. Marshal was in almost the same condition as my dining room, and the two other inhabitants of the detached building seemed no better off. Back in my house, I got from Lt. Col. Powell a few details on their misfortunes. Mr. Marshal and his young wife had not opened their door since Sunday. Their only communication with the outside is through the door of their kitchen. And they had to open it with the shovel in a mass of snow which blocks them completely. Last night their last window was buried like the rest, and they had to provide themselves with light by candles until a trench was opened to bring them daylight. The worst of it is that a lot of snow came in between the roof and their canvas ceiling and down into the chimney and drum of their stove, which they had to empty before relighting a fire in it. Then the heat made little cataracts on all sides, and sometimes they had to take refuge from them in the kitchen.

This is a hardship that everyone but me had to suffer. This fortunate exception in my favor is due to the fact that only I had expected it and had avoided it by hanging my lodging with canvas, by having all the holes and cracks stopped up, and by having mud puttied on the walls again when it melted. Because they neglected this precaution, all the other officers have felt tenfold the inconveniences that I had the blindness to complain about when I moved into my new lodging. I know I am guilty of pure ingratitude.

Worse yet has happened to Lieutenant Walborn. In his room where he lives with his wife and two young children, the door, which they undoubtedly tried to close forcibly without first taking the snow out of the way, broke and fell down inside. An avalanche invaded the conjugal domicile, the snow came in everywhere; the family took refuge in the kitchen, and when at last the damage could be repaired and the outside door re-hung, the snow coating began to thaw and to run off. One can guess what the condition of the apartment has been for some time. The tribulations of Lt. Marshal are small compared with those of Lt. Parsons, who also has his young wife with him, and moreover, a piano.

[*Feminine heroism*] The ones whom I admire as much, at least, as I pity, are these young women who brave all these mishaps—and for them I could even say suffering—with courage and even an heroic gaiety. If they complain, it is with a rather resigned manner that clearly indicates that they foresaw all this and do not regret that they have exposed themselves to it. But most of the time, they have the good spirit to be the first to laugh at their misfortunes and prefer the funny side of things to the tragic. American women really have blood: courage in danger, constancy in sacrifices, resignation in privations, self-sacrifice in devotion seem to be virtues inherent in their character. None yield more resolutely to circumstances, adapt themselves better to unexpected events, and brave the roughness of military life on the frontiers with a more even temper. The officers' wives are especially distinguished by these characteristics. Of course, I am not thinking of the belles of New York and other fashionable centers. I should not deny that among them there are some capable of such merits; but in general, I should believe it wiser not to put them to the test.

For the moment, our great need is firewood. The detachment sent out this morning to get some could not open a road for the sleds and wagons across the river, all the firewood being on the other side where twenty or thirty cords are cut and measured, waiting for them to go for it. Everything combustible has been used up at the fort. If the weather does not clear up by tomorrow, we face the threat of having to sacrifice some lumber all cut for the construction of one of the officer's houses. As for me, thanks to the indefatigable Dupont, I have no difficulty in keeping up my fire, and one of the carters of the quartermaster was able to bring us a load of coal on a sled, at the price of a frozen ear and nose. But that does not prevent me from thinking of the others, especially when I see my officers, axe in hand, pegging away at some logs they have succeeded in dragging out of the snow.[104]

Almost all the cattle are saved. They finally got to them. It was high time! They were literally packed up in snow, having hardly more room to breathe than the place their breath melted. There is a silver lining to the dark cloud. If they had been uncovered, all of

[104] A letter from Fort Berthold that appeared in the *St. Paul Daily Pioneer* told of the terrible hardships suffered by the garrison at Fort Stevenson. Such reports became so exaggerated and widespread that De Trobriand wrote letters of protest to the Department and to the *Army and Navy Journal. St. Paul Daily Pioneer,* February 29, 1868; *Army and Navy Journal,* February 29, 1868, May 23, 1868; Régis de Trobriand, Fort Stevenson, D. T., to Bvt. Brig. Gen. O. D. Greene, Department of Dakota, St. Paul, April 25, 1868. Department of Dakota, War Records Division, National Archives.

them would be frozen to death. The snow protected them against
the twenty-four below zero wind, and they retained enough inside
heat to survive. They were still able to walk to our canvas-roof houses
which we left at the camp and which are still standing. They distributed the animals in them, and they will be better off there than
anywhere else; they gave them all the hay they could get off the large
stacks through the snow that covers them. The cow that provides the
milk for our table (Mjr. Furey's and mine) is in the old office of the
adjutant, and my old lodging shelters a half dozen cud-chewers. Of
course, as they recover their strength a little, our cattle will be (part
of them at least) slaughtered. They will keep infinitely better and
more easily dead than alive.

It is quite unpleasant for me to hear again this evening the wind
take up its song in the chimney of my stove.

Thursday, January 9. Daylight came to me this morning through
a very small triangle in one of the upper corners of my window. All
the rest was buried under a compact mass of snow piled up by the
wind in the night. The trench opened in front of my door was filled
in as high as ten feet; that is, level with the roof. Faced with the
obstinate perseverance of the wind which filled in all the trenches
as fast as they were dug out in the snow, we have had to change the
system, and the trenches have been replaced by tunnels. This system
of communication is so much more feasible because the drifts have
become enormous. The one which crosses the interior of the fort
has become a high plateau flanked by drifts which vary little, except
for increasing in height and thickness. The entire detached building
housing three families has disappeared under a mountain of snow,
except for a wing on the angle where the roof of Mr. Marshal's kitchen
is still visible, like the wreck of a ship three-quarters submerged under
the waves. One now goes to my adjutant's house through a tunnel six
to seven feet high and four feet wide which makes an angle with its
mouth opening on the flank of the drift about ten paces from the
entry door. Mr. Walborn and Mr. Parsons have been forced to turn
to this kind of work in order to keep their communications open
with the outside world. I have a temporary ceiling of boards placed
above my trench, level with the roof. The snow covered it three to
four feet deep in a few hours, and so I find myself with a sloping
tunnel opposite my door, four or five yards long, not counting the
open part that keeps on lengthening and that still must be cleared
out five or six times a day. But at least I can open my door freely

without the snow rushing into my room, and this is a great advantage. The only window through which I get light had to be protected by similar means. It now opens on a covered blind alley, the entry of which requires the intervention of the shovel from time to time.

The servants have dug out another tunnel extending from their door to the side of the drift. Neither they nor the cook could get out this morning before a passage was dug up to them from the outside. And this is just the beginning. The biggest job will start tomorrow. The different tunnels, the one from my room, the one from the kitchen, and the one from the servants' room, are going to be joined by a corridor under the snow extending from Mjr. Furey's door to the servants' passage and branching off to the dining room. It will form a right angle, and will not be less than seventy feet long, forty on one side and thirty on the other. These dimensions give some idea of the proportions of the drift which has swallowed up half our buildings. It is fifteen to eighteen feet at the highest point, about fifty feet wide, and more than one hundred feet long from the east side of the detached building. As for the back side, it is completely snowed under, and in the direction the wind blows from the drift stretches out as far as the eye can see and widens proportionately. The fact is that the whole neighborhood of the fort is just like the interior, uneven as if the surface of the soil had been shaken by some underground convulsion. The musicians' quarters, spared until today, is banked with snow up to the roof. They can get to the guardhouse now only through a narrow passage which is always blocked. From a distance, the sutler's cabin and Gerard's resemble debris floating on the sea. In making a tour of the buildings, I looked around for the big haystacks and did not see them. As they are on comparatively low ground, the snow has covered them over. Farther away, the old hospital tents and some buildings of the camp are still visible, but one can hardly make out the contours of the corral under the great waves of snow which cover it.

[*Loss of cattle*] Yesterday I wrote that almost all the cattle were saved. The *official* truth is that twenty-two are sheltered in camp, and seventeen are buried under the snow for good, unless some of them, taking advantage of being left to their instinct the second day of the storm, succeeded in finding shelter in the thicket, where they will be searched out later. When the survivors were dug out of the corral, the poor beasts had lost their bovine form. Five or six inches or more of snow stuck to their hides like a crust, and they moved painfully, wearing their frozen turtle shell and looking more like shapeless blocks of snow than animals. Two mules perished last night, but the others are much better off than the horned animals. Those roaming around the stables have their shell of snow, too, but they wear it gaily and move under it as if it were an equestrian harness of the Middle Ages.

And in conclusion, let us note that the sun shone all day in the sky and that the air was very cold at a certain elevation, but the weather was fair. It makes no difference to us if the snow falls from the clouds or the sun lights up a blue sky. The important question is whether or not we have wind. Today is the fifth day that it has been blowing violently and continuously. During this period of time, the sky has been in various conditions, except for the temperature, and the state of things did not change for us. We are constantly sprinkled with a fine, thick snow which piles up around all the obstacles it meets in its course and which has already half buried us. The wind on the great plains picks it up, drives it, whips it, carries it hundreds of miles, piles it up at its will in such compact masses that one can excavate it like sandstone. For the fine sand of the Sahara deserts substitute the fine snow of the Dakota deserts, and you have the terrible simoon, icy here, burning there. But anyway, the phenomenon occurs the same way and behaves in the same manner. One buries caravans, and the other buries encampments. And by way of this, today, January 9, we are without news of the men sent to bring the mail packet from Fort Totten last December 10, twenty days ago. In ordinary weather the trip to the midway station and back would have taken them but six days at the most. Those who left for the same destination January 1 have not returned either. One cannot think about them without being uneasy, and one does not like to speculate on what could have happened to them. The answer would too quickly be formulated from a terrible probability. Because of this double delay and the persistence of bad weather, the courier who is to leave on the tenth will not go tomorrow.

Ten o'clock in the evening. In this stubborn battle which has lasted five days, the snow still has the advantage, and defeats all my efforts and ingenuity. I have just opened my door to see how things are outside. My tunnel is blocked, hermetically sealed at its entrance. It was still open at six o'clock. So it took the snow just four hours to pile up a seven-foot drift there. From there I go to my window— blocked, too, in the same way. So here I am, buried, or rather, snowed in alive, separated from the world with my lamp like a vestal who has broken her vows. It is fortunate that I foresaw this possibility and gave my instructions to Dupont. Instead of opening my tunnel again, he will dig a new one from Major Furey's door to mine, running along the building, and clearing my window. In any case, I shall see daylight tomorrow several hours later than those *on the surface.*

Friday, January 10. And in the night, in the death-like unbroken silence, in pitch blackness where not a ray of light penetrates, I began to think of all those on whom a tomb had closed while living, and especially of the inhabitants of Pompei[i], its terrible secrets kept by death for eighteen centuries. They were buried in cinders as I am in snow. But cinders and snow, what a difference!

This morning the first sound that came to me was that of human footsteps cracking on the snow above my roof. Soon afterwards a muffled conference at Major Furey's door revealed to me that my neighbor was blocked too. What's the use of getting up? The best thing to do was to wait in bed. A little later, the cracking of shovels biting the snow told me that they were at work getting us out; but the sound was far away and muffled, from which I concluded that they would be at work for some time before reaching me. Finally, when the sound of voices and shovels was close enough, I lit my light. It was almost nine o'clock. I dressed, lit my fire, and waited, eyes fixed on a black cavity that the snow had left behind two of my panes. It was through here that I saw break the first white light, which penetrated through the thin layer of snow. It grew rapidly, and finally the shovel made a hole, and I noticed first Dupont's hands enlarging the opening, then his head looking at my candle. When he noticed me, he shouted: "We are coming, General!" And in a few minutes, there was daylight in my lodging again. There were still four feet of snow to clear away to get to the opening, the only trace of the trench which was filled in before my door. The work took half an hour, and I was set free just a little before ten o'clock. The first use I made of my liberty was to have my breakfast brought in.

The work went on all day. Four men, not counting the servants, worked at it energetically, and this evening we were able to have dinner in the dining room again. We get to it through a covered passage or tunnel six feet high and four feet wide, curved on the top. It starts from an open trench at Major Furey's door, passes in front of my window, which gets daylight from it, (not as much light as you think) and on in front of my door, and from there it extends to the door of the dining room. That room was half filled with snow which had to be cleared out.

Philippe Régis de TROBRIAND

This room was in darkness, which they remedied by clearing one of the windows on the side where the drift is the smallest. The same thing had to be done for my back window because the one which opens on the snow passage gives the only light in my room. Now, I have enough daylight to read and write without tiring my eyes. I feel that I am back in the world of the living.

Experience teaches many things. In the corral, they dug out the stables in the mountain of snow which piled up there, and in this way they will free the most useful part. The animals will be completely sheltered there and warmer than behind board walls which let in the snow and the icy wind from the plain. The cold itself will not get into these buildings (although that seems strange), for the snow is at freezing temperature, which the presence of the animals will raise a few degrees; this coats the inside walls with a humid layer. But when the mercury is at twenty below outside, there is a difference of fifty-two degrees Fahrenheit, and comparatively, of heat. So where the walls of wood or adobe are not sufficient protection against the outside temperature, they bank them on the outside with a thick mass of snow. It is the best means of securing a warm temperature inside.

The wind was still blowing today, although not as hard as these past days. In a tour that I made to examine the changes made in the night, two big ravens, a solid, glossy black, with bright intelligent eyes, came flying above me, so tame that they alighted twelve or fifteen feet away to pick up some nourishment out of the snow. The exigencies of hunger dispelled their usual caution. I am not one who wishes to abuse their relative tameness. For ravens I have nothing but fine feelings, associated with memories of childhood long ago. Whenever I meet the raven, it inevitably reminds me of the paternal house of my youth. Isn't it strange that in the depths of the Dakota desert when the whole winged tribe has flown away to milder climes at the approach of winter, the only two birds which keep us company faithfully are the raven and the magpie, these two old friends of childhood from the other side of the globe? I have already noted elsewhere that the magpie I found on the banks of the Missouri is unknown in the Eastern Atlantic States. But the raven is found everywhere. In every country of the world where I have gone, I have met him. I am convinced that man and raven are the two inhabitants of this globe spread over the surface most universally, the only ones which are able to adapt themselves to all climates and make their home in them.

This evening, the weather is changing. The wind is dying down, the thermometer is rising. Are we finally coming to the end of this siege?

Nine o'clock in the evening. Doctor Grey [*sic*] has just rapped on my door and called me outside to have a look at a very rare and strange phenomenon, *three* moons in the sky. It is the same refraction as the parhelion, only it is produced by the rays of the moon instead of those of the sun. One is to the other as the lunar rainbow is to the solar rainbow. The disk of the moon was surrounded by a double disk of luminous vapors, which produced a beautiful effect. The sky is clear and calm; the stars are brilliant. It is very cold. The five-day storm is ended, and the parhelion shines in the heavens like the rainbow after the *deluge.*

Friday, January 17. Eight days have passed since the great storm abated. Since then, the weather has stayed very clear and cold, except for a cloudy day when the wind was a little threatening. The thermometer has stayed between twenty below and twenty-two below until yesterday, when, because of a breeze from the south, it went up to fourteen below. Today this softening of temperature has become much more noticeable because of a splendid sun, and at two o'clock in the afternoon the mercury had gone up to twenty above; that is, only twelve degrees below freezing point. For us it is almost a spring day, comparatively. However, in spite of these eight days of fair weather, we are still without news of the four couriers sent out, two on December 29 and two on January 1. From now on, it is to be feared that they all have perished, lost in the snow. Their trip coming and going takes six to seven days at the most, and they have now been gone seventeen and twenty-seven. No packet was sent out for Totten the tenth of this month; but if the weather continues to be as favorable, we shall send out another one the day after tomorrow or the twentieth, under the leadership of La Bombarde, the last half-breed we have.

Monday, January 20. La Bombarde came back yesterday with his two Indians from his expedition on the Fort Rice route. It is clear that the dangers, sufferings, and privations of their first trip have not discouraged them. They met the couriers from Fort Rice at the midway station, exchanged their despatches and correspondence, and returned with no incident save the loss of one of their horses, probably from weariness and the cold. The packet that they brought back consists simply of a dozen different newspapers and a few letters, all our correspondence having been sent by Fort Totten. This was one more reason to try again to open our communications in that direction, and, encouraged by the success of the couriers from Rice, we sent out this morning for Devils Lake five men, four of whom are on horseback and one with a sled. Among them, La Bombarde and Martin. They left at daybreak, and came back at three o'clock in the afternoon, after trying in vain to break through the barriers of snow massed on their route. The drifts at the foot of the heights and in the valleys are fifteen or twenty feet high or deep. The surface is icy, but it breaks under the weight of the horses, which immediately go down up to their bellies and can go no farther. Several times the men had to dig out the snow to get their mounts loose. They tried to get to high ground, but failed; they tried to get to the plain, but were unable to cross the valleys. When one obstacle was overcome or circumvented at great trouble, another showed up a little farther away. In brief, after six or eight hours of useless struggles, concluding that the country was in the same state almost everywhere, they had to retrace their steps.

Their reappearance on the edge of the horizon of snow was the signal for some scurrying around at the fort, for at a distance out on the plain it was difficult to make out, even with the best glasses, if they were our men or men sent from Fort Totten. But when we could finally recognize four men on horseback and one in a sled, we knew who it was. Nothing could be more disappointing, for from now on we must resign ourselves to being without news from our families and friends until spring, that means about three months, and it is now more than a month since we have received any. Since all our correspondence is routed by Fort Totten, the Fort Rice route—if we succeed in keeping it open until the end—will be of use only to get a few newspapers and send news to those from whom we receive none. It is always something, and since we can do nothing about it, we shall try to be satisfied.

Saturday, January 25. Let's try again. Once again, yesterday morning we sent out La Bombarde and Martin for Fort Totten, alone this time, and without soldiers, for they are a hindrance rather than a help to them. The soldiers are not used to the country as are the half-breeds. They cannot endure the same hardships and privations. The two couriers left on horseback, for God knows where the dogs and sleds are since last month. It is doubtful if their mounts will get them to their destination, but if they are forced to abandon them, our men will continue on foot, though it takes them—as Martin told me—fifteen to twenty days to get there. That is all very well, but at that rate when will they be back? Not before the beginning of March and then the time will be approaching when communications by water can be opened. However, it will be two months yet before the arrival of the first steamboat, and if we get our letters then we shall have a fine stack of correspondence to go through.

Meanwhile, we keep on sending out to Fort Rice every two weeks, and the day after tomorrow morning, two Indians will take our letters away by that method.

The weather is not unfavorable. We have had no more than a day and a night of storm for a week. Of course there is snow that must be cleared away, but everything now seems insignificant in comparison to the great five-day storm. Yesterday it was magnificent, the air perfectly calm, and the cold moderate; that is, twelve above. Today the wind is blowing, it is cloudy, and the thermometer is going down fast, the wind having shifted from the east to the north. Everything indicates that we shall have one of the coldest nights.

NOTE: [*Silver wedding*] Today, January 25, 1868, I have been married twenty-five years. A quarter of a century! It seems only yesterday. The Duke de Clermont-Tonnerre and the Marquis de la Roche-jacquelein, my two witnesses, are dead, and how many others since then! After all, a quarter of a century goes by quickly, and how many big and little things happen in this period of time! One thing at least would console me for the flight of these twenty-five years, if I needed consolation: I have turned them to good account, and not one of them was swallowed up in the past without making its contribution to the business of living. People talk of wasted days: of course I have wasted some; but not a great many altogether, considering that they were used in one way or another for an objective, sometimes one, sometimes another, better or worse. A mixture of vicissitudes, good or bad, of favorable or adverse currents, of sunny days and rainy ones; but in retrospect, more good than bad, more pleasure than pain, and whatever happens, when the end comes, I shall have *lived my life fully. Vixi!*

Sunday, January 26. Our two savages left this morning with our correspondence for Fort Rice. Before getting under way, one of them came to show me that he was really without any clothing other than a buffalo robe which he held around himself. The rest consisted of an old flannel shirt and two leggings which reached only above the knee. I had both of them given a pair of trousers, a jacket, and a military greatcoat (overcoat), and they left, delighted with their good looks and especially the comfort they felt. Until now, they had endured the rigors of winter without any protection but their buffalo robes. And this morning when one of them showed me his bare legs and his body in just a shirt, the thermometer showed twenty degrees below zero. And that without having a cold!

By way of this, I should like to remark that we ourselves are singularly acclimated to all this. Even in this Siberian cold, I rarely put on my fur overcoat, and we come and go in the fort and the neighborhood in just a light overcoat such as we would put on to go out in New York in a temperature forty or fifty degrees higher. Really, the wind is our worst enemy. When it blows, we must wrap up as warmly as possible; but if, as today, the air is calm, we hardly feel the cold.

The sun on the icy, sparkling snow of this region is terribly tiring to the eyes. It causes dazzling and colored hallucinations which end in what is called snow-blindness, and one finally sees nothing. He is snow-blind, and remains in this condition until the eyes, rested by half a day in the house, recover their power of vision. It is one of the things that greatly shortens our walks and prevents any hunting on sunny days, as if the depth of the snow and its looseness are not enough to keep us from it anyway.

Monday, January 27. Two half-breeds arrived from Fort Buford bringing some despatches which aren't very important. They succeeded in making the trip without trouble from the Indians. Because they knew the place where Brown and Gardepie had been stopped before, they carefully avoided it and made a detour across the plain instead of following the banks of the river. Moreover, it isn't certain that the *Gens de La Feuille* are still there.[105] Hunger could have chased them out and sent them to join the band gathered on the Yellowstone where it seems there are many buffalo.

Bt. Major Clarke, who now commands Fort Buford, made a raid on the half-breeds from the Red River who are trading munitions and whiskey to the hostile Indians.[106] He broke up their establish-

[105] A part of the Mdewakanton Sioux were called *Gens de La Feuille*. Edward Colhoun mentions them in his diary and calls them *Gens des Feuilles*. Colhoun Diary, typescript, p. 60, Minnesota Historical Society.

[106] De Trobriand reported on September 2 to Department headquarters on the munitions trade between the half-breeds of the Red River and the Indians. General Greene instructed him to put a stop to it, but this permission was granted

ment, seized their merchandise, peltries, provisions, and kept every-thing for the disposition of the government. The reports and official papers prove that everything is much improved at the post under the authority of the new commandant. It could not be otherwise.

The wind is still raging. The thermometer stays below zero F. Bad weather for our couriers en route for Rice and Totten.

Tuesday, January 28, 1868. At sunset, some black specks appear-ing on the edge of the horizon of snow told us that a party of a few men was coming in our direction. Immediately, everyone hoped it was the band of couriers from Fort Totten who had succeeded in getting through in spite of the difficulties. Before night, with the help of the glasses, it was possible to make out two men and four horses. The optimistic hopes were not of long duration. The two men were La Bombarde and Martin, bringing back, in addition to their own mounts, the horses of the couriers who left January 1, under the following circumstances, which were reported to me by Martin himself.

The two half-breeds had left on horseback, as I noted above, the twenty-fourth of this month, last Friday. The first evening, they had to bivouac on the open plain. With their shovels, they built a kind of snow cabin, and spent a tolerable night in it. The horses were already very tired, although the distance covered was only about ten miles. But they had to plow their way through the snow where the animals sometimes sunk in up to the neck. The icy crust had already cut their pasterns to the quick, and they had left behind them a trail marked with long streaks of blood. Nevertheless, the twenty-fifth they got under way. The obstacles seemed to get worse and more difficult, for the ravines were so filled up in certain places that no visible trace of them remained, and in others, the drifts were of such proportions that they resembled hills, and put our two couriers in continual doubts about the route to follow. It must be remembered that these plainsmen to whom the country is familiar orient themselves by landmarks such as mountains of a certain shape, a chain of hills, and lakes or ravines identified by certain marks. But because of the un-usual piles of snow of this winter, they cannot orient themselves by these natural features. In the distance, the mountain had completely changed in appearance; the chain of hills had almost vanished; the drifts piled up on its flanks; the frozen lake had disappeared, and

on February 25, after Major Clarke's raid. O. D. Greene, Department of Dakota, St. Paul, to Régis de Trobriand, Fort Stevenson, February 25, 1868. Department of Dakota, War Records Division, National Archives.

was blended with the valley under the snow; there was no ravine. Thrown off the track in this way, but still not discouraged, they arrived the second day at the locality where the first station cabin was supposed to be. They searched for it in vain. There appeared no vestige or sign of it on the vast and silent expanse. However, certain that they were not mistaken, they left their mounts to rest and went out on foot to look for the station. After a hard and painful search, they finally noticed, some distance away on a hillock the sides of which merged with the surrounding cliffs, a horse which seemed to have come out of the ground, but which really emerged from a hidden coulee.

Under this hillock, the station was buried. Our men ran to it (metaphorically), and to their great surprise found themselves face to face with two horses in the most pitiful condition, just skin and bones, and the lower part of their legs literally hacked to the quick— horses which, despite everything they recognized immediately as the ones which our couriers had ridden out from the fort last January 1st. How these unfortunate animals have been able to live twenty-five days there on the snow, with no shelter and no forage, through the great storm, is a puzzle that seems difficult to solve. It must be that by scraping the snow with their hoofs in some exposed places where it was not so thick, they got down to the dried grass, which probably kept them from dying of hunger. As for the cold, all that can be said is that they must have a terribly thick skin and a very tenacious hold on life. But there they were, quite alive, and probably very happy that help had arrived.

At first our men had some trouble in finding the exact location of the cabin. They saw indications of it in a depression in the snow above the opening left in the roof to let the smoke out. It was entirely filled with snow. They began to dig with more than ordinary energy, since they feared they would find the bodies of their two comrades buried in some corner. They enlarged the opening, and cleared out the whole inside, but they found only the saddles and bridles of the two abandoned horses. There they spent the night around the fire, and the next day (twenty-sixth) at daybreak, the first thing they did was to begin the search for some indication of the fate of their predecessors. If they had perished in the snow, the wolves would have scraped it away to devour their remains or those of the dogs they had with them. But their search revealed absolutely nothing to them, although they covered an area of five or six miles, from which they concluded—and it is certainly most probable—that because it was impossible to take their horses farther, the two couriers had abandoned them there and pushed on with the sled and the team of three dogs; for the fourth had escaped and had returned to Fort Stevenson the day after they left. What became of them then? We shall find out later; but we do not like to remember that the next day after they left the station, they had to battle against the terrible storm which scourged the plains for six days.

La Bombarde and Martin did not have any dogs. During their exploration, their horses had more than once gone down in the snow or had lain down, refusing to go on. Then they had to continue their search on foot, becoming more and more convinced of the impossibility of finishing the trip they had undertaken. Meanwhile, the wind came up, the air filled with whirlwinds of snow; all objects some distance away disappeared behind a thick veil, and the two half-breeds had no alternative but to abandon their horses, too, in order to make an impractical attempt on foot or to return to the fort with the four animals, and without delay. They wisely decided to return, and they came back to Fort Stevenson this evening, but not without new labors and more dangers during the storm.

From which we must conclude with more certainty than ever that no more correspondence will get to us from Fort Totten before the middle of April. It is extremely vexing, but what can be done about it? With inevitable reverses, the wisest thing is to be resigned and to have patience.

Thursday, January 30. This is a red-letter day. In spite of our contrary predictions, a packet finally arrived from Fort Totten today! Our men who left December 20 and January 1 have finally returned. Not one perished, which is the big thing. After that, the recitation of their privations, labors, and suffering becomes secondary. It would take too long to tell. I shall say only that they arrived at Fort Totten almost frozen, and naturally they had to have time to thaw out their hands, or feet, or noses, or ears before starting back. One of the men from Fort Totten who was more seriously affected is still in such a condition that it is doubtful that he will recover from it. The six-day storm having held them captive in one of the stations, their provisions ran out. They had already been forced to abandon their two horses, as was seen above. They had a mule left, which became food for the dogs; and two of the dogs (the youngest and most tender, poor beasts!) became in their turn food for the men. When they met the ones who had left from Devils Lake at the same time as they did, they were in no condition to return to Fort Stevenson, and consequently they pushed on to Totten, to which they were closer, and they all arrived there together.

Today they brought back only a very few letters and papers, and everything up to the end of November; that is, two months before the present date. It is evident that the same interruptions in the service have occurred on the other side of Fort Totten and between Ransom and Abercrombie. Our letters and papers from December and January must now be scattered at the different posts on that part of the trail.

[*Affairs at Fort Totten*] The *military* news is, on the other hand, quite important. Bt. Colonel Whistler arrived at Fort Totten at the end of December and took command of the post. By orders of General Terry, the first action he took was to institute an inquiry into the conduct of Captain Wainwright during his command, and especially into the serious disorders and group acts of insubordination and mutiny caused by the habitual drunkenness of the command of the post: Wainwright, Captain Piatt, second in command, and Lt. Leonard, then the adjutant.[107] These disorders took place the last two weeks in August, the time of my arrival at Fort Stevenson. I believe that I put down in these notes that when the rumor of these actions reached my general headquarters soon after, I addressed a severe reprimand to Captain Wainwright, and asked immediately that Captain Hill, then absent on detached service, be sent back to his company. Until he came back I could do nothing, for, since Captain Piatt was of the same stripe as his superior, and the adjutant completed the trio, I had no officer to replace them if they were put under arrest. At this time there were only five officers at Totten, and four absent. Three of the latter arrived at Stevenson at the end of October on one of the last boats of the season. Among them was Captain Hill, who carried to Totten my verbal instructions to find out the facts, to send me the report, and to formulate the charges and specifications against Wainwright and Piatt, if there were any. But Captain Hill and Lieutenant Lockwood, who had previously received the same instructions from me, did not dare to put an accusation against the commandant of the post in the hands of the person in the hierarchy through whom it must pass to get to me.

So they did nothing until Bt. Col. Whistler arrived. Then, pro-

107 The arrest of Wainwright was ordered by De Trobriand on January 31 in a letter from J. M. Marshall, Fort Stevenson, to J. N. G. Whistler, Fort Totten. Department of Dakota, War Records Division, National Archives.

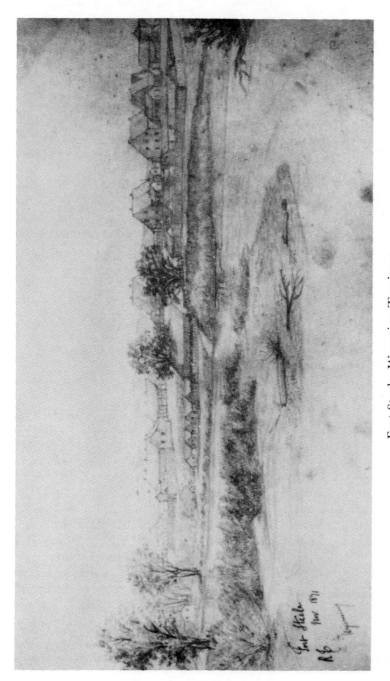

Fort Steele, Wyoming Territory

tected against any injustice from Wainwright, they made a detailed report of everything that has happened. A copy of the report was sent immediately. One can imagine nothing more shameful than the drunken follies of Wainwright and Piatt, especially of the former. A sergeant paraded before the garrison for having saluted according to regulations and not according to the whim of his drunken superior; men sent with ropes around their necks to the woods to be hanged because they were not working to the satisfaction of this satrap. And more than this—acts of mutiny, prisoners freed with impunity, a keg of whiskey stolen from the captain's tent, and nine-tenths of the garrison drunk by evening. After my reprimand, the men still lacked discipline, but these shameful scenes did not occur again. When Wainwright got drunk, he shut himself up in his tent with Piatt (*ariad[n]es ambo*) or Leonard, and sometimes remained there two or three days, not available for even the most urgent business—hoping that in this way there would be no witness to his degradation.[108] All these facts are included in the report sent to General Terry, as well as the charges and specifications formulated by Captain Hill against Wainwright and Piatt, for cases of drunkenness after his return to Totten. The result will be a court-martial; there can be no doubt of the outcome. Wainwright and Piatt, like Rankin, will be broken and expelled from the army, and there will be three positions open for the promotion of the three ranking lieutenants. Leonard will be lucky if he escapes. The case of Captain Little is more doubtful. In a word, the drunkards will be swept with one stroke from my corps of officers. Good riddance. Sooner or later I would have gotten rid of them, for I will not tolerate one of them in my regiment as long as I command it.

Saturday, February 1. Because of the information received that couriers will be sent out today from Fort Totten to meet ours halfway, La Bombarde and Hamlin (two half-breeds) left this morning with the mail. They took with them two teams of dogs (those which had been eaten were replaced at Totten). The trail is marked in the snow by the men who arrived the day before yesterday. The weather is cold, but fair. Everything encourages us to believe that this expe-

108 After Pomeroy, the paymaster, visited Fort Totten, he told De Trobriand that the men had banded together and had the run of the post. However, he declined to make an official report on the condition of the post. Régis de Trobriand, Fort Stevenson, to Bvt. Brig. Genl O. D. Greene, AA Genl, Department of Dakota, St. Paul, December 21, 1868. Department of Dakota, War Records Division, National Archives.

dition will be luckier than the preceding ones. Wind from the north-west. Thermometer, six degrees F. below zero.

Tuesday, February 4. Today for the first time since November 23, the thermometer went above freezing point. Toward two o'clock in the afternoon, it reached thirty-nine above, F., and the air was filled with a humidity due to the thaw. At the edge of the roof, icicles formed, and the snow grew dark and soft on the trails made by the traffic coming and going. By sunset, the temperature was going down rapidly. By nine o'clock in the evening, it has already fallen to ten above, F., and will be below zero before midnight with the cold wind from the N. W. blowing harder and harder.

[*Famine among the Indians*] The old chief of the Rees, White Shield, came with some warriors to ask for provisions. I had him go to the commandant of the post in order to get rid of Indian begging. The reports from Fort Berthold are distressing. The Indians who have gone back there are literally starving to death, having exhausted their supply of corn. Those who are still in the camps or who are wandering around on the plains are no better off. The migration of the buffalo to east [west] of the Yellowstone River leaves them almost without game and consequently without food, for deer and antelope are much more difficult to hunt and kill. Bows and arrows are useless against them, and only those who are armed with guns can surprise them. The fleetness of these animals makes any pursuit impossible, while, on the contrary, the buffalo can be easily overtaken by a horse of average speed. This is why the Indian lives on buffalo meat and why, when there is no buffalo, the Indian must disappear.

The pity that one would feel for the periodic famine that deci-mates a part of the Indians almost every winter is dulled consider-ably when one remembers that it is caused by their incorrigible laziness and their incurable dislike for all work. The most severe ordeals teach them nothing. At Berthold they agreed to grow corn because they themselves did not have to turn a hand. Their women, those two-footed beasts of burden, do all the work of cultivation, planting, hoeing, harvesting, husking, and packing of the corn, while their lords and masters, draped in their blankets, sun them-selves, smoke, and watch them work. In vain the government has offered them all kinds of seeds, animals, and tools as *gifts*. No, they prefer food and articles of clothing, and refuse to raise animals of any kind or to grow produce that would impose the least bit of labor on them. According to them, to make themselves independent by putting a hand to the spade or plow would be dishonorable, a disgrace; but to beg humbly and incessantly for their living from the whites and to steal if need be does not injure their pretended dignity at all, for they are devoid of any moral sense.

The trader Gerard tells us that recently four redskins at Berthold have literally starved to death. More will undoubtedly suffer the same fate before the end of winter. The others see but one remedy for this: beg for help at Fort Stevenson. But when in the spring they find in the ground breadroot and *assiniboines,* wild tubercles which they use for food, they will refuse the hogs, calves, and plows offered by the Indian agent. Instead they will ask for blankets and flannel shirts, all the things that they would certainly be able to buy in quantity with their produce from their agricultural labors if they would consent to get at it and raise more supplies than they need.[109]

[*The race is dying*] But the race of American Indian seems to have had its day and to have fulfilled its fleeting mission in the march of humanity. Its resistance to any assimilation with the whites is a seed of destruction which the race carries in itself and which grows with great rapidity. The American aborigine, no longer protected as the African race has been up to the present by the vastness of impenetrable deserts, will be the first to disappear from the great human family. It will die out in the age of man just as so many created beings have died out in the ages preceding this one, even after having been dominant on the face of the earth. And to take its place in the chain of eternal progress, some other race will rise in a future time, as superior to the Caucasian of today as that race was to the American which is now dying out.

Wednesday, February 5. Just as we thought, the mildness of the temperature yesterday was only a passing incident. This morning, the mercury went back to its average of ten degrees below zero F.

Thursday, February 6. Some officers braved the depth of the

109 In a letter from Fort Berthold dated February 2, Frederic Gerard informed Father de Smet of the destitute condition of the Indians at that place and asked for his help. Gerard said that the commanding officer at Fort Stevenson had given the three tribes eighteen cattle and some mules that had frozen during the winter, but they were not sufficient to ward off starvation. White Shield was then preparing to go to Fort Stevenson to beg provisions. The *St. Paul Daily Pioneer* reported that by March 2 thirteen Indians had already died of starvation; that all the dogs had been killed, and that the Indians were killing their mules and horses to keep alive. F. F. Gerard, Fort Berthold, to Rev. P. J. de Smet, [Washington, D. C.] February 2, 1868. Office of Indian Affairs, Record Copy of Letters Received, National Archives; *St. Paul Daily Pioneer,* April 17, 1868.

snow to go out hunting prairie chicken. They saw a great many of
them, but they did not kill a one. What a surprising difference there
is in the speed of these birds! Two months ago I told about the stupid
confidence with which they let themselves be approached and killed
on the trees where they were perched. Now it is an entirely different
thing. They almost never perch in the big trees any more, but keep
in the underbrush to look for their food which from now on is more
difficult to find. There is no way to get up to them there. The far
away crackling of the snow under the feet of the hunter or of the
twigs in his path is enough to give them the alarm, and immediately
the whole flock flies away out of range to alight again at distances
which make any pursuit futile.

They gather in very great numbers now. The other day I saw
some flying very high, and they passed from sight in the distance.
There must have been not less than two hundred of them in the flock.
I suppose that since they have become accustomed to the cold, they
are no longer susceptible to that lethargy which made them so lazy
after the first snowfall.

Friday, February 7. Unless there are new atmospheric catastrophes, our communications with Fort Totten seem to be firmly re-
established. The two men sent out with the dogs last Saturday arrived
around seven o'clock in the evening, bringing with them letters and
newspapers from New York up to December 21. The trip to the midway station and back was made without incident. Bitter cold again.
This morning fifteen below, F.

Saturday, February 8. Last night was the coldest of the winter.
This morning at seven o'clock, the thermometer registered thirty
below, F. The mercury had not gone down so low before. Fortunately,
the air is perfectly calm, which makes the temperature more en-
durable.

Tuesday, February 11. Winter is a deplorable season in Dakota.
Its excessive severity keeps us captives in our huts, and there the days
go by in monotonous uniformity. Reading is a great resource. So we
devour the fifty or sixty volumes scattered among the officers of the
garrison, English novels for the most part. There are a few volumes
of science, geology, astronomy, precious things that enlarge our education haphazardly.[110] When the couriers arrive, we have newspapers

110 By the following winter the garrison at Fort Stevenson was well supplied
with reading material. Dr. Matthews says that the post library was designed as a

and some reviews to read for two or three days. So we spend the clearest days reading.

My military duties are reduced to almost nothing. Going through the official correspondence with my A.A.G. when each courier arrives, drawing up some orders and reports when there is an occasion for it, examining the requisitions and conditions of the different posts, and endorsing and signing the official papers which pass through my general headquarters, before going through the proper channels to the higher echelons, to the general headquarters of the Department and to the Secretary of War. All of this does not take me more than a few hours a week. So this is how my days go by, almost all on the same pattern:

[*Daily activities*] At seven o'clock in the morning, my servant comes into my rooms, lights my fire, and retires to let me dress. At nine o'clock, I have breakfast. My orderly brings me the weather bulletin and the degree of the thermometer at nine o'clock in the evening (the evening before) and at seven o'clock in the morning (the day). I prolong my stay in the dining room by smoking and reading, while my servant makes up my room. Then I go back there, and I read and smoke until lunch. Lunch takes me ten minutes, after which I return to my room, light up my pipe, and go back to my book.

Around four-thirty, when it begins to grow quite dark in my cabin—still rather badly lighted by two half windows, one opening on the tunnel under the snow, the other at the bottom of a funnel-shaped hole in the snow—I close my book, put down my pipe, and stretch out on my bed to wait for dinner. I sleep if I want to, but usually—almost always—with my eyes open I daydream about a thousand different things, past memories, present affections, and I build my castles in Spain for the future. Night comes, however, and at six o'clock it is announced that dinner is served.

Dinner doesn't take long. Little time is required to eat soup, a piece of beef or rabbit, some canned vegetables (we don't have any fresh vegetables, fruit, or eggs), and a slice of pie. At six-thirty I go back to my room for the last time that day. My lamp is lit, my fire is stirred up, and my dressing gown is ready.

reading room for the men, with tables, chairs, bookcases, and 850 volumes of science, travel, history, biography, fiction and poetry. At Fort Buford, there were 394 volumes in the library. Among the authors represented were Sir Walter Scott, Charles Dickens, Nathaniel Hawthorne, James Fenimore Cooper, Henry Wadsworth Longfellow, and Bayard Taylor. *Report on Barracks and Hospitals*, p. 399; Fort Buford, Medical History of the Post, 1868. Department of Dakota, War Records Division, National Archives.

The evening is reserved for my writing. It is in the evening that I write these notes, or my private correspondence, or my official communications. But the work is not enough to fill the emptiness of the hours, and almost invariably I go back to my reading for an hour or two before going to bed—and I go to bed around ten o'clock.

People visit one another very little at Fort Stevenson. Some officer may at long intervals come to spend half an hour in my lodging with a definite object for a visit, such as borrowing or lending a book, some advice to ask of me or some paper to submit to me, that's all. As for myself, I must confess laziness in visiting the four ladies who are at Fort Stevenson. I fulfill only the demands of courtesy in this respect, but the conversation is so banal and so invariable every time —there is so little of common interest and such a great difference in lives and in ideas among us that to get together, we must comment on the condition of the weather, calculate the time when the first steamboat will arrive, say a word about the Indians and the two half-breeds who serve us as couriers—and when the same things have been said on these same subjects for the twentieth time, one can imagine that saying them for the twenty-first has no attraction. The resources for conversation with the husbands are not much more extensive or varied. Only military questions have more of a place, but the conversation rarely goes beyond the orbit marked out by the profession and by our position on the Upper Missouri. Politics are hardly mentioned. It seems that we all are thoroughly disgusted with them from reading the newspapers that we get.

Such is our existence in the winter; that is, since the first of December. Two months of it have gone, and there will be two months more.

Oh, *patienza!* as the Italians say.

Sunday, February 16. There has been an unexpected change in the temperature. Thursday evening it began to soften considerably, and the day before yesterday, Friday, the thermometer got up to forty-three above F., toward two o'clock in the afternoon. It was a real thaw, and the snow softened rapidly in the shade and melted in the sun. In the following night, the mercury went down only seven degrees below freezing point (twenty-five below [*sic*]), and in the day, Saturday, (yesterday), reached forty-five above. Today the temperature has been the same, with calm air and bright sun. It was the third day. The ground began to show through on the top of the bluffs or on the slopes in the places where the covering of snow was the least thick.

Douglas Creek broke out from its prison of ice in some places and began to run on the flat lands which border its mouth. The Missouri, too, filters through the ice which imprisons it (ice three feet thick), and little streams of water are already visible on the surface.

These forerunners of spring will undoubtedly come and go, but their coming is none the less pleasant. It affords us some variety in the countryside and at least a few days' skating. Personally, what I gain from it is seeing the sky through my windows again. Because the thaw disturbed the consistency of the snow under which my tunnel was dug, wisdom demanded that it be demolished. So it was changed into a narrow alley, but open to the sky. For the same reason, the trench which admitted daylight to my other window was considerably enlarged, and for the first time in six weeks, the rays of the sun have brightened up my room on one side in the morning and on the other in the evening. Comparatively, light of day has been given back to the prisoner. I could add freedom, too, considering my walks these last three days.

Wednesday, February 19. The weather continues fair. The temperature is very mild during the day, and the snow keeps on melting in the sun. Yesterday at two o'clock in the afternoon, the thermometer went up to fifty-one above. Every night it freezes again, but very moderately considering the season. Thus, this morning at seven o'clock the mercury was at sixteen below, [*sic*] F., and a thaw started the moment the sun came over the horizon.

[*Visit of the Mandans*] The Mandans, brought back to Berthold by the lack of big game and by the resulting famine, came to visit us yesterday to ask for some assistance in the form of provisions. Today we distributed to them some boxes of crackers, quite moldy, hominy, and a few barrels of salt pork, somewhat damaged. These provisions, which were condemned by a board of survey and consequently cannot be given to the troops as rations, find their most natural and useful disposition. They are distributed to the Indians, who appreciate them as much as if they were of good quality and willingly consume them.

These Mandans are certainly peaceful people and easy to handle. Today I attended the distribution of the supplies that were given to them in one lot. The chiefs and the warriors on one side and the old women on the other completed an inside circle around the supplies. The young women with their children and the young girls formed an outside circle at a distance of six or eight feet from the first. Everyone, men and women, was seated on the ground. Three or four warriors chosen *ad hoc* came and went and distributed to every one in the circle his share of each thing. All this went on in silence and in the most orderly way. No one thought of demanding or asking for anything, no one evidenced the slightest discontent or seemed to think of comparing his share with any other. It must be said, too, that the distributors did their job with discrimination and absolute impartiality, the two chiefs being the only ones a little favored. Each ate in silence, waiting for what would come next, and there was no chattering among the women. The horses—thin, sorry-looking things —bearing the too evident marks of the sufferings of winter, grazed on the blades of grass which stuck up through the snow or lay down in the sun in quiet resignation. The dogs hitched to their sleds stretched out their long, pointed muzzles on their mistresses' shoulders in the dubious hope of getting some scraps from the feast, too.

When the distribution was finished, everyone went back to his horse, passed the long leather thong that is used as a bridle through the horse's mouth, placed on his back the pack of provisions, and the whole band went down on the ice and in a long column took the road up the river for Berthold.

Friday, February 21. The interlude of good weather with the softening of temperature lasted just eight days. It is just that much gained on the enemy. Yesterday evening the wind was fixed at east-northeast, the thermometer went down rapidly, and after a very cold night, it was thirteen above, F., this morning. The day brought but little change. The wind kept on blowing rather strongly from the east, and the sky remained too overcast for the sun to come out.

Thursday, February 27. The sun came through today for the first time in eight days. During this time we have had very cloudy and cold weather. The wind, which almost stopped blowing from the east and northeast, became a real storm on Saturday evening. A great quantity of snow fell, and since then the thermometer has ranged between zero and twelve above.

Today the weather is very fair, but the temperature has not become any milder.

[*Hunting party*] Yesterday Bt. Col. Powell, Bvt. Maj. Furey, and Lt. Norwell went out to hunt big game in the woods below the fort. Unfortunately, there was an unexpected flood somewhere on the upper river (probably a result of the few days' thaw last week), and the water is running on the ice, particularly near the banks. So

our hunters could not cross to the other bank where the big game is
more plentiful. Nevertheless, a Berthold Indian called Bloody Knife
who accompanied them killed a deer just after they left, and so they
did not come back empty handed.[111] The guide from the post and one
of the sutler's men were with them. They were on sleds and were
supplied with buffalo robes, provisions, and a tent, in which they
spent a horrible night. This morning they returned, exhausted and
famished, and convinced that the game wasn't worth the candle.

There are great numbers of white rabbits here. They saw many
of them and killed some in passing. The snowbirds which made their
appearance two or three days ago will also improve our dinner menu.
These birds are small and white, heavy and fat as ortolans, marked
with gray-brown on their back and on the tips of their wings and tail.
They fly by the thousands, and we kill them by twenties. They come
to us here toward the end of winter and disappear with the snow.
I do not know if their plumage remains white during the summer or
if this color is just a winter livery like the rabbit and screech owl and
the traders and scouts, whose greatcoats are made from white woolen
blankets.

Saturday, February 29. The sun, after coming out Thursday for
most of the day, undoubtedly thought it had done enough for the
week. We have not seen it since then; wind, snow, and bitter, penetrating cold—this is our lot.

Sunday, March 1. How tired I am of this interminable winter!
Of this everlasting snow which for more than three months has hidden the color of the earth from us and blinds our eyes with its un-
changing whiteness; of this eternal cold weather which let up for
eight days only to rage again with as much bitterness at the end of
the month of February as at the end of December; of these monotonous days which follow each other and are just alike, with no variety,
no incident, like large drops of boredom falling one after another
into the dead sea of the past; of this isolation from the rest of the
world to which we are bound only by irregular communications at

111 Bloody Knife was the son of a Hunkpapa father and an Arikara mother.
He carried the mail from Fort Stevenson to Fort Totten in the months of 1868 when
the Hunkpapa almost succeeded in severing communications between these two
points. He was with General Stanley on his Yellowstone expedition of 1873, with
General Custer in the Black Hills in 1874, with General Terry in 1876, and with
Major Reno at the Custer Massacre as one of the Arikara scouts organized by
Gerard. He was killed on Reno Creek while trying to stop the Indians from cross-
ing. Hodge, *Handbook*, 1:155.

twenty- to forty-day intervals, and which leaves us with no news of our relatives, with no correspondence with our friends; of privations of all kinds, the natural result of our location in these deserts; of being deprived of exercise in a place where the snow makes it impossible for a pedestrian and the cold for a horseman; of the limitations of fare which because of the absence of fresh vegetables, eggs, fowl, veal, mutton, and even game has reduced us to a diet that brings scurvy to the soldiers and takes the edge off the appetites of the officers; of the lack of active occupations for the mind in this enforced captivity in which we have to struggle against the hours by the reading of every good or bad book we can find among us; of the limitations set on any study because of the lack of means and materials; of an existence where the hours of sleep become hours of deliverance as they are for a prisoner; of this absence of all distractions of society which keeps me in my miserable log hut fifteen feet square, alone during the day, and alone in the evening, for when sometimes on Sunday I do pay a visit to the homes of the officers I usually have had enough for two or three weeks.

How tired I am of all this! But what can be done? Duty has marked the path, and it must be followed up to the very end. Next winter I shall be in my house, I shall have my crayons and brushes, I shall have the materials for serious studies, books of geology, a microscope, books of astronomy, of mathematics, and I shall be able to turn to profit this boring leisure against which, for lack of experience, I did not make sufficient provision last summer.

After all, we have hardly more than another month to endure these conditions. April will certainly bring some changes, and May will complete our deliverance.

Today I received the first information of the publication of my *Quatre Ans de Campagne à l'Armée du Potomac.* The work must have appeared in Paris in the middle of the month of November and have been in New York in December, but postal communications are such that I have not yet received word of it. The news was brought to me by Doctor Gray, who found mention of it in a newspaper from Missouri brought the other day by the courier from Fort Rice.

The next mail from Fort Totten, by which all our correspondence and most of our journals come, will undoubtedly tell me more about it. It ought to have been here the twenty-fifth or twenty-sixth of last month. But our couriers wandered around in the snow, and losing their way, fell back on the instinct of their dogs who brought them straight back here. During this time, the party they were to meet halfway to exchange correspondence returned to Fort Totten. The twenty-fourth we sent our two half-breeds out on the trail with the order to push right on to Devils Lake if they did not meet the others on the way. If they had met them, they would have been back yesterday, and as they have not appeared yet, we cannot expect them now before next Saturday, *more* than a month after the arrival of the last mail, which was even then delayed.

Tuesday, March 3. For some days the rumor coming from Berthold has been going around here that a courier from Fort Buford had been stopped and badly abused by the Indians; that the despatches he was carrying had been destroyed, his dogs killed, his sled ruined, and that he himself, despoiled of his weapons and almost all his clothes, had arrived with frozen feet and in a most pitiful condition at the winter camp of the Gros Ventres. As the Indians are constitutionally the biggest liars I know, I had hoped that this was a story such as they usually tell. Unfortunately, this is not so; and this time the report is confirmed by the following excerpt from a letter from Gustave Cagnat, brought this morning from Fort Berthold: "Some Gros Ventres arrived here, and with them Joseph the Spaniard, who was seized and beaten by the Sioux while bringing the mail from Fort Buford. All the mail is lost, and the man had difficulty in saving his life. He arrived here with his feet still a little frozen. Hunger and suffering have almost driven him out of his head, and I am unable to find out exactly how the accident did happen, but as soon as I have more of the details, I shall let you know without delay." Through some of the Gros Ventres, it is known merely that the guilty ones belong to the tribe of Santees, hostile Sioux who played a very active role a few years ago in the Minnesota Massacre. They beat the courier terribly, struck him on the head with the butt-end of his gun, pulled out part of his hair and beard, and abandoned him in the snow with only his trousers and a woolen shirt. Since they did not kill him on the spot, they must have taken him for a half-breed; but they probably believed that the condition in which they left him would mean only prolonging his agony. The fact is that it is almost miraculous that he was able to get to the Gros Ventre camp alive; they thawed out his feet and restored him sufficiently to make it possible for him to be transported to Berthold, where, it seems, his reason still bears the marks of the terrible suffering he had to undergo. In two or three days, he will probably be able to tell us more about it.[112]

112 On March 2 a letter was written to the *St. Louis Republican* telling the

Wednesday, March 4. The morning of the day before yesterday, Col. Powell, Maj. Furey, and Lt. Norwell accompanied by Jack and Bloody Knife, went on a hunt in the hope of being more fortunate this time than on their first expedition. A sled followed them carrying a tent, buffalo robes, and even a little sheet-iron stove. Today they returned, worn out, and swearing, a little too late, that they would not go out again. For two days of painful and determined hunting in the underbrush and through two or three feet of snow, not counting two nights under open sky, they saw neither elk, deer, nor antelope. (A buffalo is out of the question.) The lowly rabbit is the only quadruped that showed up, and they just caught a glimpse of some prairie chicken, very wild and keeping out of range. So what has happened to the big game? Has it emigrated like the buffalo this year?

A new thaw began yesterday and continued most of today. Since there was no sun, there was another general freeze, and the mercury went down from forty or forty-five above to fifteen or twenty above during the night. So the effect on the snow still isn't very noticeable.

P. S. The mail from Fort Totten has just arrived. We were not expecting it until tomorrow or the day after. It is an agreeable surprise. A dozen letters and as many newspapers; that is something to prolong the evening and to fill the hours for a few days—not counting the official communications which will make work for me from now until next Tuesday, the day the next courier leaves.

Friday, March 6. The courier who was captured and abused by the Indians was brought to me this morning by Gustave Cagnat. He is a poor Mexican devil who goes by the name of Joe the Spaniard. For seven months he has been in the employ of the mail contractor, Ruffee, and during these seven months has not received a cent of his wages, and like the others, never hopes to get a penny of it.[113]

story of the capture of Joe the Spaniard. The correspondent says that the Santees who captured the former employee of Ruffee & Co. were led by White Bonnet and Fish Head. Joe the Spaniard may be Guiseppe Marivelli who came to Sioux City around 1853–1856 and who was commonly called "Joe Spaniard." *St. Paul Daily Pioneer,* April 17, 1868; *South Dakota Historical Collections,* 4:260.

113 Major Charles A. Ruffee was awarded a government contract for a pony express between Fort Abercrombie and Fort Benton in 1867. His mail service operated regularly in the summer and fall of 1867, but in the winter of 1867–1868, the carriers were robbed, beaten, and threatened with death. *St. Paul Daily Pioneer,* July 4, 1867; November 16, 1867; March 24, 1868; December 17, 1868; August 10, 1869.

Information about Ruffee's early career as an Indian trader, his positions in the Indian service, and his trading establishment at Fort Totten are found in the

Military Life in Dakota

[*The misfortunes of Joe the Spaniard*] He was at Fort Buford when the service was interrupted, and Major Clarke proposed to resume communications with Fort Stevenson at government expense. But the threats of the hostile Indians to the two couriers who were stopped during the winter and the fear of being killed by them kept the half-breeds from accepting the proposals. Only the Mexican, who was in dire need, made arrangements with the commandant of the post to make two trips (going and coming) to Stevenson with the papers that would be entrusted to him. What was most surprising was that he undertook to make the trip alone, on foot, with only a dog dragging that sort of frame that I have described elsewhere and that is called *travois*. After he had placed the mail and the food supplies needed by him and his dog on the net, he set out February 13. Everything went well up to the Knife River, almost two-thirds of the way. He avoided three encampments of Indians by staying away from the river and following the ravines of the prairie in order to keep out of sight. Unfortunately, this initial success gave him too much confidence, and knowing that he had between him and his destination only a camp of Gros Ventres, he stopped near the mouth of the Knife River in a log cabin which last summer served as a station for the couriers and which had to be abandoned at the beginning of winter. Since he decided to rest there, he lit the fire and set about getting a meal and a cup of hot coffee. It was a bad mistake, as it turned out. The smoke rising from the chimney attracted the attention of a hostile Indian party which was roaming around or hunting in the neighborhood, and they advanced on the cabin, surrounding it. There were thirteen of them, but the three in the lead came to the cabin door ahead of the others. Our man was captured.

After a few words were exchanged, one of the Indians addressed himself to the Mexican, and pointing toward the packet attached to the *travois*, asked him to whom it belonged. The man answered that it was the property of Mr. Ruffee.

"You lie," said the Indian. "It is the mail of the soldiers of the Yellowstone (Buford)."

Saying this, he took his knife, cut the cords, emptied the sack, and ripped out the despatches. It seemed that Joe the Spaniard, believing that he was dealing with only three Indians, and hoping

Mississippi Valley Lumberman, June 2, 1892; C. A. Ruffee, St. Paul, Minnesota, to General Sibley, St. Paul, December 15, 1869, Sibley Papers; C. A. Ruffee, St. Paul, Minnesota, to Bishop Whipple, Faribault, Minnesota, December 29, 1867, Whipple Papers.

to get rid of them, then reached for his revolver. Thereupon they jumped him, snatched the weapon from his hands, struck him again and again, and threw him to the ground. He succeeded in drawing his knife, but that was seized, too, and the blade cut him along the inside of his fingers. Then one of his enemies dealt him a violent blow on the back of the head with the gun-butt, which put an end to the battle. Joe lost consciousness, and lay on the ground covered with his blood, which was flowing freely from his two wounds. A sharp pain in the face brought him to after a time. The savages, in order to bring him out of his faint, had amused themselves by pulling out a part of his beard and mustaches, and his face was torn and bleeding, as was his head and his right hand. In his condition, these amiable redskins (there were thirteen of them now) forced the poor devil, who was half dead, to cook for them the little coffee and the few supplies he had with him, beating him mercilessly when he weakened. They killed his dog before his very eyes, hacked up the *travois,* and threw the correspondence in the fire, burning it up to the last scrap of paper. They had taken his weapons from him; they had eaten his provisions. Now they despoiled him of his clothes, took away his moccasins, woolen socks, drawers, woolen shirt, overcoat, fur cap, and blanket, actually leaving him with only an old pair of trousers and a worn-out antelope-skin jacket stripped of hair to cover his nakedness.

When the Mexican realized that they intended to leave him there in the middle of the snow-covered plains with no food and nothing on his feet or head and almost without clothes, he preferred instant death to the long agony he had before him, and he begged them to put an end to him immediately and kill him before going away. Upon which one of them took an arrow, adjusted it on his bow, and was going to shoot it through him, when another one, stretching out his arm, prevented the murder from being done. Thereupon all of them went away, without even looking back at their victim. As Joe has Mexican coloring and could easily pass as an Indian with his shock of long, straight, black hair, the savages must have taken him for a half-breed; otherwise they probably would have done away with him at the outset.

When he was alone, a strong instinct of self-preservation awoke in him. If he was to die, at least it would not be without making a supreme effort to save his life. And although weakened, bleeding, bruised, bareheaded, and barefoot, he started out in an effort to get to Fort Berthold. Certainly the man must be as stout in body as in spirit, for in the condition that I have just described, he walked all evening and all night. He walked all the next day, too, and both his feet were frozen and bleeding. To add to his misery, the wind came up, which increased the intensity of the cold. Soon a blizzard was raging; the snow filled the air, obscuring the horizon. No way to orient himself. Dying of cold, hunger, and exhaustion, the unhappy man hopelessly lost his way; his deranged mind ceased to be any help to him, and as long as he had strength to move, he wandered around in the snow. When his strength finally completely gave out, he lay down to die. A party of Gros Ventres found him in this condition, close to death, beyond the abandoned station he had left. The unfortunate man must have walked all day in the opposite direction from the route he had taken the night before.

The Indians have certain efficacious remedies for the ills to which they are most exposed. They picked up the dying man, made him take some nourishment, dressed his wounds and his frozen feet, wrapped him up in a buffalo robe, and revived him enough to enable them to put him on a horse. They kept him with them for a few days, and since they were going to leave winter camp to return to Fort Berthold, they brought him there the third where, as you see, he recovered his health rapidly. Gustave Cagnat gave him a knitted vest, a woolen shirt, and a pair of fur moccasins—and this morning he came to give me his report.

Joe the Spaniard (so named because he is a Mexican) is short, thickset, and energetic. His face is the color of burnt sienna; his mane of hair is black as jet and serves as a frame for his face, to which his brown, squinting eyes give a somewhat fierce expression. He is firmly resolved that his tormentors will pay for this if he ever finds them, for he paid close attention to their appearance—in particular the one with the bearded chin and a scar at the corner of his right eye whom certain indications seem to mark as a half-breed rather than an Indian. But Joe is reticent about this, as if he were jealous of his vengeance and as if he were afraid that the sweetness of it would be taken from him. I am convinced that if he succeeds in catching up with the man with the scar, he will not fail to square his account with him.

The most extraordinary aspect of the whole affair is that far from being discouraged by the horrible ordeal he has been through, he now thinks of nothing but setting out again for Buford, and he has already designated *tomorrow* as his leaving date! "If you want to furnish me with a horse," he told me, "I'll take the mail with me, and this time I'll take it there in such a way that the Indians won't get it. Otherwise, I'll take a few letters, which I'll sew in the lining of my coat, and go on foot." Like the rest of his story, this was recited with perfect composure in a calm voice, his language composed of a bad mixture of Spanish and a kind of English in equal doses.

"So," I said to him, "you are not disgusted with carrying the mail?"

"No," he said, "I have contracted to make two trips for which I am to receive $200, and I am resolved that I'll have my $200 or leave my bones out there."

Good heavens! Let it not be said that I shall let a fellow of that mettle leave on foot. I gave the necessary order for the mail to Buford to be given to him and that a horse be furnished for him to carry it. I made him a gift of a blanket; Major Furey gave him one, too, and tomorrow Joe the Spaniard, warmly dressed and provided with the necessary supplies, will set out for Fort Buford, loaded with despatches and correspondence. Will he arrive safely this time? I hope so, and I even have a feeling he will. The future will prove if *"That oracle is more sure than that of Calchas."*

Saturday, March 7. The Gros Ventres, back from their winter quarters, came to pay me a visit. The Mandans and the Rees (Arikaris) had already received provisions from us. Now it was their turn. I sent them to the commandant of the post, who really has charge of these distributions. But, before leaving, they insisted on having a conference with me, and I received the four principal personages, with Pierre Gareau as interpreter. They were: Crow Belly, first chief; Poor Wolf, second chief; and the leader of the warriors with his second. All four were in full regalia: jacket of deer or antelope skin covered with porcupine decorations and fringes made partly of slashed leather and partly from a mesh of horse hair or of human hair. The chief wore a necklace of pendants on his chest and in addition to his earrings of pearly shells there were rings passed through the upper part of his ears. All four had bunches of feathers on top of their heads.

I have already described in detail the ceremonial custom, which consists of the preliminary silence, the pipe going from mouth to mouth, the handshake of the exordium. I shall not go into that again. The main purpose of the discourse was to bring to my attention that more than half of the supplies that had been distributed to them were spoiled (which I knew very well). But the Indian could not limit himself to this detail, and many other things between us had to be brought up.

[*Crow Belly's complaint*] For example, to get to the point, just as Little John and Intime finally got to the ground around the county seat, he began *ab ovo,* if not "before the birth of the world," at least at the appearance of the first white men on the banks of the Upper Missouri. "The Great Spirit," he said, "made the white man very farsighted; he sees far and his mind thinks up and invents extraordinary things; but the red man was given only short sight. He sees nothing but what is around him and does not know what his father knew, except what the whites have told him. They are the ones who brought the horse to the plains and taught us how to grow corn. They gave us earthen pots and iron kettles to cook our food, and they furnished us with guns and powder to kill more game." Then came the distinction between the good and bad savages; the ones who have always been the friends of the whites, who have never broken their word, and who have made nothing but good use of the presents they have received; and those who have made treaties only to violate them, who have stained their hands by killing white men and stealing from them, and who have used the guns and powder against those from whom they have received them instead of against game. Among the former are the Gros Ventres; among the latter, the Sioux. "But what has happened? The Sioux, liars, thieves, and murderers, have received presents in quantity and guns which they have used to kill us, and they are rich in horses and in all things, while we have remained poor because we have not received all the things that our Great Father sent us, and we have hardly enough to cover ourselves and sometimes nothing to eat. But, when the great chief (Gen¹ Curtis) came to visit us a few years ago, he said to us: My children, be faithful to the whites, obey your Great Father, keep the peace, and do not break your word, and the smoke of your fires will go straight up to the sky. We did what our Great Father commanded, and despite everything, the smoke of our fires, instead of going upward, has gone down toward the ground and has been blown about by all the winds. The enemy Sioux are rich, powerful and numerous; the friendly Gros Ventres, as strong and more brave than the Sioux in the past, are now poor, weak, and few in number."

All this, of course, is a skillful mixture of truth and falsehood, combined to encourage the generosity of the government. It was not hard for me to find an answer to it. The chief went on to tell that when a company of soldiers was stationed among them at Fort Berthold, the Sioux had come to attack the village several times. The Gros Ventres had fought them bravely, had always chased them away, although inferior in number; but the white soldiers had never come to their aid. They were simply drawn up, under arms, before the fort, and had remained at a distance, passive spectators of the fight. After several repetitions, Crow Belly's speech ended with the recounting of the care given to Joe the Spaniard, whose life his men had saved.

The purpose of my answer was much more to point out to Crow Belly the road to follow in the future and to try to make clear to him and to his people their true interests and the exigencies of their present condition than to dwell on the past and follow Crow Belly in his review. So after reminding him that by his own admission the whites had given them annual presents of everything they needed to live, household utensils, arms, munitions, clothing, blankets, and food of all kinds, we had in addition paid generously for their friendship and for the cession of land fifteen miles long and two or three wide on which Fort Stevenson was going up right now.[114] After reminding him that when they were short of food, we had freely given them some several times a year; and finally that the difference between the Sioux and the Gros Ventres, far from being in any way the work of the whites, was the result of the terrible diseases (smallpox and cholera) which had almost exterminated, by the will of the Great Spirit, three tribes who were powerful in the past and who are still brave, even in their reduced condition; then I came to what seemed to me far the most important:

"There was a time," I told them, "a very long time ago, for the fathers of your fathers were not yet born, a time when all the vast lands which stretch from one sea to the other, from the north to the south, from the rising sun to the setting sun, belonged entirely to the red men. One day, some white men who had crossed the sea, in the direction of the rising sun, arrived in the red men's country. They were but a few warriors, not more than the grains of corn I could hold in my hand, and the nations on the seaboard had thousands more. However, the white men established themselves on the lands where they had debarked from their ship; more and more came, and they spread out everywhere, either by living in good friendship with the friendly tribes or by fighting and exterminating the hostile ones.

---

[114] The three tribes ceded land to the United States in the unratified treaty of July 27, 1866, and then by agreement on December 14, 1866. Hodge, *Handbook*, 1:798.

Now they are sole masters of lands so vast that in comparison, all the hunting grounds of my children are like a fistful of earth, and they have become so numerous that my children could not count them, even with their notched sticks, and the red nations which made war on them have disappeared, and their names are forgotten. How did this happen, and why did the white men multiply and become so powerful, while the red men became fewer and lost their power? I am going to tell you. Here is the reason for it (listen to me carefully): The white man always works; the red man never does. The white man cultivates the land; the red man hunts. The white man builds houses and lives without changing locations in great cities or in the midst of the land of which each one owns a part; the red man lives in tepees which he carries with him across the plains over which he moves continuously."

[*The necessity of work*] And after stressing as simply and as forcefully as I could the advantages of work, to which the whites owe all their riches, inventions, and power, I tried to make them understand the absolute and immediate necessity of labor for the three tribes of Berthold. "When the Indians occupied all the hunting grounds by themselves, and when the prairie was black with herds of buffalo, when game was plentiful in every season, the red men could feed and clothe themselves by hunting alone; but those times have passed. The buffalo are becoming fewer and fewer. They are disappearing toward the setting sun, and during the whole winter, not a one has been seen between the great lake (Rice) and Medicine Water (Totten), between this post and the Yellowstone (Buford), everything is on the other side of that river. So my children who were camped on the banks of the Missouri have suffered cruelly. They do not bring back any skins for trade, except a few elk skins; they have hardly had enough to eat, and in order to get food, several of them have been forced to sell even their own horses. And what has kept them alive during this time? The corn that they harvested last summer. How many would have starved to death if they had depended on hunting alone for food? So, the lives of many of you, particularly of the old people and children, were saved because you cultivated the land a little as the whites have shown you. And, moreover, almost all the trading you have done this year has been in corn, which has furnished you the means of doing it.

"In spite of this, you are poor and you suffer from hunger because you do not plant enough, and you plant so little because only your women work, and you who are strong and vigorous, you scorn work and spend every day smoking in the sun when you are not hunting. It would be entirely different if you changed your habits and if you yourselves cultivated the land so that you might harvest fruits of all kinds that you do not even know about, and if, like the whites, you raised cattle and hogs, and kept cows and chickens.

"I will tell you this: your Great Father wants to furnish you all the grains, animals, and implements you need if you decide to use them. Listen to the voice of the Great Spirit. It is he who wishes his red children to live differently from their fathers. That is why he is destroying more and more of the big game and why he brings the white men to the Missouri in order to show the red men how to be happy, how to become rich in horses, animals, grains, how to be warmly dressed in winter, and how never to lack food and always have enough to trade with the traders or with the tribes. All this you will have if you obey the will of the Great Spirit; otherwise you will live in misery and need, and you will die the same way, not through the fault of the whites, but through your own."

In substance, this is the little sermon I preached them on the necessity of work.

Incidentally, concerning the completely neutral attitude our soldiers took in watching their fights with the Sioux, I told them the fable of the horse who wanted revenge on the stag. "So," I said, "nations which in the past were warlike and powerful have been annihilated because they called white warriors into their quarrels or because they meddled in their wars." Whereupon, I related the fate of the Iroquois, Hurons, Delaware, Mohicans, and so many others, at the time of the wars between the French and the English on the frontiers of Canada. Then I added: "Our Great Father, who does not want his red children to perish, but to live in peace and to be happy, forbids his soldiers to help the Indian warriors destroy each other. For if he sent them to fight with one tribe against another, everyone would ask for his help, and many would be annihilated, while those who were victorious would be weakened and more dependent than ever. So it is only in the interest of his red children that our Great Father forbids his white warriors to mix in their quarrels."

My Gros Ventres listened to all this with serious attention and apparently with great interest. The outcome was that through their agent they were going to ask for new seeds and farm implements, and they will beg Father de Smet, for whom they have a great veneration, to send them a missionary to teach their children to speak the language of the Long Knives, to cultivate the soil as they do, and to live and work like the white men. Will they keep their word, and will they carry out these good resolutions? This is a big question. The answer will depend, I believe, on circumstances. If the buffalo return and game is plentiful this year—goodbye agriculture. But if there is no hunting, and they are faced with starvation and misery, at least a partial conversion is possible, and the possibilities are even stronger since the first step, the building of a village and the growing of corn, has already been made by the three tribes.

In any case, I recommended to them as well as to Pierre Gareau, their interpreter, to repeat my words to the men of their tribe, and to the Rees and Mandans, which they promised me they would do. This promise will be easier for them to keep than the other. So I hope it won't fall in the water on their trip back to Berthold.

Sunday, March 8. Yesterday, when the conference with the Gros Ventres ended, Crow Belly begged me to have some repairs done on two single-barreled guns, one flint, the other percussion. Since the work was not finished this morning when the band left, the chief remained behind with two of his warriors to wait for the guns. He unceremoniously installed himself in my room and began a conversation in pantomime in which, among other things, he showed me a certain number of scars on his face, hands, and on one foot, explaining to me how he had received them, and depicting eloquently by gesture the various combats of which he bore the marks, how this was an arrow wound, this a bullet wound, this a tomahawk wound, and these knife wounds. Usually, the story of each combat concluded with a Sioux thrown to the ground, the gesture (knife in hand) of him plunging the blade into his breast several times, with a fierce expression, then as finale, the gesture of seizing the hair of his enemy with the left hand and cutting it loose by a circular incision made with the right. After which, he sat up on his chair again, and, sheathing his knife, looked at me with the placid smile of accomplished triumph.

When the telegraphic conversation began to languish, the chief asked me for something to eat. I quickly conducted him to the dining room where I had him served with some thick corncakes, three or four slices of bread and molasses. Everything was dispatched with a promptness and ease that indicated a huge gastric capacity. We returned to my room, and not knowing what to do with my Indian, who, for a digestive, was peacefully smoking my pipe, which he had taken possession of, I showed him my full-dress epaulettes and my arms, which he examined with obvious interest.

But what excited his curiosity most was a photograph album of the principal generals of the Army of the Potomac, among whom I showed him that of General Grant, who, I told him, was the great chief who commands all the other chiefs. He examined it closely, then putting the open book on his chest, he lowered his head, closed his eyes, and seemed to give himself up to a mental invocation. Several times, he went through this "medicine" routine at different places in the book, and I understood that by this mystical application, he sought to infuse in himself the bravery, wisdom, and talents of those of our generals whose faces he admired the most. Finally the guns arrived; he called his two warriors, gave me a handshake accompanied by a "How!"—very emphatic—and at last I was rid of my visitor.

Thursday, March 12. Yesterday two Assiniboin Indians arrived bringing a mail packet from Fort Buford. Nothing but official communications relative to service details. Today a courier arrived from Fort Rice. Some newspapers, few or no letters. Our personal and official correspondence will come tomorrow evening or the day after tomorrow by the courier from Fort Totten.

Friday, March 13. It arrived early this afternoon after a trip over the shortest route between the two posts, and with it the newspapers containing the details of the war declared between the President and the general-in-chief over the reinstatement of Mr. Stanton as Secretary of War.

For a week there has been a thaw, a pleasant thaw with a shining sun, blue sky, and temperature which goes up to more than fifty above, F., during the day, and at night goes down to only a few degrees below freezing point. The effect of this shows up on the countryside. The bare ground shows through on the hills, and big green spots grow larger from one hour to the next on the white blanket of the prairie. The banks of sand along the edges of the river, where the wind-whipped snow did not have sufficient lodgement to pile up, are already completely bare. The water of the river and that of Douglas Creek is cracking through its thick covering here and there and is running on the ice, which in places is beginning to crack and thrust up in little hills. Because of these signs, forerunners of the breakup, all our wagons sent to the woods on the other bank have been kept here or recalled. It was high time, for yesterday the last one crossing on the ice broke through up to the axle, and it was extricated only after it was unloaded and taken apart.

At the fort, some detachments are busily at work providing for the quick drainage of the water, without which we should all certainly be flooded. It is a matter of making an opening through drifts ten to twelve feet high, of clearing the masonry with deep trenches, and of directing the run-off of the water in conformity with the slope of the ground. The work is arduous because of the numerous excavations covered up by the snow; but work which heralds the return of spring is welcomed by everyone.

Sunday, March 15. The wind has shifted to the north; the thermometer tumbled down to ten above, F., and did not go higher than twenty-six above today, and that in the sun. This is definitely the end of the thaw. The water, which was running on the ice, has itself become ice, and the surface of the river has regained its uniform immobility.

The other day, one of the Rees was at Fort Rice in the camp of the friendly Sioux. They had given him or sold him four horses, and he was smoking the calumet in one of the lodges when suddenly, with no quarrel, provocation, warning, or threat, he fell, shot through by an arrow. The one who had done the deed was a Brulé, who was also visiting in the camp.[115] He jumped on his horse, and galloped away. It was in the evening. I do not know if they chased him; but he escaped. The most curious thing is that this cowardly assassination is regarded by the Indians as an act of bravery. The guilty one will glory in it, and count the murder among his exploits. If there is any disgrace connected with it, it will not be on the assassin, but on the band which failed to protect the victim and whose hospitality was violated with impunity.

In announcing this misfortune, they informed the Rees that they were to send some of their young men to get twelve horses that they would offer as a sort of reparation. From now on, the blood that has been spilled will remain between the Rees and the Brulés. If the two bands meet, the relatives of the young warrior who was assassinated will paint themselves with white (sign of mourning) and will go to howl and sing their lamentations for the victim before the friends of his assassins. Then the latter will buy back the misdeed

115 The Brulés, "burnt thighs," are a division of the Teton Sioux. They were good hunters of the buffalo and the wild horse and made many excursions into the Arkansas and Platte country. They signed the treaty of 1868, but they participated in hostilities after the treaty. Hodge, *Handbook*, 1:166–168.

by offering buffalo skins, horses, or other presents, each one giving what he wishes. Then the blood will be washed away; the Rees will in return give gifts, and peace will reign between them until the next individual or group killing. But if the Brulés do not wish to buy back the blood, the Rees will be on the lookout and will find a chance to avenge him and will always kill any of the enemy band who fall in their hands. In the meantime, seven of them left for Rice this morning to get the twelve horses.

Friday, March 20. So today is the first day of spring. It is good to know that the sun is crossing the equator, but one would hardly suspect it. We have not seen the sun for three or four days. The weather remains cloudy, and the wind blows first from one direction and then from another. The mercury moves uncertainly around freezing point, and it would be hard to tell if it were thawing or not if it were not for the river. There, a rise of four to five feet, resulting from the partial melting of the snows up toward Buford, lifted up the vast sheet of ice, cracked it, and cut it off from part of the bank. The running water gushed out through all the openings and flooded the surface of the ice, which was then between two sheets of water. The river is running above and below. If this continues, the break-up will not be long in coming. The snow has partly disappeared on the prairie and on the slope of the bluffs, and we have a country-side streaked with green and white. As for the piles of snow which buried our lodgings and still surrounds them, it will take quite a few days of sun to finish them off, although they have already shrunken in height two or three feet. Finally, spring is born in heaven and in the almanac, *Primavera gioventu de l'anno.* Let us hope it will not be too long before it puts in its appearance at Fort Stevenson. However, a sign appeared with rather curious punc-tuality. The first flocks of geese and ducks returning from the South showed up today, and some of these winged travelers lighted for the first time this year on the banks of the river and the creek.

Saturday, March 21. After all, spring in the air was only a day behind spring on the calendar. It put in its appearance today in wonderful weather, a rejuvenated sun, and temperature which went up to fifty-six degrees F. Consequently, it thawed more than ever, the snow melted more and more, and the water began to run in streams in all directions. To prevent it from coming into our lodg-ings, we had to hurry to dig outlets for it. The narrow alley separating the front of our rooms from the big pile of snow has been enlarged by more than a foot, and a trench has been dug at the foot of the wall of snow to lead the water to the nearest slope. Although the temperature has gone down noticeably this evening, it does not seem as if it is going to freeze tonight, unless a wind from the north comes up, which is unlikely in the present calm. Two or three days more like this one and the retreat of winter will be quite far along.

Following the ducks and geese, the first sparrow hawk came back and obligingly showed up this morning around the fort.

Tuesday, March 24. I cried victory much too soon. The thaw continued yesterday and the day before, it is true, but more slowly because the winds from the northeast sent the temperature down during the evening and brought a big freeze in the night. But yesterday evening the snow began to fall after sunset, and this morning it was a foot high. The would-be spring was but an illusion; here we are sunk back into winter, and back to a uniform whiteness like that of January. The storm goes on without letting up for a moment. Are we going to be buried under the snow again? This is a cruel disappointment, all the more so since it threatens our communications with Fort Rice, and since tomorrow or the day after we are expecting a courier from there with more impatience than usual. This is the reason: Yesterday a letter arrived at Berthold for one of the traders; it was brought by an irregular way, for no courier was expected. It was from Father de Smet who wrote to Mr. Gerard, telling him of his next arrival and of his plan to communicate with the hostile Indians in order to prepare the way for the commission charged with concluding a treaty of general peace.[116] After dealing with Indian

---

116 Father de Smet, planning his annual visit to the Indians, offered to visit for the peace commissioners the bands of Sioux who did not intend to come into the rendezvous to talk with the commission. In letters to Sherman, General Harney, and N. G. Taylor, Commissioner of Indian Affairs, he tells of his plan to go with Mr. and Mrs. Galpin and Running Antelope into the hostile camps. Since he left St. Louis with General Sherman at the end of March, he must have been making his preparations for the mission as he wrote this letter to Gerard. For fuller information on his expedition, see these letters: P. J. de Smet, St. Louis, Missouri, to General W. T. Sherman [Washington, D. C.], January 28, 1868; W. S. Harney, St. Louis, Missouri, to N. G. Taylor [Washington, D. C.], February 8, 1868; N. G. Taylor [Washington, D. C.], to P. J. de Smet, St. Louis, Missouri, February 17, 1868; P. J. de Smet, St. Louis, Missouri, to N. G. Taylor [Washington, D. C.], February 27, 1868; N. G. Taylor [Washington, D. C.], to P. J. de Smet, St. Louis, Missouri, March 4, 1868; P. J. de Smet, St. Louis, Missouri, to N. G. Taylor [Washington, D. C.], March 13, 1868; C. E. Galpin, Fort Rice, Dakota Territory, to P. J. de Smet, St. Louis, Missouri, May 29, 1868; P. J. de Smet, St. Louis, Missouri, to N. G. Taylor [Washington, D. C.], May 30, 1868. Office of Indian Affairs, Record Copy of Letters Received; Record Copy of Letters Sent, National Archives.

affairs at some length, Father de Smet closes with a few lines which tell us that the greatest commotion in Washington now is over the impeachment of the President. "But," he adds, "you get the papers and politics is not my business." This means that he does not add any details. Now, since we have not received any papers since the thirteenth of this month, and since they were dated before this extreme measure was taken, you can imagine with what impatience we are awaiting the couriers from Fort Rice. If because of the thaw or the succeeding snowstorm, we fail to get any news, we shall have to wait until April 4 for the first mail expected here from Fort Totten. The devil take the snow!

Wednesday, March 25. The snow lasted twenty-four hours. Yesterday evening the sky cleared up, and we could see the stars. This morning the temperature was mild enough after sunrise, and it went up rapidly in the succeeding hours. The snow had had the entire advantage for twenty-four hours; but the sun has taken its turn, and the thaw has begun again.

During the night and morning the river showed a considerable rise. The water, swollen by the thawing of the snow the past days and by the storm, lifted the vast layer of ice which held it prisoner, and gradually loosened it from the two banks. Around noon, the time came when the river, overflowing its banks, swept impetuously across the flat bottoms, lowlands formed by inundations, at some points doubling the width of the river bed. As soon as the vast shell of ice began to move, the debâcle came. At first the ice floated adrift in enormous cakes. One of them was not less than half a mile long. Soon there appeared long fissures, with continuous rumblings; the cakes split, were shattered when they crashed together, and pressing closer and closer together, they swept down toward the sharp bend in the river less than a mile below the fort. There its course is narrowed down between the sharp bend of the left bank and the vast point of high sand which almost parallels it. It is on this point that the breakup produced the most impressive sight and showed its whole power. The big cakes of ice, squeezed between the two banks and pushed on by the ones behind divided, subdivided, and broke up into big blocks. These blocks pressed against the ones in their way, bumped together, went over each other, upset each other, and piled up so that soon this part of the choked-up river became a vast chaos of ice. At some points on the bank, the piles rose to twelve or fifteen feet. Many of these blocks, which were not less than a foot and a half thick, certainly should weigh several tons. But the force of the current and the pressure of the ice pack was so great that these heavy masses were raised, mixed up with, and carried on top of the others like little pebbles. The piling up finally blocked the river, and made a formidable barrier across it. The ice blocks which were coming on crashed against it one after another with deep rumblings and piled up in new heaps. The jam slowly extended over a wider area, and between four and five o'clock in the afternoon the river for more than a mile looked like a gigantic but motionless chaos. In contrast, all the lowlands covered with willows through which Douglas Creek flows to the river looked like a calm lake where the colors of the setting sun were reflected in luminous serenity. The ice blocks had not come in there; only the water which had broken over the barriers. Once it reached its level, being outside the stream, it formed a mirror around the trunks of the willows and reeds in which they could admire themselves complacently. The breakup stopped this evening, but will probably continue in the night.

It is worth noting that this year it came three weeks sooner than last year. Its usual time is the first two weeks in April, and it seldom comes in March. As I have noted above, the spring of 1868 is early. The thawing of the snow is the decisive cause in the breakup of the ice, for without the rise in the river, the layer of ice which is still more than a foot thick would have held a week or two yet in spite of the sun. Be that as it may, today we have witnessed a grand and impressive spectacle.

Thursday, March 26. The flood rose to ten or twelve feet in a few hours yesterday, and disappeared in a few hours during the night. This morning, the river had returned to its bed and was drifting along moderately. The enormous blocks of ice deposited on the lowlands by the current which had flooded them in the evening before were still stranded there. One might say that the Missouri, feeling herself overburdened with ice, deposited half her load on the banks, intending to come back to pick up what had been left behind when she was rid of the first half. These enormous ice blocks, spread along the whole length of the sand banks in a compact mass, look like an iced cake whose white crust had been crushed into a thousand pieces, all about the same size. Along the banks, which do not drop sharply to the water, the piles of Pelions on icy Ossas rear up like a rampart, the crest of which goes higher than the level of the plateau where our wharf is situated. In other places, on the broken and irregular surface of the ice which follows the undulations of the terrain beneath dead trees, roots, stones, and branches brought down by the breakup are cast up among the ice blocks. In the willow grove, which I compared to a calm lake yesterday, the water was frozen solid before it could drain off. The layer of ice, not less than an inch thick, was held up by the dense willows which it surrounds, and broken up into pieces which touched each other. These remained suspended in the air, two or three feet from the ground. A most singular sight. This morning, everything was covered with a thick, white frost, for last night the thermometer went down to ten degrees F.

The courier from Fort Rice arrived this evening. He brought nothing but a few papers, February 22 the most recent date. They report that the plan of impeaching the President has been given up by the committee. Did a sudden change come about in the four following days, or was the letter of Father de Smet, which was dated the twenty-sixth, misunderstood?[117]

Friday, March 27. The weather, which was very cold yesterday, became much milder today. A brilliant sun speeded up the thaw, and the prairie went back to the condition it was in last Monday before the snowstorm had laid down its white mantle again.

Tuesday, March 31. The thaw continued without interruption these past days; yesterday the mercury rose to sixty-five above, F., and the snow has almost completely disappeared. The river is still filled with drift ice, more or less, according to whether it rises or lowers. The flocks of wild geese and ducks are becoming more and more numerous, and the prairie chicken are leaving the woods to mate and nest in the grass. The doors are open, and there is no fire in the stoves.

The Indians, who have left their winter camps on the Yellowstone River, are taking the road for the posts where they live in the summer. The day before yesterday, the first party of about forty lodges arrived. Some of them are Yanktonahs belonging to Black Eyes' band. This is the group which was near Fort Buford. With them were some Sissetons of the old band of Won-ta-na-han. Medicine Bear's band came to join them today. All of them have put up their lodges (skin tents) on the prairie behind the wharf. Their horses are grazing at the foot of the hills, their women come and go, gather-

117 On February 13, 1868, the House Committee on Reconstruction, Thaddeus Stevens, chairman, by a vote of six to three disapproved a resolution offered by Stevens to impeach the President. Not until February 22 did this committee bring in a report containing the articles of impeachment. Ellis P. Oberholtzer, *A History of the United States since the Civil War,* 2:71-80.

ing wood, bringing water, leading the animals, etc., and all this commotion gives the prairie unusual activity. Tomorrow, they will get under way for Fort Rice, and in a few days they will be followed by the band of Two Ribs of Bear and Running Antelope (Unkpapahs). We distributed provisions to them, and this evening there is a celebration, singing and dancing, in their camp, to rejoice over their good luck. The poor devils suffered cruelly this winter, they, their families, and their horses. The latter bear the marks of it. They are so weakened that the Indians are unable to hunt buffalo with any success until they recover. However, the game they like has come back with the return of life to the prairie. The great herds of buffalo, which had gone to the other side of the Yellowstone at the beginning of winter, came back to us with spring. Several bands have showed up in our neighborhood. The Gros Ventres and Rees, whose horses are in better shape, killed several of them; but the Yanktonahs had no success in the hunt, and their mounts made futile runs. We know that buffalo do not run fast and that a horse of average speed can easily overtake them.

The Sioux camped near us today bring good news of the hostile bands with whom they wintered. At the beginning of the winter, they entertained evil plans. They spoke of nothing but continuing the war, attacking the soldiers, and stealing horses and mules as soon as spring came. Great discussions took place about this, the tribes of Unkpapahs and Yanktonahs dividing into friendly and hostile bands. The Santees are almost all hostile, but because of the Minnesota Massacres in which they played the principal role, they have been pursued and punished so severely (some hanged, others shot) that they cannot do anything by themselves any more.[118] The friendly chiefs, Medicine Bear, Running Antelope, the son of Two Ribs of a Bear, stressed the advantages of the peace which they now enjoy, and the misfortunes the others would draw upon themselves by resuming hostilities. A good part of the hostile bands were already tired of the war and ready to put an end to it. So the advocates of peace found themselves in the majority, and, reinforced by misery, they came to the conclusion that they would abstain from new hostilities and would wait for the arrival of the government commissioners to conclude a general treaty of peace and friendship if the terms offered were acceptable to them.

[118] The Santee were removed to Crow Creek in 1863. After three years, they were moved to their reservation at the mouth of the Niobrara River. Folwell, *A History of Minnesota*, 2:260–261.

I am sending this information by tomorrow's courier to General Terry who will have a great interest in them since he is a member of the commission charged with treating with the hostile Indians.

NOTE: Dined on fresh buffalo tongues and a beaver tail seasoned with small wild onions, table delicacies that an Epicurean could not get in Paris even for gold; the Cambacères, Rothschilds, Vérons, and the other celebrated gourmets of Europe cannot imagine what they missed or what they will miss in dying without a taste of them.

Wednesday, April 1. The information brought by Medicine Bear was not long in materializing. This morning, a chief of the Cut Heads (Sissetons) named Red Horse (Ta-shunka-douta) arrived with about forty lodges.[119] This chief had not yet come in to the military authorities. In 1862 or 1863, because of the Minnesota Massacres, he left his hunting grounds around Dog Den, near Devils Lake.

Since that time the tribe has been wandering around on the plains, particularly in the north near the border of the British possessions, where they spent last winter with a group of Assiniboines. Long sufferings, severe hardships, scarcity of game, and hunger now bring them in to listen to the voice of their Great Father and to submit to his direction. They lost a great many horses during the winter, and those they still have are not strong enough to run the buffalo. They are going to Fort Rice, and from there will go to the Santee reserve below Fort Randall, where they probably will settle down to plant corn in the summer. Their tribe is so scattered that Red Horse does not know how many lodges there are left or where they are right now. But he accepts unconditional submission for himself and his warriors and will go to the meeting place fixed by the commissioners solemnly to conclude a final peace. As one might guess, the outcome was a distribution of badly needed provisions, and tomorrow they will get under way, probably more satisfied than they have been for a long time.

Around noon, the three tribes of Berthold were summoned and arrived to receive a certain amount of supplies, too. The chiefs, warriors, and women were in the group. The distribution was made on the prairie behind the post, after which they all went to camp

119 The Cut Heads and the Sisseton are not two names for the same tribe. For a note on the Cut Heads, see above, p. 140.

The Sisseton, whose name means "lake village," are one of the seven original tribes of the Dakota. Although they are usually included in the eastern division of the Dakota, they form a link between the eastern and western tribes. Hodge, *Handbook,* 2:580–582.

on Douglas Creek, where they will spend the night, and tomorrow morning they will return to Berthold.

Running Antelope came with them. He tells me of the different bands coming next, some to make their submission; others to renew the bonds of friendship.

Although the wind has shifted to the north, and as a result there has been a return of the cold, the river is open today, and there are no ice blocks.

Thursday, April 2. I had a long talk with Running Antelope this morning. He furnished me with the most exact details on the bands which wintered on the Yellowstone. Almost all the chiefs will attend the peace conference when they find out the place and the time. Meanwhile, they will come to make their preliminary submission at the various posts nearest their country. The most doubtful are the Unkpapahs, in the past hostile under the leadership of Black Moon, Red Horn, Four Horns, and Sitting Bull.[120] Those with whom peace seems to be certain are: the Sans Arcs, commanded by One Horn (about four hundred lodges); the Miniconjous, who have not yet made any treaties with the whites (six hundred to seven hundred lodges); the Brulés, and the various small bands of Santees or Mississippi Sioux; and the Assiniboines.[121] This is good news, and if, as everything seems to indicate, a general peace is concluded, life in these military posts of the Upper Missouri will certainly be much more pleasant than before.

Running Antelope was charged by the chiefs he named to bring to me personally these messages of peace, and he did not fail to let me know that they had particular confidence in me because I was of French birth. For some reason or other, the Indians of this region have always kept up friendly relations with the Canadian-French. I do not believe that anyone else has ever understood the nature of these savages as well and has known how to maintain such consistently friendly relations with them. In contrast, the Anglo-Saxon or

120 Sitting Bull, warrior, chief, and medicine man, was the leader of the hostiles in the years covered by this journal. After the Custer Massacre in 1876, he fled to Canada and remained there until 1881, when he returned to surrender at Fort Buford. He was killed by the Indian police at Standing Rock in 1891. For a sympathetic biography, see Stanley Vestal, *Sitting Bull.*

121 The Sans Arcs are a band of Teton Sioux whose name is the French translation of "Itazipcho." They were closely allied with the Hunkpapa, Sihasapa, and Miniconjou. Hodge, *Handbook,* 2:453.

The Miniconjou were signatories to the peace treaty of Fort Sully, October 10, 1865. Hodge, *Handbook,* 1:868; Kappler, *Indian Laws and Treaties,* 2:883.

American race has used against them little else but brute force, demoralization, and oppression. From this comes the difference with which the redskins regard the Canadians and Americans. The longer I live among these children of the desert and the more I read the official documents relating to Indian affairs, the more I have modified the ideas I brought with me. The sum total of the wrongs done to these poor redskins surpasses any conception. "You must see it to believe it."

(Running Antelope [Tatokana] had his whole body as well as his arms slashed transversely, with long red lines, scars of gashes he inflicted on himself as a sign of mourning for the death of a son nineteen years old who died of sickness last winter. Fifty or sixty gashes, and in the dead of winter!)[122]

Friday, April 3. Continuation of the north wind brought us back a temperature of twelve degrees F. last night. Twenty degrees below freezing point in April; *that is going strong.* But since the wind has shifted to the S. W. today, we are getting back to less wintry weather.

Medicine Bear arrived this morning with about forty lodges. Another conference and another distribution of supplies. As this is becoming monotonous, I left this unpleasant job to Bt. Lt. Colonel Powell. One of the hostile chiefs who wintered on the Yellowstone accidentally killed himself. In a fall from his horse, his knife, which he carried in his belt, went into his side, and the wound was mortal. The name of this chief was Ishetan-Otanka[?] (Hawk-bustard).

Monday, April 6. For three days, the temperature has been hovering around freezing point, more below than above, and what is left of the snow remains the same. The river is completely free, and there is no drifting ice.

The day before yesterday, Saturday, the mail from Fort Totten, which we were awaiting so impatiently, finally arrived and with it a disappointment we had not expected. The mail service by contract has been abandoned, the contract nullified, and until a new company is formed to carry the mail between Fort Totten and Saint Paul, our correspondence remains en route at Fort Ransom where, it seems, there is a great deal of it. Notified of the fact, Bt. Col. Whistler sent

122 The material in parentheses was written in the French manuscript as a marginal note.

Running Antelope's Indian name is "Tatokainyanke" rather than "Tatokana."

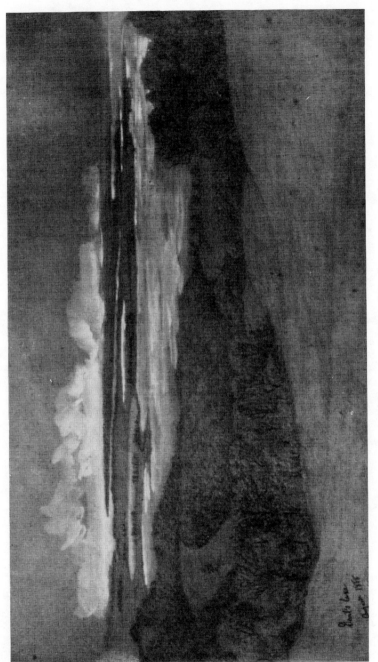

Devils Lake, Dakota Territory

a small detachment of soldiers to get the delayed mail and will send it to us the fifteenth instead of the tenth, the day set for the next courier. But at this last date, the delayed mail will still not be at Devils Lake. So the number of letters and newspapers which got to us is very small. As for myself, I received a single letter and four comparatively old newspapers (February). At least the newspapers give all the details of the impeachment of the President and the circumstances leading to this measure just when it was thought to have been abandoned by Congress. So Father de Smet's letter was correct. According to his date, the news must have just arrived by telegraph in St. Louis when he informed Mr. Gerard about it. Right now, I do not know if it isn't better to be at Fort Stevenson than in Washington when one is of high rank in the army. Here, at least, we have nothing to do with politics, and politics is like a bottle of ink. It is black inside, and there is hardly any way of getting into it without getting dirty fingers.

Tuesday, April 7. Howkah, the brother (or uncle) of Ishta-Sapah, arrived this morning on his way to Fort Rice after a trip on the prairie toward Devils Lake. I had provisions distributed to him and the little band with him, which numbers about ten lodges. Medicine Bear, who is still camped near Douglas Creek, had his share of our bounty on the same occasion. He warns us not to trust the band of incorrigible Unkpapahs, led by Red Horn, Black Moon, Sitting Bull, and Four Horns. These are the same ones who committed the depredations last fall and the only ones who still have evil intentions and say that they want to stay "on the warpath." Some of Medicine Bear's men discovered burned-out fires and some thongs in a clump of woods where we send our men out to cut poles for the palisades of the new corral. They think that these very recent traces may be indications of hostiles and promise that if the enemy band shows up, they will fight with us. However it might be, a warning has been given to the wagons and the escort to redouble their vigilance and to keep themselves on the lookout.

In order to emphasize the need he and his people have for provisions, Howkah quietly uncovered his chest to show me that he was now just skin and bones. This silent commentary on his request was not without its eloquence. A cannibal would find his ribs hardly worth nibbling at.

Wednesday, April 8. Yesterday, in the afternoon, two of our men died; one from a heart disease complicated by scurvy, the other from just scurvy. This sickness weakened our garrison considerably during the winter and reached its height last month. Right now we have in the hospital thirty-two sick with scurvy, and thirteen more are exempt from service in their company, having only a light touch or just getting over it. In addition there are six employees of the quartermaster who are being treated at the hospital, which makes a total of fifty-one cases of scurvy, equal to one-fourth of the garrison.[123]

These regrettable health conditions are the result of being without fresh vegetables for a long time and of having rations of fresh meat distributed only twice a week. The principal food of the men is salt pork, salt fish; and so there is sickness. Nevertheless, it may be presumed that it would not have reached the proportions I have just indicated if our men had had good quarters from the beginning of winter. Unfortunately the work was begun too late last summer, and as I have related, one of the two companies was not comfortably installed until the last days of December, and the other in the first days of January. Until then they were exposed to the rough weather of the end of November and the whole month of December, with no shelter but miserable edge tents. When the snow and ice came, they dug out the inside of their quarters three or four feet deep, and built themselves small earthen fireplaces, which had the inconvenience of producing stifling heat when the fire blazed and freezing cold when it was out. Moreover, sleeping on the ground wasn't good for them. Add to this and to the salt rations the constant fatigue from the hardest type of daily work, and it is no wonder that scurvy has been so prevalent, with upset stomachs, tired limbs, and sorely taxed constitutions. Fortunately the ordeal is just about over, thanks to the imminent arrival of the steamboats and the supplies they will bring us.

To combat this evil, and especially to forestall it, we have in addition to the usual remedies of the pharmacy, a small, wild, white onion, or shallot, tasting very much like garlic, which grows in abundance on the prairie. The Indians gather much of it for us in exchange for small quantities of biscuits, and so the monotony of the usual fare is agreeably and usefully varied by this natural condiment, of which we are all very fond. The Indians supply us with a cylindrical tuber as thick as a thumb, which the Canadians call artichoke, I do not know why, for nothing is less like an artichoke. In form, it is more like salsify. Raw, it is almost without flavor; cooked, it

[123] Dr. Matthews reported that in 1868 seventy-nine men at Fort Stevenson had scurvy. In 1869 the number of cases dropped to five. *Report on Barracks and Hospitals*, p. 399.

tastes like a parsnip or like the most insipid turnip. The wild shallot is infinitely preferable.

Our two dead men were buried this morning side by side on the prairie with military honors. A detachment of twelve armed men and forty others unarmed accompanied and followed the wagon carrying the two coffins. The officers brought up the rear, in full dress and unarmed. When the bodies were lowered into the two graves, Lieutenant Hooton, officer of the day, read the funeral service, a sergeant threw the shovelful of earth at the proper moment, "earth to earth, dust to dust"; three volleys were fired, and while the fatigue party filled in the graves, everyone hurried back to his lodging, for the weather was very cold, and although the wind blew from the S. E., we shivered in our overcoats. Thermometer below zero centigrade.

NOTE: With our new breechloading guns equipped with a mercury fulminate cap replacing the powder in our fixed cartridges, we cannot fire blanks any more; we must always fire the bullet. The escort had to fire in the air this morning, which is no inconvenience in our desert. But what will be done when the interment is held in a populated place as, for example, in a city cemetery?

Friday, April 10. The wild geese are coming north in great numbers. They pass over our heads in their regular *order of flight,* that is, in the form of a V, one side always longer than the other, taking turns in the leading position at the apex of the angle which breaks the air. Every day some flocks alight to rest and feed either on the bank of the river or along the creeks and on the ponds of water in our neighborhood. On the flat bottoms, the mud left by the last flood and the melting of the blocks of ice which the river left there make it very difficult to get into the reeds. On the prairie, as this is right out in the open, the geese very seldom come within gun range. These geese are more experienced than the young ones which come back to us in the fall. So one can hardly shoot them except with a carbine. The Indians, who have nothing but poor guns, lie flat on their bellies under their gray blankets, and in this way crawl on their hands and knees to get up to them. It is a good way, but so slow and *dirty* that the whites do not do it, and prefer to let the geese go rather than pay this price to get near enough to kill some.

This morning an Indian slid along like this with a double-barreled gun toward a small pond formed by the melting of the snow behind the fort. On the other side crawling in the grass was a lynx on the hunt, too, and he was quite near. So the quadruped got up within fifteen to twenty feet of his feathered prey without being discovered, and springing suddenly, he grabbed one of the birds; then, believing that he was sure of a good supper, he ran for the neighboring hills. Unfortunately for him, he had not seen or did not understand what was concealed by that gray body which resembled a piece of rock when it was motionless. When the lynx, carrying away his goose, got about forty feet away, the blanket lifted up, and the red man appeared with one knee to the ground and his gun to his cheek. Two shots rang out, and the lynx and goose lay dead on the grass side by side.

Doctor Gray traded some provisions for both. The animal is a very large Canadian lynx. Its head is just like that of a tiger, leopard, jaguar, or cat. It belongs to the same family. Only its fur is uniformly gray and its ears, which are proportionately longer, end in a little tuft of dark hair shaped like a brush. Its legs are remarkably long and powerful. Its teeth and claws are long, thin, and sharp; its paws large and furred. It is the height of the most powerful hunting dog, but its body is thinner and more supple. It is taller on its legs than most felines. Its tail is quite different, for in the lynx, that appendage is only five or six inches long. It ends in a tuft of black hair like that of the deer or elk. This is the first of its kind to be killed at Fort Stevenson.

Saturday, April 11. The news brought from Berthold is not as peaceful as that received before. It would seem that the band of hostile Unkpapahs has succeeded in making two other bands (the Blackfeet Sioux and a part of the Miniconjous) go back on their good resolutions and involve them in a general plan of hostilities for the next summer. Some Miniconjous came to offer thirty horses to the three tribes if they would leave their village and take to the plains, renouncing their treaty of friendship with the whites. This they refused to do. Then some families of Miniconjous, refusing to run the risks involved in a state of war, left their tribe to come to Berthold to live with the Arikaras. I attach very little importance to this news. Even if it were true, all that the three bands could undertake would be to steal a few mules and kill some wagoners by surprise; but we are taking measures so that in such a case the ones most surprised will be these red plunderers, because of the reception they will be given.

[*Sitting Bull*] This band of incorrigible Unkpapahs is led by four or five chiefs, such as Dark Moon, Red Horn, Four Horns, and

Sitting Bull. A few years ago the latter was wounded by bayonets in a battle. Bloody Knife, who was fighting with the soldiers, seeing that the wounded man was still breathing, jumped off his horse, and was ready to cut his throat and take his scalp when the officer commanding the detachment had the unfortunate but charitable inspiration of forbidding them to finish off Sitting Bull, who was playing dead. The result was that the rascal escaped, recovered from his wounds, and since then, bent on vengeance, he has always done us every harm in his power and is the spirit or arm of all the coups attempted or accomplished against us. It is he in particular who inspires the others with his hate and who keeps on the warpath the unsubdued band of Unkpapahs, which is always joined by young aspirants from other bands, in search of adventure, scalps, and renown.

These young braves make up the turbulent faction in every tribe, and often the chiefs have a good deal of trouble in keeping them under their authority. Here is the reason: young men who reach the age when they are counted among the warriors can acquire attention, influence, and position among the people only by prowess in war. If they are satisfied with being intrepid hunters, rich enough to have several wives and to own a dozen horses, feathers, necklaces, and a good supply of dried meat, they will not be admitted to the council fire and will not rank with the chiefs. So if they have any ambition at all to satisfy, they will go on the warpath, and they do this on their own if their tribe is at peace with the whites and with their neighbors. They will start out some night, either alone or in small bands fired with the same spirit, and begin to scour the plains. As I have explained elsewhere, bravery to them does not mean exposing themselves to danger for difficult or uncertain outcome; on the contrary, their exploits are considered much more brilliant if they can gather in more scalps or steal more horses or mules with the least possible risk. So they operate by ambush and refrain from open attack; this explains why it is possible for us to establish, build, and maintain with impunity our little post of two companies exposed on all sides, without defences of any kind, separated from Totten by six and from Rice by four days' march, right in the heart of the Sioux nation whose combined tribes number around thirty thousand souls.

But woe to the man out alone, white or red, who meets on the plains some one of these bands in quest of scalps. Even though his tribe may be at peace with the one to which the roamers belong, they will have no scruples about assassinating him, stealing his horses and his weapons, and taking his scalp back as a trophy. If the man hunt is not successful because they are too few, they will go to join some other band, and they will scour the country together or will approach the military posts to lie in wait for some wagon going for wood or some soldiers straying off into the woods.

When one of them has made a successful attack and has brought back a certain number of scalps and some booty, when the tribe has danced the scalp dance several times in honor of his return from an expedition and celebrated his exploits and perpetuated the memory of them by a name, the aspirant to the title of chief throws off his clothes piece by piece, distributes at random his horses, supplies, ornaments, and even his wives, and is proclaimed *chief* to the accompaniment of dances, shouts of joy, improvised chants, and the beating of drums. This does not mean that he will command the tribe or take the place of the second chief or the war chief. He simply acquires the title and the rank of chief; he enters the councils; his influence will be recognized. He is promoted by brevet, as it is understood in our army, with this difference—he had to do something to get the said brevet, while with us, it is the least necessary condition. If for the purposes of running buffalo, making winter camp, or any reason, the tribe separates into several bands, some families will probably put themselves under his leadership, and then he will have command of a few lodges. His campaigns will be over for the present, and the odds are that unless there is too tempting a chance, he will remain at peace.

Nevertheless, if he has higher ambitions and if young rivals by their prowess acquire a renown and influence that threatens to put him in the background, he will, in order to maintain his position in the tribe, go out on new raids, this time leading some warriors, and will strive to make some coup to refurbish his prestige. So he will stay on the warpath as long as his ambition is not satisfied, after which, if he reaches his goal and is invested with an important enough command, he will rest on his laurels and will preach peace to the young men in concert with the ancients of the tribe and the retired chiefs (unless in looking for scalps he has lost his own).

[*Four Bears*] Warrior exploits are of such paramount importance in the choice of a tribal chief that no other consideration stands in the way. Thus, the old chief of the Gros Ventres, Four Bears, had not in his veins a drop of the blood of the tribe he was commanding. He was Assiniboine by birth. Taken prisoner when still a child and brought up among the Gros Ventres or Hidatsa, he grew in importance among them, and so distinguished himself in the battles against the Sioux to whom he belonged by blood that he achieved the highest rank in his adopted tribe, and acquired a renown that lived after him.

An election or proclamation is not always necessary to establish the authority of a chief. Some have imposed themselves by their reputation and the strength of their fists. A few years ago, a chief of the Mississippi Sioux (I have forgotten his name) did this and, like all usurpers, he ruled his band with an iron hand, wielding the knife or the club at the least sign of insubordination. The last exploit which raised him to the command is rather characteristic.

A numerous band of Rees or Arikaris had surprised three Sioux on the prairie, and the poor devils took shelter in the underbrush where not one of their assailants, although outnumbering them twenty to one, dared pursue them. They made a great uproar, shouted, galloped around, shot arrows or bullets into the brush, but did not risk entering. Two Sioux came up and asked the reason for all the noise. When they found out, they dismounted, armed themselves with their knives or tomahawks, and went resolutely into the brush. They killed the three fugitives, although they were of their own nation (but not of their tribe); one of the two perished there. The other brought back the three scalps and for this deed was considered such a hero that when he went back to his tribe, he took command of it without opposition.

Among the hostile Unkpapahs, almost all the chiefs must either go to war or lose their position to others who are more audacious or more obstinate. Two of them, Red Horn and Four Horns, were friends of the whites at one time and in this period contributed greatly to saving the life of Mr. Gerard, one of the Berthold traders.

This was some years ago. At that time, the military posts did not extend farther than Minnesota. Gerard, with some horses and a wagon of trade goods, had fallen into the hands of the Unkpapahs. He was on their hunting grounds, and they all agreed to confiscate his merchandise. There was no opposition to the theft. On the question of murder, it was another thing. When the proposition of putting the unfortunate whites (there were two of them) to death was brought up, some voices were raised in their favor; but evidently the advocates of death were in the majority, and they were going to proceed with the execution when Running Antelope came to the rescue.

Running Antelope, it is well to mention, was young then and had been involved as one of the leaders in the attack on a stage, the stealing of mails and a large sum of gold, and the murder of the agent,

the driver, and, I believe, some passengers. Pursued and captured by
the troops, he was tried and condemned to death. He owed his life
only to the clemency of the President, who pardoned him and allowed
him to return to his people. He, at least, has showed himself grateful,
and since then has always remained a friend of the whites. "Which
doesn't mean," Gerard still asserts, "that I should trust him with
my skin more than any other Indian when he could profit by detach-
ing my hair from it."

However that may be, on this occasion Running Antelope
jumped up on the captured wagon and harangued the warriors, declaring that Gerard was his friend and that he would not allow him
to be put to death. At the same time, his wives and those of his kin
began a certain war chant, the aim of which is to excite their husbands or brothers to battle and to inflame their fervor in difficult
situations. At this call, the relatives and friends of Running Antelope began to run to their lodgings, and came out armed, to range
themselves around him. The opposition did likewise, and the battle
was on. Gerard and his companion took advantage of it and unhitched their horses quickly. They lost their merchandise, but got
out with their lives. There were three or four Unkpapahs killed and
a good many wounded in the melee. After this, since the causes of the
uproar had made their escape, everyone went back to his tent.

So, as this example shows, Indians are as ready to fight among
themselves as to battle the whites. From tribe to tribe, the wars, or
rather the hostilities, go on indefinitely. Twenty times they will make
peace, twenty times they will smoke the calumet together and bury
the hatchet. These are just momentary truces, and at the first chance
they will kill each other and steal from each other more than ever,
provided that one party is much stronger than the other, and in particular that one side or the other can surprise isolated hunters and
take their scalps without running any serious risks.

Since yesterday, strong wind from the N. E., very cold, and much
dust. Spring comes at a snail's pace. We haven't had a single night yet
when it has not frozen quite solid, even when the day was mild.
So nothing gets green, and there are still patches of snow on the countryside.

Sunday, April 12. Easter! It is a good thing that the calendar
marks the day, for here nothing distinguishes Easter Sunday from all
the other Sundays. For us especially "the days follow each other and
are all alike." Great flock of pelicans on the river. Like many human
bipeds, this bird lives on the reputation which has been made for it

and fiction which has made it a symbol of maternal love. Before visiting the Missouri, I had seen them only in painting or in sculpture, always pictured as they are on tavern sign boards:

Se déchirant les flancs
Pour nourrir ses enfants.

The little pelicans who depended on this kind of nourishment would soon starve to death; but they have something much more certain, a supply of small fish that their parents distribute to them, not from their stomach, but from the pouch which nature has put in their long, wide beak for this purpose. This pouch is the pantry of the household. It is here that they put and carry the surplus provisions and the baby food.

Monday, April 13. The band of Medicine Bear, which had been camped on the bank of Douglas Creek for about ten days, got under way this morning to hunt buffalo, for their horses are in better condition after this period of rest. Their departure was marked by one of those acts which demonstrate what I wrote yesterday about the insubordination of a number of young men in each tribe. Some of them, knowing that they were to break camp early this morning, stole during the night two cattle tied to Gerard's wagons near the house he built for his merchandise, a hundred yards or so from our quarters. When day came and they noticed the theft, the trader and his employees got on their horses and scoured the prairie. They found the track, and two of them were hot on the trail when the fugitives, aware that they were being pursued, set fire to the prairie to blot out the track. The pursuers came to report the incident, and Gerard himself left with one of his men. Lieutenant Walborn is accompanying him with four mounted men. It is improbable that Medicine Bear is an accomplice in the theft; but Gerard believes he will have to promise him the gift of a horse before the two cattle will be returned. Will the chief have enough authority to carry out the restitution, or will they get to the thieves before they have killed the cattle to make a grand feast? That is the question. Note that this *neighborly* procedure is the act of a *friendly* band which entertains no idea of hostility toward the whites.

P. S. Medicine Bear has kept his word. This evening he returned with about ten of his warriors, bringing back one of the cattle and what meat of the other he had been able to save. The deed was done by an Unkpapah and his son who were living with the Yanktonahs of Medicine Bear. The latter pursued them and reached them in time to save one of the animals, but too late to bring the other one back. The culprits hid in the brush, Manto-Ouakan [Manoouakan] explained, and that is why he did not bring them back with him. This may be true, but I doubt it. In any case, the band received coffee, sugar, pork, and biscuits from Gerard, and they departed very satisfied with the reward given for their virtue.

Tuesday, April 14. First rainy day of the year. This phenomenon is something of a novelty for us. We have not had any for six months and a half (October 1, 1867). At Stevenson, one cannot say, "Boring as a rainy day." On the contrary, rain is too rare here not to be welcomed. Our drifts of snow will disappear more quickly.

NOTE: Now we know that the theft of Gerard's cattle was the punishment inflicted on the trader by the Indians for having set fire to the prairie a few days ago and in this way driving away the game, which is their principal resource.

Thursday, April 16. A train of twelve wagons arrived this morning from Fort Totten, under the command of Lt. Lockwood. He comes to get some grain stored here since last fall and which the cattle and draft animals greatly need at Devils Lake where the supply of forage is exhausted, although the rations have been reduced to a minimum for some time. Nevertheless, the animals are in good condition because of the care they were given and because pasture seems to have been a good substitute for fodder.

The condition at Fort Totten is completely different from what it was at the beginning of winter. Since his arrival in the first days of December, Bt. Col. Whistler has put everything on a new footing. The disorder and demoralization which prevailed in the garrison has disappeared with the evil influence of an incapable and drunken commandant. Discipline and order have been re-established in the service. The men spent the winter in good quarters, and the sanitary conditions of the post are certainly much better there than they are here.[124] Scurvy has affected only a few men, and not until recently. The cases are not serious. Briefly, the report of Lieutenant Norwell who had gone to Fort Totten the first of this month as district inspector and who came back with the convoy, is most satisfactory.

[124] In August, 1868, Dr. King wrote that 126 of the 281 men at Fort Totten were under treatment. The most prevalent diseases were diarrhea, gonorrhea, acute rheumatism, constipation, headache, and boils. Fort Totten, "Record of the Medical History of the Post." Department of Dakota, War Records Division, National Archives.

Many Indians and half-breeds wintered around the fort. The former received rations from time to time, and the latter bought some from the companies. Now they have all gone hunting, and there are none on the reserve.[125]

Colonel Whistler had the excellent idea of sending us a supply of pike from the lake, which seems wonderful to us because we have been without fresh fish for so long and our ordinary fare has been so monotonous.

The difference in climate between Devils Lake and Stevenson is rather remarkable. Here, the snow has almost completely disappeared; over there, it still covers the ground, and the cold is still very keen. The convoy passed over ravines filled in with snow without breaking through the frozen surface, and although the wagons were empty, the weight of the carts and six mules drawing them proves how little the crust has softened. It is only on this side of Dog Den that the snow has disappeared from the prairies and is now seen only in the bottom of the coulees and behind the slopes where the sun rarely penetrates.

Saturday, April 18. The convoy which came from Totten the day before yesterday left again this morning, reinforced by five wagons with their teams which I am transferring from one post to the other. Here they were surplus; there they are needed.

This evening, along toward sunset, the expected mail arrived on the dot. It contains a number of letters, official communications, and newspapers which have accumulated at Fort Ransom since the contract mail stopped service on that line. A new company is going to be organized soon. General Terry has informed me that he is putting forth every effort to get a line established by four-horse relay, which would probably go to Devils Lake, and, if possible, as far as Buford, passing by Stevenson. It will certainly come, but I do not believe

[125] The Indians, Wahpeton and Sisseton for the most part, began arriving in November at Fort Totten, where no provision had been made for them. Bishop Henry B. Whipple, Colonel Whistler, General Sibley, and Joseph R. Brown all worked to get provisions to the Indians and to prevent them from starving to death. During most of the winter, rations were issued to about six hundred of them. S. D. Hinman, Santee Agency, Nebraska, to Bishop Whipple, [n.p.] August 17, 1868, Whipple Papers; Major Thompson, St. Paul, Minn., to H. H. Sibley, St. Paul, Minn., January 5, 1868, J. W. Daniels, Fort Wadsworth, D. T., to Bishop Whipple, [n.p.] November 2, 1868, General Hancock, St. Paul, Minn., to Bishop Whipple, Fairibault, Minn., May 30, 1869. J. R. Brown, Lake Traverse, Minn., to H. H. Sibley, St. Paul, Minn., February 16, 1868, Sibley Papers; *St. Paul Daily Pioneer,* April 30, 1868, July 1, 1868; *Report of the Commissioner of Indian Affairs for the Year 1868,* p. 195.

it will materialize soon. Be that as it may, and until a new order, Bt. Col. Whistler will send for our letters once a week to Fort Ransom, which in turn receives them from Fort Abercrombie. Between Totten and Stevenson the exchange will be made once a week, too, and will correspond with the arrival of the couriers from Ransom, and so (during the summer, at least) we shall in the future have four couriers a month instead of three.

Sunday, April 19. Among the official papers brought by the courier yesterday, I regret to see an order from General Terry withdrawing the licenses from the traders at Fort Totten, no matter on what authority they hold them, beginning next July 1. An order from the War Department established freedom of trade at all our posts, *subject to the restrictions which might be made by the commander of the Department.** General Terry has made use of this reservation to suppress the commercial establishments themselves rather than the articles for sale: he has done this to create a monopoly at Fort Totten for *his brother* and an associate who are the only ones authorized to trade there. This is using power arbitrarily to further a family speculation. I had thought General Terry above such things. But, since his brother doesn't have a cent, it seems that he wanted to help him get some money by the means he had at his disposal. The brother made an arrangement with a trader who had money and merchandise. His contribution to the association was the monopoly of the sutlership at Totten. It remains to be seen if the garrison will not lose in proportion to what the Terry family gains.

* Correction: This order does not apply to Fort Totten, which is on this side of the 100th degree of longitude. It stays under the ordinary system of sutlers. Therefore the nomination is strictly legal.[126]

Major Furey, quartermaster of the district, is ordered to St. Paul to organize the transport of part of our supplies by land. He will leave with the mail May 1. The quartermaster of the regiment, Lt. Parsons, will replace him while he is gone.

[126] The correction appeared in the margin beside the false report. The material on the Terry family was scratched out with ink of the same kind as that used in writing the bulk of the manuscript, and was therefore probably done by De Trobriand.

Colonel Whistler received notice of the trading permit of R. G. Terry and E. W. Breuner on March 21. O. D. Greene, St. Paul, AA Genl, Department of Dakota, to Col. Whistler, Fort Totten, March 21, 1868. Department of Dakota, War Records Division, National Archives.

Monday, April 20. In reading extracts from French newspapers about the new law concerning the press now under discussion in the Chamber of Deputies, I often see an allusion to the actions of the government against the political newspapers and today, as under Louis-Philippe, "the arousing of hate and contempt of the government" by moderate criticisms or rather harmless jokes plays a major role. What would they say and what would they do in France if they published a hundredth part of what is published here everywhere and every day, under every administration? For example, the article from a Chicago newspaper which came to my attention begins thus: "If the ineffable contempt and hatred of a loyal people would scathe, and blast and wither a public traitor, *Andrew Johnson* (the president) this day would lie as prostrate in life as he does in the estimation of the American people, a miserable, an irreparable ruin, an object of loathing, an object of horror to all beholders, etc."[127] Note that in Congress, the epithets applied to the President by the fiery radical orators are scarcely more moderate. However, no one would think of calling for legislation to check this brand of eloquence. The world does not stop going around because of it, and government is just as stable. Liberty has in itself the cure for its own excesses.

Wednesday, April 22. Great activity at the fort. At nine o'clock in the morning, the white smoke of a steamboat was sighted above the trees at the point where the hills hide from us the course of the river. Everyone was outside immediately, all glasses were in use, and in a few minutes the movement of the smoke left no doubt. Hurrah for the first boat of the season!

An hour later, we were gathered near the wharf; the boat had rounded the two points forming the great bend of the Missouri where it changes its course from east to south. But there was disappointment after all. The boat (it was the *Cora*, serving the Pacific Railroad line) did not have any freight for us, and passed by the wharf without stopping. After saluting the fort with a cannon shot, she continued her direct course toward Berthold and Buford. Everyone went back to the fort laughing about the mishap, and the servants took back the sacks and baskets as empty as they brought them. They had brought them so they could buy potatoes, onions, and other supplies which they hoped to procure on board. Now the boats will come one after another. When one has gone by, others will come in a steady stream.

[127] The material quoted appeared in the French manuscript in English.

Friday, April 24. The warm sun today has melted the last traces of the great drift of snow which covered my lodging this winter and which last month was piled up before my door and blocked any view from my window. They went at it several times with the spade and pickax and spread out the pieces in the sun, in this way speeding up its disappearance; unless this were done, it would have lasted a week or two more, for its base formed a solid layer of ice four or five inches thick. At last it is all gone. Some white spots scattered here and there in the hollow of the ravines and behind the slopes where the brush grows still adorn the countryside, but they are shrinking and rapidly disappearing. In a few days, no trace of the winter snows will remain. As for the chaos of huge, broken blocks of ice, the river did not go back to get them from the lowlands where she had deposited them. They have melted in the sun, too; except on a few points where what remains of them, mixed with mud, still marks the places where the piles had risen to the greatest height. Two or three more days like this, and the sun will finish its work on these, too.

Saturday, April 25. Red-letter day. First, the day has been wonderful and the temperature decidedly warm. Then around nine o'clock, the *Deer Lodge* came to tie up at the wharf. Although this is the second boat to pass Stevenson, she is the first this year to stop. She brought Lieutenant [James E.] Macklin and his wife who spent the winter at Fort Rice and are on their way to Fort Totten, their final destination.

The *Deer Lodge* brought us from Sioux City a new and complete assortment of instruments for our military band. The musicians, transported with happiness and inspired by this realization of all their hopes, had a general rehearsal on the spot, and this afternoon for the first time the band, complete and very resplendent with its shining instruments of *German silver,* played for an hour on the parade ground before my unfinished house. For a first performance, it wasn't bad, and it bids fair for a regimental band of eighteen musicians. All the officers and ladies of the garrison sat on their doorsteps to listen to the music. What a contrast this is with the fort of scarcely a month ago!

[*Current prices*] The arrival of the *Deer Lodge* enabled us to vary our table menu by purchasing some supplies, with not much consideration as to price. For example: butter, eighty cents a pound; eggs, seventy-five cents a dozen; potatoes, seven dollars a bushel, that is, eleven to twelve cents a pound. Tobacco in proportion.

Sunday, April 26. The steamboat *Success* arrived this morning, stopped a minute, and, not having anything for us, left after an exchange of civilities: a drink and some apples. I have not tasted anything like this for five or six months. I can say the same for the glass of champagne that the captain of the *Deer Lodge* offered me yesterday.

We were complaining about the cold, and we were asking for heat; for two days, we have had just what we ordered. The thermometer has gone up to seventy-five degrees. For the month of April, that is something. We were complaining about the snow; now we have dust to complain about. For us, there is no middle ground because of the frequent winds which sweep across the plains. The wind is the scourge of this climate, which, without it, would be superb, for it rains so seldom that it really is not worth mentioning.

[*Fire on the prairies*] During the past two days, the wind has spread the fire on the prairies around Stevenson. In this season of the year, the long, dry grasses of last season are very inflammable, and when it is accidentally or purposely set on fire, the flames, driven by the wind, sweep along with great rapidity. This morning, a column of smoke appeared in the west on the other side of the river, from where a strong breeze was blowing. The fire spread out, and running all along the hills, plunging into the ravines, climbing the escarpments, licking up the dry lands, and devouring the brush, it passed in front of us, and went out at the bank of the river below the bend where it turns south. This evening, the whole line of the bluffs facing us is blackened, a bed of burnt cinders, while the columns of smoke indicate that in the distance the fire is still running on the prairies far away.

Monday, April 27. The steamer *Nile* stopped a few minutes at the wharf this morning. She is the fourth of the season.

Major Furey, quartermaster of the district, received by the last courier the order to report to the general headquarters of the department in St. Paul to assist in the organization of the provisioning by land and to superintend the transport. He left this morning for Fort Totten with Lieutenant and Mrs. Macklin and an escort. The party is composed of a wagon with six mules and an ambulance in reserve. It will take them five or six days to get to Devils Lake. From there, Furey will go on his way with the couriers to Ransom, Abercrombie, where he will take the relay on to St. Cloud, where he will reach the railroad. They could not have had a better day to start out. Perhaps they will even find it too warm, for the thermometer has gone up (in the shade, of course) to eighty degrees F. It is curious to feel such great summer heat in the midst of a wintry countryside where there is not a touch of new growth on the prairies, nor a bud on the trees at the edge of the river. Probably the spring vegetation will come out suddenly because of the hot sun, and from one day to the next, dormant nature will come out of its shroud, full of life like the daughter of Jaïrus: "She is not dead; she is only sleeping."

Wednesday, April 29. Yesterday the fire was still running here and there on the prairie, driven by a strong wind from the S. W. In the evening, a thunderstorm extinguished the glow which reflected ruddy lights in the clouded sky. Today, only the good results of the storm can be seen, for it has laid the dust and brought the first touches of green to the prairie, especially on the blackened lands which the fire passed. Nowhere is there more new growth. This first awakening of nature, the heat of the sun which brings it, the military band which is now heard twice a day, one hour in the morning at the relieving guard and one hour in the evening before retreat at sunset —all this gives Fort Stevenson a new face and a much more agreeable one than the cloak of winter and the burial under the snow. The military band in particular has a most happy effect on morale, and I should almost say on the physical condition of the men, who, their day's work done, like to listen to the music, resting in a group in front of company quarters. It puts them in good humor, and the number of sick at the hospital is decreasing.

Friday, May 1. If the month of May fulfills the promise of its beginning, it will live up to the reputation it universally enjoys. Nothing could be more delightfully spring-like than today, which has been marked by some incidents outside the regular routine. The Arrikaree Indians were enlisted as scouts for six months, and will serve as scouts at the fort or with escorts which we will have to send out. They receive the pay and the rations of a soldier, and the uniform, that is, a cap with a dark feather which they like very much, the jacket, overcoat, trousers, and woolen shirt. (Through habit, all of them keep their moccasins.) In addition they get forty cents a day for their horse, which each of them furnishes. At the same time, Pacquenaud was hired as an interpreter. He is a valuable man who has spent thirty years on the plains, and he speaks with remarkable facility French (Canadian), English, Sioux, Ree, Gros Ventre, Mandan, Crow. He arrived in the country at the age of fifteen as an employee of the fur company of Mr. Chouteau of St. Louis. At this time, there were few whites in Dakota, and all of them came to trade with the Indians, who invariably gave them a warm welcome. Although the tribes did not stop fighting each other, which is an immemorial custom among the redskins, the whites were not involved in their quarrels. They could cross the deserts in security without weapons, and they were never mistreated. When they met some savages, they sat down together around the fire, smoked the peace pipe, did some trading, exchanged news with each other, and parted as they had met, friends. At that time, nothing could be more inoffensive to the whites than the plains tribes. From them, they received nothing but hospitality; every promise given was rigorously kept, and as transactions were carried out in good faith, there was the best of feeling between individuals. If theft, deceit, murder, and war have come since those days, the fault is definitely that of the whites alone. The trading posts, encouraged by the savages, multiplied rapidly, as well as secondary meeting places established on the course of the small rivers to serve the distant tribes who could not conveniently bring their peltries to the banks of the Missouri.

The great profits from the trade bred rivalries among the traders; these rivalries resulted in stratagems of all sorts and perfidies by which each made great efforts to attract the Indians and to turn them away from competitors. So to harm one another, the whites began to stir up the Indians and encouraged them to steal. The redskins learned from them bad faith, then theft, then the murder of the traders or their employees. Whiskey was introduced among them to encourage them in evil and to despoil them more easily. So Pandora's box was opened on the plains, and the vice, injustice, bad treatment sown by the whites produced this bloody harvest, which for ten years has cost so much in blood and money. The discovery of the gold mines in Montana aggravated the situation by bringing a flock of gold seekers, uncontrolled bandits, men on their own, far from the jurisdiction of the law and the dictates of civilization. The Minnesota Massacre in 1862 resulted in the expulsion of the Santees far from their hunting grounds, and brought together all the Sioux on the west bank of the Missouri. This concentration of all those at war with the whites produced these hostilities which have increased of late because the treaties concluded with the tribes of the Plat[t]e have not been observed by the government. Nevertheless, tired of the war, miserable, harassed, and hungry, most of the tribes have made their submission as I have explained elsewhere, and the rest, except, perhaps, for a band of Unkpapahs, will do likewise when the government commissioners come out to conclude a lasting peace on the Upper Missouri.

[*The number of Indians in Dakota*] Here are the names and numbers of the Indian tribes of Dakota, according to the report of the Indian Bureau to Congress in 1866. Although the count is not absolutely exact, the number approaches the truth as closely as is possible among the nomadic tribes who are strangers to statistics:

	Lodges	*Persons*
Minniconjous (Sioux)	360	2220
Brulés (Sioux)	200	1200
Two Kettle (Sioux)	200	1200[128]
Blackfeet (Sioux)	220	1320
Yanktonahs (upper) (Sioux)	400	2400
Yanktonahs (lower) (Sioux)	350	2100
Unkpapahs (Sioux)	300	1800
Sans Arcs	280	1680
Ogallalas	350	2100[129]
Mountain Crow	400	2400
Assiniboines	440	2640
Plains Crow	250	1500
Gros Ventres of Berthold		400
Arikarees of Berthold	common village	1500
Mandans of Berthold	——	400
	4,060	26,360

To this must be added the tribes of the Mississippi Sioux, or what is left of them, Santees, Sissetons, Cut Heads, etc., crowded into Dakota. All this adds up to a total in round numbers of 30,000 Indians (women and children included).

The Gros Ventres, or Hidatsa, and the Crow are tribes belonging to the same stock, divided by circumstances, but speaking the same

[128] The Two Kettle, whose tribal name means "two boilings," are a division of the Teton Sioux. Although they usually were on good terms with the whites, they occasionally went on the warpath with the hostiles. Hodge, *Handbook,* 2:136.

[129] The Oglala are one of the principal divisions of the Teton Sioux. They made incessant war against other tribes and against the whites, and participated in the massacre of Lieutenant Grattan and his men at Fort Laramie in 1854. Throughout the sixties, they attacked emigrant trains, Missouri River traffic, and detachments of soldiers. Hodge, *Handbook,* 2:109–110. De Trobriand uses various spellings of the tribal name, usually "Ogallala."

language, with a little variation. The Mandans spring from the same stock as the Winnebago in the Great Lakes region. The Arrikarees and the Pawnees of Nebraska are of the same origin and belong to the same nation. One of their bands remained in the southern region for thirty years and kept its language and organization distinct. Another has been lost sight of completely. The *Arrikaris* have different names: *Arrikaris* in Mandan, *Arrikhar'hos* in Gros Ventre, *Pananis* in Sioux, and *Rees* in the American abbreviation. Elsewhere I have explained the misfortunes through which the three tribes of Berthold, powerful and warlike in the past, had been reduced to their present condition.

Saturday, May 2. Good hunting in the marsh: plovers, curlews, snipes, and ducks, which have not yet mated. The geese are very wild and more difficult to approach than the ducks, probably because of the length of their necks.

When the Rees who enlisted as scouts came to get their uniforms at the quartermaster's storehouse yesterday, each was given the various articles of clothing on the assumption that they would take them to their tents to put them on at their leisure; but no. The joy of getting a uniform, trousers, and a hat with a black feather fastened up on one side by the American eagle and bearing in the front two crossed sabers above the yellow cord of the cavalry—the joy was too much to brook the slightest delay. Scarcely were they out of the store, when right in the middle of the parade ground, they threw off the buffalo robe or blanket, old shirts and leggings, and in a flash appeared in *naturalibus,* to put on the uniform of the *Isatankos.* Some women were looking through their windows or were in front of their doors, hardly expecting such a surprise. You can figure out for yourself whether they hurried to close the curtains or dash into the house.

These Indian recruits and the enlistment of Paquenaud caused me to make an unpardonable omission in my yesterday's notes. I hasten to make amends for it by mentioning that in the night of April 30th to May 1st, Mrs. Marshal was safely delivered of a daughter. "Mother and child are doing nicely."

Monday, May 4. The mail from Totten arrived this morning. It brings me the first news of the appearance and success of my *Quatre Ans de Campagne à l'Armée du Potomac* in New York. My daughter wrote that the copies sent from France were snatched up in a few days; that the newspapers immediately began to publish long articles and excerpts, which makes her believe that since the book was adopted and praised by the principal organs of the Republican party, it will be mercilessly criticized by those of the Democratic party. So much the better; the clamor of discussion will give the work great publicity. Since it was successful at the outset and since the demand is growing with the exhaustion of the imported copies, a new inexpensive edition (French) is going to be published in New York by Brentano (whom I suspect to be the agent of La Salle). The whole affair brings me, it seems, more reputation than money, and more publicity than profit in America, for in the absence of a treaty between France and the United States regulating author's rights, the reprinting of my book in French gave me no rights. But the translation, made under the reservations of the copyright in my favor, will give me at least half the profits. In any case, I suppose that La Salle will immediately send from Paris a second printing of the original edition larger than the first.[130]

Yesterday it was cold and rainy all day, following a storm which Friday night put an end to the premature heat which in the preceding days had brought the mercury up to 84 degrees F. The Gaillardet letters from Paris are very complimentary about my book, although decidedly opposed to my political point of view. He reproaches me with being more American than the Americans and with carrying severity to injustice in regard to Jeff Davis and MacClellan [*sic*]. Gaillardet sees too many things through the distorted spectacles of *Le Courrier des Etats Unis.*

Tuesday, May 5. Following instructions from the general headquarters of the Department, I have relieved Lt. Col. Powell of his duties as post commandant, and from now on I have the double command of the District and of Fort Stevenson, although they remain distinct from each other. It was announced from St. Paul that a new fort, the finest in Dakota, they say, is going to be built at Devils Lake by contract.[131] It ought to be finished before the end of summer, and the general headquarters of the District would be transferred there. If this happens, I shall have to go there with my general

[130] *Quatre Ans de Campagne à l'Armée du Potomac* appeared in France in February and in New York in April. Several of the reviews and some of the letters about the book appear in *The Life and Memoirs of General de Trobriand*, p. 352–359.

[131] The contract for the building of the new post had already been awarded when De Trobriand made this entry in his journal. It was given to J. W. Smythe and Patrick Nash, said to be the most energetic contractors in St. Paul. By April, Nash was trying to get together a party of 250 men. *St. Paul Daily Pioneer*, March 15, 1868; April 5, 1868.

staff and military band. By this move, we should miss the arrival and passing of the steamboats; but we should gain the advantage of a much finer country, abundantly wooded, with a magnificent lake dotted with islands, excellent fishing, and we should not lose any good hunting.

Wednesday, May 6. Still cold (between forty and fifty degrees F.) and still rainy. Disagreeable weather that keeps us indoors. For some days, the wind has been blowing, always from northwest to northeast. The steamer *Only Chance* arrived at the wharf around ten o'clock in the morning.

Friday, May 8. Two steamboats at the wharf for half an hour each: the *St. Luke* and the *Sallie,* both en route for Benton.

Saturday, May 9. The steamboat *Miner* of the Northwest Fur Company arrived. I was awaiting it impatiently, knowing that it was bringing me a hunting gun, a carbine, all my painting equipment, oil colors, water colors, crayons, canvases, paper, etc. So from now on, I am well equipped to keep busy on summer days. Everything arrived in good order, even a copy of my book, which I had not dared to count on too much, not knowing if it could be sent on time. One of the members of the Company, Mr. Seaman, was kind enough to assume responsibility for it. Naturally, the first thing that I shall do will be to read it in order to be sure that F. Gaillardet corrected the proofs conscientiously.

Sunday, May 10. Medicine Bear came to the fort to bring us a government horse found on the prairie by his people. This is an act of honesty and good friendship which deserves a reward. I had him and the five warriors with him given a good supply of salt pork and biscuit, coffee and sugar. The horse had been abandoned some time ago near Dog Den by an escort detachment, which it could not follow any more. It seems quite recovered and no longer limps.

NOTE: Since yesterday, I have run through my book. Alas! It is full of printer's errors. If I ever publish another one, it will be on the condition that I correct the proofs myself.[132]

Yesterday, my Lt. Colonel Bowman was on board the *Miner,* on his way back to his post at Buford. He is an old officer out of West

---

132 By May 16 De Trobriand had discovered over four hundred errors in the book. When the volume was translated into English by George R. Dauchy in 1886, De Trobriand asked him to correct the errors. *Life and Memoirs of General de Trobriand,* p. 348, 364.

Point who followed a career in the regular army. Since he was on the Pacific Coast at the time of the War, he could not take part in it. He was then a major in the 9th infantry. Six months ago, he was promoted to lieutenant colonel in the 31st. The season was too far along then for him to go to his post, and so, back from California, he spent the winter with his people. We spent an hour together on board the boat. What I have seen of him pleases me very much. Lt. Norwell, district inspector, goes to Buford on an inspection tour, and so he is accompanying Col. Bowman.

Wednesday, May 13. The steamboat *Antelope* stopped at the wharf today; on board were Captain and Bt. Major Dickey, who is now relieved of his duties in detached service (recruiting) and is on his way to Fort Buford to take command of his company.

Thursday, May 14. Day of steamers: no less than four came to Fort Stevenson today. The *Henry Atkins* brought a quantity of merchandise for one of the sutlers, Mr. Gerard. Next, the *Huntsville* passed without stopping. The *Peninah* brought thirty-eight barrels of potatoes for the garrison, which were very much needed. Finally, the *Mountaineer* stopped a quarter of an hour to give us a packet of letters from its passengers for us to send by post.

A rather serious incident marked this spate of steamers. In spite of the sentinels who, in such cases, guard the gangways of the boats and prevent the soldiers from coming near, and especially from going on board, two employees—one a mail courier and the other a carter—succeeded in slipping on board the *Henry Atkins*. Of course they were after whiskey. Without waiting to get off the boat, they proceeded to get drunk on the spot. Lieutenant Walborn, officer of the day, having noticed them, made them get off, and gave the order to the corporal of the guard to take them to the post. As they put up some resistance, a struggle followed, with the result that one of the drunks, pulling out his revolver, fired on the corporal of the guard. The bullet went through his uniform, and broke the butt of his gun. The corporal shot back. In the scuffle, other shots were fired. Miraculously, no one was wounded. The two drunks were arrested and taken to the post, where they were put in irons and will await trial before the military court. The result is that from this day on, even stricter measures will be taken to prevent the introduction of whiskey among the men, who are beset by the devil to get it.

Friday, May 15. The *Octavia* put in here today. She is a large, fine steamer with two wheels and three decks, not counting the pilot's cabin. There were on board a number of passengers who looked like people of comfortable circumstances, and many ladies elegantly dressed. All these people are on their way to Montana to settle at Helena or Virginia City. At Fort Benton, they will take the stagecoach line to get there.[133] A three-foot rise in the river makes navigation easier for all these boats and makes it possible for even those most heavily loaded to go almost anywhere with little difficulty.

Yesterday the *Henry Atkins* took away from here a fine horse belonging to Colonel Reeve of the 13th infantry. This horse had escaped last year, and had been captured on the plains by the Indians who brought it in. Since the colonel had to go to Fort Shaw in Montana, where he is in command of the district, the horse stayed at Fort Stevenson during the fall, then during the winter, awaiting the instructions of the owner. In accordance with a letter from him, I loaded the animal for Fort Benton, from where he will be sent overland to Fort Shaw.

Saturday, May 16. A convoy of twelve wagons arrived today from Fort Totten, led by an escort commanded by Lieutenant Smith. It comes to get the grain (corn and oats) which is still stored here.

The Indians are gathering at Fort Rice in great numbers to meet the commission sent by the President to make peace with the hostile tribes and to renew the treaties with the others, in particular with the Sioux. The commission, which is made up of generals Sherman, Sheridan, Terry, and Harney, will probably not arrive before June 1st.

Undoubtedly the Indians will relieve the boredom of waiting by quarreling, stealing from each other, and fighting among themselves. A few days ago, a Mandan was found dead on the prairie, his body slashed with a knife and his scalp lifted. The poor devil was hunting antelope. No one knows who committed the deed, although the band of hostile Unkpapahs who refuse to go to Fort Rice are under suspicion. Always the same gang of incorrigible bandits.

Sunday, May 17. The hostile Unkpapahs put in their first appearance before Fort Stevenson today. About a dozen of them, slipping up the coulees, stole from the Ree Indians two or three horses, which were grazing on the other side of Douglas Creek. They hoped to get their hands on Gerard's horses and cattle, too; but these animals were guarded by two armed Indians, who fired on the marauders

133 A stagecoach line was in operation over the Mullan Road between Fort Benton and the mines.

while bringing in their cattle. When some soldiers who were hunting in the neighborhood put in their appearance, the Sioux drew
back to the hills. The skirmish had attracted our attention, and I
immediately sent out twenty-five men led by Lt. Ward to reconnoiter
the enemy. Our soldiers deployed themselves in skirmish lines and
went to the top of the highest hill without seeing anything. The
Unkpapahs, seeing them come, had hurriedly withdrawn to the country to the east. There they met our Arrikaris scouts who were reconnoitering from that side. Some shots were exchanged. While our men,
who though inferior in numbers, were going after the nearest of the
enemy, Bull Head, one of them, was violently thrown onto the rocky
ground by his horse, which was shot from under him. The others could
not rescue him, and he remained stretched out unconscious at the
mercy of the enemy. When the news was brought to the fort, I immediately sent out Lieutenant Hooton with his company to recover the
wounded man if he were still alive, or his body if the Sioux had
finished him off. But soon we could see our man coming back by
himself with some of his people, ahead of the soldiers. While he was
unconscious, the Sioux had been satisfied to despoil him of *all* his
clothes and his weapons, leaving him only the strip of cloth that our
savages seem to wear even under trousers. For some reason, still not
explained, the Sioux had not scalped him, so he will get out of this
with a bad bruise on his head and another on the hip. The hostile
Sioux had already disappeared.

Another attack less dangerous but more irritating is that of the
mosquitoes, which put in their appearance two days ago. This is two
or three weeks earlier than usual. They are very numerous and apparently have a good appetite. From now on, we must live with
this enemy for four months; but at least it is easier to keep them
out of our log houses than our tents in which we lived last year.

Thursday, May 21. A newspaper from St. Louis, which came
this morning by the Fort Rice courier, informs me that about a
month ago there appeared in the *Intelligencer* of Washington a letter
signed *Thomas Egan,* written in answer to a very complimentary
article in the *Chronicle* about my book, and in particular about my
evaluations of General Hancock, which were made in it. In it an
allusion was made to certain people who did not possess any military
merits, but for whom the general showed partiality because of political considerations, and allowed them to influence him too easily.[134]

[134] This passage, with other comments about Hancock as a leader, is found
in *Quatre Ans de Campagne à l'Armée du Potomac,* 2:237.

Now I identified this Egan immediately. He is, in reality, a barroom politician, a man with no scruples or character, capable of any dirty trick, who had escaped court-martial for horse stealing and similar crimes only by the death of the two principal witnesses for the prosecution, both killed at Fredericksburg before his trial could be held. He had convinced Hancock that he had considerable political influence in New York, and by this representation assured himself of his special favor; with the result that Hancock promoted him and made him bvt. major general. The quality of his tools did not matter much to him if he could use them. It seems that this same Egan, who is nothing now, carried over into civil life his relations with his old chief, who used him on this occasion to direct a diatribe against me, which is a characteristic trait. As my evaluation was perfectly justified and very moderately expressed, it was difficult to deny it; as for the facts, they were incontestable. So they were not denied. The weapon used against me was simply shameless lying, the only way Tom Egan could find of satisfying his personal grudge and resentment against me for the scorn I had for him when he was serving under my command. He claims that I was *drunk* the evening of the engagement of Boydton Road, that an officer from his general staff found me wandering near the enemy lines, and that General Hancock himself *had to do part of my duties.* Imagine a corps commander himself doing the work of an officer of the day instead of one of his brigadier generals! He claims he commanded the 38th, my old regiment, with which he has never had any contact. According to him, I never had any military qualities and I advanced only through intrigue; I have never led my troops in an attack, etc., etc. Never was there a cruder lie spread around in the face of the best-known facts and the knowledge of the truth by all the officers who knew me in the service.

I do not know if in my absence any one of my friends has taken the trouble to refute the lie; but it is more probable that they have done what I myself would have done, oppose it with scornful silence. This brings me to the following remarks:

[*Slander in the United States*] The complete freedom of the press in the United States, the violence of political enmities, and the baseness of the weapons used, make slander very common. No one can be before the public, whether as a writer, as a government employee, or a politician, without immediately being exposed. There is no accusation, no matter how absurd or worthless, that has not been made and repeated against almost all public men, journalists, officials, generals, and candidates for some office, especially that of the President of the United States. Trials for slander are no cure for it. Such trials promise no certain reparation, and they mean wallowing in the mud and often giving great publicity to obscure calumnies to which no one has paid the slightest attention. So what is the redress for such a great wrong? In public opinion itself, which is taught the worth of these attacks by long experience and takes no notice of them, or, if it does listen, forgets all about it by the next day. Unless candidates for high positions of immediate interest to the community are involved, denials are useless, for personal arguments do not concern the public, and especially when it is a question of flagrant lies which contradict themselves and are sufficiently refuted by the known character of the person who is attacked. The best thing for this person to do is not to worry about it. This is what I am doing, with no hesitation, in this case, and I do it even more willingly since my book is itself the clearest account of my military career and my conduct. There are names cited on almost every page, and this host of witnesses who, with me, took part in the events and deeds I have recounted is there to unmask the lies and bear witness to the truth.

In France, such an attack would of necessity be followed immediately by a duel or a slander trial. Here, the challenge would necessarily involve dismissal from the army, and a trial would be considered stupid by everyone. Such is the difference in habits and ideas.

Friday, May 22. Two steamships came by here very early this morning and did not stop: the *Lacon* and the *Guidon*. They were held up two or three days, moored to the bank above Fort Rice because of violent south winds which have been blowing constantly since last Tuesday and so hard that the dust they raise has kept us inside all day.

We have received no mail from Fort Totten. It should have been here Wednesday afternoon, and we still have no news of it. The convoy, escorted by Lieutenant Smith, left Tuesday morning to return to Fort Totten, forty-eight hours after the courier. The presence of hostile Indians in our neighborhood makes us worry some about it, but we prefer to suppose that since Col. Whistler is on leave and the command passed to Captain Hill, the couriers, because of some omission or error, were not at the midway station, and ours have been forced to push on to Devils Lake, in which case they could not get back before Sunday evening. These delays in the arrival of the mail are always vexing to us, for we always await them with great impatience.

Monday, May 25. A little steamboat with no passengers passed by here today, the *Hiram Wood*. She has on board a supply of potatoes which she is peddling from post to post, and probably freight for Montana. As we were already supplied, she just stopped, and then went on her way.

Tuesday, May 26. There was good reason to worry about the absence of MacDonald and Joe Hamlin, who took the mail eight days ago Sunday. Both have perished, killed by the Unkpapah Indians who had put in their appearance around the post on the afternoon of the same day they left. This is how we found out the sad news today:

[*Mail captured by the hostile Unkpapahs*] The day before yesterday, Sunday, two of our couriers left with the week's mail to meet those from Totten halfway. They were Brown, an Irishman recently enlisted in government service, and Martin, a half-breed employed since last year. Both knew the country well, spoke Sioux fluently. Toward evening of the first day, they were approaching Clear Lake when they noticed in the distance something that looked like buffalo to them. In reality, it was Indians, who, in order not to betray themselves, lay on the necks of their horses, which made them look like the animal for which they wanted to be mistaken. So our men went on their way, while the Unkpapahs set an ambush for them. Arriving at a narrow ravine through which they had to pass, the two couriers suddenly found themselves surrounded by Sioux coming in on them from all sides crying, "Don't shoot! We are Medicine Bear's men (an allied chief). We are friends." And the first ones exchanged handshakes with Joe Martin, who was nearest to them. Brown's horse took fright and ran away, and some young men ran to bring it back. The pack mule with the despatch pouch and supplies galloped off in an opposite direction, his speed accelerated by fear. When Martin was so surrounded that he could not defend himself, an Indian slapped his hand on the withers of his horse, uttering a cry of triumph, the meaning of which the prisoner could not mistake. He felt that he was doomed. He was immediately stripped of everything, weapons, equipment, and clothes. His horse had been taken from him first. Brown was brought back and promptly suffered the same fate. He had been brought back by an enemy riding the well known horse of Charley MacDonald, which set him thinking. When they were in just their boots and drawers, the chief gave Martin an old overcoat to cover himself (for it had poured all day, and it was still raining), and he easily recognized it as Joe Hamlin's.[135] The overcoat was pierced by two bullet holes in the chest and two rents in the back. The chief asked the prisoners who they were and what they were doing on the prairie. They answered that they were half-breeds from the Red River and that they were going to St. Joseph to hunt. Their chief then told them that his men had killed two men and a soldier a few days before; our two couriers and a man from the convoy commanded by Lt. Smith. "I would not have had the two men from the Red River killed," said the chief, "but the young men killed them before they found out who they were." "I am the one who killed one of them," said one of the savages, coming forward armed with Mac-Donald's sixteen-shot carbine (Henry system). "I shot an arrow through his body; he fell from his horse and I finished him off on the ground with a revolver." Then the two prisoners noticed that the chief was wearing MacDonald's watch chain and recognized several pieces of his clothing and Joe Hamlin's on the backs of the Indians. "Let's kill them," several of them were saying. "Why waste time talking? Let's do to them what we did to the others." At that the chief took the prisoners aside and said to them: "The young men are saying evil things and are ready to do an evil deed. Take advantage of the night that is coming and run away quickly before it's too late." He did not have to tell our men twice, and, half naked, they hurried off. Instead of following the direction they had first taken, they ran to hide in the marshy underbrush, making a circle calculated to throw off pursuit.

It was well for them that they did. The chief had given them life only because he did not yet know that they were couriers. As I have said before, the mule carrying the despatches had run away. It took some time to capture it, and those who did feasted on the supplies they found in the saddlebags. When they came back bringing the animal and the packet of despatches, our men had already left. They took up their trail intending undoubtedly to put them to death; but night had come on, or at least dusk was falling, and they were unable to find them.

They wandered around part of the night, and at daybreak found

[135] *North Dakota Historical Collections*, 3:180–81, names Rolette rather than Hamlin as the mail carrier killed with MacDonald on the trail May 15. De Trobriand, in his report to headquarters on May 30, says it was Hamlin and Mac-Donald. Régis de Trobriand, Fort Stevenson, to Bvt. Maj. Genl Terry, Fort Rice, May 30, 1868. Department of Dakota, War Records Division, National Archives.

themselves still in sight of the enemy. By sneaking in the ravines and hiding themselves as well as they could, they hurried away in the direction of Stevenson, where, completely worn out, not having had a mouthful to eat since the morning of the day before yesterday, they arrived today at sunset with no further misfortune.

MacDonald leaves a wife and three young children. He was a fine man, still young, energetic, and brave. He was hired as chief guide of the couriers at a salary of one hundred dollars a month. His wife's parents live in Minnesota, where they are quite well off with at least enough so that his family is not left destitute. Joe Hamlin was a bachelor and does not leave any family.

[*Sitting Bull or Sitting Buffalo*] The band which committed the triple murder and stripped and despoiled our last two couriers is the hostile Unkpapah, which is constantly scouring the plains, plundering, marauding, and killing whites, especially soldiers and employees of the government, every time they get a chance. The principal chief is Sitting Bull, one of the most dangerous and evil Indians in Dakota. A price was put on his head by the authorities in Minnesota and Montana successively. Now, Dakota has become the theater of his depredations and killings. It is a nice game, the government leaving us in our posts without cavalry, without horses, and absolutely powerless to pursue and punish him. So, he can wander freely and in perfect security on the prairies which he stains with blood wherever he wishes.

He is a man about forty years old, medium height, and somewhat inclined to be fat, a very rare thing among the Indians. He is vigorous and wears his hair cut at the base of his neck; that is, short for a Sioux. His fierceness is masked by a good-natured manner and a conversation abounding in good humor. To judge by appearances one would believe him to be the most harmless of the redskins. In reality, he is a ferocious beast who seems to be laughing when he is showing his teeth. When he passed by near Fort Berthold, he told some Rees that he was going to establish himself for a time on the route from Stevenson to Totten, because many people passed there, whites and soldiers, and that he would stay there as long as he could find evil deeds to do. We see he has kept his word. He seems to like to talk, for in the little time that our couriers spent with his people, he entertained them with his exploits and his plans. He is not much worried by the commissioners sent by the government to make peace. His business, he says, is to kill whites, and he will kill them as long as he and his band last. He boasts that war is more profitable to him than peace; that it brings him arms, ammunition, clothing, and especially great numbers of horses and mules, while the tribes who have submitted are dying of misery and hunger in the places where the whites have penned them up. With him is Pisi (Gall), another fierce warrior.[136] There were thirty-two men in all, and they had with them fifty-four animals, including the four horses and two mules taken from our couriers.

So that means that our communications by the Totten route are cut off for some time. We have left the Rice route and the steamboats going down the river.

[*Misery at Berthold*] The chiefs of the Rees and Mandans, accompanied by a few warriors and women, came to ask for some supplies, which I had distributed to them. Tomorrow it will be the Gros Ventres' turn. These poor devils are starving to death because of the disappearance of the buffalo from these parts, and because the severity and length of the winter has exhausted their supplies of corn and leaves them almost without resources in the spring when they have to plant their corn. The job is almost finished, and now they are going to hunt again and are dispersing to follow what game they can find. They will come back when the harvest is ripe. It is with the savages as it is with civilized man: "When the rack is empty, the horses fight." Between the Gros Ventres and the Mandans on one side and the Rees on the other, there appear to be grievances which are rankling and which could easily degenerate into a bloody quarrel. The first reproach the second with having taken advantage of their absence during the winter to tear down their lodgings and to use the materials for firewood—which is true—and with stealing their reserves of corn for seeding, at least part of it—which is probable. The plan is to bring the Indians in to live in peace and friendship with us, when even those who do live together cannot get along among themselves for very long. I am not talking about private quarrels, which are always going on, although sometimes they extend to families and give the chiefs a great deal of trouble in smoothing out. The upshot is usually a killing which would start a feud if the blood were not redeemed. One of the most common causes for these quarrels is the bragging with which warriors are accustomed to speak of their coups, or deeds of war. If one of them believes that he has a higher standing than another, who does not share this opin-

136 Gall, the warrior, received his name when he was found eating the gall of a freshly killed buffalo. Hodge says that Gall's military genius was of the highest order. Hodge, *Handbook*, 1:482.

ion, they must decide which is the better man. So each enumerates before witnesses what he has done, the number of horses he has stolen, the enemy he has killed, scalps he has taken. The one whose superiority is thus established declares it by scooping up a handful of dirt or mud, which he throws in the face of his humiliated rival. Although he may be resentful, the latter submits to this lesson without threats, for it is not considered as an insult which must be washed away by blood. But it is another matter when the victor in the contest, stirred by hate or incited by anger, strikes his adversary or cuts from his forehead some of the hair which usually hangs down to the eyebrows. Such an outrage calls for vengeance, unless some fine present accompanied by apologies buys back the evil, in which case, the price of a horse, for example, settles the matter.

[*An Indian vengeance*] Pierre Garault [*sic*], half-breed interpreter at Berthold, had a brother who died a victim of private vengeance. Having become involved in a quarrel with an Arrikaree about the relative value of their exploits, and having been declared the better man, he rose, drew from the fire a brand, and began to beat his competitor unmercifully on the back, the shoulders, etc. The man did not move, did not say a word, and when the other had stopped striking, he wrapped himself in his buffalo robe and withdrew to his lodge, not betraying his emotion in any way. From this day on, he was not seen among the other members of the tribe; but almost every day, they saw him in the distance, alone on the top of some hill overlooking the village, crying out, imploring the Great Spirit to give him his vengeance, and trying to make himself worthy of it by fasting, atonements, and mutilations. After he had worked himself up to a fever of despair, he completely cut off the little finger from each hand. In the dark of the night, he went back to his lodge, where he lived alone with his mother. Then he ate a light meal, the only one in twenty-four hours, and in the morning, before sunrise, he left again to continue his sacrifices on the neighboring cliffs. What he wanted to obtain from the Great Spirit was the chance to meet his enemy all alone, so he could kill him by surprise. He had not attacked him when he was with his relatives or accompanied by his friends because they would have meted out justice to the murderer on the spot, and, in such a case, vengeance would not be satisfied.

Months and months went by like this. Garault had gone out hunting with some Gros Ventres. They were coming back with a good supply of robes and meat, and had camped for the night near the badlands, seven or eight miles from Berthold. Garault, in a greater hurry to get home than the others, went on alone although it was night. As he approached the village, he noticed a man on foot ahead of him on the trail, and, not knowing who he was, he said: "Comrade, step aside a little to let my horse by; it goes faster than your legs can carry you." The Indian who was addressed stepped aside without answering. As Garault passed, unaware that this man was his enemy, the latter, who had positively identified him, struck him down with an arrow through the body, finished him off with his knife, and throwing himself at the corpse, scattered the members and pieces of it on the prairie, taking with him only the liver and the heart for his evening meal.

Back in his lodge, he told his mother that the Great Spirit had finally hearkened to him, that he had killed his enemy, and advised her to leave the village as soon as possible. As for himself, he cooked his cannibal feast the same evening, devoured it with an appetite sharpened by the exultation over a deed of vengeance long and fervently sought and finally achieved. Before daybreak, he had left the village, never to return. He went to join a band of Sioux with whom he has always lived since then.

Wednesday, May 27. Yesterday evening, two Rees arrived at Berthold from the other side of the river. They were bearers of a letter from Lt. Col. Otis, commandant at Fort Rice, informing me that a strong war party composed of Sioux from the Two Kettle band and of the lower Yanktonah, has just left the neighborhood of Fort Sully and Fort Thompson for an attack on the Gros Ventres, Rees, and Mandans at Berthold. Warned, too, by a letter from Mr. Galpin, trader at Fort Rice, to Mr. Marsh, trader at Fort Berthold, our Indians immediately brought in all their young people to prepare for the fight.[137] Those who had come yesterday to receive provisions left hurriedly this morning. The Gros Ventres, who were to come today, will probably stay in the village, for their enemies must be near.

---

[137] In 1839 Charles E. Galpin came to the Dakota country where he acted as interpreter, trader, and sutler until his death at the Grand River Agency about 1870. He was with General Sully in his campaign of 1863, and was instrumental in rescuing some of the captives held by the Sioux. Married to a Yanktonai woman, Galpin was one of the most influential men among the Sioux tribes. Father de Smet frequently called on him for information, and both he and his wife accompanied the missionary on his peace mission to the hostiles in 1868. Geo. E. Spencer, Macon, Missouri, to H. H. Sibley, St. Paul, Minnesota, August 20, 1865, Sibley Papers; P. J. de Smet [n.p.] to W. T. Sherman, [Washington, D. C.] January 28, 1868, Office of Indian Affairs, Dakota Superintendency, Letters Received; *South Dakota Historical Collections,* 1:364–365.

Great Falls, Missouri River, Montana Territory

Early this morning, several Indians were sighted passing on the heights. They are probably the scouts of the band. This is an affair between Indians, for both hostile parties are at peace with the whites and are their friends, which means that we must let events take their course without meddling.

Early this morning, the steamboat *Yorktown* passed by, going up the river; she is the eighteenth of the season. She had nothing for us.

Friday, May 29. Five steamboats have gone by today; among them the *Benton,* with a great quantity of merchandise on board for one of the sutlers, Mr. Marsh. The paymaster, Major [Valentine C.] Hanna, got off to pay the officers and the garrison. After which he re-embarked and went on to Fort Shaw in Montana, where he is going to reside. We were paid for seven months: from September 30 to April 30.

Saturday, May 30. The steamboat *Cora,* which was the first of the season to go up the river, is also the first to go down. She passed very early this morning, stopping only to take a few passengers, although she was already loaded. Several of our workmen whose enlistments had run out left by the *Cora.* Colonel Reeve of the 13th infantry was on board. He is going on a six months' leave. Lieutenant Ward took advantage of this opportunity. He has a three months' leave to go to St. Louis to get married. He will come back at the beginning of fall, bringing his young wife with him.

The *Columbia* is passing at sunset.

Sunday, May 31. Steamboat *Viola Belle* went by this morning. The Sioux, whose threat to go on the warpath had been announced a few days ago, suddenly showed up at Fort Berthold. This afternoon, a battle took place. We shall have news about it either tonight or tomorrow morning.

Monday, June 1. In the middle of the night, a great disturbance took place among the Rees, men, women, and children, who live around the post on the scraps from the soldiers' table and on what they can get out of the waste thrown from the kitchens. They sleep in the willow grove below the bank where the buildings are going up. They do some fishing, and this helps them out, too, for they either eat the fish they catch or sell it. So after midnight, when everyone is usually asleep, chants and strange cries came from the willow grove. There were repeated comings and goings and the voices of women screeching, mixed with the chants of the men and the howling of dogs.

A messenger had just arrived announcing the victory of the three tribes and the retreat of the Sioux.

This morning at daybreak I received more detailed news. The Sioux, numbering fifty or sixty, dashed out on the prairie on the gallop, and at first succeeded in running off about twenty horses from the pasture. The Gros Ventres, Rees, and Mandans immediately pursued them and there followed one of those Indian battles in which the participants scatter in every direction without any order, every man for himself. This results in a succession of forays in groups of two, three, or four, in which the horsemen race around, sometimes pursuing, sometimes being pursued, with an exchange of shots and arrows. The Indians of Berthold got back part of their horses, killed five or six of their enemies' horses, and, great triumph of the day, killed a Sioux! It was a young Mandan mounted on an American horse who made the coup. Of course he scalped his adversary, whose body could not be carried away by his people. Rees, Mandans, and Gros Ventres immediately flocked around and cut up, dismembered, hacked the body. The Canadians call this *détailler*. Each one took away a piece of it, and these human scraps figured in the scalp dance and similar rejoicings celebrating the victory.

Here, too, we have had the indispensable celebration. Our scouts, on horseback and in full regalia, appeared at the post before seven o'clock in the morning, emitting chants and enthusiastic howlings. In the afternoon, the whole band from the willow grove came first to the officers' quarters and then to each of the traders, faces smeared with black and red, carrying an imitation scalp at the end of a long stick, and going through ferocious pantomimes, dances, and various chants, the women playing the principal role rather than the men, who were satisfied to be the chorus. However, since it was raining very hard, the presentations were cut short. But what a celebration for a scalp! Now that they have been attacked on their own ground, our Indians are going to go on a raid to get from the Sioux more horses than they lost and to bring back more scalps. This means that during the summer, active hostilities will probably be kept up between redskins.

[*Father de Smet*] As you see, nothing is less peaceful than the state of the country at the time when the commissioners are coming to Fort Rice to make peace reign in these regions! One cannot believe that they will succeed. The hostile Sioux are not answering the call, and the others, since they have already submitted, are going to the meeting place just to put in complaints or to ask for favors. What will be done for them will not have any influence on those they want to pacify. Father de Smet, who has great influence over all the Indians of the Dakota, has come out ahead of the commission. He stopped at Rice in order to have a conference with the chiefs who were there. Then he lost himself in the plains with some interpreters to make contact with Sitting Bull, if possible, and with the other hostile Indians who are wandering around the country. He has great courage and a great devotion.[138]

The mail by the Rice route left this morning in a wagon with six mules escorted by ten soldiers under the command of a sergeant. Reconnoitering ahead are two scouts, who, with the two couriers and the driver, bring the detail up to sixteen armed men. Under these conditions, the mail party can defy the Sioux. There is no danger that they will be bothered.

Tuesday, June 2. The *Only Chance* passed by here this afternoon, the second boat back from Benton. She tells us that the hostile Indians are very active in the Montana country. It seems that there were animals stolen and some men killed at Fort Shaw. At Fort Union, opposite Fort Buford, two men, one a Negro, who had gone out without an escort to get a cart of hay, were surprised and killed by the savages. But no matter how great their hostility may be against the whites, there is not the ferocious bitterness that characterizes their battles among themselves. One of the employees of the N. W. Fur Company at Berthold had gone out with the Gros Ventres the other day to get a shot at the Sioux when they made their foray. They chased the latter for about five or six miles, and it is then that a young Mandan, jumping off his horse, shot one of the enemy who charged him. It was vengeance for some men of the tribe killed last year. The victor scarcely had time to lift the scalp of the conquered, who was still breathing when all the other Gros Ventres, Rees, and Mandans who were closest ran up, and, although the victim was still alive, began to hack him up. He literally died under the knives with which they were cutting off his hands and feet, opening his stomach and chest to pull out the entrails, the heart, liver, etc., while others were tearing off his extremities. As I have said, these human scraps were carried to the village in triumph, and dragged around in the mud at the ends of cords in the hands of enthusiastic women and children.

138 In the John B. Sanborn Papers, there is a full report by Father de Smet on this expedition. The report is not in De Smet's handwriting, but the signature is his.

It is clear that although they are our friends, and loyal ones, too, the Indians of Berthold have lost none of their natural ferocity and enjoy vengeance as much as if they had never heard of civilized whites.

The *Only Chance* takes away the six men of the escort who came with the paymaster and who are returning to Rice. Lt. Ellis goes there, too, to meet General Terry and give him two despatches with which I have entrusted him. He will also ask for a duplicate of a three months' leave which was to be in the mail destroyed by the Indians and which he would not be able to get in time this season if he had to wait for the leave to be re-expedited from the War Department through the regular channels. Six of our sick men discharged from the hospital, several of our workmen whose term of enlistment is expired, have also taken advantage of the opportunity to return to the States.

Finally, Mrs. Parsons, wife of the quartermaster of the Department and commissary of the post, is leaving the same way, to go back to her family for her confinement. Fortunately, Dr. Matthews, who is going to New York to take his examination as military surgeon, will be with her as far as St. Louis.

Wednesday, June 3. Early this morning, the *Success* stopped here, coming back from Benton. She had on board Bt. Lt. Col. Rankin who was arrested by the marshal of the territory and turned over to civil jurisdiction for having freed by force a prisoner arrested on board a steamboat at Fort Union.[139] Lt. Col. Rankin will have to undergo his trial before the jury; after which he will be turned over to military authority and come before a court-martial for offenses of which he is accused as commandant of Fort Buford. He is already an old man, and his health seems to be seriously impaired, in part, perhaps, because of the weight of the accusations arrayed against him, of being under arrest for several months, and of the prospect of two criminal trials.

Since the federal marshal was on board, I took advantage of the opportunity to put in his hands one of the two men who, last May 13, got drunk on board a steamboat and resisted the guard. He is the one who drew his revolver on the corporal ordered to arrest him. Because at the time of the scuffle his enlistment had expired a few days

139 Rankin was taken by the marshal to Yankton, Dakota Territory, for trial. Régis de Trobriand, Fort Stevenson, to Bvt. Brig. Genl O. D. Greene, AA Genl, Department of Dakota, St. Paul, October 26, 1868. Department of Dakota, War Records Division, National Archives.

before and he was waiting to be transported, the case of attempted murder belongs to civil jurisdiction.

A little after the *Success,* the *Deer Lodge* arrived. She takes away to the address of Kin[tzing] Post a box of Indian curiosities, some furs for my daughter and granddaughter, and a letter describing and explaining the contents of the box.

Lt. Norwell came back this way from his inspection of Fort Buford. Everything is in good order there.

From Rice, I received by the steamboat *Importer* an invitation from General Terry to meet him there. I shall go there after Lieut. Ellis returns, if the letter he carries does not persuade General Terry to change his plans and to visit Fort Stevenson in person.

Thursday, June 4. The steamboat *Sallie,* passing by this morning, stopped to leave some letters from Buford. The mail arrived from Fort Rice. Many newspapers, very few personal letters. The couriers noticed some Indians in the distance. None of them came near. The presence of the escort keeps them at a good distance.

Friday, June 5. The *Miner* passed by this morning, coming back from Benton. This evening another boat went by, going up the river. From now on, there is no interest in noting their comings and goings. A serious accident happened this morning to Bt. Lt. Col. Powell, who was thrown from his horse and dragged for some distance with his foot caught in the stirrup, according to all appearances. The runaway horse returned to the stable, the saddle turned under its belly. Colonel Powell was left unconscious, stretched out on the prairie. He was brought back on a stretcher. The doctor bled him and then gave him all the care his condition demanded. However, the patient still has not regained consciousness. His breathing is heavy and labored. His face is swollen and skinned, as well as his hands, arms, etc., but apparently there are no fractures.

Sunday, June 7. Yesterday, some suspicious-looking Indians appeared on the bluffs, and in the night came down onto the rolling prairie near the corral. A little before, some Rees had come to the post to report that a considerable band of Sioux was approaching along the high ground. Our scouts posted themselves in front of the corral flat on their bellies in the grass, eyes and ears alert. The employees who live in the corral kept on guard, and I gave the order that twenty men, in addition to the guard, should sleep fully dressed, arms ready, so they can go into action at the first signal. Nevertheless, these precautions were of no use. The Indians that they heard exchanged rallying cries, disappeared, and at daybreak there wasn't a trace of them.

An hour later, the mail for Fort Totten got under way. The party is composed of nine soldiers, a sergeant, corporal, two couriers, an Indian scout. They have a wagon with six mules. With the driver, they total fifteen armed men. They are enough to hold off the hostile Indians and will not allow the route to be blocked.

They were not en route for more than three or four hours when a courier arrived from Fort Totten, something which we were not counting on at all. This courier, a young and alert white man named Frank Palmer, agreed to risk the trip alone and did not meet an Indian on the way.[140] He brings me a letter from Captain Hill, who is commanding the post in the temporary absence of Col. Whistler. By this means and through information obtained directly from the courier, I learned the following facts:

May 17, the two couriers from Totten left as usual and met Mac-Donald and Hamlin halfway. They exchanged mail and returned without learning anything since then about the fate of the last two. The convoy, commanded by Lieut. Smith, reached Fort Totten after them and saw nothing of their remains. The convoy had been followed by the Unkpapahs, who had not dared to attack it. Only, at Strawberry Lake a carter belonging to the N. W. Fur Company, and who had joined the convoy, remained behind to let the two mules of his wagon drink; and the Indians, who were on the lookout, swooped down on the wagon, wounded the man, and stole the two mules. This in full view of the convoy. This is what I can't explain: Why did Lt. Smith suffer this insult without punishing the aggressors, without even allowing his men to fire over them? Perhaps the official report will furnish me with the solution to this puzzle.[141]

140 Frank Palmer was born in Ohio. He enlisted at the age of fourteen in Company B of the 57th volunteer infantry, and fought at Shiloh. He was engaged as post guide at Fort Totten after the failure of Ruffee's mail company left him unemployed. From 1877 to 1907 he was an Indian trader. *North Dakota Historical Collections*, 3:226.

141 On May 23 a letter on the hostilities around Fort Totten was sent by a correspondent at Devils Lake to the *St. Paul Daily Pioneer*. He reported that on May 23 a band of Sioux made an attack on the herd at Fort Totten and captured a few mules. When the alarm was sounded, the Indians retreated, and in their retreat they met the supply train coming from Fort Stevenson. They gave the train a wide berth, but wounded Flury, the driver of the Northwest Fur Company wagon. Flury, a Frenchman from Redwood, Minnesota, was in critical condition at the post hospital when this letter was written. *St. Paul Daily Pioneer*, June 2, 1868.

On Sunday the twenty-fourth, the two couriers sent out with no escort spotted some Indians, before whom they fled and returned to Totten, not daring to push on farther. This is the same date that Brown and Martin from our side were captured by the band of Sitting Bull, as I related before. Captain Hill then decided to send the mail under an escort of ten men in a wagon. They passed by the station and arrived at Dog Den. There five Indians came to meet them, exchanged handshakes, and told them not to go on farther because their band was camped a little farther on (seventeen lodges), and would prevent them from passing. On this simple warning, the sergeant who was commanding and who is, it seems, a big coward, consulted with the couriers, and with no further attempt, turned back.

Palmer was one of the couriers. Stung to the quick by the jokes aimed at him when he came back, he wanted to prove that he was not afraid of Indians, and through pride offered to go on alone and carry a despatch to Fort Stevenson without an escort. His offer was immediately accepted. Leaving Totten, he arrived here today around noon, having met no one on the way except our men and their wagon.

Col. Powell has not regained consciousness during the fifty-four hours since his accident. Everything has failed. It is probable that he will never come out of it. From now on, the doctor expects that he will die at any moment. The whole right side of the patient is paralyzed, which indicates that the spine is affected. There was still some blood in the bladder yesterday, proof of some internal injury of a dangerous kind. He has had violent attacks of convulsions. His face is swollen, his eyes are bluish, and they give off matter which comes through the partly closed eyelids. His left arm waves almost all the time, coming toward the stomach as the seat of a pain he is not conscious of. His left leg doubles up and straightens out by automatic movement. The members on his right side remain inert and motionless. The officers take turns watching by the bed in which the dying man is lying, a most pitiful sight.

Wednesday, June 10. The steamboat *Big Horn* finally arrived this morning, bringing a full cargo of supplies for Fort Stevenson and Fort Totten. On board is General Terry, who, finding that he was at Rice ahead of the other members of the peace commission, complied with my request to come to spend a day here in person. I showed him the post carefully, explaining to him the condition of everything and what our most urgent needs were.[142] The outcome

142 De Trobriand had written to General Terry on May 30 that because of

is that a company from Fort Buford will come to take up its summer quarters here, which will give us a reinforcement of a hundred men for our work. In order that no time be wasted, I immediately sent by messenger an order to this effect to Lt. Col. Bowman, who will send me the company by the first steamboat. General Terry, on his part, is sending an order directly to St. Paul to send out a machinist, six carpenters, and some masons. Finally, I received the authorization to have transported here by steamboat all the grain left at Berthold. While General Terry was resting in my lodging, Lieutenant Colonel Powell died in his quarters a little before one o'clock in the afternoon. Since Friday, the day of his fall from his horse, he did not regain a flicker of consciousness, not even for an instant. So the struggle of life and death went on for 116 hours, without his being conscious of it.[143]

Thursday, June 11. Col. Powell was buried this afternoon with full military honors on the prairie where he had gaily gone out on horseback six days ago and from where they brought him back on a stretcher, dying. His death opens the way to promotion to captain for Lt. Stephen [*sic*] Norwell, the oldest of the first lieutenants in the regiment. This will be followed by the promotion of second lieutenant Mitchell to the rank of first lieutenant. Although he takes command of his company, Mr. Norwell will still keep the duties of inspector gen[l] of the District.

Monday, June 15. I have returned from an impromptu trip to Berthold. Wednesday morning, the steamboat *War Eagle,* J. B. La-Barge captain, stopped at Fort Stevenson on her way to Berthold where she was taking the annuities for the three tribes at that post.[144] As she was going no farther and had to come back empty, it was an excellent chance to bring here all the grain left in the storehouses of the N. W. Fur Company for more than a year. Since I had received instructions from General Terry concerning this, I embarked on the

the shortage of men, provisions, horses, and building materials, work at the post had almost stopped. Many of the men who would have been available for work had scurvy. Régis de Trobriand, Fort Stevenson, to Bvt. Maj. Genl Terry, Fort Rice, May 30, 1868. Department of Dakota, War Records Division, National Archives.

143 In the *Army and Navy Journal,* July 25, 1868, p. 774, there appeared an order issued by General de Trobriand for officers of the regiment to mourn Colonel Powell by wearing a badge of mourning for thirty days.

144 For the story of Jean Baptiste and Joseph LaBarge, see Chittenden, *History of Early Steamboat Navigation on the Missouri River.*

War Eagle, taking with me Lieutenant Norwell, my orderly, my servant, and *Marco* (my dog). At the same time, I sent overland three wagons and ten men to carry the grain from the fort to the wharf. The outfit was accompanied by Paquenaud, the interpreter, and escorted by five Indian scouts to lead the way. They arrived ahead of us. Leaving around ten o'clock, we tied up the boat at Berthold at three o'clock in the afternoon, and my men were already at work, as a pile of oat sacks going up on the bank testified.

The chiefs, who had been in this way warned of my coming and of the cargo the boat was bringing, immediately came to meet me in full regalia, some of their warriors being painted with black, a sign of war, because of their recent victory over the Sioux. While the men were unloading the cargo, which consisted of flour, biscuits, pork, plows, wagons, a forge, iron, farm tools, and implements, I went to the fort to estimate, approximately, the amount of oats to be loaded. I quickly saw that with ten men and three six-mule wagons, it would be a several days' job. In order to cut the time down as much as possible, I asked for sixty women, twenty from each nation, and immediately I had more than eighty of them to load and unload the wagons. However, since the work was going too slowly, I hired a trader's cart for the next day. The interpreter did more than I should have asked. He had the strongest squaws carry the sacks of oats themselves. Now the weight of each sack varies from 130 to 160 pounds, and the distance from the fort to the boat was not less than five or six hundred yards. These Indian women are so accustomed to hard labor, particularly to carrying loads, that tiring as it was, especially under a scorching sun, they did not seem to consider the task too hard. So, single file, they went down the hill on which the fort is located, following a rather steep path, bent over under the burden which was held on the back by a double thong of buffalo hide, fastened around both the forehead and the upper part of the chest. For this hard work, I promised only to feed them while they worked. It lasted two full days (Saturday and Sunday), three hours Friday afternoon and two hours this morning, two days and a half in all, during which time 4,039 sacks of oats were taken from the storehouses, loaded on the wagons, and hauled to the wharf. The crew of the steamboat took charge of loading them. I have distributed to the squaws three barrels of biscuits and three quarters of bacon, weighing forty-four pounds each. Then, when the work was finished, I had divided among them thirty sacks of damaged oats, the canvas having rotted and the grain molded. But what is not good enough for our horses and mules is still all right for the Indians, who even now are cooking oat cakes. They consider this a piece of good luck, for want is so common among them.

We left Berthold at seven-thirty this morning, and we arrived here at nine-thirty. The trip to Berthold was most pleasant. Not that the business that took me there was in itself very attractive; but once the orders were given, the execution of them was left to Lieut. Norwell and the interpreter, and I was free to use my two days as I liked. I took advantage of the opportunity to make three sketches of Fort Berthold and a part of the immense view over the surrounding countryside and the course of the Missouri that one has from the top of the bastions. I also sketched the portraits of two Mandan and Arikara chiefs. I had already done one of the Gros Ventre chief.

However, this diversion was not what made the trip the most pleasant, for nothing could be more pleasing than the society I found on board, which consisted of the captain's family and that of the supercargo. As the steamer was chartered by the government and had on board no passengers but the man in charge of the Indian presents, the Captain (Jean-Baptiste) LaBarge, had brought with him on this trip his wife and his daughter-in-law, whose husband is one of the pilots on the boat. With them was Mrs. Thorndike, the young and pretty wife of the supercargo, and one of their friends, Miss Alice Whitman. These ladies are all persons with excellent manners, and even elegant in their toilettes and bearing. Furthermore, they are of excellent people—a family quite representative of the good old stock of the former French city of St. Louis. The time could not be spent other than pleasantly in such good company, and during these three days that I received hospitality on board, we became as intimate as old acquaintances. I say that I received *hospitality* on board, for the transport order did not include my passage or that of my *attendants,* as the papers say. However, Captain LaBarge not only took us on board, but gave Norwell and me a place at his table, and fed my orderly and servant without hearing of any payment. This afternoon, I went to get the whole family in the carriage and brought them to the fort while they finished unloading the boat. We served them dinner, lunch, and tea at my table. The band played its best airs, and the evening ended with ices made and served by Mrs. Walborn.

Tuesday, June 16. The steamer *War Eagle* left this morning between nine and ten o'clock. The ladies from the fort went on board to say goodbye to the ladies from the steamer, everyone delighted with this little interlude in the usually monotonous life of the garrison. Captain LaBarge is one of the oldest and best navigators of the Upper Missouri. He was the first to take a steamboat up to Fort Benton. There is not a piece of the vast banks of the Missouri which is not familiar to him. There is not an Indian chief frequenting the country through which the river goes whom he does not know personally; not a pioneer of the region, not a traveler of note with whom he has not been in contact. On his steamer he carried the famous English hunter, Sir George Gore, with his whole outfit consisting of men (sixty), horses, hunting dogs, wagons, etc., which were out on the plains for two years. There were also Ct. D'Otrante, Lord Mortimer, Ct. le Pindère, and a hundred others. So his stories are most interesting, and as original as they are picturesque. His memory retains an inexhaustible fund of anecdotes and adventures, and one can listen to them for hours without being bored.

I can say as much for his eldest brother, Captain Joseph LaBarge who commands the finest ship on the Upper Missouri, the *Octavia*. This boat passed by Berthold while we were there. He was coming back from Benton and tied up his boat by ours for an hour or two. So I had a chance to become better acquainted with him, for I had just caught a glimpse of him as he passed Stevenson, and of his wife and two daughters whom he brought with him on his trip. He is a man of very good breeding, such as is rarely found among the captains who make this long and sometimes dangerous trip. I can say the same for his family as I have said of his brother's.

One of his daughters is married to Captain Ashby, who is a former member of the Confederate army and is now supercargo of the *Octavia*. When one knows the two brothers and their families, there is no reason to be surprised that their boats are in great favor and are much sought after by all the passengers, especially by those who are taking their families with them to Montana.

Today, in the middle of a terrible storm, with thunder, wind, and rain, the mail from Fort Rice arrived. It brings me nothing interesting in the way of letters or newspapers.

Wednesday, June 17. Today, the mail from Fort Totten arrived, escorted by the guard I sent out for that purpose a week ago Sunday. Nothing in particular marked this round trip. The Indians they met were not hostile, and, moreover, they were not permitted to come near the wagon. There were a number of letters and newspapers covering the month of May. The communications with Fort Totten which were broken for two weeks are re-established, and from now on will be kept up, protected from any interruption. The best news for me is the letting of the contracts to furnish wood for construction and heating, as well as hay for the post. We have received the copy of the contracts awarded to Mr. Anderson, a local man who is very energetic and who understands such matters. This arrangement will spare many men and teams for work on the fort. Had it not been for this, I should have had to send fifteen or twenty miles above Fort Berthold to cut the wood needed for our building and to bring it down the river on rafts. The logs must be at least sixteen inches in diameter and twenty-five feet long, and trees of these dimensions can not be found closer than thirty or forty miles from here. The contract for the firewood calls for twelve hundred cords; another saving of work for our men. Under these conditions, the completion of the post will go along rapidly, and at least we shall have good winter quarters.

Thursday, June 18. Company F, expected from Buford, arrived this morning under command of its captain, Bt. Major Clarke. But the wind, which was blowing violently, drove the steamboat more than half a mile beyond the wharf, and pinned it to the bank, from which it could not budge all day. This evening, the wind has not died down, and the troops are still on board. However, we hope there will be a calm tonight, and then the company can debark tomorrow morning.

John B. Gerard, who arrived from St. Louis two weeks ago and who was left in charge of the store of F. F. Gerard, his cousin, one of our sutlers who is gone for a while, clandestinely sold whiskey to some noncommissioned officers and soldiers, who immediately got drunk. He even had the impudence to drink some with the sergeant major, sergeant quartermaster, and others in the office of the adjutant of the District, where he was found at ten o'clock in the evening by the adjutant of the post. So, yesterday I ordered that he be told to leave the post and the reserve within a few hours, under pain of being arrested and put in the guardhouse if he were seen around after retreat. He immediately went to Berthold, and from there he will go wherever he wishes; but he will not set foot in Fort Stevenson again.[145]

145 Gerard was expelled from Fort Stevenson by Special Order no. 56, issued on June 17. Special Orders, 1868, Department of Dakota, War Records Division, National Archives.

Friday, June 19. Company F debarked this morning at daybreak with all its camp equipments, its laundress, a cow, etc. The company set up its tents on a place chosen for them between the old and the new corral, a hundred yards from the fort. Now we are supplied with a sufficient number of workers for the summer. They will begin work Monday. We shall begin by making adobes, while waiting for the contractors who must furnish us with wood for construction.

Tuesday, June 23. Double arrival: by land a train of thirty wagons to transport the supplies for Fort Totten which come to us by river. These thirty wagons have come from St. Paul by Fort Totten. Sixty others, which they were to meet here, are coming directly from Fort Ransom, but have not yet arrived. This brings to ninety the number of wagons furnished to the government by the contractors of the work. Each of them is drawn by two oxen. Those arriving today were under the protection of an escort of twenty men, a sergeant and two corporals, all commanded by Lieutenant Mac[k]lin. On the way, they killed a suspicious-looking Indian who had followed the train and who was evidently trying to steal horses or do some mischief.

By water, at the same time that the train was arriving at the post, the steamboat *Ben Johnson* was pulling up to the wharf, loaded with some 1,900 sacks of grain for us, and with 222 for Fort Totten. This is the most useless thing in the world. Since the storage of the 4,039 sacks brought from Berthold, we already have more grain than we know what to do with. All this crowds us, and we have no place to pile these supplies sent to us, which we do not need, but are just for the greater profit of the contractors. This grain is even more superfluous since draft animals of the post have been reduced to a bare minimum. We have received the order to ship twenty-eight to Fort Shaw (Montana) at the first opportunity, and to send to Fort Totten, for transfer from there to Fort Ransom and Fort Abercrombie, five complete teams of six mules each, with wagon, harness, etc. When these are sent off, we shall have six wagons and thirty-six mules left. That means our stock will be reduced two thirds, and so this would be the time they would choose to send us grain, as if we had a regiment of cavalry here! On the other hand, the complement of supplies of the commissariat has not arrived. Too much for the animals; not enough for the men.

Wednesday, June 24. The mail from Totten has arrived. The trip was made without incident or accident, except that the corporal commanding the escort killed his horse when his pistol went off accidentally.

Because the train yesterday brought letters and newspapers addressed to me and the officers, the mail today is reduced to very little. Very violent wind all day.

The *Deer Lodge* passed by yesterday. She is the first steamboat making her second trip of the season to Fort Benton. The Indian agent, Mr. Wilkinson, was on board. This time he is coming to reside at Fort Berthold, where he has the responsibility of civilizing our Indians, if it is possible to do so. They say that he is bringing with him a man who is going to open a school for the young redskins. A farmer, a carpenter, a blacksmith are coming to settle at Berthold.

Thursday, June 25. After loading up yesterday, the train of thirty wagons left for Totten this morning, carrying grain and supplies. Eight men deserted last night, probably in connivance with the men from the steamboat *Ben Johnson,* which got under way yesterday at five o'clock in the evening. But she had gone downstream only a few miles to a place where she was to get wood and spend the night. The deserters knew it, and they certainly must have been taken on board, for they had only a day's rations, which made it impossible for them to try to cross the plains. The Indian scouts sent out to look for them found no trace in the direction of Totten or of Rice. This is the result of the system of paying off the men followed in the frontier posts. The men who received *seven months'* pay last month do not have to worry about money if they wish to desert, and with the money, they can easily find a way of getting on the steamboats which may stop for the night anywhere near by.

Sent seventy-five guns, breechloaders, and six thousand metallic cartridges to Fort Totten. While they wait for arms to arrive for the three companies which form the garrison, these seventy-five guns of the new pattern will be enough for the escorts, the guards of the cattle, etc.

Sunday, June 28. The additional convoy of sixty wagons arrived, not directly from Fort Ransom as announced, but from Fort Totten, which it must have passed. With the convoy, Bt. Major Furey has returned to us. He is coming only to transfer the public property for which he is responsible to Lt. Parsons, who replaces him as quartermaster of the District, of the depot, and of the post. He is now appointed to Fort Totten, where a new fort, much more important than the first, is being built. The workmen assigned to Fort Stevenson are on their way, but Major Furey brings none of them with him. They are probably coming with the train of the contractor supplying construction wood, hay, etc., which ought to have been here two weeks ago.

Thursday, July 2. The paymaster, Bt. Lt. Col. Pomeroy, arrived this morning, coming from Buford, where he went for a long tour of the posts in Montana. From here, he will go to Fort Totten, coming back to take a steamboat going down the river. This is just the reverse of the tour made by Paymaster Hanna.

Saturday, July 4. With us, the celebration of the national holiday consisted of the usual program at a frontier post. The military band played national airs at reveille. After the mounting of the guard, target practice by company (three bullets per man). To the best shot of each company, a prize of $10. Then the three winners competed with each other for another prize of $10, with five shots each, counting the total run of the five shots. At noon, an artillery salute of thirty-seven guns. At four o'clock in the afternoon, a two hundred yard foot race. First prize $10, second $5. Then a sack race, also for $10. This last one amused everyone so much that the officers immediately made up a new purse to start a second race with two prizes, one of $10, the other, $4.[146] But the part of the program which evidently pleased the soldiers the most was the last two months' pay which was given to them, since the paymaster was here.

Unfortunately, the holiday was clouded and saddened by a serious accident. One of the gunners who served the pieces which were firing the salute had his right arm shot off by the premature discharge of the cannon into which he was ramming the charge. Of course the accident happened through the fault of number three who had the responsibility of sealing the vent hermetically and who let the air get in through negligence or distraction. This is always the way these accidents happen. I was present at the amputation of the arm, which was the inevitable result. The operation was done by Dr. Gray with a great deal of skill and composure. The patient was under the influence of chloroform and felt absolutely nothing. He is getting along as well as could be expected this evening. His name is Ch. Ray. During the war, he served in the artillery. It is a real tragedy

146 At Fort Buford, the day was celebrated by games like pole climbing and by the opening of the theatre. The soldiers at the post regularly gave performances, but there had been an interruption of several weeks in the entertainment. Fort Buford, "Record of the Medical History of the Post," 1868. Department of Dakota, War Records Division, National Archives.

to have to come through deadly battles only to be mutilated while firing a peaceful salute.

Sunday, July 5. Paymaster Pomeroy left this morning for Totten with his clerk; Maj. Furey and his clerk are in the party. They have with them three wagons carrying the baggage and furniture of our ex-quartermaster. In addition to the mail escort, I have given them nine men and a corporal, who will accompany them to their destination; twenty-six armed men in all, including two soldiers who are going to rejoin their company at Devils Lake; and as there are four persons and two servants, this makes a party of thirty-two men, more than enough to travel the plains in perfect security. However, I had a great deal of difficulty in making this understood to the paymaster, who seems to have a terrible fear of Indians. If I had listened to him, I should have given him a whole company, and we should have had to suspend part of our work. But I had no intention of listening to him, and because he was afraid of more laughter at his expense, he did not dare to insist, and started out dressed in deerskin like a half-breed, with an embroidered belt, etc. Could it be with some hidden motive of finding increased security in this outfit?

Monday, July 6. The steamboat *Argonaut* arrived this afternoon, loaded with supplies for us, a part of them for the quartermaster: articles of clothing, buffalo shoes, steam engine for the sawmill, a new model ambulance for the hospital, etc.; part for the commissary, food supplies of various kinds. All this will be unloaded tonight, and tomorrow the boat will return empty to Fort Rice, where it must stop to take on seventy-five passengers, chiefly the members of the Indian peace commission. It seems that the commission has finished its work. The captain reports that right now there are from seven to eight thousand Indians camped around the fort. He says the bluffs along the river are literally covered with their lodges. What was the outcome of this great gathering and the succeeding conferences? We don't know yet, but we shall soon find out.

Tuesday, July 7. Thermometer at ninety-eight, F., in the shade! Ouf!

Thursday, July 16. During the week which has just gone by, two boats, the *Peninah* and the *G. B. Allen,* loaded with supplies for Fort Stevenson and for Fort Totten, came to unload their cargoes at the landing. There are assortments of medicines, supplies for the commissariat, and a quantity of construction materials, cement, fir boards, lime, laths, shingles, etc., and a quantity of grain, corn, and oats. The trains from Totten had returned, so we got rid of a good share of all this. One left yesterday (seventy-five wagons), the other leaves tomorrow (eighty and some wagons). When they come back, the number of each convoy will be brought to almost one hundred by the addition of thirty wagons brought to Totten for the business. With two hundred wagons, the transport will go along quickly, and by fall, we shall probably have nothing left of what is intended for Totten.

The paymaster returned and is waiting for the first boat to continue his tour by going on to Rice.

[*Excursion into the badlands*] Last Sunday (twelfth) I spent my day painting a study of the badlands half way to Berthold. This region has a bad reputation and is frequented by the Sioux because it has great advantages for surprises and sneak attacks; but the Sioux were far away. Moreover, I had with me Dr. Gray, Lt. Norwell, an escort of five men, and ten others who came to take advantage of the chance to hunt in the badlands. If the Sioux showed up, we were a large enough force to give them a good reception. Our outfit was composed of my ambulance, and an army wagon, and the little expedition was led by three Indian scouts. We came back without an incident, I with my study and two pencil sketches, the men with no game, since it was impossible to get near the antelope. But the day was spent pleasantly, and everyone had a good appetite for the picnic lunch.

The order has come with the last mail for me to go to Fort Totten to preside over a court-martial which must judge captains Wainwright and Piatt, and Lieutenant Leonard. Lt. Col. Bowman makes up part of the court, along with Dr. Gray. The Lt. Col. will probably be here by the first boat. The three of us will leave around the twenty-fifth or twenty-sixth, the court starting its session on the third of August. In addition, I shall take along with me Lt. Marshall, my adjutant, and the regimental band for escort. It will be, everything taken into consideration, a pleasant excursion across the plains. The men of the convoy assure us that there will be plenty of waterfowl and fish. We shall get along all right.

Friday, July 17. The paymaster, who has been back from Totten for a few days, embarked this evening on the *Silver Lake,* on its way back from Benton. She will carry him to Rice, with his clerk, Mr. Webber, and Dr. Benjamin, assistant surgeon detached here temporarily. The arrival of Dr. Bean relieved him of his duties for the interim. Oppressive heat; clouds of mosquitoes. Around noon, the mercury went up to above one hundred Fahrenheit.

Saturday, July 18. A day of rest in memory of the death of Mr. Buchanan, ex-President, and in conformation with the orders from supreme headquarters. Program: salute of thirteen guns at reveille;— a gun every half hour until retreat, which ends with a salvo of thirty-seven more guns. This liberal expense of powder in honor of a man who—but he is dead: *nihil de mortuis, nisi bonum.* So be it. At ten o'clock in the morning, the order of the President and that of the general in chief was read before the troops assembled under arms. At this rate the soldiers would not mind if a former President died every week.

Three Sioux from the band of Medicine Bear arrive from Fort Rice and announce the outcome of a general peace. They claim that Sitting Bull came to the meeting.[147] Red Horn, Four Horns, Gall, and Black Moon did not dare to trust themselves there in person, but would send their people, assuring Father de Smet, who had gone out to find them, that they would accept the peace as if they were present, on the conditions agreed to with the other chiefs. As a pledge, they restored to him the horses, mules, and harnesses taken from our men whom they had murdered. In this way we recovered part of the papers stolen by Sitting Bull from the mail carried by Brown and Martin. What Indians say must never be accepted without reservation. Let us wait to find out if things are so satisfactory. The commissioners left Rice eight or ten days ago, and the crowd of Indians gathered there was scattered in every direction, carrying with them presents, ammunition, supplies, etc., gifts of the Great Father of Washington. Now the question is to find out if the treaty of peace will be observed by all the parties agreeing, and for how long.

Monday, July 20. It does not seem that the great treaty of peace with the Indians has produced any immediate effects. Yesterday or the day before yesterday, two whites cutting wood for the steamboats were attacked by the Indians: their mules were stolen, and a Gros Ventre who was with them was wounded in the foot by a bullet. The incident took place opposite Berthold. The attackers are unknown;

[147] Vestal says that Sitting Bull did not go to the meeting and did not sign the treaty of 1868. There is a Sitting Bull who signed the treaty, but this Sitting Bull was an Oglala, not Hunkpapa. There is no signature of a Sitting Bull on the Hunkpapa treaty. Stanley Vestal, *New Sources of Indian History,* p. 430; Kappler, *Indian Laws and Treaties,* 2:1004, 1006.

but of course they are a part of the same Sioux whom the government has just fed for more than a month at Rice, to whom the government gave presents, ammunition, etc., in exchange for words of peace, the worth of which can be judged by this deed.[148]

Did I mention before that fifteen or twenty days ago seven whites, settled above Buford to cut wood, were massacred by the savages? A steamboat discovered the scalped and mutilated bodies, and they were given a decent burial.

The herd of cattle for Stevenson and Buford finally arrived: 166 head for us, and 210 for the Buford garrison, which is going to send an escort of 60 and some men to get them. With the cattle has arrived Mr. Anderson, the contractor, who has agreed to furnish construction wood and hay for our post. For this, he brings with him thirty men whom he is going to put to work immediately thirty miles from here. The logs, bound into rafts, will be sent down the river, and the sawmill will cut them to the form and size needed to finish our buildings, particularly the roof.

[*Agent and trader*] More news: The Indian agent at Berthold, Mr. Wilkinson, tells me that since F. F. Gerard's license has expired and has not been renewed, he has ordered his representative to leave the Indian territory under his jurisdiction with all his merchandise. This representative is Beauchamp, who is very puzzled and does not know what to do in the absence of his employer. He does not have any way to transport the merchandise here. I advised him to take an inventory and to give the key to Wilkinson, who can hardly refuse to take charge of it. Gerard's other employees can easily find employment with Mr. Anderson, who needs additional men to speed up the delivery of his supply of wood and hay. The cause of this severe

148 De Trobriand had doubts about the success of the peace commission both before and after the meeting at Fort Rice. He wrote to headquarters in September, 1868, that "none of the hostile Chiefs of any consequence in these parts, went to Fort Rice . . . the Commission made peace there with the Sioux which were *not* at war with the Government. *Sitting Bull, Black Moon, Four Horns, Red Horn, The Man Who Jumps in the Middle, the Gall* . . . kept away from the conference. They listened to Father de Smet merely out of condescension for his character of 'Man of Medicine'; but for all that, none of them could be made to budge an inch from the position they had assumed from the beginning." "The men killed and wounded in this Command before the meeting of the Commission at Fort Rice," De Trobriand continued in the same letter, "were *all* shot with arrows: the men killed and wounded in the Command since arms and ammunition have been distributed among the Indians are all shot with bullets or buckshot . . ." Régis de Trobriand, Fort Stevenson, to Bvt. Brig. Genl O. D. Greene, AA Genl, Department of Dakota, St. Paul, September 6, 1868. Department of Dakota, War Records Division, National Archives.

measure is the report that Gerard sent to Washington at the beginning of last winter to set forth the claims of the Rees, who were complaining of being cheated by the agent Wilkinson in the distribution
of the annuities. The political influence of Wilkinson's friends caused
his commission as Indian agent to be renewed, without the facts
charged against him being taken into consideration, and now he is
using his power for personal revenge on F. Gerard by refusing to sign
his new license, and by ordering him, at the expiration of the old one,
to leave Berthold with all his merchandise. The houses built by
Gerard as a home and as storehouses would undoubtedly be very
convenient for Wilkinson. In them, he could install the personnel
and store some goods of his agency. This expulsion from Berthold
takes in all the employees and white residents, except those who are
in the pay of the agency or the fur company of Durfie [Durfee] & Peck.
This is a monopoly for Wilkinson and the trader, Marsh; by avoiding all surveillance, they have the Indians and their interests at their
mercy without any possible appeal. I do not think it is difficult to
foresee what the outcome of this will be, or rather, what the immediate consequences will be. What will then result from the discontent of the Indians is a rather serious matter. And this is how all
the efforts and expenses of the government and of its commissioners
are incessantly compromised by the political intrigues and private
speculation of the Indian Bureau. The power given to the agents
to keep or expel whomever they wish is excessive and can result in
most flagrant abuses when its exercise is not restrained by guarantees
of justice.

This is the day for incidents: The cattle had scarcely arrived
with its escort of a mounted company under the command of Captain [William] Stanley (brave officer who lost his left arm at Coal
[Cold] Harbor) when 300 lodges of Indians from Rice appeared on
the horizon. These 300 lodges consisting of 1200 to 1500 people, form
a part of seven bands whose chiefs are: *Manto Ouaken* [Mahtowakan]
(Medicine Bear); *Ishta Sapa* (Black Eyes); *Ta Shunka Douta* (My Red
Horse); *Ouanatah* (meaning unknown); *Ata Sapah* (All Black); *Tath'-
anka Khi* (Carrying Buffalo); *Tath-ankatchie* (Weeping Buffalo).
With them is the son of *Black Cat Fish,* who died last winter. His
name is *Mato-Pahre* (Bear Nose). All these people are coming from
Rice and are going to hunt the buffalo, which, they say, are going
down the Yellowstone.

[*An old treaty*] The camp made, the chiefs, followed by two
or three hundred of their people, came to see me, no need to mention

the reason. With Indians, it is always a question of getting provisions. But it is impossible for them to ask for something to eat without an oration, which invariably takes the same pattern. To give a sample of it here would be mere repetition. So I was forced to receive the seven chiefs and to submit to their eloquence. Four of them had not yet met me, a special reason for displaying their talents in oratory. They were not lacking in them. The only compensation I found was examining the original of a peace treaty concluded with the Indians in 1820 on the Three Rivers at Travers[e] de[s] Sioux, which was then a complete wilderness and which today is so far back in the States that the interpreters themselves do not know where it is. This treaty, signed by about twenty officers and twenty-seven chiefs or Indian personages, contains provisions that were not carried out by either party; but those who signed it have been dead for a long time and won't come back to complain.[149] This document was given to me to read by *Weeping Buffalo,* whose grandfather was one of the principal signatories.

As a conclusion, I had distributed twenty-two boxes of biscuits, three for each band and one to divide among the seven chiefs, each one of whom received in addition a pound of coffee, two pounds of sugar, and a piece of salt pork.

Another incident occurred during the day, which I cannot leave out here: the heat was overpowering; the thermometer went above 105, F., or from forty to forty-one degrees centigrade. Around noon, clouds of grasshoppers began to show up in the sky. A multitude of these fearful insects flew skimming along the ground, and the layers seemed to thicken as they rose in the air. In the direction of the sun, these innumerable multitudes, more visible to the naked eye, looked like a thick dust of white specks which drifted, passed each other, and multiplied in the air. Finally, the last and fatal symptom, a great murmur like the steady rumble of far away carriages filled the air all around. It was the droning of this traveling ocean of winged insects. Our gardens and pastures would be all gone if this cloud came down to earth. Two or three hours would be enough for complete and absolute devastation; everything would be devoured, and nothing could prevent it.

149 There is no recorded treaty with the Sioux at Traverse des Sioux in 1820. Early treaties were signed by bands of Sioux at Portage des Sioux in 1815, at St. Louis in 1816, at Fort Lookout in 1825. In 1837 the Sioux signed a treaty at Washington, D. C. ceding all their lands east of the Mississippi. In 1851 the Sissetons and Wahpetons signed a treaty at Traverse des Sioux on the Minnesota River. Kappler, *Indian Laws and Treaties,* 2:113, 114, 128, 227, 493, 588.

At this time, a black storm began to come up on the horizon to the north. Heavy clouds mounted one on the other, lighted by brilliant and repeated flashes of lightning, which were followed by rolling thunder, nearer and nearer. The noise of the grasshoppers seemed to be its feeble echo. When the storm came up almost above our heads, blasts of violent wind began to blow in squalls, sweeping everything before them, and great flashes of lightning rent the air. Then all that winged dust which was making the sky white passed over us rapidly. Carried by the storm, it crossed the Missouri, and scattered far out on the plains. Our gardens and pastures were saved, at least this time.

The storm, before reaching its zenith, went east, and swept around far toward the south, where it finally disappeared, without moistening the soil of Fort Stevenson by a drop of rain, although it fell in torrents in other places. Great blasts of wind, fierce bolts of lightning, one of which killed an Indian mule grazing on the prairie; finally, a great roar of thunder; all the storm did for us was to drive away the grasshoppers, but it did not water our vegetables.

Tuesday, July 21. The Indians did not leave until this morning; but the grasshoppers came back. Around ten o'clock in the morning, their vanguard arrived, and soon the air was filled with them. For more than six hours, they passed over, flying low, many of them almost touching the ground and all going uniformly from north to south. On their way over, a great number, insignificant in comparison with the enormous total, lit on the grass, on the roof, on the boards, the walls, on the posts, and formed in places gray, crawling, moving masses. Fortunately, our windows are equipped with mosquito netting, which was put there to protect us from mosquitoes and which this time protected us from the grasshoppers, without which we should either have had to suffer their invasion into our quarters, or to have closed the doors and windows at the risk of being suffocated by the heat. The flying host swept on relentlessly, flecking the sky like snowflakes driven by the wind; and if one looked at the effect of the wings of these right in the sun, he would have said that it was snowing grasshoppers. Going out was very unpleasant. These cursed insects hit us in the face, caught in our eyes or in our beards, got into our clothes, and jumped from the ground in swarms at our every step, like big hail stones bounding on the hard ground. So again we must worry about our vegetables and pastures, and nothing, absolutely nothing, can be done to save them from destruction!

314

Thank God the sky clouded up for a second time. A little after four o'clock, a strong wind, sign of a new storm, began to blow from northeast. The effect was almost instantaneous. The millions of grasshoppers which were flying low seemed to be lifted up by this powerful blast into the upper atmosphere, and while the surface of the ground was almost completely swept clean, the living cloud became thicker above. It is no exaggeration to say that the sun was darkened by it, while, from the air, the great rustling noise I mentioned yesterday came again, stronger than ever. Evidently the effect of the windstorm was to thicken the mass considerably by pushing the multitudes it met back onto the others. This heavenly broom swept the winged dust and rolled it into larger and larger masses. At the end of a few minutes, the swarm was darkening the sky, and although it was moving very fast, half an hour went by before it cleared. Finally, it gradually disappeared, leaving behind only a number of insects which stuck onto some tree, stragglers of the great army, which can be annoying but not dangerous.

These grasshoppers do not vary in any respect from the common insect found everywhere on both sides of the Atlantic. Same shape, same size, same color; I have not been able to discover the slightest difference. It is simply our grasshopper multiplied *ad infinitum*. What a shame our Indians do not feed on them like St. John in the desert, and like certain African tribes, as we are told! In these two days, there would be enough to feed all the tribes of Dakota. The hens and chickens stuffed themselves. In the beginning, there was great activity and feasting among the feathered tribe; but they gulped down so many that finally they were stuffed with them, and when their stomachs could not take in any more, they looked at the hopping around them with a mournful and indifferent eye. Perhaps more than one mother hen will grieve at the effect of the indigestion suffered by those of her chicks who were too greedy or too recently hatched.

P. S. This evening, the gardeners report that only the onions were seriously damaged. The corn is intact, and the potatoes scarcely touched.[150] The rain came, although late; undoubtedly it will help

150 There is no record of the size of the garden at Fort Stevenson. The surgeon at Fort Buford, however, described the garden of that post in some detail. It covered five acres and produced lettuce, radishes, lambs quarters, cabbages, turnips, beets, potatoes, green peas, cucumbers, and onions. Dr. Kimball considered that the health of the troops depended on the success of the garden. Fort Buford, "Record of the Medical History of the Post," 1868. Department of Dakota, War Records Division, National Archives.

to repair the damage, unless we have a third invasion. But we shall not be a prophet of misfortune, and we shall hope for the best.

Sunday, July 26. The Indians left Wednesday morning; good riddance. Friday they were followed by Mr. Anderson's thirty wood-cutters. I gave them an escort composed of a sergeant, a corporal, and ten men to protect them in case of trouble with the Indians. However, it was not from the Indians, but actually from their agent that trouble was to come. When he saw the party arrive, he gave them notice that he was reserving all the wood between the reserve of Fort Stevenson and the Little Missouri for his agency, and ordered them to refrain from cutting any tree there. I found the conduct "cool," as they say in English. The joke was just too much. So I gave Anderson a written order to go ahead and carry out his contract with the government to cut wood wherever he found it without paying any attention to orders from another authority commanding him to do the contrary.

I believed the incident closed when yesterday morning, Marsh, the trader, arrived from Berthold with a letter in which Mr. Wilkinson, the Indian agent, informed me that a party of men led by J. Anderson came to his agency to cut wood there; that he is reserving this wood for the buildings that he plans on putting up at Berthold, and that consequently he sent Anderson the order of which he is sending me a copy (the one which had been sent to me the day before). He finished by telling me that since this order had no effect, he was asking me to furnish him with a military force to carry it out. In this action, the confidence and presumption of Master Wilkinson reaches lofty proportions. This is impudence raised to the third power. So I answered him in strong terms with a letter ending this way: "It is a great surprise to me that you asked me to obstruct the carrying out of a contract with the government, which it is my duty to protect, and to furnish you with a military force against my own soldiers. You will probably be much less surprised to know that in answer, I refuse to comply with your request."[151] And, as a result, right now Anderson's men are busy cutting construction timber for us above Berthold.

Yesterday, Saturday, Captain Stanley, his two lieutenants, and

[151] There are differences between the letter quoted above and the letter on file in the Indian Office. However, the substance of what De Trobriand wrote to Wilkinson is the same in both letters. See Régis de Trobriand, Fort Stevenson, Dakota Territory, July 25, 1868. Office of Indian Affairs, Dakota Superintendency, Record Copy of Letters Received, National Archives.

his mounted company got under way for Fort Wadsworth, the garrison to which they belong, leaving us to guard the 210 cattle which belong to Fort Buford.

Last night, the body of Col. Powell, which his brother came to claim in the name of the family, was disinterred to be put in a metal coffin, hermetically sealed. Disgusting! I do not understand people who, in order to have it near them, are so set on raising from the ground a thing as foul and disgusting as a body in full decay. The operation was most sickening. The details I got the next day are enough to turn the stomach. Who in the devil can find sentiment in that!

In contrast, a wedding was celebrated tonight at eight o'clock, a simple and primitive ceremony in keeping with our country and our position in the desert. A musician named Hantz married a young girl, sister of one of the laundresses of Company I. She was in the employ of Mrs. Walborn, in whose home the wedding took place. When the officers were gathered in the main room, and the adjutant took his place a little in advance of the group, prayer book in his hand, the future husband entered, offering his arm to the future wife, and both took their places facing the official. Then, addressing the couple: "Do you, of your own free will, take for your legitimate wife this woman?" "Yes Sir." "Do you, of your own free will, take as legitimate husband this man?" "Yes Sir." "Join hands. All right, I now pronounce you man and wife in the name of the Father, and of the Son, and of the Holy Ghost. Amen."

After this, everyone shook hands with the couple, and cakes and refreshments went around. The company drank to the health of the newly-weds, who then withdrew into an apartment prepared for them for the night by one of the traders, at the request of the officers. And that was all. After a few gay remarks and insinuations, required by the event, "everyone went home," as did Marlborough. It is certainly impossible to reduce the celebration of a marriage to a more simple form. A formula pronounced, and everything is said: but Hantz and Annie Noble are just as legitimately and firmly united as if priests, ministers, magistrates had taken part in it, with all the pomp of ceremonies and all the solemnity of formulas, masses, prayers, readings from the law, speeches, etc. It is the same with most things in civilization. A great many complications and useless things. One must come to live in Dakota to get things back to their real value and primitive simplicity.

Sent six men and a sergeant on board the *Urelda*, whose crew attempted mutiny. They will go as far as Buford, where they will be relieved by an equal number of men, just as they themselves relieved the squad from Fort Rice.

Lt. Col. Bowman has not shown up yet; he was to be here today. I am waiting for him so I can go to Fort Totten, where I must preside over a court-martial of which Dr. Gray is also a member.

Trip to Fort Totten

(DEVILS LAKE)

Tuesday, July 28. Lt. Col. Bowman arrived from Fort Buford in a boat which the first steamboat going up the river will take back with the men who make up the crew. This happened yesterday; and since there was no one else to wait for, we got under way in the afternoon today, to avoid the midday heat. The little expedition is composed of four officers: myself, Lt. Col. Bowman, the surgeon major, Dr. Gray, and Lt. J. Marshall. The latter is not a member of the court-martial, but I am taking him with me in his capacity of Acting Assist. Adjt. Gen¹ of the District, whose general headquarters are moved to Fort Totten with me for the time I am there. The head clerk of the office goes with us for the same reason. Three sergeants and a cook complete the personnel, except for five wagoners and the regimental band (nineteen men) which forms the escort and performs its duties on the way. In all, thirty-three people in an ambulance, a char-a-banc, and three wagons. In such numbers, and armed as we are, the hostile Indians, if they come on us, will respectfully let us pass.

I have no intention of hurrying. The wild fowl are very plentiful on the way in this season of the year; the court does not open session until Monday, August 3. So we have time to make of this trip a pleasure expedition. Our first bivouac will be only fifteen miles from Stevenson, on the edge of a lake called Spring Lake, because of the spring which flows at the place where we are going to spend the night.

Wednesday, July 29. We arrived there at nightfall, after having crossed a region of rolling prairies, where there is not a tree on the horizon. To make up for this, we noticed a wolf and three antelope, but too far away to try to approach them. The dusk was still light enough to allow us to park the wagons and to set up the tents with no difficulty; but in addition to growing darkness, we had another more urgent reason for hurrying. For about an hour a threatening storm had been growing in the west. The sun had set behind a thick mass of black clouds which portended nothing good. This somber curtain climbed up the horizon and spread across the sky. Every minute or so it was split open by long flashes of lightning which were followed by thunder, sounding from every point of the compass.

[*Storm*] Everyone kept turning first to watch attentively the

319

progress of the storm, and then to the supper which was cooking over an improvised fire. The question was: which would come first, the storm or the supper. Fortunately, it was decided in favor of the supper, which we enjoyed in the open without any difficulty. We had scarcely given our place to the servants when the first gusts of wind quickly breaking into squalls began to shake the tents as if testing their stability. In a second everyone was at work driving the stakes in deeper, tightening the cords, and in general redoubling precautions against the storm. Nothing was neglected. A few minutes later, we were in the clutches of a furious hurricane mixed with torrential rain, accompanied by incessant lightning and deafening claps of thunder. For a quarter of an hour, which seemed long to me, I believed that everything was going to be blown over and carried away. My two hunting dogs, squatted on the floor of my tent, crouched down as much as they could, stretching out their muzzles on the edges of the buffalo skin which I was using as a bed, as if to get more protection from the unleashed wind which shook our shelter furiously, causing the canvas to flap terribly. I heard my three terrified traveling companions fastening down the tent that they shared next to mine. Seated on my valise, I was philosophically waiting for some catastrophe when finally the fury of the sky seemed to abate. The assault on our tents and covered wagons, where our men who had had no time to set up their canvas shelters had taken refuge, lost much of its force. Little by little, the air grew calm, the stars began to come out, shyly at first, then brilliantly in the clearing sky. The storm had passed, and during the rest of the night nothing disturbed the peace of the camp.

This morning, after a breakfast eaten in the first hours of dawn, we got under way at four-thirty, just as the sun was coming up. Soon we were joined by the two Indian scouts who were to have left Stevenson at the same time we did, but who were delayed and could not join us before nightfall. They slept in sight of our fires, wisely putting off joining us until this morning for fear that in the darkness our sentinels would shoot at them before they had time to recognize them. On the plains, it is always good to be cautious. So our band is increased to thirty-five.

Around seven-thirty, we halted for an hour on the banks of a chalybeate watercourse, which is named Red Water because of its color. I immediately began to hunt, and without going more than half a mile, we killed twenty ducks, plovers, and snipes of the large variety.

A little before noon, we arrived at our destination for the day, and we made camp on a kind of projecting point between two lakes separated only by a strip of land fifteen to twenty feet wide—lunch and rest at midday —. Toward evening, the doctor and two or three men from the escort went fishing. They caught nothing but small fish, but a great many of them, and they tasted very good fried for supper. They were, for the most part, small perch. I took my gun and, accompanied by four men, I went out to look for the remains of Ch. MacDonald and Joe Elmla, our two couriers killed by the Indians in this neighborhood last May.[152] A report coming from some Sioux Yanktonahs who passed by here indicated that the remains of the two victims were to be found at the edge of a clump of brush adjoining the divide between the two lakes. I searched the spot and the country around, and I found nothing but some elk bones which perhaps could be taken for human bones, and farther on, a sock which seemed to be pierced by a bullet and soaked with blood, at least it appeared to be. Convinced, after useless search, that what we were looking for was not there, I went back to the shores of the lake where I killed a few ducks before returning to camp. Not a sign of Indians or quadrupeds. We are really right out in the desert. In every direction, the eye ranges across empty space, yellow in color, the edge of which is lost in the heat of the sun and is merged with the sky. Only from the east the lonely silhouettes of the sinister heights of Dog Den can be made out against the milky background of the horizon.

Thursday, July 30. Early this morning, we passed rather close to Dog Den, probably given this name because of the great numbers of prairie dogs which must have made their homes there. They must have emigrated, for we have seen no more of them there than elsewhere.

[*Prairie dogs*] This little animal does not resemble a dog in any way, although it bears the name. It is a kind of ground squirrel, red in color, the size of a gray squirrel, but with a less furry tail. It digs its home in the ground, and the earth it throws out forms at the entrance a little mound above each dwelling. It particularly loves to sit on this mound, watching what is going on in the neighborhood. It is very quick in its movements, and although it isn't wild, letting

152 When the news of the death of the two couriers was first received, Mac-Donald and Hamlin were the names given by De Trobriand. The *North Dakota Historical Collections,* 3:181. See above, p. 298.

itself be approached within a few steps, at the first cause for alarm it disappears into its hole, at the bottom of which it keeps its provisions and where it remains buried under the snow and probably hibernates all winter. These pretty little animals live together, sometimes in such large numbers that the collection of thousands of mounds takes the name of Dog Town in the language of the country. When one sees them sitting in the sun, each on the top of its dwelling, one would say they were a gathering of little gossips chatting on the steps of their doorways. They have a sharp bark which is somewhat like that of all young dogs. It is said they are very friendly with reptiles, and it is even claimed that they live on very good terms with snakes, toads, etc., when these come to share the underground homes with them; but I doubt it very much.

Dog Den is called by the Indians The Mountain Which Looks (*La Montagne qui Regarde*), a name which is much more exact and with a much more real meaning. In reality it is a height composed of a collection of rather abrupt hills, separated by deep ravines well covered with trees, or by narrow winding gorges filled with rocks. This height rises alone in the middle of a vast plain. From the top, there is an unobstructed view for a considerable distance in all directions. No terrain could be better laid out for ambushes. So the raiding Indians, in search of evil deeds to do, make it their rendezvous. They can easily hide in the depressions of the terrain, as if they were in a boat scanning a rough sea. Their keen sight can detect from there clear to the edge of the horizon travelers or white or red hunters. Then, according to the circumstances, they can either remain hidden or come down in the ravines to surprise, kill, or steal from their victims. This is the way the Unkpapahs killed Ch. MacDonald and Elmla. This is the way they surprised and robbed Brown and Martin. Because of the bad reputation of the place, the trail does not cross it, but circles some distance away.

[*Rocky Creek*] We halted for an hour on the other side of Dog Den, on Rocky Creek. It runs between steep banks; but it is three quarters dried up in this season of the year. There is much brush in the ravine, and also a considerable number of trees. I did not find any game; only young pigeons scarcely out of the nest, which our men were able to catch on the run. As we went on, I killed some plovers on the ponds of water along the road. We met half of the train going to Stevenson empty to load up supplies for Fort Totten: this train is made up of slow-moving ox carts. Because of their great number (there are more than 120 of them) they are divided into two trains, following each other at a day's interval. There is a driver for every three or four carts. Moreover, all are armed and protected by an escort supplied by the Totten garrison, under the command of an officer who travels with the second train. A sergeant and fifteen men accompany the first. The convoy slowly unwinding in the distance looks rather picturesque in the middle of these desert plains. A wolf and some antelope showed up so far away that we were unable to shoot at them.

[*Middle Station*] Arrived around one o'clock at the middle station, so named because it is the point where the couriers from Totten and Stevenson meet midway and exchange their mail sacks. This point is surrounded by five lakes very close together. When we got there, their surface was dotted with wild birds. One in particular, completely surrounded with high and thick rushes, seemed to be the preferred spot of the feathered tribe, and here was a nursery for geese, ducks, and teals. A number of young families not yet able to fly were swimming in flocks on every side, each one led by the mother. The water of these lakes is alkaline, and consequently horrible to drink; but two pure springs gush out at the ends of one of them. Here we pitched our tents, and here we found that the second empty supply train, under the command of Lieutenant Lockwood, was making its halt for the day. The wagons were brought into a circle with an entrance and an exit left open opposite each other. The oxen were grazing at the edge of the lake under the guard of drivers and the protection of half a dozen soldiers in scattered outposts. They left around four o'clock in the afternoon, leaving us the field free for the evening hunt. No need to ask if we got much. We killed as much as we could eat, but were ourselves devoured by millions of mosquitoes, which spoiled our pleasure considerably. (My dog, Marco, does marvels. He is only nine months old and hunts like an old dog already. With him, I have not yet lost a piece of game, no matter what distance from shore it drops.)

Friday, July 31. Near the five lakes, the undulations in the prairie completely disappeared and we entered a perfectly flat plain, with no variation in terrain, stretching as far as the eye can see. Its uniformity was hardly varied by the swelling of a hill near Buffalo Lake, which we reached at seven-thirty this morning after a trip of thirteen or fourteen miles. We made more than an hour's halt here and killed a number of large golden plovers, curlews, teals, etc. Our larder filled for the rest of the day, we continued our trip, still on a flat plain.

Some distance from there, at the edge of the trail, two crossed sticks mark for us the exact spot where Coon was recently slain. His pillow was still there on the ground. Coon was a white man who had stayed at Fort Totten for some time and, when spring came, he started out *alone* in a wagon with two horses for Fort Stevenson, where he planned on taking one of the Missouri steamboats to go to Fort Benton, and from there to the Montana mines. He had with him a large sum in gold and had unwisely let it be known before setting out.[153]

[*Murder of Coon*] His murder was blamed on the Indians, but there is no lack of clues to place suspicion of guilt on others, whites or half-breeds. In fact, all the gold hidden by Coon in his wagon, cooking utensils, and everything that could contain it, and his harness was stolen; his pillow and other articles were opened up in the search. The skin sack which contained it was found empty some distance away, and the harness, wagon, kitchen gear, all of which could be recognized, were left there. Only the horses were stolen. All this is quite different from the Indian ways and as still more conclusive evidence, the body was not pierced with arrows, and the scalp was not taken. Finally, on the trampled ground where the murder took place, prints of *shod* horses and shoes *with heels* were identified. Nothing could be less Indian. These circumstances, added to a coincidence in dates, have produced a suspicion I have heard expressed that perhaps Ch. MacDonald and Elmla are neither dead nor strangers to the murder of Coon. Of course, this idea does not hold up under examination, for even if it is true that up to now the remains of these two victims have not been found, still on the other hand, all their things, weapons, clothes, etc., have been found in the hands of their murderers, who did not hesitate to tell the details of their murder to Brown and Martin whom they held prisoners and threatened with a similar fate. Isn't it enough that the poor devils have lost their lives without having their memory smirched after their death?

The vast, flat plain brought us to a ravine, winding and deep, where there is a spring of excellent water beside a half dried-up stream. This is called "Big Coulee." Around noon, we made camp there for the rest of the day and the following night. Not a tree, not a stick of wood to burn, except what is left of that which we had brought for this purpose. The men found some dried buffalo dung, the usual fuel of the prairies.

[153] Abram Coon left a half-breed wife, who, by instructions of De Trobriand, endorsed on February 7, 1869, was to receive his property. Department of Dakota,

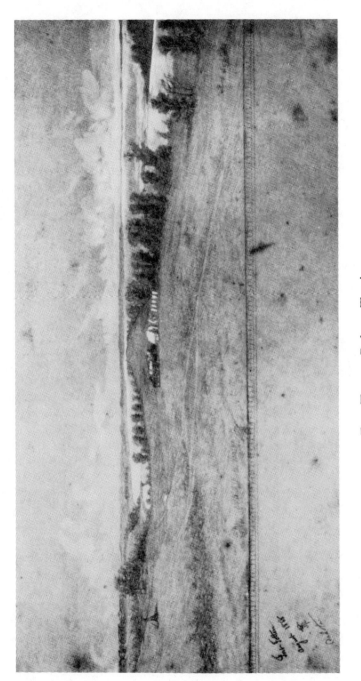

Fort Totten, Dakota Territory

Trip to Fort Totten

Saturday, August 1. The plain is still just as bare, but a little more rolling. It is cut by some coulees, much smaller and shallower than the one where we spent the night. These coulees form the source of the Shayenne [Sheyenne] River. We found the water there palatable.

[*Crow Island*] Our usual halt to water and to rest the teams was made twelve miles from Fort Totten on the bank of Stony Lake, which really has very rocky banks. The Canadians and half-breeds call it "Crow Island," although there is no island. But in their figurative language, the whites of French blood who frequented these bare plains gave, by way of analogy, the name "island" to any rare clump of wood which showed up on this motionless ocean, the green undulations of which look like waves.

So Crow Island is a clump of trees and brush rising on the slope of one of the shores of the lake. Here the crows caw around their nests in emulation of one another, and here, as everywhere else, there is an abundance of waterfowl.

[*Devils Lake*] Around noon, we reached the end of Devils Lake, the blue surface of which we had seen for some time. From this point, it extends north out of sight, with the prairie coming right down to the water. Trees cover some islands and peninsulas on the side followed by the road. There, too, the shores are shaded by oaks. Soon we left the shores to cut off toward Fort Totten, where we arrived around one o'clock, happy to get to our destination at last and to be done with that long ride across the monotonous uniformity of the vast plains.

Fort Totten does not look very charming to us, although the lake does form a background for it. It is a long parallelogram formed by a palisade, with the guardhouse, the prison, saddlery, and mule-drivers' room at one end; and along the sides, the stables, company quarters, hospital, storehouse, and offices. Opposite the entry, at the farther end of the parallelogram, there are the officers' lodgings. The latter are laid out almost as they are at Stevenson: two lodgings to a house, separated by a common corridor. At Stevenson, each lodging has its corridor and is completely separated from the other by a thick partition. The cattle corral is on the opposite side from the one by which we entered, below the high plateau where the fort is located, and at the edge of the water. All the buildings are alike; not very attractive-looking log houses, made of tree trunks and mud.

War Records Division, National Archives. Coon was buried at Fort Totten. *St. Paul Daily Pioneer,* June 2, 1868.

In short, seen at a distance, Fort Totten looks like a collection of large stables. When one gets there, the impression changes because of the lake and its banks shaded by trees which overlook it. Yet, to have a good look at them, one must go out of the palisade which surrounds one on every side. This precaution, which we have always scorned at Fort Stevenson, does not seem necessary to me. It makes the post look like an unpleasant prison. Accustomed to living right out on the open prairie with no barriers of any kind, I felt crowded and seemed to breathe less easily in this enclosure, which is twice as large as Stevenson.

Tuesday, August 4. Court-martial went into session yesterday. General Marcy arrived, charged with the inspection of the posts of Wadsworth, Abercrombie, Ransom, Totten, and Stevenson, and with the examination of the possible need for a new fort near the frontier line around Pembina. He comes from there. His outfit is composed of five wagons and two ambulances with a suitable escort.

Saturday, August 8. General inspection of the post and the garrison took place the day before yesterday. Gen¹ Marcy was to leave for Stevenson yesterday morning, but a night of storm and torrential rain, which did not end with daylight, held him up twenty-four hours and he did not get under way until this morning, when the weather cleared up considerably. The meetings of the court-martial go on continuously every day from nine o'clock in the morning to one or two in the afternoon, which leaves me some time early in the morning before breakfast for hunting and in the afternoon an opportunity to do some sketching. The waterfowl are very plentiful, and there is no lack of scenes to reproduce. So we take trips into the surrounding country. With Mrs. Whistler and her family, we visited the top of a high hill where one can enjoy a broad view of the lake and the plain in every direction. As General Sully seems to be the first white man of note who tramped on the top of it, it was named for him (Sully's Hill). The road leading to it is charming. First, it runs along near the pine grove in which the fort is situated, and then crosses a tangled clump of oak, near which there is a fine natural park which could exist in civilized countries only by the expenditure of money and art. With the exception of Dr. Gray, who takes his meals with Major Furey, we dine with Col. Whistler and his family. No one could be more hospitable than they all have been in their welcome to us.

Sunday, August 9. A courier coming from Stevenson informed me that the hostile Indians attacked my cattle the day after my departure, but they were repulsed and given a good chase, and did not get a single animal. The Rees conducted themselves well. Lt. Cussick, who came with 50 men to get the 210 head for Buford, had a skirmish with the Indians himself, but it did not amount to much.[154] It does not seem that the treaty with the redskins is having any great effect.

The climate of Dakota seems to be unsettled. The rain and cold which marked the day before yesterday continued in full force last night. Terrible day. Incessant rain. The rain filters through the badly kept earth roof and runs in little rivulets in our miserable rooms. I am one of the best off, and I have only a place for my bed in a corner protected from the rain. What to do? Sleep under a buffalo robe? All right, but still one can't always sleep. What boredom, gloom, cold, humidity, darkness! And no company! Everyone stays in his den, just the reverse of snails, which go out when it rains.

Thursday, August 13. The supply train has come back from Fort Stevenson. The first half arrived yesterday and the second today. Lt. Leonard arrived this afternoon, too, coming from Fort Buford. He is called as witness for Captain Wainwright and for Captain Piatt, after which he will be summoned for judgment himself. Last Sunday, when the steamboat *Lina Leoti,* on which he was traveling, was stopping at Fort Berthold, about forty Sioux suddenly appeared on the opposite bank and fired two volleys at the boat. No one was hit except a Mandan on the bank. The passengers armed with carbines gave a spirited reply. The Indians of Berthold did likewise, and the assailants quickly withdrew into the brush, where they disappeared. There is no doubt that the firearms used by the Sioux were a part of those that the peace commission so generously distributed to them. The results of this absurd policy of the government become more and more evident. Hostilities have flared anew among the Sioux, whom we intend to pacify by a generosity that was naturally taken to be fear. They accepted everything that we were willing to give them, and now they are using it to make war on us with more confidence and energy than ever. The only way to put an end to it is, first of all, to punish them soundly. As soon as they are convinced that we are the stronger, they will keep the peace. Until then, no.

Monday, August 24. The mail, which left for Stevenson yester-

154 Cornelius Cusick's name is sometimes spelled "Cussick" by De Trobriand in the journal.

day morning, was attacked by Indians at midday at Big Coulee. The men had unhitched the mules from the wagon, and with the blind imprudence which is characteristic of the soldier left to himself where there is no danger evident, they had left their weapons in the wagon. The sergeant had not placed any sentinel, thus disobeying the orders given him. That disobedience cost him his life, as well as those of his two men. Six Indians ambushed near there, seeing how our men neglected to protect themselves, waited until they were sitting on the ground eating their dinner before they approached by crawling up behind a rock situated about twenty paces away. From there, they fired on the group simultaneously, and, as I have just said, killed three men, among them the sergeant.

The other three ran for their arms, but it was too late. They could fire only from a distance on the assailants, who fled, taking advantage of the depressions in the ground. They ran off with the mules, which were lost in the encounter. Palmer, one of the couriers, arrived last night, bringing the fatal news. Immediately Colonel Whistler sent Captain Hill with thirty men in three wagons to bring back the mail wagon, if it has not been destroyed, as well as the soldiers who escaped being attacked. But the latter arrived in the evening. They had left on the spot the unharmed wagon, the mail, and the bodies of their three comrades, whose weapons they hid so they would not fall into the hands of the Indians if they came back, which is probable.

Tuesday, August 25. Captain Hill returned this morning, bringing the three bodies, which were not mutilated by the savages. The latter were satisfied with taking what they wanted from the wagon. They left the letters, correspondence, and newspapers, which were brought back today, and which we shall take with us when we go back to Fort Stevenson. Half of the detachment pushed on to meet the mail from Stevenson, and they will bring it back with them. Having been told about what has happened, our men will be on the lookout and will protect themselves, so the Indians will not have a chance to repeat the performance.

The session of the general court-martial, over which I presided, is closed, after having completed the trial of the three officers who were referred to it. So, without losing any time, I have decided to leave tomorrow for my general headquarters. Here are the distances between Fort Totten and Fort Stevenson, measured with the odometer:

From Totten to Big Coulee	35 miles
From Big Coulee to the Midway Station	28½ miles
From the Midway Station to Clear Lake	27½ miles
From Clear Lake to Stevenson	34 miles
Total	125 miles

(Equal to about 200 kilometers.)

Arrived here August 1, and we stayed twenty-five days, quite long enough to appreciate the good and bad features of the post. It is indisputable that the situation here is pleasant. Hunting is easy and plentiful, especially waterfowl of all kinds. The principal fish is perch, with which the lake is teeming. They weigh on the average, from six to ten pounds, and more than enough can be caught by trolling in a light skiff or by throwing out the line and bringing it it to the bank in little jerks. A piece of mother of pearl, metal, or even a rag is enough for this voracious fish. But for deep fishing, a piece of bacon or fish makes good bait.

[*The new post*] Since the government has decided to make Fort Totten a permanent post, probably because of its proximity to the border of the British possessions, the present temporary fort is going to be replaced by a much more important one, built by contractors who right now are busy with a host of workmen. They are making the necessary brick two or three miles from here. An abundance of timber for construction can be found in the surrounding country. The new fort will be built for eight companies, in case they are needed. Because of this, all the buildings are to have two floors, with an artesian well in the middle of the parade ground. In general, the plan is conceived on a large scale. The storehouses are huge, and the officers' quarters will leave nothing to be desired. Each of them will be large enough for one family and will have as many as possible of the comfortable contrivances which make the American home superior. The present fort will be left standing, and it will make a wonderful corral for the employees of the dept. of the quartermaster and for the animals and equipages.

The new fort is going up behind the old one, which it overlooks. So the view is more beautiful and interesting, for it takes in part of the lake and a great stretch of the prairies.

There are few Indians living near Fort Totten. These are half Sioux, Sissetons, and Santees, all more or less miserable, and living like dogs from the scraps of the garrison kitchen. In the winter they are more numerous, attracted by the hope that provisions will be distributed. Winter and summer, they live from hand to mouth and from day to day, not having any agriculture like our Indians at Berthold, who at least harvest corn, pumpkins, and other fruits of the earth.

Despite the work of the court-martial, the pleasures of hunting, and the temptations of fishing, I found time to make three oil paintings and some pencil sketches. They are something to add to my souvenirs of Dakota.

Wednesday, August 26. I postponed the time of leaving two or three hours to attend the burial of the three victims of the Indian ambush. The ceremony is going to take place this morning with military honors. The presence of all the officers had a good effect on the survivors.

Our party is more numerous going back to Stevenson than it was coming. It is reinforced by several officers: Major Furey, who is going to general headquarters with his clerk to settle some accounts with his successor; Lieutenant Lockwood, transferred to one of the companies in the garrison at Buford; and Lieutenant Leonard, who is returning to his post. This makes one more wagon added to our caravan.

P. S. The funeral ceremony took place; the three bodies were committed to the earth, which will not give them up. So, there are three for whom the troubles of this life are no more. Do they already know what we on this side of the tomb do not? And the great *perhaps?* Is it already decided for them? Questions with no possible answer, and therefore useless.

The wagons are hitched, the men at their posts. Goodbye to Fort Totten, its hospitable commandant, and the garrison. Everything is ready? Yes? Then let us be on our way, on our way to Stevenson. And here we are, off.

☞ ☞ ☞

Tuesday, September 1. And here we are back at Fort Stevenson. I feel the pleasure of a traveler home again. The stay at Fort Totten, in spite of the hunting, fishing, the lake, and the woods, does not make me sorry that the general headquarters for the department were not transferred there. All in all, I prefer Stevenson. The passing of the steamboats, the new faces that are seen from time to time, the news that they bring us from Montana or from the States, keep things moving here, unlike Totten. One feels bound to civilized life through those who come and go. It is a connection which for six months binds us to Sioux City, Omaha, St. Louis, and through these points to the rest of the world.

It was Saturday (August 29) when we arrived. Since we left July 28, we were gone a month. Nothing unusual marked our return, except a little way from Fort Totten, we met the mail from Stevenson, which Captain Hill had sent twelve men and a wagon to meet.

The sack was opened to take out the despatches addressed to me. The most important was given separately to the sergeant, who carried it on himself and hastened to give it to me, telling me that it was brought from Fort Buford by two Indian messengers with the recommendation that it get to me without delay. It was marked "Important," and the contents justified the label. It was the summary report of an attack by hostile Indians and their theft of almost the whole herd of cattle sent for the supply of fresh meat for the garrison during the winter and the next spring. Along with this was a requisition for a new herd of two hundred cattle to be sent immediately, before cold weather. I signed and approved the requisition on the spot, and gave it to the sergeant to be sent tomorrow morning to the general headquarters of the Department.

Now here are the facts in brief as they were given in the second, detailed report which arrived here by steamboat.

[*Indians steal cattle*] August 20, about three o'clock in the afternoon, two or three hundred Indians, divided into two bands, suddenly sprang out from the ravines in the badlands neighboring Fort Buford, near which the herd was grazing that day. At the first sign of attack, the mounted guards hurried to push the animals toward the fort; but they were soon forced to turn and face the band of redskins, which was coming on them. They were just twenty men against one hundred or one hundred and fifty. In spite of this, they would have been able to hold off their assailants long enough to save the cattle if the second band, which they had not yet noticed, had not come between the herd and the fort. These last, by making a furious clamor, shaking their buffalo robes, firing at the cattles' noses, threw the herd into panic and disorder, and it fell back pell-mell on the drovers, through whom they passed, mad with terror, chased by the redskins. The two bands then came together to surround the twenty guards, while the others ran the cattle toward the gorges of the badlands. Our men fought bravely and in close combat, for several were struck with war clubs, among others, Lieutenant Cussick, officer of the day, who had rushed up at the first alarm. But all they could do was to fall back by cutting their way through the Indians to the infantry, which dashed up to the rescue.

At Fort Buford, as at Fort Stevenson, everybody was busy with construction work. All the men were at work. They ran for their arms immediately and dashed at the attackers; but they were all mounted, and so it was impossible to come to close quarters with them. So they had to be satisfied with recovering all they could of the cattle which had strayed from the herd. Some of the animals were rather seriously wounded; others had been killed by the Indians who shot with arrows those which stayed behind.

Major Dickey, commanding the post in the absence of Lieutenant Colonel Bowman, immediately mounted all the men he could find horses for, and a running skirmish went on for several miles. It was no use. We were able to save about forty cattle from about 240 to 250, the number of the herd.

The next day, Bt. Major, Captain Little was sent with two companies to try to gather up those of the stolen animals that were left on the way. He found nothing but a number of carcasses. In the evening or early in the morning, the herd had been taken to the other side of the Missouri. In addition to the loss of around two hundred cattle, this affair has cost us three men killed and three seriously wounded. Lieutenant Cussick will get off cheaper than that. They say that he owes his life to one of his men who ran up to rescue him when he was grappling with the redskins, and this man was himself killed for this act of devotion.

Although the first despatch received en route did not contain all these details, our knowledge of the outcome took the joy from our homecoming. It was the day for solemn consideration. Around noon, or one o'clock (August 26), we arrived at Big Coulee, where the three men from Fort Totten had been killed three days before. The first thing I did was to dismount and examine the ground. The spot of the murder was clearly marked by three spots of blood where the victims had been hit and where the bodies had been found by Captain Hill. It was on a small projecting plateau surrounded by a ravine. The six Indians had slipped up the slope and then had crawled behind a large rock. From this point they had fired at a distance of twenty paces on the group of soldiers who were nonchalantly eating their dinner, sitting on the ground near the unhitched wagon. Not one of them had his gun. The arms were all in the wagon. One of the couriers who had just gone to water his horse at the neighboring spring and who had taken his carbine with him had for this act been the butt of the soldiers' jokes. So he was afraid the Indians were coming to attack him? He was a cautious man, etc. Scarcely five minutes had passed before three of the jokers were struck dead by Indian bullets. They perished, victims of their utter carelessness in protecting themselves and of their disobedience to orders received. If the sergeant had only placed a man on watch at the edge of the plateau, not an Indian could have approached without being seen, for the ravine is as bare as your hand, and there is not a bush where a rabbit could hide. But the Indians posted somewhere in the neighborhood saw right away that our men did not have their weapons and that they were not keeping watch around them; they got the idea of surprising them, and this in full daylight on the open plain, although they were only six against eight. It is probable that they figured they would come up as friends to exchange handshakes and beg some bits of provisions if they were discovered. But everything going as they wished, they fired their shots and fled, running away with the mules, which were frightened by the gunfire.

We spent the night by the spring, on the same spot where we had camped before on the way to Totten.

The next day (August 27) we met near Buffalo Lake the first half of the transport train, between the two posts, about eighty wagons. In the afternoon, we camped at Five Lakes (midway station) where we killed a good supply of game for our table. (Among other feats, I brought down five ducks with one shot.)

In the night there took place an incident that is, unfortunately, too characteristic, one which proves the extent of the vice of drunkenness among a number of officers, especially among the old officers of the regular army. Lt. Col. Bowman filled himself with whiskey and became so drunk that he made a scene by yelling, insulting the sentinels, and disturbing the peace part of the night. And this without temptation, without provocation, all by himself, simply for love of the thing. Until then he had slept in my tent; I have sent him to sleep out under the stars. The next day I forbade him to use my ambulance, and I sent him to another wagon with the lieutenants. Finally, when we got back to Fort Stevenson, where he will have to stay for a time because of the lack of means of transportation, my first official act in reassuming command was to put him under arrest, until a new order, "for drunkenness and riotous conduct at middle station, during the night of twenty-seventh–twenty-eighth of August, 1868." This order written, entered at the post, sent to the general headquarters of the Department with the others, ought to bring him a humiliating and beneficial punishment; but one cannot count on the reform of drunkards. Already at Fort Totten during the session of the court-martial of which he was a member and where he was sitting in judgment of other officers being tried for drunkenness, he had slipped twice—*on Saturday night* (notice the precaution; the court did not sit on Sunday), to drink enough to be noisy and to make a spectacle of himself before the lower ranking officers. I had severely reprimanded him for forgetting decorum and duty, and he had solemnly promised me that if I would pardon this first offense, he would not do it again. And see what has happened five days later! He certainly deserves to be called before court-martial; but it is so difficult to call together a court for an officer of his rank in our frontier posts that we are forced to have recourse to it only as a last resort. Nevertheless, this will happen to him if he does not mend his ways, and although he does not come to trial, the fact that there are charges and specifications against him will be enough to deprive him of his command at Buford. Let's hope, however, that the sinner is converted rather than killed.[155]

The day of the twenty-eighth was terrible. A biting, damp, penetrating cold kept us wrapped in our blankets and buffalo robes until we got to Clear Lake, where the weather became milder and the sun finally began to shine. The second part of the transport train passed us in the morning. In the evening, some Indians were spotted in the distance, but they hurried away. They acted wisely.

Finally, the twenty-ninth, at three o'clock in the afternoon, after a halt at Spring Lake and another at Red Water, both marked by more killing of ducks, plovers, curlews, etc., we set foot on Stevenson, happy to have reached the end of our trip and with the prospect of "rest at home" before us. I had some idea of reporting at Fort Buford; but I shall be satisfied with sending my district inspector there. I have had enough of traveling for the time being.

Captain (Bt. Major) Clarke, who commanded the post in my absence, lived up to his reputation. He pushed the work forward energetically, and the appearance of the fort has changed since my departure. My future house, which had only bare walls standing all year, is now covered with a roof. The chimneys are built, the partitions and windows in place; everything lathed and covered with the first layer of gray plaster, well made of mud, cement, and lime. Of course the floors are in place. A second house is covered too. It contains two complete apartments for officers. A third, which still had only its stone foundation, is now erected, and the framework for the roof is up. I

155 By special order no. 24, August 29, 1868, Bowman was placed under arrest. He was released by special order no. 30, September 12, 1868, then placed under arrest again, for drunkenness on duty, by special order no. 21, January 16, 1869. Special Orders, Department of Dakota, War Records Division, National Archives.

relieved the band for a while and put the musicians in extra service in the depot of the quartermaster for lathing and shingling roofs, work which is familiar to them, for they did it last year. This reinforcement of workers will shorten that much the time of the work and will effectively speed it up. The new wing of the hospital is built, too, but still does not have its roof.

All these jobs would be even farther along if two unfortunate accidents had not happened, one right after the other. The quarters of the band, the lodging of the bandmaster, and the different offices were constructed in a new building divided into three main parts. One would think that the walls would be solid enough and that the framework could be dispensed with since they were made 18 inches thick, that is, increasing to 18 to 8¾ the dimensions of the new adobes, which were 12½ up to 6 before. But it so happened that when the walls were built, a devilish storm came, with a torrential rain lasting 24 hours. The adobes dissolved quickly, parts of the wall crumbled, and the rest of the work had to be torn down. They had worked ten days at it. After this experience, we are going back to framework and to the 12-inch adobes, convinced more than ever of the truth of the adage that better is sometimes the enemy of good. We had believed that we were introducing an improvement by imitating what was done in New Mexico, country *par excellence* of adobe. But we had reckoned without the climate, which down there easily hardens them like brick and which here, considering their 4-inch thickness, just dries them slowly and not enough. Since the smallest kind is the thinnest, it is much better for Dakota, especially in a calamitous summer like this one.

Troubles never come singly. The second accident is the result of an unexpected three-foot rise in the river. We had several rafts tied up at the wharf, which completed Anderson's contract for supplying the timber. The rise and the proportionate increase in the strength of the current shook the logs from the rafts, frayed and broke the tie ropes, and so two hundred logs were carried away by the river. It was impossible to recover them. So, another contract must be made with Mr. Anderson. The thing is settled, and he will go out again to cut down more trees and repair the loss; but this means stopping the sawmill for a week and a corresponding slowing down of the carpenter work.

In spite of everything, the time will not be wasted, and the work on other things will be pushed, the corral, for example, where there is a granary to be built and immense shelters to protect the cattle in the winter. The slabs were put aside for this purpose; and when the work on one thing is stopped, it can be continued on another. Right now the post looks less like a military post than a huge construction yard. Arms are replaced by the trowel, saw, plane, etc.

The paymaster, Major [Jesse] Bowen, came from Rice *by land* to pay the garrison for the last two months. The last company will be paid tomorrow morning, after which he will return with the escort which brought him, and will leave for Omaha, still by land, as he came, after paying on his way the garrisons of Rice, Sully, and Randall.

Wednesday, September 2. Departure of Doctor C. C. Gray. The doctor is transferred to Fort Sully and is replaced by Dr. [Charles E.] Goddard, who was at Rice before and who arrived here during my absence. Dr. Gray's leaving is regretted. He is a distinguished surgeon and a man of pleasant manners. Mrs. Gray is a charming person, whose departure will leave a great void in our little society. The steamboat *North Alabama* took away the doctor, his family, and all his belongings.

Friday, September 4. We had an alert during the day. It was rumored that the Sioux were crossing the river in great numbers opposite the badlands. Consequently, we got ready to receive them, but, as it turned out, there were no Sioux. The Indians spotted by the men working on the prairie for Gerard were Gros Ventres, Rees, and Mandans, and they had not crossed the river. They had come down in great numbers to a point opposite the badlands because this morning seven Sioux, believing themselves sufficiently protected by the river, came to the bank across from Berthold, more for bravado than anything else, and shot at our Indians who were on the other side. Immediately the warriors of the Gros Ventres, Rees, and Mandans ran for their horses, and crossing the Missouri in their bull boats, gave chase to the seven impudent Indians. They overtook one of them across from the badlands and, according to the custom, killed him, scalped him, and hacked him up. The steamboat *North Alabama* passed by Berthold just as they were returning, bringing back the feet and hands of the victim in triumph. This is the way we got the first details of the affair. There will be dances and celebrations at Berthold for a week. It is a rather strange fact that the one who killed the Sioux is the same young Mandan who killed the other one at the beginning of summer. Here is a young fellow who will become chief if his career is not terminated.

Tuesday, September 8. The steamboat *Andrew Ackley* brings us news that the Indians have attacked five men located above Buford cutting wood for the steamboats. The captain, who had stopped near there to make some repairs, heard the shooting, and sent his yawl with a dozen armed men to the aid of the woodcutters. Two of the latter were already seriously wounded, not only with arrows but with bullets and buckshot. The steamboat brought them all to Buford, where the two wounded men are in the hands of the surgeons. I have prepared a long report to General Terry and Lt. General Sherman on the hostilities in my district, and in this report I have not softened the truth about the bad effects of the policy adopted by the government and the deplorable results of the distribution of arms and ammunition to the Indians, especially after the weakness shown in abandoning, in the face of their threats to reopen hostilities, the three military posts built at great expense in the valley of the Powder River. Will this report have any result? I do not know. In any case, I shall have done my duty by pointing out the evil, even if the high authorities do not provide any remedies for it.

Thursday, September 10. A band of Indians, evidently friendly, since they had with them their lodges and their families, appeared this morning on the hills some distance from the fort. Soon a number approached on foot, apparently intending to come to the post. They were promptly met by Lt. Leonard, officer of the day, who, accompanied by the interpreter, went to find out who they were. Some unarmed soldiers, a part of the supply train, the first section of which arrived from Totten yesterday, joined them, and thus found themselves among the Indians, who were not expecting this visit. It did not take the men from Totten long to recognize several redskins who were a part of the band which at the beginning of summer made an attempt to steal the mules at Devils Lake. One in particular, White Faced Bear, was positively identified by one of the soldiers. Moreover, they had with them three cattle, which must have been from the herd stolen at Fort Buford, from which place they have just come, and two mules branded "U.S.," property of the United States. The officer of the day took from one Indian a Sharps rifle which the latter claimed he had bought from Galpin, the trader at Fort Rice. But when he wanted to take the mules, he met with lively opposition, and the *friendly* Indians began to load their guns. As the officer of the day was alone with three or four unarmed men, and as the Indians promised that as soon as their camp was made they would bring the animals in themselves and explain to me how they got them, he let them go, and returned to make his report. Scarcely had he turned his back when the Indians, instead of camping as they had announced, hurriedly made a getaway with their booty. Now do you want to know which band it is that has men who have taken part in the hostilities against our posts, who have stolen cattle and mules? It is the band of Black Eyes, those friendly Yanktonahs who live at Fort Rice, where the government feeds them, clothes them, and arms them. Black Eyes himself was with them, Black Eyes, that inveterate beggar of beggars, an Indian who goes from post to post, offering his hand and protesting his devotion to the whites in order to obtain provisions. This was his fourth visit to Fort Stevenson; but this one was short and profited him little, as can be seen. If he comes back, I shall discourage him from these mercenary visits for good. Meanwhile, I am going to denounce him in a new report to general headquarters. We shall see what will come of it, and whether Lt. General Sherman, now appointed as superintendent of Indian affairs, will authorize me to punish these impudent vagabonds who come strolling around my post with the animals stolen from another post under my command.

P. S. The Sharps rifle taken from the hands of a Yanktonah Indian and placed in my lodging was recognized as the very same one that the band of Sitting Bull had stolen from Joe Martin, one of our couriers, when he was captured with Brown near Dog Den at the end of last May. Joe Martin recognized it at the first glance, and showed me double letters made with a knife on the butt end, a mark which makes any doubt impossible. Still another proof of the connivance existing between most of the supposedly *friendly* Indians and the avowed hostile ones. Besides, suppose the man told the truth (which is hardly probable), that he did buy this weapon from Galpin, it would still be interesting to make an investigation about the type of trade by which a government weapon stolen by hostile Indians was sold at Fort Rice to a friendly Indian by a trader in the employ of the government.

Sunday, September 20. Finally, a steamboat going up the river arrived. She is the first for more than a month. The *Benton* is going up to Buford. She had about twenty tons of merchandise for the N. W. Fur Company store at this post, the same amount for Berthold, and the same amount for Buford. Lieutenant Colonel Bowman, lieutenants Lockwood and Leonard, who were waiting here for a chance to get back to their posts at Buford, hurried to get on board the

Benton. Captain Clarke has gone with them to review a decision of the court-martial for which his presence was necessary, and I sent out Captain Norwell to make his second inspection of the post. These two officers will return by the same boat in about a week.

Tuesday, September 22. The equinox brings us winter. A violent and biting wind, whipping gusts of snow before it, this is what we have here from the month of September on! We had a right to expect better of fall, for the summer has been comparatively so cold and humid that there was reason to expect compensations from the months of September, October, and November. But if the two latter are like this one, it can be said that this year the seasons are really unsettled. A summer of two weeks, when usually there are three full months of dryness and torrid heat; and to make it more irregular, the whole month of September has a temperature usual for the end of October, with sharp winds from the north, and finally snow, the day of the equinox! Our workers curse and swear about this state of things; it is something to swear about.

Another steamboat: the *Bertha* arrived yesterday, like the *Benton* going to Buford. She is loaded with ammunition, engines, and other articles for each of our posts, and brought a large amount of grain to General Harney, who is setting up on the Grand River, around a hundred miles below Rice, the depot of the Sioux Indian reservation, which he commands.[156] I have received the order to send him three thousand bushels of corn, which I am going to send by these two boats when they come down from Buford. From all appearances, the *Bertha* will be the last boat going up the river this season. The early arrival of cold weather will undoubtedly stop any more trips.

Thursday, September 24. Fine weather, but yesterday morning thirteen degrees F., and this morning twelve F.; that is, twenty degrees below freezing point. And this is the month of September. That's promising for winter.

Monday, September 28. This evening the *Bertha* came back from Buford, bringing Bt. Major Clarke and Captain Norwell. They stayed there only a few hours, but this short time was enough for the one to preside over a session of court-martial and to modify a

156 The Hunkpapa, Yanktonai, Cut Heads, and Blackfeet Sioux came in to this agency on the Grand River. By September 26, when the agent made his report, 4,500 Indians had gathered there. *Report of the Commissioner of Indian Affairs for the Year 1869*, p. 318–319.

faulty judgment, and for the other to inspect the post and to condemn certain articles as beyond service. The steamboat can carry only two hundred sacks of corn to General Harney on the Grand River where he is establishing the general headquarters of the Sioux reserve. I have fifteen hundred of them to get to him. I doubt that the only two steamboats which are still up river can take them. *Vedremo*.

By the *Bertha*, I have just received a report from Bt. Major Dickey which informs me that on the eighteenth of this month four soldiers, who were hunting around the fort, about one kilometer from what is left of the herd, were suddenly attacked by a dozen Indians. One of them was mortally wounded and the others certainly would have lost their lives, too, if the mounted herders had not dashed to their rescue. The Indians were pursued, but to no avail. They hurriedly crossed the river and left only their bull boats in the hands of the pursuers.

Change in the weather. The days are warm now, as they ought to be in October, and unusually so, for the thermometer went up to seventy-four F. This sudden change produces a thick haze which fills the air and wraps us in a blue-white fog through which the sun looks like a burning red moon.

Monday, October 5. Today I moved into my new house. Finally! I am sleeping in it for the first time tonight. It is a great change, leaving that dark cavern where I have just spent more than nine months between walls made of logs and mud, under a low sod roof where the mice had chosen their home and where they had multiplied rapidly and where they put on a shindy every night by running around on the old canvases which took the place of a ceiling. From this dingy and squalid cabin, I have now moved into at least a presentable and comfortable lodging. My house has five rooms. It is separated into two parts by a hall; on the right, the living room, dining room, and kitchen; on the left, two bedrooms. Above, servants' rooms and an attic to store furniture. The walls are painted in imitation of woodwork, and of course, in different colors; white, like the ceilings, or maroon as in the living room, or lilac-gray in the bedrooms, and a grayish-red in the dining room. My furniture is quite sufficient. In brief, here I am comfortably and pleasantly installed for the winter. It's a great thing!

Tuesday, October 13. The herd of cattle from Fort Totten has just arrived under a strong escort commanded by Captain Hill, accompanied by lieutenants Smith and Hoffman [*sic*]. I was not expecting it so soon, and I was not prepared until Friday to send mine to Fort Buford where it is to replace the herd which was almost all stolen by the Indians. The one from Fort Ransom will replace Fort Totten's, and finally, the one from Abercrombie will be sent to Fort Ransom, and a new one will replace it. It is much quicker to make these changes than to send a new herd the whole distance from St. Cloud or Abercrombie to Buford. The trip would have taken the cattle about six weeks, while in this way all these posts will have a new supply in fifteen or twenty days. I am sending 110 head of cattle to Buford, and am receiving only 94 in exchange; but that doesn't matter. This last figure is entirely enough (with six cattle more than we are authorized to keep) to supply our needs for fresh meat until next summer.

Wednesday, October 14. Captain Hill did not lose a moment in getting under way this morning to return to Fort Totten with his detachment. Captain Norwell, whom I sent on his fall inspection, also left with the mail and its escort, since it was the day for the courier.

Friday, October 16. My herd of cattle started on its way to Buford this morning, escorted by the whole first company under the command of first Lt. Hooton, accompanied by second Lieutenant Walborn. Assistant Surgeon Bean is going along with the detachment in case of an encounter with the hostile Indians who, I am told, are approaching Berthold at this very moment to trade horses for corn with the Rees and the Gros Ventres there. The detachment is composed of seventy-two men, plus wagoners, a guide, and four Indian scouts. This is quite enough to take care of all the hostile Unkpapahs; but they will probably cause no trouble. The first company will remain at Fort Buford permanently, where it will replace in the garrison company K (Capt. and Bvt. Major Clarke) which I am keeping here. Lt. Walborn will bring back with him the wagons furnished to the first company for its baggage, supplies, under the escort of a party of the men who are entitled to their discharge because of the expiration of their term of service during the winter.

Saturday, October 31. The second two weeks of the month went by with no particular happenings. The hostile Unkpapahs came as they had announced to trade with our Indians at Berthold. They brought their women and their lodgings, which assured peaceful intentions on their part, made their camp on the other side of the Mis-

souri, and for a few days there was great activity as they crossed back
and forth in their bull boats. The three tribes acquired about fifty
horses in exchange for corn, after which they parted, and the Unkpapahs took the Little Missouri route.

I have explained in another place that these truces between the
savages are customary when there is profit for both sides in trading
peacefully at a stated rendezvous. They smoke the peace pipe; they
exchange handshakes and friendly speeches. Then, once they part,
they kill and scalp each other when they meet as if there had been
no friendly dealing.

This would have been a good chance to strike a real blow and
to deal out exemplary punishment to the Unkpapahs for their misdeeds, especially since the famous Sitting Bull, The Man Who Jumps
into the Fray, Red Horn, and some other chiefs were in the party.
But for this, we should have to have at our disposal one hundred and
fifty to two hundred men. They would cross the river by Stevenson,
march in the night, and at dawn surround the Indian camp, then
wipe them out. Unfortunately, the whole first company was on the
way to Buford, forty-five men of company F were discharged from
service, and almost all the rest were busily engaged in the work that
must be completed before winter, which does not give us a minute
to lose. Moreover, in the absence of specific orders, it is undoubtedly
better not to go to war right now since the government is not prepared to take on the job. The active war which is being waged
against the Indians of Kansas and Arkansas, the Cheyennes, Arapa-
hos, Kiowas, Comanches, etc., the expedition sent against them
by Sheridan, and the mobile columns sent to protect the settlers, all
absorb the available military forces in the division of the Missouri,
and there would be left nothing but our weak garrisons in Dakota in
case of a general uprising of the Sioux. So we must be patient; everything will come in time. Encouraged by the security which they enjoyed this time, the hostile Indians will come back next year, and
we shall again have the chance lost this year, and under favorable
circumstances from which we can profit. In regard to information,
the peaceful visit of the Unkpapahs near Berthold has not been without some results. It enabled us to find out that the three soldiers
killed at Big Coulee August 24 were murdered by six Indians, self
styled *friends,* from Fort Rice, three Blackfeet Sioux, and three Yanktonahs, and that the attack and stealing of the cattle at Fort Buford
was the work of the Tetons and various wandering bands gathered
together for this purpose. (See my official report on this subject.)

Sunday, November 1. Nothing but arrivals and departures. A few days ago, some of the wagons of Mr. Anderson, the contractor, left for St. Paul, taking twenty men discharged from the service. As many left by the river in two flatboats, one of which they bought, and the other they built. Tomorrow, or the day after, the five wagons furnished to transport the belongings for the first company to Buford will arrive. Fifty men coming from Buford to get their discharge here will form the escort. The others are expected at any time by boat on the river. The first ones went by last week on board the *Hiram Wood*, the last boat of the season.

Monday, November 2. The paymaster arrived from Fort Rice today. He took advantage of a convoy of a few wagons bringing us 120 sacks of potatoes. With them were 17 cattle which, added to the 94 brought from Fort Totten, will replace the 110 we sent to Fort Buford. This is even a gain, if I know how to count.

Tuesday, November 3. Col. [Edward] Wright, the paymaster, did not waste any time. Although the season was still very fine and we have been greatly enjoying St. Martin's summer for about three weeks, he fears a change of weather and the beginning of winter. Spurred on by this fear, which is certainly not without foundation, he paid everyone in one day, and got on his way to return to Rice and from there to Sully, Randall, Dakota, Sioux City, and Omaha, paying the troops at each of the posts on his itinerary. His departure was marked by an event, the possible consequences of which I still do not know; consequently, I shall not tell about it until tomorrow.

[*Prairie fire*] The event I alluded to yesterday was a great fire on the prairies, which was blown toward us by the wind and which we watched with anxiety. It first showed up in the afternoon, a drifting mass of smoke, which formed an enormous fawn-colored cloud blown along by a northwest wind. As the wind increased from one minute to the next, it was very difficult to estimate how far away the fire was. Nevertheless, it was evident even at the distance separating us from the fire that the extent of the blaze appeared to be considerable. In fact, when a strong wind lifted or parted the vast curtain of smoke which began to darken the sun, red, white, and brown columns could be clearly seen spiralling up on the horizon beyond the bluffs. This was the situation when at sunset the paymaster and his escort, commanded by Bvt. Major [William] Nelson of the 22nd infantry, started out. He was returning to Fort Rice; that is, going in the opposite direction from the fire, and he was counting on a start of two or three hours, camping on the other side of Snake Creek, ten miles away, in order to be protected in any eventuality by the stream of water. But he had scarcely left when the first tongues of fire appeared on the top of the bluffs. Almost immediately, with a rapidity that no one can imagine unless he has seen a fire on the prairies, the flames driven by a strong wind ran across the crest of the hill, and the whole line of the heights was crowned by a brilliant light, so much the more brilliant since it was already night. The flaming line reached Snake Creek much more quickly than any harnessed horse could walk, and so we began to feel quite worried about the paymaster and his escort whom we were expecting to see come back at great speed at any moment. When the flames had come down the hills and, crossing the prairie, had reached the bank of the Missouri east of Fort Stevenson, and the detachment had not showed up, the impossibility of their back-tracking certainly did not reassure us, and we knew that their only chance was to get to the ford of the little river as quickly as they could, or if they hadn't time for this, to throw themselves on the sands which on that side border the course of the Missouri in places. However, it wasn't long before we had enough worries of our own to occupy us.

The first flames appearing on the bluffs were directly north, about a mile from the fort. As the wind was blowing in an east-south-east direction, they had not come down onto our pastures, and while their vanguard was devouring everything toward Snake Creek, the rear guard was dying out for lack of fuel, and the center, driven by the wind, was going down the hills obliquely, about two miles away. So the fort was safe, and what worried us more than the fort were the four huge stacks of hay amounting to three hundred tons, the corral, and the stables and the wood yard, all of which were nearer to the fire (two hundred to three hundred meters) than our buildings.

But just at the time we thought we were getting off with only a harmless alert, a new conflagration was whipped up by the wind into a great red flame, the nucleus of which grew in intensity with every moment. Everyone had his eyes on this new danger which was advancing as rapidly as the first. But the general opinion was that this second fire, or rather, this second column of the fire, would burn itself out on the edge of the ground already devastated where there wasn't a blade of grass left. This forecast seemed doubtful to me, for this time the fire was running at us; it could get to the top of the bluffs on this side of the burned land, come down onto the plateau, and then! In any case, I gave the necessary commands so everyone would be ready to leave at the first order. All the men were ordered to their quarters, although it was not yet the hour of taps, and all the officers were on the alert. It is a good thing I took these precautions.

Scarcely a quarter of an hour had gone by when the fire came down the hills like a torrent of lava from a row of craters. It enveloped the pasture and ran crackling toward the houses of the traders on one side and toward our stacks of hay on the other.

My servant was the first to warn me. I went out immediately, and a glance was enough to show me clearly the extent of the danger. I sprang onto the parade ground and shouted in a loud voice: "Everybody out!" The officer of the day, who came out of the guardhouse, ran to his company immediately. I ran to the other, and opening the door abruptly, repeated my command to the men who were grouped around the stoves talking and who had not heard at first. At this moment, all the officers were coming out of their quarters, and the sergeants were forming their men into squads. First they ran to a pile of willows that I had the prisoners cut below the fort and pile by the guardhouse when the fire first appeared. Everyone took a handful of them to fight the fire. Those who could not get any equipped themselves with anything they could find: old sacks, old brooms, switches, etc., and on my orders, they ran out to the fire to fight it as well as they could. Naturally, the men divided into two bands to face the two advances of the enemy. I myself led one of them where the encroachment of the fire was threatening the stacks of hay. The other band with most of the officers rushed to the side where the traders' houses, their wood, and their fodder were in the most immediate danger.

One can imagine that the sixty or eighty men who were working under my eyes and under my personal direction did not spare any pains; but it is a hard job to put out a dry-grass fire when a strong wind is blowing. Everyone beat down the flames, stamped on the burning cinders, raked the flaming grass with these long willows shaped like a broom, or went at it with empty sacks, but in vain. The fire beaten out at one point immediately sprang up at another. When the wind died down a second, or changed its direction a little so that the flames were thrown back on the ashes, the whole line advanced, and the scourge was mastered for a moment. But then came a new gust which drove the flames toward us, and blinded, suffocated, and burned, we were routed. We charged again as soon as we got a deep breath of air, especially when the fire got to the places where the grass was shorter, because it had either been trampled underfoot or eaten off by the animals. In spite of all our efforts, the fire gained on us more and more and forced us to beat retreat for a hundred yards or more. Wishing to give an example to the men, I stood my ground, inhaling burning and suffocating smoke, which for a moment made me so dizzy that I saw all red or not at all. What more could we accomplish by battling this way? We got to a road made by the carts used to get stones from the bluffs for the masonry of the fort. I knew that this was our best chance, and calling to me all the men who were fighting the fire on the flanks, I placed them across the line along which the flames were racing. This first line fought the fire as it died out at the edge of the beaten road, and a second line put out in the rear all the flakes of fire or sparks which, lashed by the wind, rekindled the fire in the dry grass on the other side. Once the vanguard was stopped, we worked back, and since the ground was in the most favorable condition there, we finally stopped and put out the fire on this side.

What we had done at this point, the other detachment was doing on the side of the traders' houses. But since the grass was shorter and thinner on their side, their task was less difficult. In spite of everything, they were unable to stop the fire until it got to the cemetery, about two hundred yards from the first building. Farther on, the fire crossed two beaten roads and did not stop until it got to the edge of the embankment, below which are the willow thickets. There it went out, and what had been our danger became our protection. In fact, from this time on, the fort was completely surrounded on three sides by a large zone of ashes and burnt earth. Since the Missouri and its banks of sand formed the fourth side, from then on the fire could run in any direction on the prairies. No matter which direction the wind was blowing, it could not get to us, and had to go out at the edge of that black sea of burnt ground, in the middle of which Fort Stevenson and the surrounding lands for a radius of about a hundred yards rose like an island. From then on, our isolation was our security. I stayed on with several men to put out the little fires which still smoldered under the ashes for an hour or two, either in the roots or tufts of grass, or in dried dung. At the hour of taps (eight o'clock), everything had returned to normal. Everyone could go to bed with no worry and in perfect security.

The paymaster and his escort were safe, too, on the other side of the mouth of Snake Creek on the sands of the river. Two Indians sent out on reconnaissance brought back this satisfactory news.

Since the wind had shifted to the north, we still had a few hours to admire the wonderful sight of the flames running like infernal squadrons on the crest of the bluffs, on the prairie, on all the undulations of ground on the other side of Douglas Creek. There it did not lack fuel. It was a splendid and many-colored illumination, something like a distant city going up in flames. But no, any comparison is inaccurate because of the speed of the fire's course, which can be seen only on the plains in this season of the year. The night was still glowing when I went to bed. The next day when I got up, the whole countryside was in mourning, and from east to west and over to the north, as far as the eye could see, there was nothing but black ashes and burnt earth. There is nothing more dreary, but the countryside will not be saddened long. It won't be long before the snow with its white mantle will cover the traces of the fire.

Sunday, November 8. We did not have to wait long for the predicted snow. It fell during part of the day and hides from our eyes the blackened grass which like crepe seemed to put the countryside in mourning.

Tuesday, November 10. The snow continued to fall spasmodically yesterday, with the result that on the average, the total depth is not more than three or four inches. Today the weather is clear, but terribly cold. This morning the thermometer went down to below zero Fahrenheit (eighteen degrees centigrade). This is promising for the first two weeks of November.

Wednesday, November 11. The cold continues. Very soon the soldiers will stop escorting the mail by wagon, and the couriers will carry it with dog teams hitched to small sleds *ad hoc*. So today I sent out a detachment of four wagons and twelve men to build three cabins for stations, the first at Sulphur Spring Lake, the second at Clear Lake, and the third at Stony Creek. At the same time, I sent Col. Whistler an order to send out another detachment to build a cabin at "middle station" and at the other intermediary points in the direction of Totten. The men take with them all necessary materials: the cabins are built of slabs under the direction of Brown. The river is filled with much drift ice. It will not take long to freeze if the cold continues.

Friday, November 13. The cold is letting up considerably. The snow is melting in the sun, and the blackened ground left by the fire is showing through everywhere. Our men will have much better weather to build their shelters.

Monday, November 16. Yesterday it was colder than ever; the river which was almost free of ice is beginning to freeze over. Brown and his men are back after building their three shelters. They did not see an Indian. Now it is the season when we can feel confident that we are rid of them until spring. Nevertheless, we had a false alarm this morning. Around noon, one of our Indian scouts who had gone toward Snake Creek looking for some of their ponies that he thought had wandered away in the brush, found a sack of corn, a load of wood, and a picket rope of the mule which our two couriers had taken with them as usual in the morning when they left to pick up the correspondence from Fort Rice. Red Dog, that is the name of our Indian, came back on the gallop, bringing these articles to give the alarm in case it was as they feared, and our two couriers had been attacked, robbed, and perhaps captured or killed. However, Red Dog did not return before he thoroughly examined the spot, and he assured us that he had discovered no trace of Sioux, although he had scoured the brush and prairie. I immediately ordered two wagons and a detachment of twenty men under the command of a sergeant to scout around and to capture or kill any Sioux they met in the neighborhood. The herders on horseback and the Indian scouts left with the detachment, but they did not go far. Half a mile away, they met a hunter who had seen the two couriers at Snake Creek in the morning. They had told him that since the mule was lame and was slowing them up considerably, they were going to leave it behind with its saddle pack, asking him to bring it back and report when he got back to the fort. Before returning, he continued his hunt all morning, and so caused the false alarm. The detachment turned back immediately, pleased to see the expedition over before it started, for a twenty degree cold made it quite unpleasant.

Tuesday, November 17. The ice blocks pressed in the narrow confines of the double channel, which is formed by a huge sand bank in the middle of the river (the water is very low) stopped and joined together last night between nine and ten o'clock. However, it cannot be said that the river is completely frozen over, for there are still spaces of running water here and there through the barrier of motionless ice blocks. But with this exception, the natural bridge of ice which joins the two banks all along the Missouri is now in place. In two or three days, unless the temperature becomes too mild, we shall be able to cross on foot and hunt in the thicket over on the other bank.

Thursday, November 19. A courier from Buford brings us mail and will take back letters and official documents. Nothing new from there. Some of our men crossed on the ice today to go hunting on the other bank of the river. And so the river crossing is regularly opened for the winter.

Monday, November 23. Lieutenant Walborn died this morning after a few days' sickness—a victim of whiskey. He was only twenty-three years old and seemed to have a robust constitution. I do not know where or when he acquired the habit of drinking to excess; probably during the war in volunteer service; but the fact is that he was fatally encouraged in the habit because of the way his constitution resisted the effect of liquor. When he had consumed enough to make two or three ordinary men drunk, he still had full use of his brain, his tongue, and his legs; his ideas were still clear, his language distinct, and he walked straight. Briefly, since the whiskey did not make him tipsy, he had confidence in this peculiarity of his constitution, and he drank terrible quantities. Here no one can buy liquor from the traders without a permit signed by me. So Walborn had to come to me often to ask me to sign for a gallon of whiskey. One day, about six weeks ago, I could not refrain from telling him that he alone was drinking more whiskey than all of the officers of the garrison together; this, moreover, was not an exaggeration, all the other officers being remarkably moderate in this respect. "That is possible, General," he answered, "but what difference does it make if my service is not affected by it?" "It is true," I went on, "that your service is not affected by it, and that I have never seen you under the influence of drink. That is why I sign the permits that you bring to me. But as friend rather than commandant, let me warn you against the sad consequences of this terrible habit, if you do not reform. You assume that whiskey does not hurt you because it does not make you drunk, even very strong doses of it. Make no mistake. You are ruining your constitution more surely and more quickly because the liquor they sell here is of the lowest quality. It is really poison, slow but sure. You will go in a year, two years, five or six years perhaps, believing you are all right. But some day or other you will pay the price; the crisis will come, and it will be all the more violent for the delay, and then you will suddenly wake up with a ruined stomach, health wrecked beyond repair, and perhaps facing an open grave."

Walborn listened to me attentively, seemed to be touched by the personal interest I was showing in him, and thanked me for it expressively. Of course his life did not change, and my prediction materialized, fatally, only much sooner than I had thought. I had given him a few years, and he did not last two months from that day. We shall bury him tomorrow with military honors. He leaves here a young widow and two small boys. At this season of the year, the poor woman cannot go back to her family. She will have to stay here all winter near the temporary grave of her husband, whose body I believe she intends to take with her when the first steamboat coming back from Fort Benton affords her means of transport. In any case, this will not be before the month of June.[157]

A report from Berthold informs us that three Gros Ventres were killed by the Sioux on the other side of the river. A small number of Sioux appeared on the bluffs across from the fort, disguised as buffalo; that is, crouched over the necks of their horses, and wrapped in a buffalo robe. At a distance their outlines can be mistaken for those of the animal. Our three Gros Ventres fell into the trap, went out to hunt the supposed animals, and did not come back. Nevertheless, since their bodies have not been found, the report lacks confirmation, and so their deaths are not yet certain.

Wednesday, November 25. White Shield, chief of the Arrikarees, coming from Berthold where he went from his winter quarters to get a supply of corn, arrived here to pay me "a visit of sympathy" for the death of Walborn, whom we buried yesterday. On this subject, he gave me a little speech which was not lacking in a certain distinction, recalling that Lieutenant Walborn was the leader of the Indian scouts and that his Ree children were commanded by him.

The chief visited my house, which he had not been in since it was finished. In spite of the reserve customary with the Indians, he did not fail to show his astonishment and admiration for what the whites can do in such things. He informed me that the three Gros Ventres believed to be dead are in very good health. When they found no game, they went on farther than they figured and consequently were gone a longer time. They did not, however, meet any enemy.

[157] In an order issued November 26, 1868, De Trobriand announced the death of R. Frank Walborn. Walborn had enlisted in the Sixth Pennsylvania Reserves in 1861. He was wounded at the second battle of Bull Run and had then contracted typhoid fever. *Army and Navy Journal,* January 2, 1869, p. 308.

The only verified fact is that twelve horses were stolen from the Rees during the night. This theft could have been made by a party of Sioux; and so the rumor got around that the three Gros Ventres were dead. White Shield left as usual with a little present of sugar and coffee. His visit was prompted as much by this prospect as by the death of Lieutenant Walborn. Savage and civilized men are alike in more than one way.

Friday, November 27. A change in temperature as complete as it was unexpected. This afternoon the thermometer went up to fifty-five F. A great thaw all about us. However, this evening the ice on the Missouri is still holding firm.

Saturday, November 28. Received today news of the death of Josephine Virfolet, news that arrived in New York a month ago to the day. "Devoted and faithful heart, courageous and honest spirit, she inspired nothing but affection during her life, and only sorrow by her death." Such will be, I think, the epitaph that her sister has asked me to write. It will have the merit of being simple and honest. Still another who has gone before. Josephine was still comparatively young (forty-one years old). She succumbed in a few hours to a complication of mortal illnesses; one of them, dropsy of the lungs, brought on by apoplexy. It is not to be regretted that her life was not prolonged, for the autopsy showed that there was nothing but days of suffering ahead for her. The world will not matter to her, for there is on high an infallible justice.

Thursday, December 10. Twenty-two degrees *below* zero.
In contrast: Thursday, December 17, + 45 F.
For three or four days, the weather has been absolutely unseasonable; hardly freezes during the night, and during the day, the mercury goes up to about twenty degrees in the shade. Yesterday, it rose to fifty F. Consequently, the snow has almost completely disappeared from the countryside; but the ice on the river does not budge. In the sun, it is positively hot, as in October.

Sunday, December 20. This weather could not last, of course. After a rather heavy snowfall, the wind held in the north and the mercury immediately fell. It is fourteen F. below zero.

Thursday, December 31. Nothing notable has marked the last days of the year 1868. The thermometer rises and falls. This is the only change that varies our monotonous existence any, and the year is dying without its last suns shining on any incident to add memories for these records.

In the succession of days, life repeats itself when the scene has not changed. Many incidents which were new last year and found a place in this journal will not be mentioned again, or will be very briefly noted, leaving out any detail or description which has already been recorded. Our military life, our relations with the Indians, etc., all this is well known and does not have the same interest that it had in the beginning. So these notes will include here and there only such incidents as are novel or such events as are important. Will this harvest be abundant in 1869? We shall see.

Saturday, January 16. The mail has arrived from Fort Buford, bringing the charges and specifications against Lt. Col. Bowman who has been so drunk that he almost never leaves his room or his bed. The document is dated October 19, and specifies that Bowman has not been sober for periods of twelve or fifteen days running. According to established rules, Captain Ch. Dickey, who signed the accusation, delivered it to the adjutant of the post to be transmitted to the general headquarters of the District and of the Department; but Bowman confiscated it in passage and gave it to a trader at the post to keep.[158] This makes the case against him still more serious. Things remained in this condition for more than two months. Finally Capt. Dickey, discovering the suppression of the charges and specifications signed by him, sent on directly the duplicate which arrived here today.

The courier returning to Fort Buford will take with him an order putting Lt. Col. Bowman under arrest until a new order. Captain Dickey, the ranking officer after him, will take command of the post. In transmitting the charges and specifications to the general headquarters of the Department, I added to them the following letter which clearly explains the situation we are in:

"Bt. Brig. Genl. O. D. Greene A.A.G. Dept. of Dakota

"Sir: I have the honor to forward by this mail a duplicate of charges and specifications against Lt. Col. Bowman. By the endorsement of Captain Bt. Major C. J. Dickey who preferred them on the nineteenth of October last, it will be seen that the original ones were intercepted and kept back. Since that time, I am informed that Lt.

158 De Trobriand found on December 28, 1868, that the original charges were in possession of Mr. Samuel Jones, a private citizen doing business at the post. Endorsement on the charges and specifications forwarded from the Middle District, January 16, 1869. Department of Dakota, War Records Division, National Archives.

Col. Bowman has been constantly drunk and unable to attend to his duties, remaining the most of the time in bed where he signs the necessary papers. I ordered him under arrest until further orders, and had the command of the post transferred to safer hands.

"I would respectfully call the particular attention of the Bt. Maj. Genl. commanding to the urgent necessity of having justice done in this case, in order to counteract the demoralizing effect produced lately by the impunity of most serious offenses in this command where, as a result, there is a tendency to suppose that the military law and justice can be rendered inoperative by certain personal influences; and that certain parties cannot be brought to trial, or if tried, and whatever be the sentence, will surely be returned to duty, a nuisance and a disgrace to the regiment.

"I need not insist upon the subject. The Bt. Maj. Genl. commanding, in his full appreciation of the case, is the best judge to decide how the ends of justice may be attained, and the vital interests of the service safeguarded."[159]

The cases of impunity to which I allude are, of course, those of Bt. Lt. Col. Rankin, who with six charges and twenty-two specifications against him, not only has not been tried but has been assigned to recruiting service, which is considered as a favor; Bvt. Maj. Little, who, as a result, has had to be released from arrest, the charges against him being signed by Bt. Lt. Col. Rankin; finally, and in particular, the case of Captain Wainwright, who, tried by the court-martial, declared guilty on all the main points of the accusation and condemned to be broken and expelled from the army, has been re-established in his duties by no less than the President, who first commuted the sentence to a relative loss of seniority rank, then completely pardoned him.[160]

In order to spare nothing in doing my duty and to arrive at some sort of justice in these cases, I have referred Lt. Col. Bowman and captains Rankin, Wainwright, and Piatt to the action of the retiring board which can pronounce their retirement from service. We shall see what will come of it. Bowman will be retired, I believe, but it will

159 The quotations from the letters appear in the French manuscript in English. This copy is identical with the original, found in Department of Dakota, War Records Division, National Archives.

160 De Trobriand was deeply concerned about the welfare of the posts left under the command of these men. He wrote to the Department constantly for instructions. See Régis de Trobriand, Fort Stevenson, Dakota Territory, to Bvt. Brig. Genl O. D. Greene, AA Genl, Department of Dakota, January 19, 1869. Department of Dakota, War Records Division, National Archives.

be more difficult with the others because Wainwright is the brother-in-law of Genl [Edward D.] Townsend, assistant adjt. genl. of the War Department; because Rankin has a young and pretty wife very active in his interest; and because both are close to General [Rufus] Ingalls, quartermaster general; finally, because Piatt has the support of political influences in his family. And it is thus that justice is sacrificed to favor. In this respect a republic, or at least the republic of the United States, is not any better, even worse, than the monarchies of Europe. Nowhere in the old world (except perhaps in England) would such vices be tolerated and perpetuated in the administration of the army. Americans are decidedly *warlike,* but decidedly not *military.*

Sunday, January 31. More mail from Buford. This time it is Lt. Col. Bowman who sends charges and specifications against Bt. Maj. Dickey because of what seems to have been a squabble between officers heated with wine on the evening of January 1st. Dickey had insulted Leonard, and finally would have struck him. Looking to the past, he also reproached him for having two serious altercations with two employees of the traders at Buford last year. These last two specifications have no value at all and prove that a spirit of vengeance and malice inspired the accusation. It seems quite probable that Bt. Maj. Dickey has been pushed into a trap. However it might be, the result is that the command of the fort has passed to Captain Little, who is himself under accusation for having struck his superior (Rankin). If he had not been released from arrest, the command would have fallen into the hands of a simple lieutenant—and we are speaking of a post of five companies in the heart of a country frequented by hostile Indians. This is what we get for the ridiculous tolerance toward drunkenness. As long as drunkards like Bowman are kept in the army, we can expect all kinds of disorders and difficulties, especially in our frontier posts so far from the centers of higher authority. What an Augean stable!

During this month, the Rees and part of the Gros Ventres came back from their winter camps to their village at Berthold. The two chiefs came, each in his turn, to pay me a visit with some of their warriors. The usual speeches were given, and the two interviews ended with what occasioned them: the distribution of some supplies, flour, salt pork, and biscuits, with coffee and sugar for the chiefs.

The big game seems to have disappeared from the banks of the river and throughout this whole region. Our Indians complain bitterly about it, for in order to find buffalo now they would have to go to the Yellowstone and beyond into the very heart of the country of their enemies, the Sioux. This is why they have come back so soon, before the end of winter. At Berthold they have corn, which will help them keep alive until spring.

Sunday, February 7. The special courier who brought the last despatches from Buford is named Kelly.[161] He is a very young, tall, straight, handsome fellow, with an intelligent and bold look. There is a mysterious story in his life, the details of which are not known, but he has revealed something of it to those whom he has met on the plains.

[*The exploits of Kelly*] It is known that Kelly is Irish and Catholic and was intended for the priesthood. On leaving boarding school, he entered the seminary for this purpose, where he completed his education. The fact is that his education, which includes Latin, is much superior to the little that the pioneers of civilization on the Upper Missouri have. They claim, I do not know on what information, that he then became infatuated with a girl who did not return his affection, either because of her own position or through reverence or dislike for the robe of the seminarian. The fact remains that Kelly cast off his robe, and like many a wounded or despairing soul, shook the dust of civilization from his feet and buried himself in the western deserts, seeking adventure and danger. He has found both. He has been known for some time for the careless courage with which he travels alone and unannounced across the plains armed only with his rifle and revolver, and unconcerned about hostile Indians. He shows up one day at Berthold, another at Buford, and still another at Benton, staying here and there as he wishes, and leaving as unexpectedly

161 Many of the conjectures about Luther S. Kelly related in this journal are probably romance. Kelly says that he attended Lima Academy in New York before he enlisted as a private in the 10th infantry. After the Civil War he was stationed at Fort Ripley, and then at Fort Wadsworth, where he learned to love the life of adventure on the plains. When his enlistment ran out in 1868, he remained on the plains to lead a wandering life. In his memoirs he recalls the meeting with De Trobriand when he brought the mail, and says that the commanding officer was "a portly man with a pleasant face." Thomas Curry, who was cutting timber for Fort Buford on the banks of the Yellowstone in the summer of 1870, describes him as "6 feet high as straight as an arrow with long dark hair hanging down his shoulders . . ." He was floating down the river on a raft, playing "Swanee River" on a concertina. When he died in 1928, his body was buried on Kelly Mountain, overlooking the Yellowstone. Milo Quaife, ed., *Yellowstone Kelly;* "Recollections of Yellowstone Kelly," manuscript in the Montana Historical Library; Telegram, David Hilger to Chas. H. Ruzica, December 28, 1928, Montana Historical Library.

as he came when he thinks he has rested enough. It would have been too bad to have this adventurous spirit buried beneath a cassock.

After bringing the despatches from Buford and resting for the few days that I kept him here to wait for the arrival of the mail from the east, he left Wednesday in the afternoon, his horse and arms in good condition.

Yesterday morning an Indian from Fort Berthold brought us the news that Kelly had killed two Sioux near the Great Bend (a point on the Missouri), that the Mandans who were in the neighborhood took the scalps and cut up the bodies, and that they were going to have a big scalp dance in the village. One must be cautious about Indian reports, and so I had very serious doubts about the correctness of this story. This afternoon when Kelly returned, he confirmed it, and supplied the details. Here is what happened to him. I shall let him tell it:

"Near the Great Bend, about forty miles on the other side of Berthold, the trail follows a sort of a narrow place hemmed in between the foot of a sharp bluff on one side and on the other by a clump of willows on the bank of the river. As I was going around a turn in the road there, I suddenly found myself face to face with two Indians on horseback coming at me. There were hardly forty yards between us. When they saw me, they quickly stopped their horses and jumped to the ground. I stopped, too, but stayed in the saddle, just drawing my rifle from the case. Seeing this, the two Indians jumped into the brush. One was armed with a good double-barreled gun; the other had only a bow and some arrows. Their action seemed suspicious to me, and I asked them in Sioux who they were and what they wanted. They said that I should not fire, that they were friends, Mandans, and that they belonged to a party from Fort Berthold that was cutting wood a few miles from there. I knew very well that they were lying because of their language and in everything else, I had recognized them as Sioux. At almost the same time, a shot came from behind a tree, and my horse began to kick and jump. I knew that he had been shot, and that it would be impossible to hold him still, so I had to jump to the ground. In jumping, I fell full length, and while I was trying to get on my feet, one of the Sioux ran up to within six feet of me, took aim, and fired. I would be dead now if the gun had gone off; but since the percussion cap missed fire, I did not lose any time in firing back, and my enemy fell dead, a bullet through his head. Then it was like a duel with the other one who kept under cover behind a tree trunk, where he shot arrows at me, as you can see (showing

Interior of Fort Stevenson

me a double hole in the folds of his jacket). I was completely exposed, so, rifle ready, I reached a rise in the ground, behind which I was in a better position. Since I could still fire fifteen shots without reloading (Kelly was armed with a Henry rifle) I started to fire carefully at my man. The last tree he hid behind was not big enough to cover him completely. On one side or the other, an arm, a shoulder, or a hip was exposed. After nicking the tree without knowing what other effect my bullets had, I finally broke his arm below the shoulder. Soon he sank to the ground, and coming near, I saw that in addition to his broken arm, he had several more bullets in his body. He confessed to me then that he and his comrade were Sioux, belonging to the band of fifteen or twenty lodges of Unkpapahs who were in the neighborhood and for whom they were out scouting when I had met them. My horse was dying; theirs had fled into the woods, so without losing time in running after them, I started on foot for the spot where I knew I could find the Mandans. It was five or six miles away.

"When I told them what had happened to me, the best mounted jumped on their horses and ran to the scene of the combat. They found the dead and the wounded Indian there, lifted the two scalps, and cut up the two bodies; after which we made a good meal of the flesh of my horse, and we all returned to Berthold together. There I was joined by two couriers from Fort Buford, and came back with them *to report here.*"

Monday, February 1. There is great festivity at Berthold where the Indians held a frenzied scalp dance around the scraps of the two Sioux who were hacked up into small pieces. Thursday, Kelly will return to Buford with the two couriers who arrived yesterday. The mail they brought does not have any important news.

Only, the charges preferred by Lt. Col. Bowman against Maj. Dickey have led the latter to bring some against Lt. Leonard. These, according to all appearances, furnish the true version of what went on Christmas night and New Year's Eve. It seems that on these evenings, Leonard, completely drunk, insulted and threatened Ch. Dickey, his superior, with a revolver, and had to be put out of the officers' room. This explains why he refused to sign the charges against Bt. Maj. Dickey, and Bowman had to sign them himself. In the spring I shall go to Fort Buford on one of the first boats of the season, and I shall see to it that all those counts are verified.[162]

162 De Trobriand made his official report on the charges preferred against Dickey by Bowman on February 1, summarizing the state of the command at Fort

Friday, February 19. Bvt. Major Little is showing energy and vigor in the exercise of the command that fell to him. Another courier from Buford. Among the official papers he brings is the report of the measures taken against J. B. Gerard. That scoundrel came from St. Louis last year as an employee or rather an associate of his cousin F. F. Gerard, one of the traders at Berthold and Stevenson. This was a bad arrangement. Because some difficulties had arisen relative to his license, the latter had left for the States, leaving the store in the care of his cousin. The first action taken by the latter was to sneak in whiskey to the soldiers of the garrison in violation of all orders and rules. A week had not gone by when he was caught one evening in the very act of drinking with the noncommissioned officers in the district office. He was ordered to leave the post and the reservation *in two hours* under pain of being arrested and put in the guardhouse if he were still seen within the limits of the post.[163]

J. B. packed off without being urged, and went to settle at Berthold, awaiting F. F.'s return.

I don't know what financial arrangements there are between the two cousins, but when F. F. returned, although warned of everything that had happened and although he had lost hundreds of dollars at least as a result, he did not hesitate to go to Fort Buford, and ask permission to establish a store there, a branch of the one he has at Stevenson. And when he obtained the permission of Lt. Col. Bowman, whom does he place in charge of this branch of his business? The same J. B., whose lack of ability and dishonesty he already knew by experience. What came of it? J. B. began to play his pranks again, undoubtedly encouraged by the habitual drunkenness of the commandant of the post who probably could see only fire. But then Bowman was put under arrest, and the command passed to Little. It did not take him a week to find out what was happening. Master J. B. not only had sold liquor to the soldiers; he had sold some to the Indians, too, and had even tried to persuade some men employed

Buford with Rankin assigned to recruiting, Little, under charges and specifications, in command, with Dickey under arrest by Bowman, and with Bowman under arrest by De Trobriand's order. Régis de Trobriand, Fort Stevenson, to Bvt. Brig. Genl O. D. Greene, AA Genl, Department of Dakota, St. Paul, February 15, 1869. Department of Dakota, War Records Division, National Archives.

163 J. B. Gerard was ordered away from Fort Stevenson on June 17, 1868, by special order no. 56. At Fort Buford, he sold liquor to the Assiniboin Indians and attempted to induce enlisted men to secure grain for him. Special Orders no. 4, J. M. Marshall by order of Régis de Trobriand, Headquarters, Middle District, Fort Stevenson, Dakota Territory, February 20, 1869. Department of Dakota, War Records Division, National Archives.

in the quartermaster's department to steal grain for his profit. Result: J. B. Gerard is expelled from the post and from the district; all his merchandise is seized and confiscated for the government, and the store is closed and will not be opened again.[164] In the meantime, F. F. has gone to St. Louis to arrange for improvements and to lay plans for the extension of his trade at Stevenson and Buford. At one blow he lost half of his business. It is his own fault. By entrusting it to a scamp like J. B., he knowingly exposed himself to what happened to him today. Served him right!

Monday, February 22. The mail for Fort Rice leaves today. The couriers will have a rough trip, for after more than six weeks of comparatively mild weather, a sharp cold set in Friday; the thermometer tumbled down to the depths of 20 below zero F., and has not gone up since then. When we are now so close to spring, are we going to pay for the mild temperature we enjoyed in the middle of winter?

I sent off in the mail a letter to Lt. Col. Otis, answering a communication he addressed to me by the last courier about some white workers who have settled about thirty miles from here to cut and cord wood to sell to the steamboats in the spring. It seems that Messieurs the Sioux Indians do not think much of that. From the reservation which has been assigned to them on the Grand River and where the government has fed them all winter, they have had their agent write to Colonel Otis ordering that this work be stopped in the place called Painted Wood. The Colonel answered that Painted Wood was in my district and consequently outside his jurisdiction. The answer did not satisfy the Sioux, who, as their agent claims, are threatening to take affairs *into their own hands.* Consequently, Colonel Otis informed me of what had happened and of the threats uttered against the whites who are cutting firewood at the spot indicated.

In my answer, I am stating that I do not know of any rights that any tribe of Sioux has on any spot in my district; that the only

164 The action of Major Little was approved on February 20. Little was ordered to maintain the seizure of the goods and to destroy the liquor if he thought that course best. The case of J. B. Gerard was to be reported to the civil authorities of the Territory. Lt. J. M. Marshall, Fort Stevenson, to Bvt. Major Little, Fort Buford, February 20, 1869. Department of Dakota, War Records Division, National Archives.

According to the records of the post surgeon, Gerard was not the only one selling whiskey. Durfee & Peck and the Northwest Fur Company had both introduced ale and whiskey by October 14, 1868. Larpenteur's store, according to the report, was the only one not selling it. Fort Buford, "Record of the Medical History of the Post." Department of Dakota, War Records Division, National Archives.

Indians who could claim rights on Painted Wood are the Rees and Mandans, original owners of this region where they still had their villages a few years ago near old Fort Clark before they came to settle at Berthold.[165] I am also warning the workers to keep on the alert and to be ready to repulse any Sioux attack and promising to help them if the need arises. I am furthermore suggesting that it would be well to let the Sioux of the reservation know how I feel about this and to warn them that any attack on the woodcutters at Painted Wood will be considered as a direct act of hostility against the whites and against the government, and that, therefore, they must expect to suffer the consequences. Moreover, I am convinced that the Sioux of the Grand River are really not worried very much about the wood cut at Painted Wood. They are urged on and stirred up by a trader from Fort Rice called Galpin, who is using them to assure himself of as much of a monopoly on the firewood from the banks of the Missouri as he can get and in this way profit at the expense of the river commerce in general and the steamboats in particular. Half a dozen poor devils work all winter long, enduring the hardships of cold and privations and exertions of all kinds, and now when their wood is almost cut and corded, it would be a fine piece of speculation for Mr. Galpin to have them chased away by Sioux Indians and to take possession of the fruits of their labor himself and to sell them for his own profit. But no matter what he can do in the jurisdiction of Fort Rice where he is established, he can give up this kind of speculation in my district before he starts. I think my letter will be enough to dissuade Galpin and the Sioux Indians from meddling in the business of my command.

Sunday, February 28. On the news that an epidemic had broken out among my Indians of Berthold, especially the Rees, I sent Doctor Goddard to confirm it and to identify the sickness. He returned this morning, announcing that it was scurvy which had been making serious ravages for two weeks. Twenty or twenty-five Indians, chiefly old people, have died of it, and thirty-two are still stricken with it. I immediately requisitioned a cart from the agency, and sent to Berthold ten kegs of sauerkraut and anti-scorbutic pickles to be distributed to the Indians every day. These poor devils are so honest, and I am always surprised, for it is such a contrast to the character of the Sioux. Among them, scurvy is the result of their hardships and miseries;

165 The letter, summarized briefly here, was written on February 18. It is in Department of Dakota, War Records Division, National Archives.

they suffer especially from cold and hunger, having only a little corn to keep body and soul together. And there are the agency cattle, running free. They wander around in the willows which border the river. They are without a guard, in reach of everyone, especially at night. And these poor Indians die of hunger near these animals rather than touch them, although the meat of a single beef would make a wonderful feast for a great number of them. I certainly would not be sure of the honesty of whites in such a case. And here are the Indians, plundered, robbed, and mercilessly oppressed by the agents of the government. Let us hope that all this trash from the Indian Bureau will soon be cleaned out, and replaced by military authority.

Friday, March 5. This morning the mail left for Totten and was accompanied by Captain Clarke, who has a three months' leave, by Richer, the head carpenter who is called to Canada by family business, and by a dozen men whose term of service has just expired. Clarke, Richer, and Vogel [Vogler], the ex-sergeant quartermaster, are in a sled. The others are on Indian horses which they bought for the trip. They left in a dry storm from the northwest and with the temperature at zero Fahrenheit. They must have the devil in them to travel in such weather when they aren't forced to.

Yesterday, March 4, inauguration of the new President. Great celebration in Washington. Rejoicing and a big time in all the States. Here, nothing at all! I chose this date of good omen to request a six-months' leave, beginning next fall when navigation on the Upper Missouri is over; that is, at the end of September. In this way I shall be able to go to France to spend my next winter and to renew my acquaintance with Brest and Paris. After two and a half years with the savages, I am in great need of this. The request for the leave went out this morning. Around the end of next month, I shall know if the talisman of March 4 has had its effect on the Secretary of War.

Saturday, March 6. Yesterday evening, at about eight o'clock, the travelers who left in the morning returned in a pitiful condition; noses and ears frozen, numb and crippled, leading a lame horse. During the day, the furious blasts of wind, which came at intervals, lifted the snow in clouds so thick that at times they could not see ten feet ahead of them. It did not take long before the travelers lost their way and wandered around in the middle of the prairies, not knowing which way to go and with the prospect of a night with no fire which would probably be fatal to more than one of them. Fortunately one

Philippe Régis de TROBRIAND

of the couriers carrying the mail had remained behind and accompanied them with the sled, planning to rejoin at the first station his comrade who had gone ahead with two discharged soldiers on mounts. Seeing that the travelers were in no condition to go on, and not being too sure of where he was himself, the half-breed courier tried to take them to the banks of the Missouri and from there back to Stevenson. After great hardship and terrible suffering, he succeeded, and they arrived at nightfall. It was on the return trip with the wind in their faces that most of them got their noses, cheeks, and ears frozen. Major Clarke did not share the common fate, however, thanks to his many fur garments. George Koeplin, the half-breed who brought them back, left this morning to catch up with his companion, if he can, and bring back with him the mail from Fort Totten. The two soldiers who had gone ahead with Richemond, the courier, have not shown up yet, and must have spent the night in one of the stations, and continued their trip today, for although it is still very cold, the weather is fair again, and the air is perfectly calm, which is something.

Sunday, March 7. Since the weather has cleared again, Richer and Vogel [*sic*] got on their way with Brown, who will be their guide to Totten, and return with the next mail. The one today brings me, among other things, a request from Captain Wainwright for four-months' leave. This is the endorsement I put on it in transmitting it to higher general headquarters:

"Respectfully forwarded *Disapproved*. Captain W—— did not perform his duty for the past twelve or thirteen months, being under arrest awaiting first his trial by gen¹ court-martial, and then the confirmation of his sentence. For his previous conduct, he was sentenced to be *cashiered*, but being pardoned by the clemency of the President, he is just returned to duty. With such a record, I don't consider it advisable to grant new favors to Captain W—— for the present."[166]

But he is a brother-in-law of Gen¹ Townsend and probably he will take no notice of it. We shall see, nevertheless.

The month of March is still terribly cold, although the weather is generally fair and there is very little snow. This morning the thermometer registered eighteen degrees below zero Fahrenheit (twenty-eight below, cent.).

[166] The letter appeared in English in the French manuscript.
On March 4, Whistler had forwarded the request to De Trobriand, "Approved." De Trobriand sent the endorsement quoted above on March 12. Department of Dakota, War Records Division, National Archives.

Monday, March 8. Today Lieutenant Cusick arrived from Fort Buford in charge of three prisoners sentenced to ten years in prison for burglary of the store of one of the post traders. One of them was a sergeant. They have already escaped twice. They gave themselves up the first time and were captured the second (or vice versa). In brief, the commandant of the post, believing that the prison was not secure enough and the guards of the prisoners doubtful, did not want to wait for the steamboat season and sent them by land under escort from post to post to their destination, which is the Stillwater penitentiary (Minnesota). Lieutenant Cusick has been in charge of fatigue duty which in this season is terribly hard; but as he has asked for a leave, he will have a chance to enjoy it sooner if it is granted to him in St. Paul. I really suppose that this is why the prisoners have been sent on. Undoubtedly it is true that great vigilance is demanded, for in their position, they are willing to risk anything to escape on the way. So I shall get rid of them as soon as possible by sending them on to Totten next Friday, the nineteenth, at the same time as the mail.[167]

Tuesday, March 9. It seems that the Indians at Berthold finally gave in to the strong temptation that the sub-agent has constantly kept before them since the beginning of winter. Reaching the end of patience and forbearance, half dead with hunger and misery, one of them killed a young veal that had been left to wander on the banks of the river with the rest of the herd. Upon this, Mr. Marsh, who replaces Wilkinson,[168] writes to me *ab irato* to ask me to take charge of the guilty one and to keep him prisoner in the guardhouse. Refused. This post is not a penitentiary for delinquent redskins, especially in this case where I consider the agent more guilty than the poor devil who killed the calf. If the greater part of the supplies sent to our Indians by the government were not stolen by the agents in

167 In the *St. Paul Daily Pioneer*, April 15, 1869, there appeared this item: "Four soldiers were brought down on the St. Cloud train yesterday, with balls and chains attached to them. They came from Fort Stevenson and were sentenced to ten years in the penitentiary at Stillwater. They were placed in the county jail in this city where they remained last night." Dr. Kimball recorded that the men who robbed the store of Durfee & Peck forfeited all pay and allowances, were dishonorably discharged, branded on the left hip with the letter "T" and sentenced for ten years. Fort Buford, "Record of the Medical History of the Post." Department of Dakota, War Records Division, National Archives.

168 The trader Marsh had a temporary appointment. Captain W. Clifford made the report for the Fort Berthold Agency September 1, 1869, and Mahlon Wilkinson was agent until September 28, 1868, when he made his report. *Report of the Commissioner of Indian Affairs, 1868,* p. 192–193; *Report of the Commissioner of Indian Affairs, 1869,* p. 312.

connivance with the traders, they would not be reduced to this horrible misery and would not kill a calf to eat.

Scurvy at Berthold has been cut down by the supplies of vinegar I sent. Since then, no one has died and the sick are getting better; I am going to send another cart of sauerkraut and pickles.

Thursday, March 18. Spring has preceded the almanac by two days. First day of complete thaw the thermometer went up to forty-six above, F. (eight c.)

Saturday, March 20. In revenge, the weather could not be more disagreeable for the astronomic beginning of spring. It snowed part of the day. Yesterday Lt. Cusick left with his prisoners and their escort. Several soldiers who received their final discharge joined the party. For the trip, they bought Indian ponies, preferring to bear this expense rather than to prolong their stay here until navigation is open on the river.

Monday, March 22. Red-letter day! The mail arriving today brings us the official information of the changes of garrison ordered at general headquarters. As far as my regiment is concerned, we shall be relieved by the 7th, which will come up as soon as the river is navigable. When it arrives, I am ordered to add to this contingent any soldiers I have left in my companies and to go with my officers, noncommissioned officers, and my military band to Newport Barracks across from Cincinnati on the Ohio. There I shall receive new orders for a further destination when the ranks of the regiment are filled again. So we leave the desert plains of Dakota and the Indian tribes to return to the States. Heaven be praised! There is a good deal of troop movement. The 13th, 22nd, and the 10th, which were also in Montana, Dakota, and Minnesota, have received the same orders and are being replaced: the 13th by the 2nd; the 22nd by the 34th; the 10th by the 16th, etc. The Texas garrisons are completely changed, and even the 9th comes back from California where it has been for I don't know how many years. Same movements in the artillery and cavalry.

The general rejoicing was sobered by more news brought by the same courier. The party composed of Richer, Vogler, Bittner, and Shank, under the leadership of Brown, was lost in the snows near Big Coulee. Only two of them, Richer and Brown, were found by the mail couriers, and they were half dead with cold and hunger, arms and legs frozen, etc. They were near their sled which they burned to make a little fire. As for the other three, they disappeared, hoping to force a route, and we do not know or know all too well what has become of them, for they had left their buffalo robes and blankets in the sled, and did not have anything with which to make a fire. Unless a miracle happens, they are dead.[169]

Wednesday, March 24. Spring definitely began today, with a heat of sixty-five degrees F., in the shade, of course. Superb weather, dazzling sun, which brings us back the migrating birds. The flocks of wild geese and ducks have reappeared. The first ones passed over the fort, outdoing each other in their cackling. I suppose that this is their way of expressing to each other their joy at seeing once more the country where they were born. The ducks are silent, but I hope they don't think any less of it.

Naturally with this spring temperature, the ice on the river is melting under our very eyes. The water is running on every side, and the surge which follows this lifts up the huge shell under which the Missouri has been imprisoned for four months; the break-up will not be long in coming. The couriers coming back from Fort Rice were stupid enough to shorten the trip by crossing the river yesterday as they have been doing all winter; but this morning when they wanted to get back on this bank, they could not cross it any more. They were forced to go on until they were across from the fort and to wait there until we improvised a skiff to go to their aid. The work was finished in less than two hours, and animals and men got back home with no accident save a few hours' delay. However, the mail is of no importance.

Sunday, March 28 (Easter). The weather continued to be very mild these last days: a strong wind from the west has blown almost continuously. It seemed to have little effect on the temperature, for the mercury did not go down to the freezing point, even during the night, and during the day came up to fifty to sixty degrees. This dry storm (it hardly brought more than a few drops of rain) hurried the break-up which came at noon today. This year it was much less of a spectacle than last year. Then a huge rise, a result of the thawing of the snow which accumulated during the winter, began from March

---

169 On April 1, John George Brown wrote to De Trobriand from Fort Totten a full report of the trip. T. F. Richer wrote for enclosure in the letter a statement that Brown was not responsible for the loss of H. O. Vogler, F. Bittner and John Shank. This statement was written for De Trobriand, March 19, in French, at Big Coulee to tell him about the trip. De Trobriand Family Papers; see also *St. Paul Daily Pioneer*, April 9, 1869.

22 on to break up the ice which was still very thick and which had
been piled into a huge, tumbled mass by the force of the current. This
time, because very little snow had fallen during the winter, the rise
is not nearly as great and the ice which was from two and a half to
three feet thick has had time to melt gradually. Today the ice blocks,
which are not more than six to eight inches thick, broke up easily
and floated down the current easily.

The bed of the river is not blocked, and this evening the greatest
part of its width is free from ice.

The men released from service this month are hurrying to put
the finishing touches on the building of the Mackinaws in which they
will go down river in a few days. Seven of them are actually going
to embark in a long canoe made of an enormous tree trunk hollowed
out, which was used by miners from Montana last year to go down
to Berthold. The impatience of these liberated men to see civilization
again after three years' service in the desert is such that I believe that
for lack of anything better they would board a raft rather than wait
two months for the return of the first boat from Benton. Now that
the river is open for navigation, none of them considers going across
the plains. They are all busy as beavers so they can get started tomorrow and the following days.

Tuesday, March 30. Yesterday, the first detachment of the flo-
tilla started out. I am afraid they have been too much in a hurry
and will have a bad time of it. In fact, last night the cold was rather
severe again, and this morning the river was full of drift ice. In the
afternoon, the channel was free, and although the weather looked
bad, two boats, each carrying seven men, were launched. They had
scarcely pushed off when the high wind threw the small boats out of
control (they are flat and have no keel). They had to land, for the
boats were already half full of water. Since then, the weather has
just grown worse, and this evening we have had a real snowstorm.
I pity our amateur navigators who left yesterday!

Wednesday, March 31. The break-up of the twenty-eighth was
only a partial one, and the river was still frozen above Berthold. The
storm broke the last shackles of the imprisoned river, and an enormous mass of floating ice cakes began to come down during the
night. This morning the Missouri was choked up with them, and
during the day their number did not seem to diminish.

The two boatloads which were held up yesterday could not
dream of starting out before the ice has gone out, and this will prob-

ably take a few days. It is still cold. The wind is still blowing from the north with the same intensity.

Thursday, April 1. Fine weather, brilliant sun, but nipping cold. This morning, the thermometer was at fifteen degrees F. (minus 9½ Cent.). All day the ice cakes have come down with no noticeable decrease.

Friday, April 2. New snowstorm during the night. Winter is still with us. The temperature, which was very cold this morning, became much milder in the afternoon. Last night's snow has disappeared, too. The river is almost entirely free from ice cakes.

The mail left this morning for Totten. The one that the couriers will bring us in exchange Monday will be one of the most interesting that we have ever received. It ought to contain the inauguration of President U. S. Grant, the composition of his cabinet, about which we have not heard a word, some orders for the carrying out of troop movements in this department, the last report about the fate of Richer and Brown's three companions, telling us if they were found on the prairie living or dead, etc., not to mention our personal letters and the news of the first days of the administration of the new President.

Sunday, April 3. Three boats taking away twenty men left this morning. The weather is favorable, and the wind, which is in the south, promises the travelers mild weather. This morning the mercury was still at twenty-five degrees F. But it did not take long for it to go up above forty degrees. The floating ice cakes have almost disappeared. There remain only those which the flood put on the banks and which will gradually melt in the sun.

Sunday, April 4. "Anyone *who relies on the future* is a fool!" The mail arrived this afternoon, bringing us all the news we were expecting and some that we were not expecting. The last is of most immediate interest to us. All the announced movements of troops have been changed. The order for them is revoked because of an act of Congress which among other measures reduces the infantry of the army from forty-five to twenty-five regiments. A new general order from the general-in-chief (now W. T. Sherman instead of U. S. Grant) prescribes the incorporation of the regiment with these and names the officers kept on the active list. I am among the twenty-five colonels chosen and am transferred to the command of the 13th regiment of infantry. The former 31st is to be combined with the 22nd, which is our neighbor in Dakota.

My new regiment stationed in Montana does not change garrison. So, instead of returning to the States, I bury myself deeper in the territories, and instead of being near my people, I go a thousand miles farther away. My general headquarters are at Fort Shaw, sixty miles beyond Fort Benton, which is the head of navigation of the Missouri.

However, distance is not everything; lines of communication mean a good deal, and in this respect, I am profiting by the change. At Fort Shaw there is a regular daily mail service. Letters and newspapers come by the Pacific Railroad, and by the string of relays from Salt Lake, the city of Mormons. Since Fort Shaw is half way between Fort Benton and Helena, its communications are open all winter, the climate being much milder than in this region.

For field officers, I have two distinguished and agreeable officers: Lt. Col. H. A. Morrow and Major R. S. Lamotte, both gentlemen of sober habits. I have not received my official nomination; but I read it in the *New York Herald* of March 17. So it is very certain. Undoubtedly I shall receive my orders in the next mail. They ought to come from Gen¹ Hancock, who will relieve Gen. Terry from the command of the Department of the Dakota. Gen¹ Terry is named to the Department of the South, general headquarters, Atlanta.

My stay at this new post ought to complete my studies of Far Western life in all its aspects. I have already lived two years among the redskins, whom I now know thoroughly. I still must acquaint myself with the miners and gold hunters who populate Montana. *Allons!* Perhaps it will be for the best after all. I shall obey fate without a murmur.

The mail from Totten also includes a detailed report on the deplorable accident which happened to Vogler and his companions. When the first news of it reached Colonel Whistler, he immediately despatched scouts to look for the three missing travelers. Two of them were found dead in the snow; one only three miles from Fort Totten, the other eight miles. They were Shank and Bittner. At the last date, Vogler had not been found.

A strange discovery was made as a result of Bittner's death. Naturally the papers he was carrying as well as the money he had on him ($9.80) were taken and sent to me. Among these papers was a forged discharge, a final report in duplicate which was also forged, and different letters to the paymaster general, etc., a whole series of falsifications through which, by forging my signature and that of his captain, Mr. Norwell, he hoped by fraud to get more than twice what the government owed him. Now, as sergeant major of his company, he had always conducted himself well, and consequently was considered an honest man on whom we could depend. So who can be trusted? To commit these forgeries, he probably had to steal, by some unknown means, the necessary forms, the parchment form for his duplicate discharge, and paper ones for the rest. For him, punishment was not long in coming. *P[o]ena pede claudo.* Death stopped him at the first step. Here is a fine text for a sermon on Providence.

Although he did not get started until March 19, Lieut. Cusick, with his escort and three prisoners, ran into so much snow on the other side of the halfway station and had such bad weather that they were forced to abandon the wagon and much of what it contained to get to Fort Totten on foot. One mule died on the way. On the plains, we can see how dangerous it is to trust the first false smiles of spring and to have confidence in any changes in temperature which come in the month of March.

These examples are far from being the only ones. The St. Paul chief of police recently wrote to ask me for some information about a man named Andrew Smith who worked for Gerard last year and whose mother had not heard from him for five or six months. Here is what happened to this poor devil.

In the first days of December, he undertook to go to Fort Buford alone to start working in the branch that Gerard had there at that time. He left on a pony which was loaned to him for this trip, and since then he has not been seen alive. A few weeks later, his body, or rather his remains, were found by the Indians from Fort Buford only seven or eight miles from the marked route. He had wandered around, and not being able to find his way on the prairies when he got away from the river, he had perished in the snow of cold, hunger, and exhaustion. The wolves had devoured him almost completely, so he could be recognized only by his clothes, and especially by his vest with which he had wrapped his feet that were probably frozen. What slow and terrible agony! His horse came back alone and was found three weeks later near an encampment of woodcutters above Berthold.

Friday, April 9. Anniversary of Lee's surrender. Four years ago on a day like this, what a scene at Clover Hill! As long as life lasts, those memories will never fade.[170]

170 For De Trobriand's description of Lee's surrender, see *Quatre Ans de Campagne à l'Armée du Potomac*, p. 382–385.

Saturday, April 10. Rather heavy snowfall during the night. This morning, the countryside was dressed, probably for the last time of the season, in its white robe, which disappeared before the sun's rays in a few hours. How many people there are in the world whose robe of innocence disappears like this before the rays of the sun of truth! Tomorrow's mail is awaited with great impatience. It will be heavy with news.

Sunday, April 11. Not at all. The mail arrived, and brought nothing new. The general orders for the combination of the regiments and my transfer to the command of the 13th infantry were already known to us through the newspapers. The detailed dispositions that we expected from the general headquarters of the Department are not a part of the despatches, so we are still waiting to find out the way in which the consolidation of the 31st and 22nd will be done, the distribution of the garrisons in the different posts, and other special points. The rumor is that the 13th will garrison Fort Buford.

Thursday, April 15. Twelve or thirteen days ago, a party of Arrikarees coming from Fort Buford passed the fort going down the river in bull boats. They were painted and armed for war, and, in fact, they were going toward Fort Rice with the intention of surprising the Sioux there and of getting in a good coup. Today they came back. Around the middle of the day their arrival was announced by columns of smoke rising to the horizon from the banks of the river, which for a moment was mistaken for the smoke of a steamboat. They came back in great spirits, and this evening there is great rejoicing in the quarters of the scouts where the victors are singing and dancing the scalp dance. They bring back two scalps and a horse. They killed a warrior from whom they captured a horse, weapons, and, this isn't the best part of the business, a squaw. But such is the custom of the redskins. With them, neither age nor sex has any immunity in war, and they kill children, old people, or women just as they do warriors. The victory of the Rees in this case cost them rather dearly. They picked up two of their warriors seriously wounded, one in the thigh, the other in the rump; both of them still have the bullets deep in the wounds. They are in the hospital where the doctor will extract the bullets. A third one has a slight wound on a finger of the left hand, a small bone of which was nicked by the bullet. All the Rees were on foot, and the Sioux whom they fought, Yanktonahs of Two Bears' band, were on horseback. They had to fight bravely and skillfully to bring back their wounded and the spoils of the enemy.

Friday, April 16. The aurora borealis is so frequent and so beautiful in these latitudes that it would take too long to describe it. Nevertheless, it is impossible not to note here the splendid phenomenon which we witnessed yesterday evening from nine to ten o'clock. Contrary to what I had always seen up to now, the rays or luminous discharges did not spring from the darkened vault at the edge of the horizon to the north. The center or nucleus was at the zenith, probably at the magnetic pole, where all the rays converge. So it was like a large luminous bell, and we were at the center. In all directions, the rounded sides went down to the edge of the horizon. It is an extraordinary thing, but the electric illumination was as strong in the south as the north with this difference that in the north it behaved as usual with luminous discharges, while in the south, it moved in huge waves, perfectly distinct from one another, which swept toward the zenith in waves similar to those of the sea, although they moved much more rapidly. When one of these waves reached the point of convergence, the brightness redoubled, just as a transparent wave breaks into foam against an obstruction. Luminous shadows of different kinds then formed at this point in the sky, and vanished in a few seconds to give place to others. This point, as I have said, touched at the zenith, a little above and to the right of the constellation of the Lion whose stars could be made out through this effulgent haze. The light of the atmosphere was like a beautiful twilight, but paler.

This reminds me that last month I saw a parhelion with three false suns; two to the right and left and the third at the top of the circle, the lower edge of which dipped behind the horizon. It was between seven and eight o'clock in the morning, and the sun still was not up very high. The phenomenon lasted about half an hour, three-fourths of an hour at the most.

After this unusual aurora borealis, we had the finest and warmest day of this season. The thermometer went up to sixty-five degrees F., six more than I have seen it reach before. And not a breath of air in the season when high winds blow almost incessantly.

Sunday, April 25. The orders which have been expected for three weeks finally arrived from the general headquarters of the Department. The principal dispositions which concern me are that I am relieved of the command of the Middle District, and am named commander of the District of Montana, where I am ordered to report without needless delay. The 31st is consolidated into five companies like the 22nd which will form the new 22nd. Fort Buford is transferred to the District of Montana, and will be garrisoned by three companies of the 13th which are going from Benton by the first boat to relieve the present garrison. All the posts of the new Middle District have two companies each.

And so I shall go ahead with my preparations for leaving, transfer of government property, packing, etc., after which I am on my way by the first boat which will furnish me a comfortable passage. My old adjutant, Mr. Marshall, will await orders from General Stanley to take to Fort Sully the noncommissioned staff, the band, and to transport the registers, official papers of the old District.

And so, for some time, I close my journal.

Bibliography

I. *The published works of Régis de Trobriand*

De Trobriand, Régis. *Quatre Ans de Campagne à l'Armée du Potomac.* Librairie Internationale, Paris, 1867.

————. *Les Gentilshommes de l'Ouest.* Louis Desessart, Paris, 1841.

————, editor. *La Revue du Nouveau Monde,* 1849–1850. New York. 4 v. There is a file in the University of Minnesota Library.

————. *Vie Militaire dans le Dakota.* Librairie Ancienne, Honoré Champion, Paris, 1926.

Post, Marie Caroline de Trobriand. *Life and Memoirs of General de Trobriand, U.S.A.* E. P. Dutton & Co., New York, 1910. Mrs. Post has selected letters written by General de Trobriand and letters written to him, as well as portions of "Vie Militaire," which was then in manuscript form. She has added to the papers biographical data drawn from her own memory.

Quaife, Milo M., editor. *Army Life in Dakota.* The Lakeside Press, Donnelley & Sons, Chicago, 1941. Selections from the published journal, translated by George F. Will.

II. *Manuscripts*

Armstrong, Moses K. Diary kept as secretary to the Indian Peace Commission of 1866. Minnesota Historical Society. There are in the diary data on the posts from Fort Pierre to Fort Union and on the Indian chiefs of Dakota who signed the treaties of 1866.

Colhoun, Edward. Diary kept on his trip with Stephen H. Long in 1823. Typescript in the Minnesota Historical Society. Dr. Mary D. Galligan, Minneapolis, owns the original diary.

Curry, Thomas. "Recollections of Yellowstone Kelly." Montana Historical Library.

De Trobriand, Régis. "Vie Militaire dans le Dakota." Manuscript journal in the possession of Waldron Kintzing Post, New York City.

De Trobriand Family Papers, in the possession of Waldron Kintzing Post, New York City. Some of these papers were published in *Life and Memoirs of General de Trobriand, U. S. A.*

Hilger, David, to Chas. W. Ruzica. Telegram, December 28, 1928, on the death of Yellowstone Kelly. Montana Historical Library.

"Interview with F. F. Gerard's Daughter." Library of St. Benedict's Academy, St. Joseph, Minnesota.

Sanborn (John B.) Papers. 1854–1882. Minnesota Historical Society.

Sibley (Henry H.) Papers. 1815–1891. Minnesota Historical Society.

U. S. Office of Indian Affairs. National Archives. Record Copies of Letters Sent. January 30, 1864, to March 23, 1869.

——. Dakota Superintendency. Record Copy of Letters Sent, July 22, 1864, to August 31, 1869.

——. Dakota Superintendency. Record Copies of Letters Received, May 14, 1864, to August 31, 1869.

——. Appointments Division, Record Copy of Nominations, April 15, 1862, to December, 1869.

——. Appointments Division, Record Copy of Letters Received, February 28, 1868, to April 20, 1869.

U. S. War Department. National Archives. Middle District, Department of Dakota. Record Copy of Letters Sent, July, 1867, to April, 1869. Endorsements, July, 1867, to April, 1869. General Orders, July, 1867, to April, 1869. Special Orders, July, 1867, to April, 1869.

——. Department of Dakota. Letters to Régis de Trobriand.

——. Medical Histories of Fort Stevenson, Fort Buford, Fort Totten.

Whipple (Henry B.) Papers. 1833–1908. Minnesota Historical Society.

III. *Government Documents, printed*

Annual Report of the Commissioner of Indian Affairs, 1867, 1868, 1869, 1870. Washington, D. C.

Annual Report of the Secretary of War, 1866, 1867–68, 1868–69, 1869, 1869–70. Washington, D. C.

Annual Report of the Bureau of American Ethnology, 1896–97. Washington, D. C.

Annual Report of the Bureau of American Ethnology, 1928–29. Washington, D. C.

Annual Report of the Bureau of American Ethnology, 1882–83. Washington, D. C.

Hodge, Frederick W., editor. *Handbook of the American Indian.* Washington, D. C. 1907–1910. 2 v.

House Executive Document no. 76, 39 Congress, 1 session, serial no. 1263. Report on the Department of Missouri.

Bibliography

House Executive Document no. 76, 40 Congress, 2 session, serial no. 1332. Report on the Sioux Indians in Dakota.

House Executive Document no. 97, 40 Congress, 2 session, serial no. 1337. Report of the Indian Peace Commissioners.

House Executive Document no. 124, 40 Congress, 2 session, serial no. 1337. Appropriations for Indian Treaties.

House Executive Document no. 239, 40 Congress, 2 session, serial no. 1341. Subsistence of Indian Tribes.

House Miscellaneous Document no. 37, 39 Congress, 2 session, serial no. 1302. Indian Affairs.

House Report no. 45, 39 Congress, 1 session, serial no. 1272. Military Posts on the Northern Overland Mail Route.

Kappler, Charles J. *Indian Affairs, Laws and Treaties.* Washington, D. C., 1903–1913. 3 v.

Senate Executive Document no. 26, 39 Congress, 2 session, serial no. 1277. Report on the Sand Creek Massacre.

Senate Executive Document no. 22, 39 Congress, 2 session, serial no. 1277. Report on Indians in Dakota Territory.

Senate Executive Document no. 15, 39 Congress, 2 session, serial no. 1277. Report on the Fort Phil. Kearny Massacre.

Senate Executive Document no. 13, 40 Congress, 1 session, serial no. 1308.

Report on Barracks and Hospitals with Descriptions of Military Posts, circular no. 4, War Department, Surgeon General's Office, 1870.

Roberts, Thomas P. *Report on a Reconnaissance of the Missouri River in 1872.* Government Printing Office, 1875.

Thian, Raphael P. *Notes Illustrating the Military Geography of the United States.* Washington, D. C., 1881.

IV. *Newspapers*

The Army and Navy Journal, 1866–1870, in the files of the Minnesota Historical Society.

The Helena Herald, 1866–1868, in the files of the Montana Historical Library.

The Montana Post, 1864–1869, in the files of the Montana Historical Library.

The St. Paul Daily Pioneer, 1866–1870, in the files of the Minnesota Historical Society.

V. *Articles*

Atherton, Lewis E. "The Services of the Frontier Merchant," *Mississippi Valley Historical Review,* 24:153–170. September, 1937.

Chauncey, Thomas. "Frontier Firearms," *The Colorado Magazine,* 7:102–109. January, 1930.

Collins, Ethel A. "Pioneer Experiences of Horatio H. Larned, *North Dakota Historical Collections,* 7:1–58. Grand Forks, 1925.

DeLand, Charles E. "The Aborigines of South Dakota," Part I, *South Dakota Historical Collections,* 3:271–586. Aberdeen, 1906.

———. "The Aborigines of South Dakota," Part II, *South Dakota Historical Collections,* 4:275–730. Sioux Falls, 1908.

Green, Charles L. "The Indian Reservation System of the Dakotas to 1889," *South Dakota Historical Collections,* 14:307–411. Pierre, 1928.

"Letellier's Autobiography," *South Dakota Historical Collections,* 4:217–253. Sioux Falls, 1908.

Lull, George F. "The Old Army Life," *Field Artillery Journal,* 26:307–310. May–June, 1936.

Marks, Constant R. "French Pioneers of Sioux City and South Dakota," *South Dakota Historical Collections,* 4:255–260. Sioux Falls, 1908.

National Waterways, February, 1930. This is the log of the "Deer Lodge" on her trip up the Missouri River in August, 1867.

Quaife, Milo M., editor. "The Small Pox Epidemic on the Upper Missouri," *Mississippi Valley Historical Review,* 17:278–299. September, 1930.

"Steamboat Wrecks in South Dakota," *South Dakota Historical Collections,* 9:393–402. 1918.

"Theophile Bruguier," *South Dakota Historical Collections,* 4:263–270. Sioux Falls, 1908.

Welty, Raymond L. "The Army and the Mining Frontier," *The Frontier,* 12:261–269. March, 1932.

———. "The Frontier Army on the Missouri River," *North Dakota Historical Quarterly,* 2:85–99. January, 1928.

———. "The Policing of the Frontier by the Army," *Kansas Historical Quarterly,* 7:246–257. August, 1938.

———. "Supplying the Frontier Military Posts," *Kansas Historical Quarterly,* 7:154–169. May, 1938.

Will, George F. "The Mandan Lodge at Bismarck," *North Dakota Historical Quarterly,* 5:38–48. October, 1930.

Bibliography

Wright, Dana. "Military Trails in Dakota," *North Dakota History*, 13:80–95, 103–111. January, 1946. July, 1946.

VI. *Books*

Abel, Annie Heloise, editor. *Chardon's Journal at Fort Clark, 1834–1839*. Department of History, State of South Dakota, Pierre, 1932.

Bandell, Eugene. *Frontier Life in the Army, 1854–1861*. The Arthur H. Clark Co., Cleveland, 1930.

Barrett, Jay A. *The History and Government of Nebraska*. J. H. Miller, Lincoln, 1892.

Boller, Henry A. *Among the Indians*. T. Ellwood Zell, Philadelphia, 1868.

Briggs, Harold E. *Frontiers of the Northwest*. D. Appleton Century Co., New York, 1940.

Chittenden, Hiram M. *The American Fur Trade of the Far West*. The Press of the Pioneers, Inc., New York, 1935. 2 v.

———. *History of Early Steamboat Navigation on the Missouri River*. F. P. Harper, New York, 1903. 2 v.

Collins, John S. *Across the Plains in '64*. National Printing Co., Omaha, 1904.

Crawford, Lewis F. *History of North Dakota*. The American Historical Society, Inc., Chicago and New York, 1931. 3 v.

Cullum, George Washington. *Biographical Register of the Officers and Graduates of the U.S. Military Academy at West Point* . . . Houghton Mifflin & Co., New York, 1891–1930.

Dodge, Richard Irving. *The Plains of the Great West*. G. P. Putnam's Sons, New York, 1877.

Downey, Fairfax. *Indian Fighting Army*. Charles Scribner's Sons, New York, 1941.

Fiske, Frank. *The Taming of the Sioux*. Bismarck Tribune, Bismarck, 1917.

Folwell, William Watts. *A History of Minnesota*. Minnesota Historical Society, St. Paul, 1921–1930. 4 v.

Ganoe, William A. *The History of the United States Army*. D. Appleton Century Co., New York, 1943.

———. *Selected Bibliography in the History of the United States Army*. D. Appleton Century, New York, 1924.

Grinnell, George B. *Beyond the Old Frontier*. Charles Scribner's Sons, New York, 1913.

Judd, A. N. *Campaigning against the Sioux*. Waterville, California, [1905].

Hanson, Joseph Mills. *The Conquest of the Missouri.* A. C. McClurg & Co., Chicago, 1906.

Heitman, Francis B. *Historical Register of the United States Army.* The National Tribune, Washington, D. C., 1890. 2 v.

Henry, Stuart O. *Conquering Our Great American Plains.* E. P. Dutton & Co., New York, 1930.

Hyde, George E. *Red Cloud's Folk.* University of Oklahoma Press, Norman, 1937.

Kelly, Luther S. *Yellowstone Kelly.* (Notes by Milo Quaife.) Yale University Press, New Haven, 1926.

Kingsbury, George Washington. *History of Dakota Territory.* S. J. Clarke Publishing Co., Chicago, 1915. 3 v.

Larpenteur, Charles. *Forty Years a Fur Trader on the Upper Missouri,* edited by Elliot Coues. Francis P. Harper, New York, 1898. 2 v.

Libby, O. G., editor. *The Arikara Narrative of the Campaign against the Hostile Dakotas.* North Dakota Historical Collections, Vol. VI, Bismarck, 1920.

Lounsberry, Clement A. *North Dakota History and People.* S. J. Clarke Publishing Co., Chicago, 1916. 3 v.

McLaughlin, James. *My Friend the Indian.* Houghton Mifflin Co., Boston and New York, 1910.

MacLeod, William C. *The American Indian Frontier.* Knopf, New York, 1928.

Marcy, Randolph B. *Thirty Years of Army Life on the Border.* Harper and Brother, New York, 1866.

Priest, Loring B. *Uncle Sam's Stepchildren.* Rutgers University Press, New York, 1942.

Robinson, Doane. *South Dakota, Sui Generis.* The American Historical Society, Chicago and New York, 1930. 3 v.

———. *The Sioux Indians: A History.* Torch Press, Cedar Rapids, Iowa, 1908.

Sawyer, Charles W. *Our Rifles.* Williams Book Store, Boston, 1941.

Seymour, Flora W. *Indian Agents of the Old Frontier.* D. Appleton–Century Co., New York and London, 1941.

Shambaugh, Benjamin F. *The Old Stone Capitol Remembers.* State Historical Society, Iowa City, 1939.

Spinden, Herbert J., and George F. Will. *The Mandans.* The Museum, Cambridge, Mass., 1906.

Standing Bear, Luther. *My People, the Sioux.* Houghton Mifflin Co., Boston and New York, 1928.

Bibliography

Taylor, Joseph Henry. *Kaleidoscopic Lives*. Published by the author, Washburn, North Dakota, 1902.

———. *Sketches of Frontier and Indian Life on the Upper Missouri and Great Plains*. Published by the author, Pottstown, Pa., 1889.

Vernon, Edward, compiler. *American Railroad Manual for the United States and the Dominion*. The American Railroad Manual Company, New York, 1873.

Vestal, Stanley C. *New Sources of Indian History*. University of Oklahoma Press, Norman, 1934.

———. *Sitting Bull*. Houghton Mifflin Co., Boston and New York, 1932.

Wissler, Clark. *The American Indian*. Oxford University Press, New York, 1938.

Wissler, Clark, editor. *Anthropological Papers of the American Museum of Natural History*, Vol. XVII, New York, 1916.

De Trobriand, the Artist

Oil paintings and pencil sketches owned by Waldron Kintzing Post

Missouri River

Missouri River, below Fort Berthold, July, 1868. Pencil sketch.
Dauphin Rapids, May, 1869. Pencil sketch.
Upper Missouri. Oil painting.
Upper Missouri. Oil painting.
Great Falls of the Missouri River. Oil painting.
Upper Missouri Rapids, near Benton. Oil painting.

Dakota Territory

Devils Lake, August, 1868. Pencil sketch.
Fort Totten, August, 1868. Pencil sketch.
Fort Stevenson, May, 1868. Pencil sketch.
Fort Stevenson, June, 1868. Pencil sketch.
Fort Stevenson, April, 1869. Pencil sketch.
Fort Stevenson, April, 1869. Pencil sketch.
Fort Stevenson. Oil painting.
Fort Stevenson, Traders' Stores. Oil painting.
Fort Stevenson, Winter Quarters. Oil painting.
Fort Stevenson, Douglas Creek. Oil painting.
Fort Berthold, June, 1868. Pencil sketch.
Fort Berthold, June, 1868. Pencil sketch.
The Badlands, May, 1868. Pencil sketch.

Portraits

White Shield. [Undated] Pencil sketch.
Crow's Breast, May, 1868. Pencil sketch.
Eagle Who Pursues the Eagle, June, 1868. Pencil sketch.

Montana Territory

Lewis' Ranch, September, 1869. Pencil sketch.

Sun River, August, 1869. Pencil sketch.
Sun River, August, 1869. Pencil sketch.
Sun River, near Fort Shaw. Oil painting.
Prickly Pear Canyon, September, 1869. Pencil sketch.
Prickly Pear Canyon, September, 1869. Pencil sketch.
Prickly Pear Canyon, September, 1869. Pencil sketch.
Prickly Pear Canyon, September, 1869. Pencil sketch.
Prickly Pear Canyon. Oil painting.
Prickly Pear Canyon. Oil painting.
New Mission, September, 1869. Pencil sketch.
New Mission Canyon, September, 1869. Pencil sketch.
Schmidt's Ranch, September, 1869. Pencil sketch.
Fort Shaw, June, 1869. Pencil sketch.
Fort Shaw, July, 1869. Pencil sketch.
Fort Shaw, July, 1869. Pencil sketch.
Fort Shaw. Oil painting.
Fort Ellis, September, 1869. Pencil sketch.
Fort Ellis. Oil painting.

Wyoming Territory

Fort Steele, November, 1871. Pencil sketch.
Fort Steele, June, 1872. Pencil sketch.
Fort Steele, June, 1872. Pencil sketch.
Fort Steele. Oil painting.
Fort Steele. Oil painting.
Fort Steele. Oil painting.

Utah Territory

Camp Douglas, August, 1871. Pencil sketch.
Camp Douglas. Oil painting.
American Canyon. Oil painting.

Marginal Sketches in the French Manuscript

(The pagination refers to the location in the original manuscript)

Bench Used in the Indian Theater, p. 145
Bull Boat, p. 91
Burial Scaffold, p. 127
Calumet, p. 152
Corner of Fort Berthold, p. 128

Index

Abercrombie, J. J., 44n

Abilene, xviii

Adobe, xix, 43, 74, 120, 220, 305, 335

Agency, Grand River, 339, 339n, 359

Agents, Indian, xviii, 159, 160, 181–83, 311–12, 316, 361, 363; malfeasance of, 155–57, 157n

Alexander, Edmund B., 45

Ambulances, 308, 333. *See also* Transportation, overland, ambulances

American Fur Company, xv, 22n, 45n, 83n, 87n, 91n, 98n, 141n

Ammunition, trade in, 104, 104n, 119, 122, 127, 170, 224n, 225n; Cheyenne, 102; Sioux, 102; three tribes, 101–107

Amusements, army posts, 150, 159, 175, 191, 208, 212, 232, 234, 235, 238

Anderson, Joseph, 71, 304, 311, 316, 335, 343

Animal life

antelope, 32, 35, 37, 40, 140, 151, 152, 188, 193, 230, 240, 283, 309, 319, 323

bears, 11

beaver, 40, 81, 108–11, 117, 142, 155. *See also* Fur trade

bison, *see* buffalo

buffalo, xviii, 28, 28n, 32, 35, 102, 123, 126, 148, 152, 162, 169, 175, 176, 187–88, 193, 224, 230, 240, 247, 249, 257, 258, 269, 290, 312, 355; Indian imitation of, 287, 350

deer, 32, 35, 123, 152, 175, 188, 193, 230, 237, 240

elk, 240, 247, 321

fox, 80

hare, 32

lynx, 263–64

marten, 177

muskrat, 137

prairie dogs, 321–22

rabbits, 32, 188, 237, 240

snakes, 322

toads, 322

wolves, 11, 50, 115, 119, 188, 319, 323

Animals, domesticated

cattle, 28, 42, 44, 49, 51, 60, 71, 120–21, 123, 151, 192, 210, 212, 215–16, 217–18, 248, 270, 283–84, 306, 311, 316, 317, 327, 340–41, 343, 361; shelters for, 335–36; theft of, 331–32, 337, 342, 363

dogs, 77, 78, 79, 88, 99, 119, 139–40, 154, 188, 198, 199, 227, 229, 232, 236, 238, 239, 241, 242, 300, 303, 320, 323

greyhounds, 21, 28

hogs, 20, 248

horses, 28, 48, 64, 71, 73, 88, 99, 113, 114, 115, 138, 163, 170, 176, 177, 184, 186, 192, 193, 198, 199, 221, 222, 225, 226, 227, 236, 243, 244, 245, 276, 280, 283, 303, 306, 336, 357, 361; bridles, 142; Indian, 28, 63, 64, 66, 256, 257, 258, 269, 348, 364; officers', 21; presents, 251–52; theft of, 142–43, 150, 257, 283, 287, 290, 310, 324, 351; trade in, 127, 148, 247, 251, 264, 341, 342

mules, 32, 58, 59, 60, 66, 71, 133, 192, 212, 218, 288, 295, 305, 314, 348, 369; theft of, 134, 135, 138, 172, 174–75, 257, 290, 310, 328, 337; trade in, 127

oxen, 32, 133, 305, 322, 323

Annuities, theft by Indian agents, xviii. *See also* Annuities under the names of the various Indian tribes

Army, U. S., as Indian agents, xviii; board of survey, 235; burial services, 263; cavalry, 44; changes in regiments, 364, 367; conditions on the plains, xviii–xix; Department of Dakota, xviii–xix, 44; Department of Dakota, District of Minnesota, xix, 45; Department of Dakota, District of Montana, xix; Department of Dakota, District of Southeast Dakota, xix, 21, 45, 57; Department of Dakota, District of Sun River, 45; Department of Dakota, Middle District, xix, 45; Department

383

Index

Chambers, Mrs. Alexander, 21

Chicago, 16; growth of, 11–12; railroad center, 11

Chivington Massacre, 116–17

Cholera, 102n, 246

Chouteau, Pierre, xv, 112, 141n, 277

Churches, in charge of Indian affairs, xviii

City planning, De Trobriand's comment on, 16

Civil War, xix, xxiii, xxiv, 19, 38, 49

Clark, ——, captain of the *Deer Lodge*, 19, 21

Clarke, Francis, 69, 155, 158, 193, 194n, 224, 224n, 241, 304, 334, 339, 341, 361

Clear Lake, 287, 329, 334, 347

Cobden, Richard, quotation from, 12

Cold Water, mail station, 162

Construction materials, 41, 58, 118, 308–309, 334–36, 346

Coon, Abram, 324, 324n

Corbin, ——, clerk, *Deer Lodge*, 21

Corn, 28, 88, 102, 230, 245, 247, 249, 355; caches, 350; storage of, 148–49; trade in, 148, 341, 342. *See also* Three tribes, agriculture

Council Bluffs, 12, 13–14

Couriers, 48; half-breed, 287, 362; Indian, 331; murder of, 332; wages, 244, 289. *See also* Mail service; Half-breeds; Indians; Transportation

Courrier des Etats Unis, xxii–xxiii

Courts-martial, 70, 72, 152, 154, 155, 158, 194, 203–204, 229, 285, 296, 309, 318, 319, 326, 327, 328, 330, 333, 334, 334n, 339, 339–40, 353, 362, 362n

Cozzens Hotel, Omaha, 14

Crow Creek, Yanktonai agency, 27n

Crow Island, 325

Cunard Steamship Line, 4

Cusick, Cornelius, 327, 331, 363, 364, 369

Cussick, Cornelius, *see* Cusick, Cornelius

Custer, George A., xvii, xx, 65, 65n

Dakota Territory, capitol, 27

Davis, Jefferson, 280

Deep Bottom, 38

Desertion, xix, 72, 72n, 73, 73n, 118, 186, 306

De Smet, Pierre Jean, xviii, 116, 160, 231n, 248, 253, 253n, 254, 256, 261, 292n, 294–95, 295n, 310, 311n

DeTrobriand, Philippe Régis, life, xxi–xxv, 200–202, 223, 361; in Paris, 3; trip from Brest to New York, 4–9; trip from New York to Omaha, 11–14; trip from Omaha to Fort Stevenson, 20–40; observations about Omaha, 15–20; at Fort Stevenson, 40–78, 118–300, 302–18, 330–72; at Fort Berthold, 78–118, 300–302; at Fort Totten, 319–30; as artist, x, xii, xxiv, 137, 170, 238, 281, 302, 309, 323, 326, 330; as author, x, xi, xxii–xxiv, 279, 280, 280n, 281, 281n, 284–85; opinions on communication with the dead, 54–56; opinions on woodcutters, 31–32; opinions on Indian affairs, 18, 155–56; opinions on warfare against the Indians, 64–67; opinions on women at the frontier posts, 214–15

De Trobriand family, xxi

Devils Lake, 22, 42, 44, 49, 53, 67, 121, 122, 137, 139, 140, 153, 157, 184, 186, 199, 222, 227, 239, 258, 261, 270, 271, 280, 286, 308, 325, 337

Dickey, Charles J., 69, 282, 332, 340, 352, 354, 357

Dog Den, 138, 139, 148, 162, 258, 271, 281, 299, 321, 322, 338

D'Otrante, Count, western traveler, 303

Douglas Creek, 42, 59, 76, 79, 124, 150, 158, 159, 162, 163, 175, 176, 184, 235, 250, 255, 259, 261, 269, 347

Dupont, ——, De Trobriand's servant, 210, 212, 213, 215, 219

Durfee and Peck, xvi, 312, 359n, 363n

Egan, Thomas, 284–85

Elliot, Thomas I., *see* Elliott, Thomas I.

Elliott, Thomas I., 21, 33

Elliott, Mrs. Thomas I., 21

Ellis, Philip H., 121, 123–24, 152, 154, 194, 296, 297

Elmla, Joe, 321, 321n, 322, 324

Fetterman, W. J., xxvii, xx

Fetterman Massacre, xvii, 47n

Feuilletons du Lundi, xxiii

Firearms, xviii, 17, 33, 34, 41, 61, 63, 63n, 77, 79, 81, 91, 107, 113, 119, 125, 130, 131, 133, 134, 137, 141, 150, 151, 171, 179, 180, 186, 187, 230, 242, 245, 249, 263, 281, 282, 288, 290, 306, 307–308, 311n, 321, 331, 337, 338, 356, 357

Fish
crayfish, 15
perch, 321, 329
whitefish, 32

Fisher, Thomas H., 38

385

Fishing, 281, 293, 309, 321, 329, 330
Fisk, James L., expedition of, xvii
Five Lakes, 333
Flury, ——, carter, Northwestern Fur Company, 298
Food, xix, 95, 99, 151, 207–208, 211, 212, 238, 241, 249, 258, 262–63, 271, 308; at the posts, 49; on steamboats, 59. *See also* Provisions
Fort Kearny Massacre, 38n
Forts
　Abercrombie, Fort, 44, 44n, 45, 162, 174, 228, 240n, 272, 275, 305, 326, 341
　Benton, Fort, xvi, xvii, 21n, 34, 44, 45n, 52, 75, 120, 129, 152, 240n, 281, 283, 295, 296, 297, 303, 306, 309, 350, 366, 368, 372
　Berthold, Fort, 22, 22n, 33, 42, 47, 50, 51, 51n, 57, 58, 71, 73, 80, 81, 85, 128, 136, 148, 150, 153, 156, 157, 168, 171, 179, 186, 192, 200, 230, 235, 236, 237, 239, 242, 243, 249, 253, 258, 259, 264, 273, 279, 289, 290, 291, 292, 295, 300–302, 303, 304, 306, 309, 311, 312, 316, 327, 336, 341, 350, 354, 356, 360–61, 363, 364, 366; attack of the Sioux on, 90–93; battle of the three tribes with the Sioux, 293–94; cemetery, 82–83; description of, 83; visit of De Trobriand to, 79–118
　Buford, Fort, xix, 22, 22n, 44, 46, 46n, 51, 63, 69, 70, 106, 120, 121, 122, 123, 124, 129, 130, 138, 139, 144, 148, 152, 171, 182, 192, 193, 224, 239, 241, 244, 247, 250, 252, 256, 271, 273, 281, 282, 295, 296, 297, 300, 331, 332, 334, 337, 338, 339, 341, 342, 343, 349, 352, 354, 356, 357, 358, 363, 369, 370, 371–72; conditions at, 154, 155, 158, 172–73, 172n, 193–94, 225, 357–58; 357n; construction, 132; robbery, 363; social life, 307n
　Clark, Fort, 360
　Cooke, Camp, 44, 44n
　D. A. Russell, Fort, 19n
　Dearborn, Fort, 11n
　Ellis, Fort, 45n
　Fisher, Fort, 45
　Philip Kearny, Fort, 47
　Pierre, Fort, xv, 21n, 141, 141n
　Randall, Fort, 21, 21n, 27, 28, 38, 141n, 163, 174, 258, 336, 343
　Ransom, Fort, 44, 44n, 174, 228, 260, 271, 272, 275, 305, 306, 326, 341

Reynolds, Camp, 44n
Rice, Fort, 9, 21n, 23, 23n, 37, 38, 39, 57, 58, 71, 73, 161, 162, 168, 169, 173, 174, 178, 179, 184, 189, 198, 199, 204, 221, 222, 223, 225, 238, 247, 250, 251, 253, 254, 256, 257, 258, 261, 265, 274, 283, 284, 286, 292, 294, 295, 296, 297, 299, 303, 306, 308, 309, 310, 312, 318, 336, 337, 338, 339, 342, 343, 348, 359, 360, 365, 370; Indians, 38; lodgings, 37–38
Shaw, Fort, xxv, 44, 44n, 45, 45n, 283, 293, 295, 305, 368
Steele, Fort, xxv
Stevenson, Fort, xxv, 22, 38, 40, 40n, 41, 45, 69, 70, 80, 99n, 117, 120, 124, 152, 154, 162, 171, 174, 192, 200, 227, 228, 241, 261, 271, 274, 275, 276, 280, 283, 289, 297, 300, 303, 304, 308, 311, 316, 319, 322, 323, 324, 326, 327, 328, 329, 330, 331, 333, 334, 338, 344; burial ceremony, 50, 263, 300, 350; commemoration of Buchanan's death, 310; construction of, 42, 43, 128, 129, 300, 305, 334–36; daily routine, 233; description, 41–44, 121; De Trobriand's assignment to, xv; fire, 344–47; Fourth of July, 307, 307n; garden, 313, 314, 315; health conditions, 261–63, 262n; lodgings, 20, 44, 54, 150, 151, 153, 163, 175–76, 186, 190, 194, 195–98, 203, 205, 206, 207, 208, 209, 210, 211, 212, 213, 214, 216, 217, 238, 252, 262, 274, 284, 334–36, 340, 350; officers, 43; social life, 203, 234, 237–38, 275, 302–303, 307, 317; soldiers, 43
Sully, Fort, 21, 21n, 31, 33, 34, 45, 57, 66, 163, 174, 292, 336, 343
Thompson, Fort, 292
Totten, Fort, 22, 22n, 42, 44, 53, 67, 67n, 69, 70, 71, 72, 73, 120, 121, 122, 123, 139, 140, 149, 151, 153, 157, 162, 164, 171, 174, 186, 198, 199, 200, 204, 218, 221, 222, 225, 227, 228, 229, 232, 238, 239, 240, 247, 250, 254, 260, 265, 274, 275, 279, 280, 280n, 283, 286, 287, 289, 298, 303, 305, 306, 307, 308, 309, 318, 319, 319–30, 322, 323, 324, 325, 329, 330, 331, 332, 333, 337, 340, 341, 343, 347, 361, 362, 363, 367, 368, 369; burial ceremony, 330; conditions at, 67–70, 72, 228, 229, 229n, 270–71, 362; description, 325–26, 329; half-breeds, 271; health con-

Index

Two Ribs of Bear, 257
Weeping Buffalo, 312, 313
White Bonnet, 240n
White Cloud, 192–193
White Faced Bear, 337
White Parefleche, *see* White Shield
White Shield, 95, 104–105, 106, 113, 126–27, 156, 160, 181–83, 230, 231n, 350–51
Won-ta-na-han, 256
Indians, tribes
Absaroke, *see* Crow
Arapaho, 45, 138, 138n, 144, 342
Arikara, 50, 50n, 73, 111, 142, 156, 184, 251, 252, 257, 264, 267, 289, 292, 297, 327, 350, 370; annuities, 159, 312; conferences with De Trobriand, 100–107; dress, 95; famine, 230, 290; magic, 97–98; medicine lodge, 93; music, 93–97; numbers, 95, 278; oratory, 350; ornaments, 95, 100; presents, 244, 354; scouts, 276, 279, 284; theatrical performances, 93–98; wars against the Sioux, 57, 113–15, 150, 283–84, 370. *See also* Three tribes
Arikaris, *see* Arikara
Arrapahoe, *see* Arapaho
Arrikaris, *see* Arikara
Arrikhar'hos, *see* Arikara
Assiniboin, 28, 138, 138n, 250, 258, 266; numbers, 278
Atsina, *see* Gros Ventres of the Prairie
Blackfeet Sioux, 122, 122n, 138, 144, 342; hostilities, 264; numbers, 278; reservations, 339n
Brulé, 28n, 251n; hostilities, 251–52; numbers, 278
Cheyenne, 19, 45, 65n, 102n, 116, 117, 122, 138, 138n, 144, 342
Chippewa, treaties, 11n
Comanche, 45, 342
Cree, 192, 192n
Crow, 138, 138n, 325; language, 278–79; Mountain, numbers, 278; Plains, numbers, 278
Cut Heads, 140, 140n, 258, 258n, 278; hardships, 258; hostilities, 258; presents, 258; reservations, 339n
Fox, treaties, 11n
Gens de la Feuille, 224, 224n
Gens des Feuilles, *see* Gens de la Feuille
Gros Ventres, 50, 51, 57, 91n, 98, 239, 241, 243, 249, 257, 266–67, 290, 291; agriculture, 245, 247, 248, 249; an-

nuities, 160, 246; children, 146–47; conferences with De Trobriand, 100–107, 244–49; dress, 86, 244; hair dress, 86; language, 102, 278–79; numbers, 278; oratory, 101–107, 245; origin of the name, 50, 86; ornaments, 86, 100, 244; presents, 354; wars against the Sioux, 350–51; winter encampment, 244. *See also* Three Tribes
Gros Ventres of the Missouri, 51n. *See also* Gros Ventres
Gros Ventres of the Prairie, 51n
Hedanza, *see* Gros Ventres
Hidatsa, *see* Gros Ventres
Hunkpapa, xvi, 28n, 38, 38n, 122, 138, 140, 144, 148, 179, 183, 184, 257, 278, 356–57; conference with De Trobriand, 140–46; customs, dress, 140; customs, hair dress, 140, 289; customs, ornaments, 140; hostilities, xvii, 38, 38n, 127, 135–36, 139, 142–43, 259, 261, 264–65, 267, 283–84, 287–90, 298, 299, 310, 322; numbers, 278; oratory, 143–44, 145; opportunity for attack, 342; presents, 146; reservations, 339n; thievery, 269–70; trade with the three tribes, 341–42
Kiowa, 342
Mandans, 50, 51n, 57, 57n, 98, 119, 279, 336; annuities, 160; conferences with De Trobriand, 100–107; famine, 235, 290; hair dress, 100; numbers, 278; ornaments, 100; presents, 235, 244; treaties, 57n; wars against the Sioux, 283. *See also* Three Tribes
Mdewakanton, 28n, 224n
Men of the Willows, *see* Gros Ventres
Miniconjou, 28n; hostilities, 127, 127n, 264; numbers, 278
Minniconjou, *see* Miniconjou
Mississippi Sioux, *see* Santee; Sisseton; Wahpeton; Cut Heads
Ogallala, *see* Oglala
Oglala, xvi, 28n, 278n, 310n; numbers, 278
Ottawa, treaties, 11n
Pahlanis, *see* Arikara
Pananis, *see* Arikara
Pawnee, 65, 66, 69n, 279
Piegans, xxv
Pottawatomi, treaties, 11n
Rappahoes, *see* Arapaho
Rees, *see* Arikara

389

Index

LaBarge, Joseph, 303
Lafayette Guard, xxiv
Lake Michigan, 11
Lamotte, R. S., 368
Land speculation, 24
Languages, 201; Arikara, 105; English, 248–49; French, 48, 78, 90, 109, 117; Gros Ventres, 102; Indian, 167; interpreters, 86, 102, 103, 109, 146, 164; Mandan, 105–106n; Sioux, 92, 183–84, 184n; Spanish, 244, 248–49
Leblanc, ——, interpreter, 164
Leonard, Charles H., 68, 121, 123, 152, 228, 229, 309, 328, 330, 337, 338, 354, 357
Le Rebelle, Nouvelle Canadienne, [sic] xxii
Libraries, army posts, 54, 108, 232, 232n, 234, 238
Lincoln, Nebraska, 16n
Liquor trade, 118, 122, 139, 148, 192, 224, 225, 277, 304, 358–59, 359n
Little, Thomas, 154, 155, 158, 172–73, 172n, 229, 332, 353, 354, 358
Little Big Horn, Battle of, xvii
Little Missouri River, 342
Little Muddy River, 122
Lockwood, Benjamin C., 67, 68, 72, 228, 270, 323, 330, 338
Logging and lumbering, 43, 62, 131, 304, 311, 335

McClellan, George B., 280
MacDonald, Charley, 79, 138, 139, 140, 148, 164, 287–89, 288n, 298, 321, 321n, 322, 324
Mackinaw boats, see Transportation, Mackinaws, Missouri River
Macklin, James E., 274, 275, 305
Macklin, Mrs. James E., 274, 275
Mail service, 21n, 57n, 58, 164, 203, 237–38, 271–72, 347, 364, 370; dependence of forts on, xix; mail routes, 139–40; overland routes, 44n, 162, 171; overland route, Fort Buford to Fort Stevenson, Fort Stevenson to Fort Buford, 192, 193, 193n, 224, 239, 239–44, 241, 250, 349, 354, 356, 358; overland route, Fort Ransom to Fort Abercrombie, 228; overland route, Fort Rice to Fort Stevenson, Fort Stevenson to Fort Rice, 173–74, 198–200, 204, 221, 222, 223, 225, 238, 250, 253, 254, 256, 284, 292, 295, 303, 348, 359, 365; overland route, St. Paul to Fort Totten, 260; overland

route, Fort Totten to Fort Stevenson, Fort Stevenson to Fort Totten, 138, 189, 198–200, 204, 218, 221, 222–23, 225–28, 229–30, 232, 240, 250, 254, 260–61, 279, 286–87, 287–90, 298, 303–304, 305, 306, 323, 328, 331, 361–62, 367; overland route, pony express, Fort Abercrombie to Fort Benton, 240n; Missouri River, steamboat, 118, 123, 149, 150, 282, 290, 297
Mandan houses, see Lodgings under Three tribes
Marcy, Randolph B., 110, 326
Marivelli, Guiseppe, 239, 240n, 240, 240n, 239–44, 246
Marsh, D. W., 71, 72, 87, 132, 133, 153, 179, 292, 293, 312, 316, 363
Marshal, James M., see Marshall, James M.
Marshall, James M., 21, 48, 172, 194, 214, 216, 309, 319, 372
Marshall, Mrs. James M., 214, 279
Martin, Joe, 164, 165, 167, 178, 199, 222, 223, 225, 227, 287, 288, 299, 310, 322, 324, 338
Matthews, Washington, 79, 99n, 101, 296
Meade, Lieutenant George, 69
Meade, General George G., 69
Meyer, Edward S., 19
Middle Station, 323, 347
Midway Station, 329
Milk River, 138
Mines and miners, xvi, xix, 28, 28n, 29, 46, 118, 129–30, 136, 150n, 152, 277, 324, 366, 368
Minnesota Massacre, 28n, 91, 117, 122, 167, 239, 257, 258, 277
Missouri River, 3, 9, 76, 113, 347; breakup, 235, 236–37, 250, 252, 254–56, 274, 365, 366; description, 23, 25, 26–27, 28, 29, 33, 34, 39, 75, 79, 161, 176, 348; fortifications, 21n; freight rates, 34; Indian camps, 138; navigation, xv, 19, 26, 29, 30, 34, 35, 52, 75–76, 106–107, 120, 152–53, 154, 158, 273, 283, 286, 304, 330. See also Transportation; Communication
Mitchell, George, 121, 123, 300
Montana, mines, 28; District of, 371, 372
Moreau River, 35
Mormons, xxv
Morrow, H. A., 368
Mortimer, Lord, western traveler, 303
Mosquitoes, 27, 36, 39, 50, 284, 310, 314, 323

Mott, Gershom, 38
Mountain Which Looks, 322
Mouse River, 139, 200
Musicians, 274

Nash, Patrick, 280
Nelson, William, 343
Newport Barracks, 364
Newspapers, slander, 273, 285–86
Niagara Falls, 12
Noble, Annie, 317
Nobles, William H., expedition of, xvii
Northern Pacific Railroad, xv, xviii
Northwest Fur Company, *see* Northwestern Fur Company
Northwestern Fur Company, xvi, 22n, 45n, 57, 83, 133, 157, 281, 295, 298, 300, 338, 359n
Norvell, John, 193
Norvell, Stevens F., 48, 149, 154, 194, 195, 236, 240, 270, 282, 297, 300, 301, 302, 309, 339, 341
Norwell, John, *see* Norvell, John
Norwell, Stevens F., *see* Norvell, Stevens F.
Nute, Grace Lee, xii
Officers, Army, U. S., xix–xx; drunkenness, 154, 155, 158, 172–73, 228, 229, 229n, 333, 349–50, 352, 353, 354, 357, 357n; hardships, 52, 53, 214–15, 216
Omaha, xv, 12, 14–20, 40, 123, 150, 175, 330, 336, 343; businessmen, 19–20; description of, 15–17; supply depot, 16–17; transportation, railroad, 16
Oregon Trail, xvi
Osgood, Ernest S., x
Otis, Elwell, S., 37, 57, 173, 178, 292, 359
Otter Tail River, 44n

Packeneau, Charles, *see* Pacquenaud, Charles
Pacquenaud, Charles, 91, 121–22, 146, 149, 276–77, 279, 301
Painted Woods, 359–60
Palmer, Frank, 298, 298n, 299, 328
Paquenaud, Charles, *see* Pacquenaud, Charles
Parsons, Foster E., 48, 145, 211, 214, 216, 272, 306
Parsons, Mrs. Foster E., 214, 296
Patineaude, Charles, *see* Pacquenaud, Charles
Pay, soldiers', 67, 70–71, 72n, 155, 293, 306, 307, 308, 309, 336, 343
Paymaster, 296, 336, 343, 344, 346

Peace commission, *see* Indian Peace Commission
Peace Pipe, *see* Calumet
Pease, David, 133, 133n, 134, 137, 138, 148, 157
Pembina, 326
Pemmican, 78
Piatt, John H., 68, 69, 228, 229, 309, 327, 353
Pindère, Count le, western traveler, 303
Plains, description, 20, 42, 75, 79–80, 120, 121, 124, 250, 252, 324–25
Plants, 12. *See also* names of individual plants
Platte River, 29, 45, 66n, 203
Plums, 131
Pochler, ——, contractor, 71
Politics, American, 261, 280
Pomeroy, George, 67, 68n, 229, 307, 308
Population, Indian, *see* Numbers under the names of the various Indian tribes
Post, Waldron Kintzing, xi, xiii
Posts, military, construction of, xix; equipment for, 20; maintainence of, xix. *See also* Forts
Powder River, xvi
Powder River Valley, fortification, 337
Powell, Albert M., 47, 48, 69, 76, 131, 132, 133, 179, 180, 203, 214, 236, 240, 260, 280, 297, 299, 300, 300n, 317
Powwow, *see* Indians, conferences
Prairie fires, 51, 52, 59–60, 269, 270, 275, 343–47
Prairies, Illinois, description of, 12–13
Prairies, Iowa, description of, 12–13
Prairies, population, 12–13
Pratte, Chouteau and Company, xvi
President, U. S., inauguration of, 361, 367
Prices, Upper Missouri, 34, 274
Prisoners, 296–97, 363, 363n. *See also* Courts-martial
Provisions, 41, 42, 58, 59, 60, 71, 119, 120, 121, 123, 129, 136, 150, 151, 152, 153, 154, 178, 184, 235, 244, 246, 257, 258, 260, 261, 270, 273, 274, 282, 283, 287, 299, 305, 306, 308–309, 339, 340, 343; for Fort Totten, 67, 67n; stores at Fort Berthold, 47

Quatre Ans de Campagne à l'Armée du Potomac, xxiii, xxiv, 38, 238, 279–80, 280n

Index

Rain, *see* Storms, rain

Rankin, William G., 22n, 46, 69, 123, 138, 154, 155, 158, 172–73, 172n, 193–94, 194n, 229, 296, 296n, 353

Rankin, Mrs. William G., 46, 46n, 354

Ray, Charles, 307–308

Red River of the North, xvii, 44n, 48, 115, 122, 127, 138n, 171, 192, 224n, 225, 288

Red Water, 320, 334

Reeve, Isaac Van Duzer, 45, 283, 293

Revue du Nouveau Monde, xxiii

Richemond, ——, courier, 362

Richer, T. F., 361, 362, 364, 365, 367

Rocky Creek, 322

Rolette, ——, courier, 288n

Ruffee, Charles A., 240, 240n, 241, 241n, 298

Ruffee & Co., mail contractors, 240n, 241n

St. Cloud, 275, 341, 363n; communications, mail, 44n

St. John, 31

St. Joseph, 288

St. Louis, xv, xvi, 16, 19, 34, 39, 40, 45, 52, 58, 71, 112, 120, 123, 154, 261, 284, 293, 296, 304, 330, 358; provisioning the posts, 17

St. Mary, convent, 16, 20

St. Paul, xvii, 157, 163, 260, 272, 280, 300, 343, 363, 369; mail, 44n; headquarters, Department of Dakota, 44

Salt Lake City, 368

Sanborn, John B, 45n

San Francisco, 16

Sawmills, 24, 41, 60, 118, 121, 124, 308, 311, 335

Schofield, John M., 69

Scouts, 67, 297; Arikara, 276, 279, 284; Arikara, pay, 276; dress, 276, 279; half-breed, 151, 162; half-breed, pay, 48; Indian, 57, 58, 123, 162, 173, 174, 294, 301, 306, 309, 320, 341, 348, 350. *See also* Couriers

Scurvy, 71, 238, 261–63, 262n, 270, 300n, 360–61, 364

Seaman, ——, Northwestern Fur Company, 281

Shank, John, 364, 365, 368

Shaw, Robert, 44n

Sherman, William T., xviii, 45, 45n, 169, 253n, 283, 337, 338, 367; opinions on the Indian problem, xx

Sherman House, Chicago, 11

Sheridan, Philip H., 283, 342

Sheyenne River, 44n, 325

Shields, ——, clerk, *Deer Lodge,* 59

Sioux City, 17, 21, 24, 115, 163, 330, 343; churches, 24; land speculation, 24; print shop, 24; railroad, 17, 24; supplying the forts, 17; transportation, 17, 24

Sioux Outbreak, *see* Minnesota Massacre

Smallpox, 50, 57n, 103, 103n, 246

Smet, Pierre Jean de, *see* De Smet

Smith, Andrew, 369

Smith, Edward W., 173

Smith, Oskaloosa M., 149, 153, 283, 286, 288, 298, 341

Smythe, J. W., 280

Snake Creek, 76, 119, 169, 344, 346, 348

Snow-blindness, 224

Soldiers, accidents, 122; army, U. S., xix; conditions of, 276; drunkenness, 358; duties, xix; fear of Indians, 60; hardships, xix, 72, 128, 161, 191, 204, 215, 215n, 261–63, 339; lack of military drill, 44; murder of, 342; pay, 293. *See also* Army, U. S.

Spring Lake, 319, 334

Stanley, D. S., 21, 33, 45, 57, 372

Stanley, William, 312, 316, 317

Steamboats, 281, 337; aid to woodcutters, 337; attacks on, 327; description, 24–25; deserters, 306; landings, 24, 33, 41; liquor trade, 282; mutiny, 317–18; passengers, 36, 283, 293, 303

Steamboats

Amanda, 75, 76, 118

Amaranth, 149, 154

Andrew Ackley, 337

Antelope, 282

Argonaut, 308

Ben Johnson, 305, 306

Benton, 153, 154, 158, 293, 338, 339

Bertha, 339, 340

Big Horn, 299

Centralia, 52

Columbia, 293

Cora, 273, 293

Deer Lodge, xv, 19, 20, 23, 38, 49, 51, 59, 76, 150, 150n, 156, 274, 275, 297, 306; accommodations, 21; crew, 34; description of, 24–25; embarkation on, 20; fortification of, 34; freight, 23; passengers, 23

G. B. Allen, 308

Guidon, 44, 46, 286

Henry Atkins, 282, 283

393